Women, Work & Domestic Virtue
in Uganda
1900–2003

EASTERN AFRICAN STUDIES

Women, Work & Domestic Virtue in Uganda

1900–2003

GRACE BANTEBYA KYOMUHENDO

Department of Women & Gender Studies
Makerere University

&

MARJORIE KENISTON MCINTOSH

Department of History
University of Colorado at Boulder

James Currey
OXFORD

Ohio University Press
ATHENS

Fountain Publishers
KAMPALA

James Currey Ltd
73 Botley Road
Oxford
OX2 0BS

Ohio University Press
19 Circle Drive, The Ridges
Athens, Ohio 45701, USA

Fountain Publishers
PO Box 488
Kampala

1 2 3 4 5 10 09 08 07 06

British Library Cataloguing in Publication Data
Bantebya Kyomuhendo, Grace
    Women, work & domestic virtue in Uganda, 1900-2003. -
    (Eastern African studies)
    1. Women - Employment - Uganda - History 2. Women - Uganda -
    Social conditions
    I. Title II. McIntosh, Marjorie Keniston

331.4'096761'0904

ISBN 10: 0-85255-988-7 (James Currey Cloth)
ISBN 13: 978-085255-988-8 (James Currey Cloth)
ISBN 10: 0-85255-987-9 (James Currey Paper)
ISBN 13:   979-085255-987-1 (James Currey Paper)

ISBN 10: 9970-02-586-4 (Fountain Publishers Paper)
ISBN 13: 978-9970-02-586-2 (Fountain Publishers Paper)

**Library of Congress Cataloging-in-Publication Data
available on request**

ISBN 10: 0-8214-1733-9 (Ohio University Press Cloth)
ISBN 13: 978-0-8214-1733-1 (Ohio University Press Cloth)
ISBN 10: 0-8214-1734-7 (Ohio University Press Paper)
ISBN 13: 978-0-8214-1734-8 (Ohio University Press Paper)

Typeset in 9/10½ pt Baskerville
by Long House Publishing Services, Cumbria, UK
Printed and bound in Great Britain
by Woolnough, Irthlingborough

Contents

Contents

List of Maps, Figures & Illustrations

Acknowledgements

Doing the research for this book was indeed a joint effort, involving not only its two primary authors but many other contributors. Our graduate research assistants in 2002–3, Jean Kemitare and Deus Mukalazi, went through old newspapers, tracked down dissertations in Makerere University's many departmental libraries, and helped to set up interviews. Moses Kadobera assisted with the newspaper work. Taped interviews with the district sample and preparation of detailed notes based on our chronological template were done by Jean Kemitare, Sylvia Latigo-Olal, Anita Mago-Sempa, Judith Ruko, and Beatrice Tumushabe. We are grateful for the interest, ideas, and competence that all these talented people brought to our project.

We appreciate the willingness of the 'Torchbearers' (Jackie Asiimwe, Olive Kigongo, Maggie Kigozi, Sarah Kitakule, Peace Kyamureku, Grace Mukasa, Angela Nakafeero, and Lydia Rugasira) to make time for us within their demanding schedules. Our debt is equally great to the 113 women in our seven districts who set aside their work to talk about their experiences. We thank the Chief Administrative Officers and the LCV Chairpersons of those districts for permission to conduct interviews, and we are especially grateful to the Community Development or Gender officers for their assistance in identifying a diverse group of working women and in many cases for introducing us to those women and asking for their cooperation.

At Makerere University, we were assisted by staff members in many libraries, especially those of the Africana section of the main library: without their knowledge, our research would have been impossible. The staffs at the Uganda National Archives, the Uganda Bureau of Statistics, the Education Ministry, the Uganda Nurses and Midwives Council, the Nursing Schools at Mulago and Mengo Hospitals, the archives at Bishop Tucker campus of Ugandan Christian University, Mukono, and the Public Record Office in London were likewise very helpful. Marjorie McIntosh is grateful to the Department of Women and Gender Studies at Makerere for its hospitality in 2002–3; she learned a great deal about women and their work from her colleagues and MA students. She thanks the former Vice Chancellor, Professor John Ssebuwufu, for allowing her to use a flat on campus during that year.

Acknowledgements

Our project received financial assistance as well. The Committee on Research and Creative Work and the Graduate Committee on the Arts and Humanities at the University of Colorado at Boulder awarded research grants to Marjorie McIntosh for 2002–3 and summer 2004. The (US) African Studies Association selected Grace Bantebya to receive an International Visitor Award in November 2004, enabling her to come to the ASA's annual meeting and spend two weeks in Colorado giving lectures and working on final revisions to our text.

The book was improved by the comments of Professor Gracia Clark, Victoria Mwaka Nakiboneka (Professor of Geography and first head of the Department of Women and Gender Studies at Makerere University, now a member of the Ugandan Parliament), and Dr Kathleen Sheldon. We are grateful for the ongoing interest of Douglas Johnson of James Currey Publishers, Oxford, and Alex Bangirana of Fountain Publishers, Kampala. While we take responsibility for the limitations of this study, we are happy to acknowledge the many people who have contributed to its creation.

Abbreviations & Glossary

ACFODE	Action for Development, a women's activist group founded in 1985.
A-levels	Advanced level exams, taken by children at the end of 6 years of secondary school, often as preparation for university study.
Amin, Idi	Head of a military-based government, 1971–9.
ayah	A domestic servant who took care of young children.
Ba	As a prefix with an ethnic name, an adjective referring to multiple people or the features of that group. E.g., 'Bagisu people or Bagisu customs'.
bananas	The basic type, sometimes termed 'plantains,' are cut while green, peeled, and steamed to make *matoke*, a staple starch served every day in many ethnic groups. Because banana 'plantations' or 'gardens' are used for other purposes too and have cultural significance, many families have small plots of bananas near their houses. Other species of bananas are grown for beer or to be eaten when ripe.
Bridewealth	Formerly known as 'brideprice,' this referred to the presents given by the family of a prospective husband to the family of the prospective wife. The nature of these gifts varied between the country's ethnic groups but might include cows, food, and beer; later money was sometimes expected. Traditionally, if the wife left her husband, her family had to return the bridewealth to her husband's family.
Bu	As a prefix with an ethnic name, a noun referring to the physical or political region of that group. E.g., 'In Bugisu, the famine was severe'.
CBO	Community-based organization.
CEEWA	Council for the Economic Empowerment of Women in Africa.
CMS	Church Missionary Society of the Church of England.
	CMS, *Annual Letters, year* = Church Missionary Society, *Extracts from the Annual Letters of the Missionaries for the Year 1903 and 1904.*

	CMS, Birmingham = unpublished CMS archives kept at the University of Birmingham Library in the UK. Also available on microfilm.
	CMS, *Letters from the Front, year* = Church Missionary Society, *Letters from the Front, Being a Selection from the Annual Letters from the Missions, 1911 and 1912.*
DP	Democratic Party, generally backing Catholic concerns.
DR Congo	Democratic Republic of Congo, formerly Zaire.
FEMRITE	The Ugandan women writers' organization.
FIDA	International Federation of Women Lawyers
FINCA	Foundation for International Community Assistance, a microfinance organization active in Uganda.
FOWODE	Forum for Women in Democracy.
groundnuts	'Peanuts' in US usage.
HIV/AIDS	Human Immunodeficiency Virus/Acquired Immunodeficiency Syndrome.
ICT	Information and Communication Technology.
IMF	International Monetary Fund.
IWD	International Women's Day.
IWY	International Women's Year.
Kabaka	The king of Buganda.
KY	Kabaka Yekka ('Kabaka alone'), a political party focused on Buganda concerns.
LRA	The Lord's Resistance Army, led by Joseph Kony, the main group fighting against the NRM government in northern Uganda in 2002–3.
Lukiiko	The council of chiefs or Parliament of Buganda.
magendo	A black market economy, often including smuggling goods across the border and sometimes bribes to corrupt officials.
matoke	A staple food made of steamed starchy bananas (= plantains).
MFI	Microfinance institution.
Mu	As a prefix with an ethnic name, a person from that group. E.g., 'She is a Mugisu'.
MU	The Mothers' Union, an organization of Christian women run by the (Anglican) Church of Uganda.
namasole	The queen mother of Buganda = mother of the reigning *Kabaka*.
NAWOU	National Association of Women's Organizations of Uganda, founded in 1992.
NGO	A non-governmental organization, a British term that in American usage is closer to a 'non-profit organization'.
NRA	National Resistance Army, active in the 'bush war' against Obote, 1981–5.
NRM	The National Resistance Movement, headed by Yoweri Kaguta Museveni. After taking power in 1986, the NRM became the non-party government of the country.
Obote II	The second period of government led by Milton Obote, 1979–85.
P1 – 7	The grades within primary education, which were usually started

	at around age 6.
parastatals	Semi-autonomous governmental or government-linked agencies.
PRO	Public Record Office, part of the National Archives, Kew, London, UK.
ROSCA	Rotating Small Credit Association (with voluntary membership, where each member puts in a set amount each week or month and the total sum is given to one member, in rotation).
S1 – 6	The grades within secondary education. Based on the British system, S 1-4 or 5 culminated in the General Certificate of Education or 'Ordinary-level' exams; in more recent periods, S 6 leads to the 'Advanced-level' exams.
SAP	Structural Adjustment Program, a set of economic policies required by international financial institutions.
simsim	Sesame.
SPSS	Statistical Package for the Social Sciences, computer-based software.
U	In notes, Government Publications, Uganda.
UAWO	Uganda Association of Women's Organizations.
UCU Mukono	Uganda Christian University, Bishop Tucker Campus, Mukono, Archives.
UCW	Uganda Council of Women.
UIA	Uganda Investment Authority, a parastatal body.
UNA	Uganda National Archives, in Entebbe.
UNAIDS	The Joint United Nations Programme on HIV/AIDS.
UNC	Ugandan National Congress, a political party founded in 1952.
UNCCI	Uganda National Chamber of Commerce and Industry.
UNICEF	United Nations Children's Fund.
UNMC	Uganda Nurses and Midwives Council, Ministry of Health, Kampala.
UP	In notes, Government Publications, Uganda Protectorate.
UPC	Uganda People's Congress, headed by Milton Obote and generally supportive of the Church of Uganda.
UPE	Universal Primary Education = free primary education at government-supported schools.
UPDF	Uganda People's Defence Force, the national army during the NRM period (formerly the National Resistance Army).
Ush	Ugandan shillings. During 2002–3 when the research for this project was done, the exchange rate with the US dollar was just under Ush 2,000 to US $1. A conversion rate of 2,000:1 has therefore been used in this book.
UWEAL	Uganda Women Entrepreneurs Association Ltd.
UWFT	Uganda Women's Finance Trust.
UWONET	Uganda Women's Organizations Network, founded in 1993.
waragi	A distilled alcoholic drink, similar to gin, often made locally.
WHO	World Health Organization.
YWCA	Young Women's Christian Association.

Part I

Introduction

One

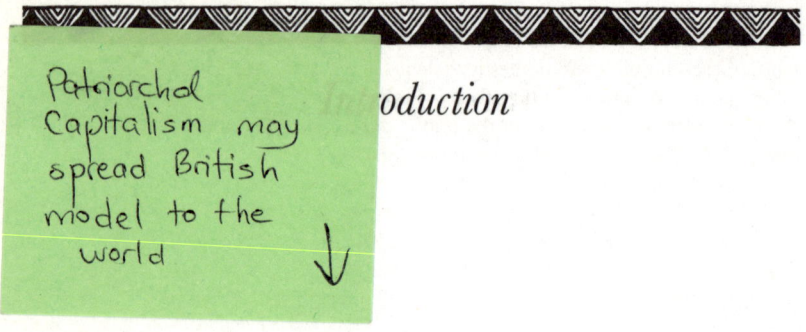

Patriarchal Capitalism may spread British model to the world ↓

~~Intr~~oduction

The history of Ugandan women and their work during the twentieth century is filled with struggle: struggle not only in practical terms but also in a personal, emotional sense. Women were caught in a tension field between two conflicting forces. Many women were pushed or pulled into the market economy by material factors or individual goals: they needed to work to feed and house their family, they wanted to educate their children, or they hoped to use their own training and skills to benefit the community and gain personal satisfaction. Yet at the same time they faced powerful ideological opposition to any work outside the domestic context. A set of expectations for women that we label 'a model of Domestic Virtue' developed early in the twentieth century. This gender definition was based upon shared African and British concerns, with roles for women clearly distinguished from those for men. Women were valued for their contributions within the family, perceived and applauded as wives and mothers who produced food and cared for their households. Husbands had authority over their wives, and women were expected to be submissive and deferential to all men. Excluded from decision-making and control over resources, women were not supposed to work outside the home. Across the generations after 1900, many Ugandan women grappled with the question of how to bring in some money for themselves and their households while at the same time conforming to that model's definition of what constituted a good and proper woman.

Domestic Virtue thinking proved remarkably persistent. Despite the massive economic, political, and cultural changes that transformed Uganda during the twentieth century, older values continued to shape the lives of rural women and to influence the options open to women in towns. As late as 2001-2, women candidates for Parliament might be expected to kneel when requesting support from men, and the country's Vice President triggered a storm of criticism from the public when she announced that she was seeking a divorce on grounds of physical abuse. But the Domestic Virtue model did demonstrate some flexibility. Twice in the twentieth century it generated variant forms in response to the challenges posed by changes in the actual nature of women's work. Each new version accommodated certain types of female economic activity so long as women conformed to

2

the essential features of the model within the domestic context and in their dealings with men. Nevertheless, the tension between women's desire to enter the cash-based economy and the ongoing strength of Domestic Virtue thinking had some negative consequences: it limited women's ability to participate fully and effectively in their country's public life and economic development, and it contributed to gender-based hostility and domestic violence.

By the late twentieth century there were encouraging signs of change. Millions of women were now engaged in the public domain, doing many different kinds of work. Though most were still concentrated at the bottom of the economic system, some businesswomen, professional women, and politicians were active at intermediate and even higher levels. Thanks to the affirmative action policies introduced by President Yoweri Kaguta Museveni and the National Resistance Movement (NRM) government after 1986, women were more equal participants in education and government. As the result of these developments, a new gender formulation was starting to emerge by 2003. It enabled successful women to maintain a positive identity even though they displayed an entrepreneurial approach at work and redefined their relationships within the family. Their husbands too were offered a wider range of roles.

This study, written jointly by a Ugandan anthropologist and a North American historian, traces the struggles and the gains of women in Uganda from 1900 to 2003. The distinctive perspective that has emerged from our intellectual partnership, integrating two different disciplinary and continental approaches, opens up new ways of understanding women in Uganda and elsewhere. Our approach is inclusive, looking not only at women's activities but also at how they have been defined and represented. Because the book covers a long span, we can follow changes over time, describe women's position in 2003, and offer historically grounded recommendations for how to improve their effective participation in the public domain. Among those recommendations are ways to hasten the development of alternative gender definitions that will enable women and men to live and work more constructively together.

We concentrate upon women's involvement in the market or cash-based economy, looking at all the ways in which they have brought in some income. Our account therefore includes not only women's place in trade but also their roles as professionals, employees, and producers of goods. In treating women's labor in subsistence agriculture and their work within the household less fully, we do not intend to downplay the importance of these contributions. Uganda's families and its national economy are heavily dependent upon women's food production and unremunerated household work; taking care of their families brings personal satisfaction to many women. But to set manageable boundaries around our project, we focus upon income-generating activities.

This book argues that the history of women's work in Uganda has been determined by the combined pressure and interaction of eight factors (see Figure 1.1.) Seven of them fall under the broad heading of material or practical influences. Some operated directly, especially economic and demographic pressures. Others functioned less immediately but were nonetheless important in facilitating or impeding women's economic involvement: political factors, women's education, their organizations, religious beliefs and practices, and legal protection of women's rights. The eighth factor highlighted in our conceptualization is ideological. An

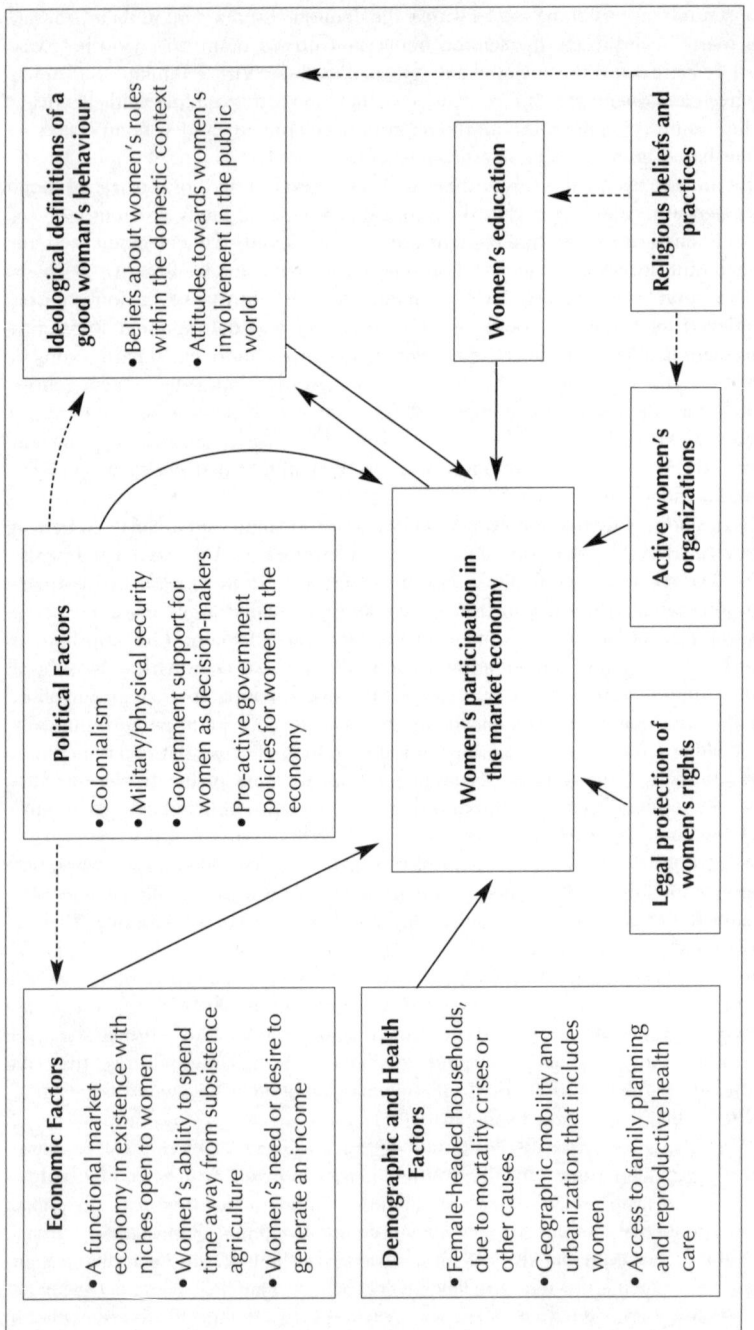

Figure 1.1 Influences upon Ugandan women's participation in the market economy

essential influence upon women's ability to participate effectively in the market economy consists of the gender definitions that prescribe the roles and responsibilities of proper women, as related to parallel definitions for men. Within the Ugandan context, these expectations were expressed primarily through Domestic Virtue thinking but were reflected also in discussion of three clusters of contested social issues: marriage and domestic relations; inheritance and landholding; and public participation by women. Heated debate concerning these topics extended from the early colonial period right through 2003.

This chapter begins by explaining how we defined and conceptualized the project and presents the analytical diagram that has emerged from it, which we believe may prove valuable in examining women's work in other contexts too. After describing our methodology and sources, we summarize our findings and argument, arranged by chronological period.

Definition, Conceptual Framework and Analytical Diagram

Uganda, located astride the Equator in the heart of tropical Africa (see Map 1.1), was selected as the setting for this study for several reasons. We wanted to examine women and their work within a country that did not have a tradition of female market-sellers and was not heavily influenced by coastal trade or the introduction of mining or plantation economies. An agricultural, inland country, we thought, would form an interesting addition to existing studies of West Africa and eastern and southern regions of the continent. Because Uganda is exceptionally well documented during the colonial period, we can explore patterns here that may have been present in other interior but less readily studied regions of the continent as well. Since Independence, Uganda has shared many political and economic experiences with other African countries, developments with a strong effect upon women. Its history thus opens up a poorly understood aspect of women's lives in colonial Africa – their ongoing and often exclusive participation in subsistence agriculture – but also illustrates some common features of the decolonizing period.

The scope of our study expanded from a narrower original definition. When we first began discussing the project, our objectives were to describe the history of women's participation in the Ugandan market economy since 1945 and to identify the constraints that currently limited their economic involvement. As we moved more fully into the research, however, we realized that we had to go farther back in time to trace the roots of the patterns visible in the mid-twentieth century. We therefore extended our chronological span to around 1900, when information about women becomes available in written sources.

We found also that we could not explain women's economic roles without considering other aspects of their lives. There is no existing history of Ugandan women, nor are they commonly mentioned in modern histories of the country.[1] The latter explore political developments and economic change, often from a nationalist, neo-Marxist, or structural dependence perspective, but they seldom touch upon women. A few articles have appeared that deal with the history of women from particular ethnic groups or in certain periods; and several recent books examine Ugandan women's political participation, educational opportunities, and

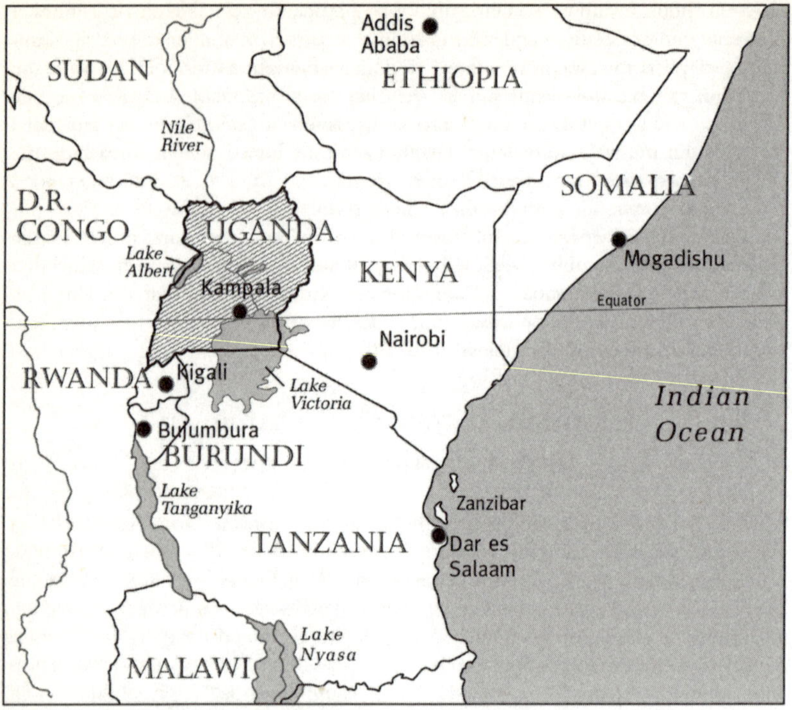

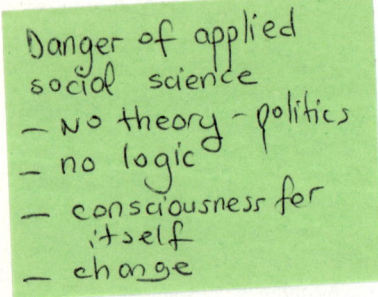

Map 1.1 Uganda and its neighbours

Danger of applied
social science
— No theory - politics
— no logic
— consciousness for
   itself
— change

aspects of their health care.[2] Christine Obbo's pioneering anthropological study of women's demographic, social, and economic situation in a poor region of Kampala, published in 1981, is now hard to find; Nakanyike Musisi's Ph.D. thesis on the history of Baganda women is likewise not readily available.[3] Because no one has attempted to identify the range of roles women have played from early colonial times to the present, we widened the scope of our own research to include the diverse factors that have affected women's work.

The final expansion of the project came only as we began to analyze our material. Whereas we had initially focused primarily upon the practical factors that affected women's income-generating activities, we became increasingly aware that we could not explain the patterns we observed without devoting more attention to the power of gendered expectations about the roles and behavior of good women. We therefore looked more closely at all the sources that shed light on gendered attitudes and expectations, and did additional research on the early colonial years, the period in which women's issues came under active debate and the Domestic Virtue model appeared.

Conceptually, this study is grounded in feminist and gender-based concerns. It emphasizes female agency and is sensitive to differential division of roles, responsibilities, and benefits within families and households. We have not assumed that patterns identified in studies of male Ugandans will be the same for women. Resisting any simple equation of patriarchy and capitalism, we explore how the particular forms of male dominance present in Uganda around 1900 were in some respects reinforced but in other ways challenged by the values and institutions introduced by capitalism, colonialism, and Christianity. We trace changing definitions and representations of 'good women', showing how the mass media, mainly newspapers, have reinforced or challenged stereotypic images based upon the original Domestic Virtue model. In discussing political factors, we look at women's roles in opposition to colonialism, in national self-definition and armed conflict, and in an affirmative action system that ensures their participation in government. In examining women and development, we consider how Structural Adjustment Programs, privatization, and globalization have affected Ugandan women.

Our book attempts to minimize Western epistemological and academic assumptions so as to trace Ugandan women's experiences in their own terms. The debate raging within international feminism concerning Western vs. African-centered analyses reinforced our decision to develop our own stance, one that selectively integrates features found in diverse approaches. We draw upon those feminist formulations that seem relevant to Ugandan women but have discarded others. For example, we did not find useful the commonly proposed theory of a dichotomy between public and private spheres, with women's roles confined to the latter.

Insofar as possible, we wanted to allow Ugandan women to occupy a historically constituted place specific to their situation. Shying away from historical 'master narratives', we have focused upon particular periods and changes over time. The standard economic and political conceptualizations (e.g., Marxism, modernization or dependency theory, or a political economy stance) proved too generic – too blunt-edged – to highlight the complexities of Ugandan women's lives. Rather than choosing an existing theory and exploring how it could be applied to our topic, we have therefore used our evidence to generate an independent analytical framework. We hope that we have succeeded in producing culturally specific knowledge while at the same time helping to lessen unequal relations between African and Western scholars in the creation of feminist understanding.

Our analytical diagram displays the influences that we see as essential to a historicized analysis of women and their work. These factors can either draw women into the market economy or constrain their participation, in Uganda and probably in other settings. In Figure 1.1, direct influences are shown as solid lines and indirect ones as broken lines. We describe here how the factors operate in general terms, reserving for later chapters more specific analyses of individual periods.

Economic pressure commonly brings women into income-generating activities. The primary push force for many poor women is simple necessity: the need to help their families survive or provide for their children. In more recent periods the latter may include basic schooling. Pull factors are more important for educated women, who frequently seek a higher standard of living, better opportunities for their children, and the chance to use their skills in personally satisfying and socially valuable ways. The particular types and level of economic activity that women enter depend upon the nature of the local economy and its relationship to the national and international economy. If women are to move beyond subsistence agriculture, a functional market economy must exist in their region, including adequate transport and market demand. Even if these conditions are present, women may be excluded from participation by culturally defined gender expectations and/or by the domination of trade and manufacturing by foreigners.

Women living in rural settings must have time and energy to engage in activities other than agriculture. So long as women are expected to do all or most of the agricultural work, in a setting that lacks other forms of power, and so long as their household relies upon the food they grow, they may not have the opportunity to partake in additional activities that would bring in cash. They can only do the latter if someone else is growing food for their household, if technological advances enable them to do their work more easily, or if they can use part of their earnings to buy food.

In settings where the market economy, commercial agriculture, and the manufacturing sector are weakly developed, poor women may have few ways to earn money other than engaging in the lowest levels of food and drink production or trade. To succeed at middle or higher levels of business or to enter a profession, one needs capital, connections, and/or education, requirements that are beyond the reach of most African women. During the later part of the twentieth century, outside economic influences intensified, among them the Structural Adjustment Programs that typically worsened poverty at least temporarily and pushed more women into small income-generating activities. Privatization and globalization privileged large businesses and forms of communication and commerce with international ties, making it difficult for women to compete.

A few political factors are particularly important to women's economic activity. Our model suggests that the impact of colonial rule on women was largely indirect. It affected their market participation through economic decisions such as taxation, forced labor for men, and the introduction of cash crops; it helped to re-define the dominant image of good women and their proper roles. In a secondary fashion, colonialism worked through demographic decisions such as opposition to urbanization and women's geographic mobility, through its stance on female education, and through its impact upon legal patterns. Military and physical security is desirable, but women may have to work even during – or *especially* during – unstable periods. Civil war or other types of armed conflict cause not only high mortality but also the temporary disappearance of men, the mass migration of families, and violence against women. If women are left as household heads, they may be obliged to find ways of bringing in cash, no matter how high the danger. But when a government maintains peace and physical stability, women are better able to participate in activities outside the home, obtain training, and travel safely to other parts of the country or world. These conditions contribute to a favorable environment for women's work and may help at least a few to participate in intermediate or higher levels of the economy.

Government support for working women operates in different ways at various levels of the economy. Women may well need or want to work even if political leaders do not support their participation, as was true in Uganda between 1971 and 1985, during the regime of Idi Amin and the second government led by Milton Obote (customarily described as 'Obote II'). Economic necessity can thus outweigh a negative political environment. But under those circumstances, most women will be forced to take whatever work they can find and will remain clustered at the bottom of the economy. A different climate is created if a government promotes a wider belief that women should take part in all aspects of the public sphere and in decision-making bodies, perhaps implementing its support through affirmative action measures that give women a visible and secure place in all ranks of political activity. Particularly in settings that do not have a tradition of female participation in the market economy, pro-active government policies that privilege women in economic terms may be needed at least temporarily to help women compete more successfully. Such measures are especially conducive to women's entry into middle and upper levels of the economy.

A cluster of demographic and health-related factors have a powerful impact upon women's work. The most direct is the presence of female-headed households, often caused by mortality crises or war, which may force women to generate their own income. In Uganda many women were left in charge of families by the fighting of the Amin/Obote II period, by armed conflict in the north of the country between 1986 and 2003 (during the government of the National Revolutionary Movement or NRM), and by HIV/AIDS. Even households that grew most of their own food needed at least a little cash. This led women to develop income-generating activities in rural areas or to move to urban communities in search of work. But the existence of a market economy that women are allowed to enter is a necessary pre-condition, as are cultural patterns that permit widows or unmarried women to head their own households. As was demonstrated in Uganda at the time of the terrible epidemic of sleeping sickness early in the twentieth century, this pressure will not operate if there are no niches for women in the cash-based economy, or if widows and orphaned daughters are inherited by or absorbed into the household of male relatives.

If geographic mobility and urbanization include women, these factors promote their economic involvement. When women are free to move in search of work, it expands their options. Towns offer a greater range of economic and social benefits, including access to information about economic conditions, better educational opportunities for children, and readier participation in women's organizations. The low level of urbanization in Uganda has therefore been an obstacle to women's work. But female mobility is also likely to trigger male anxiety and heightened control: fear of the breakdown of established family patterns and a weakening of male authority, unwelcome competition for male workers, and uncontrolled female sexuality. In many contexts, both colonial and African authorities have attempted to keep women – especially unmarried ones – out of towns.

Women are able to enter the economy more readily and to perform more successfully within it if they have access to family planning services and good quality reproductive health care. If cultural pressure in favor of large families is strong (as was true in Uganda even in 2003, with an average of 6.9 births per woman), and if women do not receive good medical care during pregnancy, delivery, and lactation, their ability to devote consistent time and energy to their income-generating activities is impaired.

Education can pull women into the economy. Through formal schooling women gain information and skills that will be useful to their work and in some cases a desire for economic independence. Receiving even a primary education leads women to seek their own income and prepares them to enter the economy at more than the bottom level. Women with a secondary or university degree are frequently eager to use their training in business, government, or the professions, sometimes perceiving their work as a contribution to society. Education brings secondary benefits as well. In most cultures, women who have completed a primary or secondary education are less likely to marry at a young age and will have fewer children, freeing up time that can be devoted to income-generating activities. Educated women are more likely to join women's organizations and become leaders within their communities. The decision of the NRM government to assist women in university admission policies and to institute free primary education was therefore a significant investment in the future participation of women in the economy as well as in other public arenas.

Women's groups – whether organized by churches, community-based organizations (CBOs), or local or international non-governmental organizations (NGOs) – similarly encourage women to enter the economy. Even if an organization has apparently conservative goals, such as teaching domestic skills, the fact that women come together to talk and work gives them access to knowledge and builds both individual and group capacity. Organizations that work to improve conditions for women can put pressure on private and public institutions because their members have learned how to define goals and work collectively toward them. The independence and effectiveness of women's associations diminish sharply if they must be authorized by the government or are tied to the dominant (or only) political party.

Another factor that promotes female economic activity is a favorable and clearly articulated status for women in the law. Legal protection of women's rights provides a substructure that helps them to move into income-generating activities. They are more likely to venture into the public domain and to thrive once there, if their legal position as independent actors is secure and if they enjoy well defined rights within the family. In Uganda, these protections were not fully in place. As late as 2003, proposed reforms that would have increased women's rights over family and marital property and made domestic violence a crime were not supported by the government and appeared to have little chance of being approved by Parliament.

In our formulation, religion functions indirectly. Religious beliefs and the teachings of the organized churches have a profound effect on cultural definitions of the roles and responsibilities of good women, both within the family context and in public arenas. Because most colonial education was offered within a religious context, attitudes about what girls should learn were shaped by religious concerns; in some cases these patterns have continued into the post-colonial period through the social prominence of church-run schools. The legal position of women is also heavily influenced in many cultures by religion. In Uganda, religion was a power-ful force during the colonial years but declined thereafter.

The final influence upon women's work, one to which we assign great weight, consists of culturally defined gender expectations. These include definitions of women's economic and social roles within the domestic setting as well as ideas about their involvement in the public domain. The central question for our purposes is whether a good woman, one who fills the designated roles at home and acts properly toward her husband and/or male relatives, is allowed to participate in the broader economy. What types of outside activity, if any, may she pursue and still be seen as respectable? Those issues are of course intimately tied to male status. Is it acceptable for a woman to interact with – and even compete with – men at work, and what happens to marital relations when [...]
own money? How can men maintain a positive [...]
functions are being progressively taken over by wo [...]
other parts of the world, such problems have not [...]
demonstrates that when women have sufficient nee [...]
even in the face of strong gender-based opposit [...]
Amin/Obote II years. Their participation is facilita [...]
tions accord with the changing realities of women's [...]
arrow in Diagram 1.1, new patterns in women's [...]
influences can lead to modifications of the dominan [...]

> DL is totally ignored and reduced to ideology
> VAW is also ignored
> patriarch = ideology

Methodology and Sources

Our study combines a historical perspective with a cross-sectional anthropological design to capture the key issues that have affected women and their work over the past century. This approach required that we integrate information from archival sources with material gained from interviews. Whereas the former shed most light on educated, elite women, especially for the first half of the twentieth century, interviews allowed us to expand our horizon in more recent periods, covering a broader range of experiences. They also permit us to give women's own voices a prominent place in the book. McIntosh did the research with written sources, while Bantebya took the lead on the interview side of the project.[4]

Written sources include a wide range of unpublished primary materials as well as printed books and articles. For the colonial period, the main archival sources were records of the British and Buganda governments and materials produced by the Church Missionary Society (CMS) in Uganda.[5] For the post-Independence years we gathered information from: government ministries in Kampala and

Entebbe; unpublished research reports from the 1960s–70s preserved at the Makerere Institute for Social Research and the Africana section of the Makerere University Library; interview-based dissertations done by students at Makerere University starting in 1968; and nursing records.[6] From 1920 onward, we gained additional material from English and local language newspapers, examined for one or two sample years per decade. The newspapers were quarried by graduate research assistants who photocopied articles, letters, advertisements, and photos relevant to our project from the collection at the Makerere University Library.[7] We used contemporary fiction by Ugandan women to highlight social issues. To assist subsequent scholars, we provide extensive references to both primary and secondary sources in the notes and the Bibliography.[8]

Interviews formed the other major component of our research. We first talked with eight 'Torchbearers', important women in Kampala.[9] The Torchbearers were selected to provide a variety of perspectives on women's work and its history as seen from the top. They included the heads of women's associations, economic organizations, and government affiliated agencies. In these conversations we asked for their observations about how women's work has changed over time, what factors have affected it, and where things stand at present. We also participated in a series of meetings with 25–30 of the country's women leaders during the first half of 2003, and McIntosh interviewed four 'cultural historians': a Bakiga scholar and three officials of the Buganda kingdom knowledgeable about the traditions of their groups.[10] Material from all these interactions was analyzed qualitatively and appears throughout the following chapters.

In addition, we trained five female research assistants to interview a small but diverse sample consisting of 113 working women from seven districts across Uganda.[11] The research assistants were all graduates of Makerere, all had previous interviewing experience, and two were currently enrolled in the MA program in Women and Gender Studies. They were assigned to areas they knew personally and whose languages they spoke. The districts (Mpigi, Kabale, Hoima, Arua, Lira, Jinja, and Kampala) were selected to reflect the geographical, ethnic (or 'tribal'), religious, and economic range that characterizes Ugandan society, but because we did not use quantitative criteria, ours is not a representative sample in more formal terms. In each place we worked with the district's Gender or Community Affairs officer, who generously helped us to identify some or all of the women to be interviewed. In some cases the officer went with the interviewer on a first visit to request the cooperation of the working women.[12] To facilitate selection of the women, we prepared a checklist that made clear our interest in finding women engaged in many different kinds of work, of varied economic levels, and of a range of ages. Most of the interviews were conducted in local languages, using a guide we developed.[13] The district women were asked about their own backgrounds, their working and personal lives during the various periods examined here, their current situation, and their views about the situation of women at the present time and what could be done to assist their work.

Information from the district sample forms a major component of this study: it tells us how working women described their own experiences in 2003. Some of the interview information was analyzed quantitatively by McIntosh, using SPSS software to generate descriptive tables of key variables. Selected material from this process is summarized in Chapter 2 and laid out in tabular form in Appendix C.

The rest of the data was explored qualitatively, mainly by Bantebya, through theme and content analysis. In all cases, we arranged the material by chronological period so as to trace changes over time.

Summary of our Findings and Argument

This book begins with an account of places and people. Chapter 2 introduces Uganda and the seven districts from which our main interview sample was drawn and describes the 'Torchbearers' and the organizations they head. It turns then to the 113 women in our district sample. After presenting some key demographic, religious, and socio-economic characteristics, we offer introductory profiles of four of the women across the span of their working lives.

The following six chapters trace the history of Ugandan women and their work since around 1900.[14] The story falls into two main periods. The generations of gradual evolution consisted of the early and late colonial years, up to 1962, and the first decade of Independence. As of 1971, an era of radical change began. This period included the Amin and Obote II regimes, up to 1986, followed by the NRM government led by Yoweri Kaguta Museveni, which continued through 2003 and beyond.

During the colonial and early post-colonial periods, the lives of Ugandan women differed significantly from those of their counterparts in some other regions of the continent, especially in demographic and economic terms. Uganda remained overwhelmingly rural: as late as 1959, only 3 percent of the total estimated population of 6.5 million lived in Kampala or one of the other four towns with more than 10,000 residents. During the first half of the century, sleeping sickness and other diseases curtailed demographic growth. Urban migration was low and included few women, and family structures remained largely intact. Nearly all women engaged in subsistence agriculture, though some worked on cash crops as well. The commercial economy was weakly developed, and South Asians dominated long-distance trade and the sale of manufactured goods. African men operated only at the bottom of the market system, and women rarely participated. Because of its landlocked location and the limited presence of mineral resources, Uganda experienced few of the dislocations felt in coastal regions directly influenced by foreign trade or areas shaped by mining-based economies. The country had comparatively few agricultural plantations and almost no white settlers. In all these respects, Ugandan women lived in a different world from the heavily urbanized areas of West Africa where local trade was generally dominated by women, from east coast trading centers like Zanzibar, and from the mining, plantation, and white settler regions of southern and southeastern Africa. It is likely that, as further research is done, the stability of rural life experienced by most Ugandan women for two-thirds of the twentieth century will prove characteristic of patterns in many interior regions of the continent.

During the nineteenth century, the area that would later be included in the Ugandan nation contained some ethnic groups that were loosely structured but also some powerful kingdoms with well defined governmental systems, socio-economic hierarchies, and clan units. In the 1880s and 1890s, the kingdom of Buganda, located to the northwest of Lake Victoria, emerged as the dominant force. Its success derived in part from the willingness of its leaders to cooperate with the British. A series of wars resulted in the expansion of Buganda's territory at the expense of its main rival, the kingdom of Bunyoro-Kitara in the west. As of 1900, all the kingdoms, including Ankole and Toro, had come under some degree of British control (see Map 3.1).

Chapter 3 describes the context of women's lives during the early colonial years, from around 1900 to 1939. After summarizing economic patterns prior to European contact, we review the main developments of the opening decades of colonialism. In political terms these derive from the particular form of 'indirect rule' used in Uganda and its devolution of some power to 'Native Authorities'. An outbreak of sleeping sickness in the years around 1900 disrupted family and clan traditions and facilitated British attempts to promote economic change. These included a new form of land tenure created by the colonial authorities in Buganda, the introduction of cotton and a few other cash crops, forced labor, the gradual expansion of trade, and the taxes imposed by the British. The chapter turns then to Christianity and female education, ending with a discussion of women's limited involvement in most income-generating activities, but also the entry of a few of them into the unfamiliar fields of teaching and nursing.

Chapter 4 looks more specifically at attitudes and actions concerning women during the early colonial period. Ugandans, British missionaries and church leaders, and colonial officials struggled with three clusters of issues that were vitally important to women. The first dealt with marriage, domestic relations, and violence against women, while the second addressed inheritance, illegitimacy, and land ownership. The third asked whether women should be involved in discussion of public issues, participate in decision-making, and receive leadership training. In these debates, we observe disagreements between Buganda's *Lukiiko* (its council of chiefs or Parliament), British colonial administrators, and church people. We also explore the divisions between colonial officials and liberal members of the Protestant church in Uganda (missionaries of the CMS, an arm of the Church of England, and the early bishops and their wives). The chapter then examines the sense among African and British authorities, especially during the 1920s and 1930s, that women were acting with inappropriate and dangerous freedom, and describes shared attempts to control their behavior.

In an attempt to define women's position in a way that would re-establish patriarchal control, male leaders – both African and British – formulated a model of how a good woman should act and what her duties were. This domestically focused set of gender assumptions contained multiple elements. All women were expected to marry and provide services for their husbands, and they were to bear children and care for them. They had practical duties in the household, including providing food (usually growing it themselves), and they were to remain within the compound or its fields. A woman was supposed to be submissive to male authority – especially that of her husband – and deferential when dealing with her husband's male relatives and other men in the community. Women did not make decisions except about minor domestic matters. They could use resources, including land, but did not control them. By extension, if a woman went out into the world on her own, she might legitimately be regarded in sexual terms.

The Domestic Virtue model was based upon patterns already present in Buganda and some other parts of the country during the early colonial period, but

14

it was strongly reinforced by British colonial administrators, whose late Victorian patriarchal views accorded well with those of many African men. To some extent these attitudes were shared by British and European Christian missionaries and early leaders of Uganda's churches, who emphasized women's contributions to the family and taught domestic skills in their schools. As is true of all successful ideologies, the model was accepted by most of those whom it disadvantaged (in this case women) as well as by members of the dominant group whose interests it served (in this case men). The expectations built into the Domestic Virtue model were implemented by governments and courts: British authorities, rulers and chiefs in Buganda, and probably many chiefs in other parts of the country as well.

Some features of the Domestic Virtue model were, however, challenged by Christian teachings and practice, especially those of the CMS missionaries and the early bishops of the Church of Uganda. They believed that girls and women should learn to read and in some cases gain further academic training. They encouraged educated women to become teachers and nurses and to continue working after marriage and motherhood. Most of the first generation of African women who took up these roles came from influential families. Although the number of teachers and nurses was initially very small, their elite status and close contact with Europeans gave them considerable visibility. The 1920s and 1930s thus witnessed the appearance of the first group of Ugandan working women, a role created jointly by British missionaries and African women.

Although the early teachers and nurses came from respected families and their work was generally admired, their activity did not accord in all respects with the basic Domestic Virtue model. For the first time, this set of expectations demonstrated its adaptability, producing a variation that enabled these women to work while still being defined as good women. In what we label the 'Service Career' version, educated women were excused from growing food and providing personal care for their families if they worked in a high-status occupation that served the community. They were allowed to buy food or hire someone else to grow it, to employ female domestic help, and often to decide how to spend their own income. But they were still expected to conform to the core elements of the model, including marrying and bearing children, assuming responsibility for the smooth operation of their households, and remaining submissive to men. Over the course of the following generations, the range of occupations that fell within the Service Career category and the number of women engaged in them gradually expanded, but the restrictions continued.

Chapter 5 investigates the changes of the later colonial period, 1940-62. Here, as in subsequent chapters, we supplement material from written sources with information gained from our interviews. After examining the slow economic changes of these decades, we consider demographic patterns, including the increased migration of women into the towns. As conservatives feared, geographical mobility weakened familiar domestic patterns. Ugandan pressure for Independence was limited, but women participated in a few proto-nationalist movements. Political parties were formed and the British began to train some African men for leadership roles. A significant expansion in education for girls was accompanied by the entry of a few young women into higher education, either in Uganda or overseas. Women's organizations expanded beyond religious groups, some of them now bringing together members from diverse cultural and racial backgrounds. Women's participation in politics and government nonetheless remained very low.

The chapter turns then to the gradual expansion in women's work. During the late colonial years more women entered teaching and nursing, while a very few began to sell food or drink in the towns or worked in factories. In general, however, most women remained at home in the villages, growing food and looking after their families. A final section examines what was happening to the Domestic Virtue model and its Service Career variant, and explores what was being said in the three areas of debate about women's issues. Particularly interesting are the divergences revealed by local-language and English newspapers concerning women and their roles. Very different positions were advocated by conservatives (including most British government administrators, many Baganda men, and some other African men and women) and by progressives (including many women in Ankole, some in Buganda, and some church leaders).

Chapter 6 carries the story into the years of early Independence, 1962-71. The ending of colonialism brought relatively little change to Ugandan women: the gradual development visible in previous decades continued. Expansion of trade had limited impact on women, but increased migration into Kampala after the British left created opportunities for some women as market vendors or producers and sellers of cooked food and drink. Such work, which was to expand greatly after 1972, did not fit comfortably with either the basic Domestic Virtue model or its variation for women in service careers. Education became more widely available to girls and young women, and women's organizations expanded in number and scope. A growing number of women entered respected careers, now including government work and clerical occupations. The improved opportunities open to women were backed by the rhetorical stance assumed by the government and newspapers. Advocating women's involvement in Uganda's public life, including its economy, this approach stressed the importance of their contributions to the newly independent nation. Approbation did not, however, extend to the majority of the country's women who were still engaged in subsistence agriculture, nor did it support women's involvement in electoral politics. Further, the thorny question of how women were supposed to reconcile their roles in the public world with the ongoing strength of the Domestic Virtue model at home was ignored.

During the period between 1971 and 2003, the lives of many Ugandan women changed dramatically. They were affected by forces felt in other parts of the continent as well: political instability and military violence, a collapse of the formal economy, and, more recently, affirmative action policies that promoted women's participation in government and boosted their involvement in education. Starting during the regime of Idi Amin and culminating in the NRM period, more women entered the market economy and they undertook new kinds of income-generating activities. While similar developments occurred in many African countries, the pace of change between 1971 and the early twenty-first century in Uganda was unusually rapid because most women's lives had changed so little in previous generations.

Chapter 7 looks at the years 1971-86, during the Amin and Obote II governments, an intensely disruptive period for all Ugandans but especially for women. Political instability and military or police brutality caused hundreds of thousands of deaths and the migration of millions of people, within the country or into foreign exile. There was extensive violence against girls and women, and education and healthcare suffered. Many women were left at least temporarily as household heads, responsible for supporting their families. This happened at the very time when the formal economy fell apart due to Amin's 'economic war,' including expulsion of the South Asians. Hundreds of thousands of women were therefore forced to generate some kind of income under the most difficult circumstances, either by producing and selling food at home in the villages or by moving into Kampala or other towns in the hopes of finding better options.

Their efforts were by no means supported by the government. On the contrary, Amin's government, backed by the media, mounted a repressive campaign against women who left the domestic context. This stance was based upon an exaggerated version of the Domestic Virtue model that emphasized women's negative potential, especially their sexuality, if they were not kept at home under the control of male relatives. Yet because other people in the community recognized that many poor women sought work simply to keep themselves and their children alive, a second variation of that model emerged in response. The 'Petty Urban Trade' version stated that if a woman *had* to work to sustain her family, she could make and sell food or drink or do other kinds of unskilled or service work while still being regarded as a good woman.

Chapter 8 traces broader developments for women during the NRM period, 1986-2003. Many of the changes were favorable. Physical security was restored in much of the country, though not in the north, and a stable free-market economic system was created. Thanks to the NRM's affirmative action policy, started as soon as it took power and inscribed in the Constitution of 1995, women were guaranteed seats in government at all levels, from village councils through to Parliament. Women held top positions in government ministries and the bureaucracy. The NRM also improved opportunities for women in higher education, giving them extra points when applying to the university. The system of free Universal Primary Education, introduced in the later 1990s, resulted – as intended – in a greater percentage increase in the number of girls than of boys attending school. By the end of the century, 49 percent of all primary school pupils were girls. At Makerere University in Kampala, Uganda's earliest and most prestigious university, 41 percent of the students were women. Especially between 1986 and 1998 the Ugandan women's movement was active and effective, and the country contained thousands of CBOs and NGOs working to improve the status and daily lives of women. Some organizations focused on women's legal rights, while others addressed poverty. Microfinance institutions, many of them supported by foreign donors, loaned small sums of money to poor women.

Severe problems nonetheless remained. By 2003, women activists were discouraged by the realization that deeply rooted gender patterns could not be changed simply by government order. The NRM's commitment to women had apparently weakened, and corruption and political repression were increasing. The Structural Adjustment Programs required by the international financial institutions had intensified family-level poverty at least temporarily, with particularly severe consequences for women. Job cuts through restructuring of government public services removed positions previously held by women or their husbands. Reduced government spending in such areas as education and health meant that families had to pay more for such services. Trade liberalization policies, privatization, and involvement in a globalized economy increased the advantages of scale in business, making it difficult for most women to compete. By the end of the century, even married women whose husbands were working commonly needed to generate some income to help their families get by, and female-headed households were disproportionately represented among the very poor. The ability of women's organizations to work effectively for change diminished. The birth rate remained very high, while the ravages of HIV/AIDS brought further human suffering, left more women as household heads, and impaired the ability of female carers to carry out their own income-generating activities.

Chapter 9 looks first at women's work in the years 1986-2003. Although a higher proportion of women was involved in the public domain during the NRM period than ever before, participating in a great range of income-generating activities, they were still concentrated in petty trade or unskilled work. But educated women continued to move into salaried employment, and some business-women adopted a more entrepreneurial approach. During the first NRM decade, the government's support for women as full members of the community and decision-makers was shared by the newspapers, which represented women in favorable terms and offered serious discussion of issues that concerned them. However, the NRM period also saw increased gender tension and domestic violence due to the lack of consonance between women's new roles outside the family and the continued strength of Domestic Virtue expectations of how good women should behave at home.

By the later 1990s, a new breed of confident and successful women was starting to emerge in the higher ranks of business and – to a lesser extent – the professions and government. These women shared two characteristics. Clearly in charge of their own lives, their approach to work was entrepreneurial, looking for ways to expand their wealth or authority and competing actively with men. They also developed different kinds of relationships within their families, stemming in part from their own significant incomes and influence. Most of these women had children, whom they educated very well; if married, they generally shared responsibilities and rewards more evenly with their husbands. These successful entrepreneurs challenged Domestic Virtue thinking so severely that it could not stretch far enough to accommodate them. Their economic and often social prominence meant that they could not be dismissed as bad women, but if they were to claim a positive identity, an alternative gender formulation was needed. By 2003 a new and promising set of gender definitions was starting to appear. It offered greater role flexibility for both sexes. The only requirements still in place for women were that they accept primary responsibility for their households and children, and that – if married – they display suitable deference to their husbands and their male relatives in public settings.

The final chapter shifts to the present and future. For each of the seven practical factors that affect women's work, we assess the situation in 2003 and set out the recommendations that have emerged from this study about how to consolidate improvements and address problems. We then examine the gender-related handicaps that impede women's ability to participate fully in the market economy, looking at issues arising in the workplace and in the home and how they can be mitigated. This leads to analysis of the current impact of Domestic Virtue thinking and the potential of alternative gender formulations. We recommend a public campaign to open dialogue about gender assumptions and to facilitate development of more flexible and constructive definitions of gender roles. If gendered expectations as well as practical working conditions can be improved, women will be able to perform more effectively in the public domain and gender tension will be reduced.

Notes

1   E.g., Karugire, *A Political History*; Mamdani, *Politics and Class Formation*; and Jørgensen, *Uganda*. For women in a broader context, see Berger, 'Women in East and Southern Africa'.

2   For examples of historical studies, see Dimock, 'The Silence of African Women?,' her 'Women's Leadership Roles,' Musisi, 'Colonial and Missionary Education,' 'Gender and the Cultural Construction of "Bad Women",' 'The Politics of Perception,' and 'Women, "Elite Polygyny".' For political roles, see Tamale, *When Hens Begin to Crow*, and Tripp, *Women and Politics*; for education, see Kwesiga, *Women's Access to Higher Education*; for health, see, e.g., Wallman, *Kampala Women Getting By*.

3   Obbo, *African Women*, and Musisi, 'Transformations of Baganda Women'.

4   Most of the research was done in 2002-3, while Bantebya was Head of the Department of Women and Gender Studies at Makerere University in Kampala and McIntosh was a Visiting Lecturer there. Further work on the early colonial period, using materials in Uganda and Britain, was done by McIntosh in summer 2004. In writing the book, Bantebya and McIntosh each drafted some of the sections and chapters, sending them to each other by e-mail. During July 2004 in Kampala and November 2004 in Colorado, we worked together on revising and polishing the chapters and refining our argument.

5   The archives used were: British government records in Uganda (now at the Uganda National Archives in Entebbe) and those stored at the Colonial Office in London (now the National Archives, Public Record Office, Kew); a transcript of the records of the Buganda's kingdom's *Lukiiko* (Parliament) from 1894 to 1917; documents, publications, and correspondence of the CMS (now at the University of Birmingham Library in the UK and available on microfilm); and materials held at the Bishop Tucker campus of Uganda Christian University, in Mukono (CMS materials plus information about the Anglican Church of Uganda and the Mothers' Union).

6   Registers from the training schools for nurses at Mulago and Mengo Hospitals, and records at the Uganda Nurses and Midwives Council at the Ministry of Health in Kampala.

7   See Appendix A for a listing of the papers and years consulted.

8   To save space, abbreviated titles are used in the notes; the Bibliography provides full bibliographical information. In notes, the format 'For below, see . . . ' refers to material contained in the following sentence.

9   The Torchbearers are listed in Appendix B and described in Chap. 2 below. These interviews were conducted in English, taped, and transcribed by McIntosh. These and all other tapes have been deposited in the Women and Gender Studies Library at Makerere University.

10   See Appendix D for the women leaders and Appendix B for the cultural historians.

11   The interviews were carried out in January–May 2003.

12   See Appendix B. McIntosh went with the interviewer to Mpigi, Kabale, and Jinja to present our letters of introduction to local government officials and meet some of the interviewees; she also carried out a few of the Kampala interviews. In general, however, her presence as a white woman proved distracting. The interviews were taped and transcribed by the interviewers.

13   We were influenced by such studies as Stacey, 'Can There Be a Feminist Ethnography?,' S. Hale, 'Feminist Method,' and Patai, 'U.S. Academics and Third World Women'.

14   Detailed references are provided in the chapters themselves but are not given in this summary.

Two

Uganda
Its Districts & People

This background chapter first provides a brief introduction to Uganda and the seven districts in which we interviewed working women. After an account of the 'Torchbearers' and the organizations they head, the next section describes the 113 women included in our district sample. The chapter ends with profiles of four middle-aged or older women from this group, providing an introduction to the kinds of experiences encountered by individual working women over the course of their lives.

Uganda and the Seven Districts

Uganda is a small country located to the north and west of Lake Victoria (see Map 1.1.) It lies between Kenya on the east, Sudan on the north, the Democratic Republic of Congo (DRC) (formerly Zaire) on the west, and Rwanda and Tanzania on the south. Uganda is about 250 miles (400 km) from east to west and about 300 miles (480 km) from north to south. Its total area is 91,000 sq. miles (236,000 sq km), roughly the size of Great Britain or the state of Oregon in the United States. Its population in 2002 was 24,700,000 people.

Most of the country lies at an elevation of more than 3,300 ft (1,000 metres) and is fairly flat, with low, rolling hills. The exceptions are volcanic Mt Elgon on the Kenyan border, the mountains separating Uganda and Rwanda, and the Rwenzori Mountains that lie between Uganda and the DRC. The latter rise to 16,800 ft (5,100 m) and are snowcapped all year round, leading to the suggestion that they are the 'mountains of the moon' mentioned by the Greco-Egyptian geographer Ptolemy in the second century AD. In most parts of the country the climate is tropical but includes two dry seasons; the north is semi-arid. Fertile soils and regular rainfall mean that people rarely go hungry unless their region has been disturbed by fighting. In 2003 agriculture remained the most important sector of the economy, employing over 80 percent of the workforce. Most food crops were raised for the family's own consumption or sale within the country. Coffee was the major export crop, followed by tea, cotton, and tobacco; newer items being promoted included vanilla, flowers, and fruits. Administratively, Uganda was divided into 56 districts, including the city of Kampala.

Uganda has received conflicting forms of international attention over time. During the early colonial period, the British were impressed by its natural abundance and the high degree of organization of its indigenous kingdoms. No less a figure than Winston Churchill labeled Uganda 'the pearl of Africa' after his visit there in 1907. More recently, accounts have been less positive. Idi Amin's rule during the 1970s, including its violence and the expulsion of the South Asians, was covered extensively by the international press. During the later 1980s and 1990s the problems associated with HIV/AIDS in Uganda were widely reported. But since the coming to power in 1986 of the NRM government, led by Museveni, the country has been credited with considerable success in its attempts to privatize and liberalize its markets and to publicize and combat HIV/AIDS.

Uganda is also recognized as a global leader in working towards gender equality. It has many effective women's organizations that have pressed the government for reforms. From the beginning of the NRM period, seats have been reserved for women in Parliament, in addition to those they win through contests with men; the Local Government Act of 1997 stipulates that a third of all council members at every level must be women. The Constitution of 1995 clearly commits the government to gender equity, and legal and policy frameworks have been put in place to enhance women's participation in all aspects of development. Such measures have increased their participation in decision-making processes. The Department of Women and Gender Studies created in 1991 at Makerere University was the first of its kind in sub-Saharan Africa. It trains both undergraduate and MA students while serving also as a center for research. For all these reasons, Uganda was selected as the venue for an international women's conference in 2002, bringing 2,000 academics and practitioners from 90 countries to Makerere University.

Despite these achievements, Uganda's progress in 2003 was handicapped by ongoing problems. Poverty was a serious issue. Various plans passed in the 1990s committed the government to tackling poverty, and some success was recorded.[1] According to the government's figures, the fraction of the population living in poverty as defined by international measures declined from 56 percent in 1992 to 44 percent in 1997 and 38 percent in 2003. Yet the absolute number of people living in poverty fell only marginally, from 9.3 million in 1992 to 9 million in 2003. The majority of the very poor are women and children. These problems have been intensified by HIV/AIDS, which has killed or weakened many adults of working age, reduced the labor force, put additional strain on the women who care for those who are ill or are left as household heads, and produced an estimated 1-2 million orphaned children. Ongoing fighting in the north has intensified poverty, HIV/AIDS and other illnesses, and the myriad problems that confront displaced people.

With the exception of Kampala, the seven districts chosen for the interview sample in this study are heavily rural, as is true of the country as a whole, though they are diverse in other respects. The town after which each district is named serves as the administrative headquarters, containing 15,000-45,000 people. The economic activities of the area are concentrated there, joined by smaller trading centers elsewhere in the district. We describe here the main features of our seven districts, beginning with Kampala and moving clockwise around the country (see Map 2.1).

Map 2.1 Uganda and its districts 1996

Kampala is the national capital as well as its own district. The city plus its extensive peri-urban area contains the overwhelming majority of Uganda's urban population, with about 1,200,000 people in 2002. The central business district is Kampala's commercial heart, and most government ministries are located in the city. There is also some industry, and certain areas of the city and most of its suburbs produce agricultural products such as potatoes, cassava, and beans. The socio-economic level of Kampala's population varies greatly, ranging from large mansions on shady hilltops to very poor areas. About 10 percent of the total area can be described as slums, and these neighborhoods contain 27 percent of the city's population. Although Kampala has been described disparagingly as a collection of villages and lacking the aggressive energy of a city like Nairobi, it is nonetheless a cosmopolitan community, a melting pot of various cultures where women's participation in the public world is clearly evident.

Mpigi District is located immediately southwest of Kampala, lying along the shore of Lake Victoria and straddling the main road leading south from the capital. It supports a relatively large population – about 1,100,000 people – thanks in part to commercial agriculture fostered by demand for foodstuffs in Kampala and the ease of transport to the city. Items produced include the staples of many Ugandan diets: bananas, sweet potatoes, 'Irish' potatoes, cassava, yams, beans, maize (= corn), groundnuts (= peanuts), and sorghum. Dairy farming is also common, and some coffee and cotton are grown. Men living along the lake catch fish, often joined by women in drying or smoking it before sale. Small-scale industries include the manufacture of footwear and furniture, brewing, printing, brick-making, stone quarrying, coffee and tea processing, and bakeries.

Kabale District, with a population of 510,000 people, lies in the southwest corner of Uganda. Its elevation is high, and it contains the mountainous border with Rwanda. Agriculture includes not only staple crops but also some less common foods that can be grown here because of the altitude and cooler weather: wheat, green vegetables, and fruit. Cattle, goats, and sheep are raised, and Lake Bunyonyi offers fishing. Local industries include manufacture of wine, furniture, and footwear, brick-making, metal fabrication, stone quarrying, and a little mining of wolfram and tin.

Hoima District is situated in the middle of Uganda's western side, lying just to the east of Lake Albert, which forms part of the border with the DR Congo. With a population of 342,000, Hoima is one of the successor districts to the ancient Bunyoro-Kitara kingdom. Agriculture is again the mainstay of the district's economy, with both subsistence and cash crops grown. The latter include cotton, tobacco, and horticultural items.[2] Livestock is also raised.

Arua District is located in the northwest corner of Uganda, on the west side of the Nile river. It borders Sudan in the north and the DRC in the West. Arua's population of 860,000 includes those who are living in camps as the result of the violence against people, buildings, and crops that has continued at least sporadically since 1986 due to fighting between the Lord's Resistance Army, which in 2002-3 was led by Joseph Kony, and the Ugandan army. Arua's economy is almost entirely based upon subsistence agriculture, of types suitable to its drier climate. Only 0.5 percent of the population is engaged in commercial farming, either tobacco or cotton.

Lira District lies in the middle of the country, some 120 miles north of Kampala on the far side of Lake Kyoga and its marshes. Its population of 760,000 people has likewise been destabilized in recent years by the fighting. Lira is one of Uganda's largest producers of oil seeds, which include simsim (= sesame) and sunflowers, and of shea butter – the latter an ingredient in beauty products that is starting to gain ground as a major income earner. Fourteen percent of the district's area is under water and another 15 percent is wetland, providing good conditions for rice production.

Jinja District lies about 50 miles east of Kampala, adjacent to the point where the River Nile flows northward out of Lake Victoria. Although most of its population of 346,000 people either raise food crops (for home consumption or sale) or fish, Jinja has several distinctive features. Prior to Amin's period, Jinja town was the center of South Asian settlement, plantations, and economic activity in Uganda. With the expulsion of these residents, the community declined. Although it had still not returned to its former level in demographic and commercial terms as of 2003, it was once more producing sugar cane, coffee and cotton, in some cases on plantations owned by South Asian multinational corporations to whom the property was restored by the NRM government. Furthermore, the construction of the Owen Falls Dam on the Nile in the 1950s provided hydroelectric power that made Jinja the country's leading industrial town for several decades. Although it was later overtaken by Kampala, it still produced power, textiles and beer as well as refining sugar, smelting iron, and tanning leather. These are the settings within which working women were interviewed for our district sample.

The 'Torchbearers'

At the beginning of our research, we interviewed eight women who head important organizations in Kampala and have thought deeply about women's economic issues.[3] Of these successful women, recognized as leaders and role models by others, three directed national women's associations, while five headed groups dealing more specifically with economic matters. The following description of the women and the organizations they led at the time of the interview moves from broadly based organizations to more specifically focused ones.

Grace Mukasa was the executive director of Action for Development (ACFODE). This national women's organization was formed in 1985 as a follow-up to the international women's conference held in Nairobi (see Chapter 7). An active force in Uganda since that time, ACFODE's mission was to improve the status and lives of women through communication and networking with rural and urban women, and through close collaboration with other organizations. It sought to empower women by sharing knowledge and experiences on issues regarding health, family planning, legal rights, other social problems, and income-generating projects. In addition to advocating women's increased participation at all levels of decision-making and lobbying for legal reform and the enforcement of women's rights, ACFODE generated information about issues of concern to women. It was also a powerful player in the decision to introduce extra points for women in university admission. Grace had an MA in Gender and Development from the University of Sussex in the UK.

Peace Kyamureku was the executive director of the National Association of Women's Organizations in Uganda. NAWOU was set up in 1992 by NGOs and

24

CBOs dealing with women to function as a coordinated network of member organizations for the efficient use of resources in order to improve the status and living conditions of Ugandan women. It had the following aims: raising awareness of the needs, rights and responsibilities of women; empowering women to fulfill their potential within the family, community, and on decision-making bodies; co-operating at all levels with other non-governmental and community-based organizations and with local and international partners; networking through meetings, seminars, and workshops at national, regional, and international levels; and monitoring the status of women with special focus on legislation, implementation, conventions and human rights, and sustainable development. NAWOU had a particular interest in rural women. Peace held a master's degree in history and in 2002–3 was beginning research for a Ph.D. in Women and Gender Studies.

Jackie Asiimwe was the coordinator of UWONET, the Uganda Women's Organizations Network. A lawyer by profession, with an LL.M. from the United States, Jackie was a member of the younger generation of women activists. UWONET was established in 1993 as a way to bring together national organizations and individuals to work more effectively on issues of common concern to women through information sharing, communication, and collective action. Focusing on women's political, economic and social empowerment, UWONET advocated appropriate and relevant legislation and policies. It was, for example, at the forefront of lobbying and educating Parliament and the public about the Land Act of 2002 and the proposed Domestic Relations Bill. In addition, the organization participated in the monitoring of the 2001 elections for women's representatives in the districts and for Members of Parliament.

We talked also with two women who head major economic organizations. Olive Kigongo was the president of the Uganda National Chamber of Commerce and Industry. The Chamber, charged with organizing, mobilizing and promoting commerce and trade in the country, had been relatively inactive during the later 1990s and early 2000s. When Olive was appointed as its head in 2002, the first woman to hold the office, this poised and self-assured woman introduced a series of initiatives to revitalize the organization and move it in new directions. She was especially concerned with tapping into overseas markets and the potential of ICT. Olive was a successful businesswoman in her own right. Together with her husband, one of the leading figures in the NRM in 2003, she ran a large and expensive complex in an exclusive neighborhood in Kampala, containing rental housing, a restaurant, and other services.

Maggie Kigozi was the executive director of the Uganda Investment Authority (UIA), a parastatal (government-affiliated) body. A medical doctor by training and the widow of a prominent businessman, Maggie's positive outlook and enthusiasm were carrying the UIA in new directions. The UIA was charged with directing and promoting investments in Uganda, including licensing medium and large-scale projects. Eager to encourage the business success of women, Maggie set up a Women's Network, creating a database of women entrepreneurs and holding regular meetings on such topics as how to use one's capital and how to keep appropriate records. The members of the network, most of whom operated at an intermediate economic level, were engaged mainly in tourism, hotel and restaurant work, education (setting up their own schools), grain milling, real estate, and cargo handling.

The remaining women all worked with organizations concerned specifically with women's economic activities. Angela Nakafeero, who had a master's degree in Women and Gender Studies, was the executive director of the Uganda chapter of the Council for the Economic Empowerment of Women in Africa. CEEWA-Uganda was initiated at an NGO forum in 1994, in anticipation of the Beijing Conference. Its goals were to articulate regional and country-specific strategies to address the causes of poverty and lack of economic empowerment for women. Principally an advocacy organization, it also promoted the economic empowerment of women through training programs. The organization was particularly important in carrying out model projects and doing high quality research about women's economic activities. In 2002–3 it was running four programs: women and agriculture; women and finance; gender and economic decision-making; and women and entrepreneurship development.

Sarah Kitakule was the newly appointed, young, university-educated director of the Uganda Women Entrepreneurs Association Ltd. UWEAL brought together women who managed or owned commercial enterprises to promote their success and build up a body of sensitized businesswomen who could work for economic change in Uganda. As part of its activities, UWEAL offered training programs in various parts of the country on how to run a sustainable enterprise. In 2002–3 it had 200 members in Kampala and 500 in its countrywide network. Sarah was especially interested in promoting a spirit of entrepreneurship among women and in facilitating their training in modern business administration techniques and computer-based technologies in schools and colleges.

Lydia Rugasira was Assistant General Manager of the Uganda Women's Finance Trust Ltd. (UWFT). This organization, the first successful microfinance group in Uganda to focus on women, was established in 1984. The mission of UWFT was to empower low-income women economically in both rural and urban areas by providing a consolidated package of products and services that included savings and credit. Its clients were women who did not qualify for commercial financial services because they lacked collateral but who had the potential of using a loan to expand their economic activities. The income from their businesses could then feed, house, and educate their children. Group lending was introduced in 1991 to increase outreach and mitigate the high risks that the institution had experienced in lending to individuals. By 2002, UWFT had 20 branches and a staff of 161 members, 97 of whom were women.

The Women in our District Sample

The 113 women in our district sample covered a wide range in demographic and socio-economic terms.[4] They came from 17 different ethnic backgrounds (see Map 2.2). Baganda women formed about a quarter of the total, with the Banyoro, Langi, and Bakiga each comprising roughly an eighth.[5] The rest were more diverse. Each district except for Arua had a dominant ethnic group, and only three women had mixed ethnic parentage. In religious terms Catholics (45 percent) slightly outnumbered members of the (Anglican) Church of Uganda (40 percent). Muslims and pentecostal, or 'born again,' Christians, several of whom had converted from Islam as adults, accounted for 7–8 percent each.

Map 2.2 Ugandan ethnic groups

Only 42 percent of these women were married and living with their husbands at the time of the interview, with a slightly higher concentration among Catholic women.[6] Just over a fifth were separated or divorced, 18 percent were widows, and 20 percent had apparently never married. The high fraction of women not currently married probably resulted in part from the fact that the sample consisted wholly of women who were active participants in the market economy or had retired from it: women living with their husbands might have been somewhat less likely to engage in their own income-generating activities.

When the women who were currently or formerly married were asked whether their husbands had multiple wives or households, whether officially recognized or not, nearly a third said yes. Interestingly, although the fraction of multiple marriages or households was somewhat higher among Muslim women, it was 25–31 percent for all the Christian groups, despite their religion's official opposition to polygamy.

In age, the largest cluster of women were in their forties, followed by those in their thirties and fifties.[7] Smaller groups were in their 20s or were aged 60–92. Nearly a third had first married while they were in their teens, with 43 percent marrying at age 20–24 and 27 percent at age 25–33.

In considering the number of children and dependants of these women, we need to recognize that several factors make these figures rather approximate. Some of the women had not yet married or were still of child-bearing age, so their families were incomplete. Some women apparently gave us the number of births, while others counted only living children. Some may have included people as dependants whom they did not support fully. As reported, however, the average number of children (3.8) was low when compared with the 6.9–7.0 average births per woman for the country as a whole between 1980 and 2000.[8] Only a third had six to ten children, but Muslims and pentecostal Christians were more likely than Catholics or Protestants to have very large families. In addition to their own children, 90 percent of the women were supporting additional dependants, often within their households. Forty-one percent had one to four dependants, 29 percent had five to nine, and 20 percent had 10-18 or 'many'. It is probable that working women were particularly likely to take in children orphaned through HIV/AIDS or to assume the care of other relatives, because they had their own incomes.

In the area of education, 27 percent of the women had received no formal training or only primary schooling; 30 percent had at least some secondary education; 31 percent had a diploma or certificate (common among teachers and nurses); and 12 percent had a bachelor's or higher university degree.[9] These figures are higher than would be found among all Ugandan women of similar ages because our sample contained an atypical proportion of workers in occupations that required specialized training or advanced education. That these women had used part of their income to invest in the education of their children is demonstrated in Appendix C5b, which shows the highest level reached by any of their children. The children of only 10 percent had no more than a primary education, while 44 percent had a secondary education and 46 percent had a diploma, certificate, or university degree. These figures are well above the national averages.

If we turn to the primary type of income-generating activities in which the women were engaged at the time of the interviews, we note that 41 percent made and/or sold food or drink or were involved in other kinds of trade.[10] About a third worked in professional areas defined by local culture as well suited to women: teaching, nursing, or clerical and secretarial positions. This distribution is again unrepresentative of the working population as a whole: our selection process deliberately included a number of early workers in these fields, thereby weighting the sample. Another 9 percent did other types of skilled or high-status work, and 16 percent provided unskilled or semi-skilled labor. Half of the women worked on their own, while a quarter hired or supervised one or two other people, and another quarter hired or supervised three or more people. Only seven of the married women worked together with their husbands.

A quarter of the women mentioned a second type of work. In nearly all cases they had added business or trading activity to salaried employment. Furthermore, many of them had shifted from one type of activity to another during their lifetimes – in some cases repeatedly – as their own personal circumstances or the world around them changed.

About half of these women carried out their work in Kampala or their district's headquarters.[11] A further 29 percent lived in a peri-urban area, involving semi-dispersed housing often with large gardens located on the edge of Kampala or another town; 22 percent worked in villages. The teachers, nurses, and secretaries were concentrated in district headquarters or peri-urban regions, while small traders were scattered throughout all types of settings.

To provide a more concrete sense of these women's economic activities and the variations contained within the sample, we shall describe their occupations based upon the type of community and type of work. Any division by category of activity is necessarily arbitrary, as many women earned money in multiple and overlapping ways. In the district headquarters, women who engaged in food and drink work did so from diverse settings. Some sold in the official marketplace, offering such items as dried beans, peas, vegetables, and groundnuts. Others linked sale of food in the market with other activities: offering dried fish plus fabrics, or selling maize flour and making baskets. A few more fortunate women had indoor shops that sold groceries and other items, while some sat on the verandah outside another person's shop or along a roadside to sell foodstuffs they had grown themselves. Several women offered roasted cassava, pancakes, and banana juice to passers-by. One woman owned and operated a restaurant, while another had a tearoom at a bus park, for which she hired two women attendants. One woman ran a bar that sold groceries as well, while another barkeeper employed two girls to provide sexual services for favored clients. Some women produced foodstuffs commercially, like poultry or cattle, and a pensioner sold vegetables for extra income. One woman was a commercial tobacco farmer.

Work with textiles and clothing was a common occupation in the towns. Some women offered lengths of fabric, others sold ready-to-wear clothing, and one specialized in interior furnishings (mainly curtains). A few worked as dressmakers or did tailoring and embroidery. One ran a small shop that sold embroidery and decorations, which boomed around the Christmas and Easter holidays. Another sold clothing items but also provided hairdressing services in her shop.

Other kinds of business were less common. A few women ran carpentry work-shops, either making general furniture or specializing in coffins; they generally employed 2–4 male workers. A cluster of women sold 'general merchandise' in their local market or in a shop (two of them augmented their earnings by operating a communication bureau or holding the contract for street cleaning in the town), and one was a wholesaler of such goods. Other women sold stationery, offered photography supplies and services, or charged people to use the telephone in a tiny shop. One woman owned and operated a shop that sold drugs (medicines), supplementing her income by knitting sweaters for schoolchildren; another ran a veterinary drug shop while rearing poultry and selling eggs on the side. One woman managed her own lodging house. A prominent trader sold building hardware, while another woman ran a shop with her husband that sold spare parts for motors; they also operated a grain grinding mill, owned residential property to rent out, and had their own truck for transport.

The district headquarters offered employment in the careers traditionally seen as appropriate for educated women. Several of the women interviewed were primary school teachers and one was a deputy headmistress. A significant cluster worked as nurses or midwives, three of them employed as (senior) nursing or health officers for the district. Most of the nurses had sources of income in addition to their wages, commonly operating a drug shop. One woman was a senior medical assistant and another a dental assistant. Other women were traditional birth attendants (partially trained midwives) or prepared and sold medicinal herbs. A significant group worked as secretaries, copy typists, or office administrators. Several of them did small-scale farming as well. A few were records officers or accounts clerks for local government. Another woman offered private stenography services, doing typing at home with her own manual typewriter; one provided computer instruction.

Women were involved in other kinds of professional, skilled, or high status work as well. Local governments hired a senior labor officer, a personnel officer, the director of a vocational training center, and a community development worker. A few of these women did occasional consultancies in gender-related work. One woman was the district coordinator for a national women's organization, while international NGOs provided employment for a customer relations officer and a vehicle driver.

The rest of the town-based workers provided semi-skilled or unskilled services or labor. The largest group offered hair care. The most successful ran their own hair styling salons, in some cases supplementing these earnings by selling groceries or making and selling wine. One woman sat at the side of the street plaiting (braiding) hair and selling roasted groundnuts. Other women worked for wages. Some were employed by local governments: a manual laborer cutting grass and looking after public places for the municipal council, a woman hired occasionally as a cooking and baking instructor for the district, and a cook at a vocational training institute who brewed and distilled local alcohol (*waragi*) on the side. Another group worked as shop assistants, one of whom received no salary from her husband for helping him in his business. Other women were hired as waitresses or tailors. One worked as an attendant in a bar and lodge, renting out low-income housing in addition. One young woman, who had a diploma in commerce but was not able to find a better job, worked for the housekeeping department of a small hotel. An orphaned girl and several adults worked as domestic servants, living with the family that employed them, while an elderly woman worked as a domestic servant at a school, supplementing her income by brewing beer and doing agricultural labor. The most grueling work was done by two women who worked in a stone quarry, crushing stones in the blazing sun, using heavy wooden mallets. They also undertook casual labor when it was available, usually in agriculture. One woman was a member of the reserve force of the Ugandan army (the UPDF).

In Kampala and its immediate suburbs, despite the huge concentration of people, most women worked in ways not very different in size and complexity from those seen in the district centers. They were, however, even more likely to pursue multiple income-generating activities: only six of the twenty women interviewed were engaged in just a single venture. One woman had a cooked food stall, and another operated a kiosk in one of the residence halls at Makerere University, selling soft drinks and cosmetics, but also did domestic work for visiting European or North American academics. Three sold used clothing or locally made bridal attire; one worked nominally as an unpaid attendant in a textile shop run by her husband, but in order to have her own income she sold embroidery under the counter, without his knowledge. One woman owned and ran a veterinary drug shop, at the same time rearing poultry and renting out her vacant plot of land on a short-term basis. A former teacher worked for Kampala City Council as a divisional school inspector but did some private farming as well, while a woman in her nineties owned a school run by her children, at which she sometimes helped out. Three women were nurses. One of them also operated a drug shop, worked as a traditional birth attendant, and raised poultry, while another owned a private clinic. One woman was a secretary and one a supervisor with a health-related international NGO. Two women owned beauty and hairdressing salons, and a pensioner bred pigs and did occasional work with the Uganda Media Women's Association.

In the capital, however, a few of the women's businesses were larger than in other regions, requiring substantial inputs of capital, labor, and skills. These included a medium-scale enterprise that produced and packed fruit juices, cakes, and sweet bread, and a milling firm that processed maize, millet, grain, and soybean into human foods and feed for cattle and poultry. A large new office building situated in a desirable area of Kampala was owned and run by a medical doctor and her husband, who held other real estate as well, while one of the largest and most affluent private schools in the city was owned and operated by several women with their husbands' backing. Construction of buildings for the latter two projects required enormous capital investment, supplied by loans from commercial banks or international credit organizations.

The economic level of the women in our district sample varied greatly. When we asked what they earned monthly (from their businesses, salaries, and/or other activities), some were unwilling to talk about how much they made. Concern that the information would come into the hands of local tax assessors may have led some women to understate the size of their actual earnings, while others inflated their income out of pride. A small group did not know how much they made per month. Although the figures are therefore only approximate, 29 percent said they earned under Ush 100,000 (<US$50) per month; 36 percent said they made Ush 100,000–499,999 (US$50–249); 16 percent said they made Ush 500,000 or more (US$250 or more); and 19 percent did not answer or did not know.[12]

The women's reported earnings varied by district. In Mpigi, the lowest value for monthly earnings disclosed was only Ush 6,000 (US$3) for an apprentice tailor, while the highest was Ush 300,000 (US$150) for a computer instructor. If the top

Introduction

earner is excluded, since her income was out of line with the others, the average monthly income of the remaining women came to Ush 44,000 (US$22). In Hoima, Jinja, and Lira, women reported somewhat higher monthly earnings. The average monthly income for most of the women in these towns was between USh 89,000 and 112,000 (US$44–56), if the few women with atypically large incomes are excluded.[13] In Kabale and Arua, reported income was up one more notch. With the top values excluded, the average monthly income for the other women was Ush 158,000–180,000 (US$79–90).[14]

In Kampala only nine of the twenty-two women were willing to talk about their monthly earnings: some of the wealthiest and some of the poorest declined to say how much they made. The level of earnings nonetheless appears to have been higher and the range of incomes greater than in the district towns, not surprising given the larger scale of business in the capital, the presence of the central offices of governmental bodies and NGOs, and the increased cost of living in a metro-politan area. At the bottom of the spectrum, two women who ran hairdressing salons and one who ran a clinic and drug shop said their monthly income was Ush 40,000 (US$20). This was almost certainly net income, after expenses. At the top of the scale, a health worker and retailer reported monthly earnings to the tune of Ush 3,900,000 (US$1,950), a woman employed as a supervisor by an NGO said her monthly salary and allowances came to Ush 4,400,000 (US$2,200), and the operator of a grain mill said her gross monthly income varied between Ush 5,000,000 and 10,000,000 (US $2,500–5,000).

Because the self-reported earnings were incomplete and unreliable, we asked the interviewers to estimate each woman's standard of living, based upon where she was working, what she wore, what possessions she had, and other subjective indicators. These assessments were relative, based upon the economic norms of the particular community. Here we used four categories: very poor, living in real hardship (e.g., probably unable to afford three meals per day and living in a single rented room); low but living adequately (e.g., able to eat regularly, renting several rooms, and owning basic household goods); of middle level, living fairly comfortably (e.g., in their own home, with more household goods, and able to pay for their children's education); and well-off (e.g., living in a house with ample furniture and some conveniences, able to afford a boarding school education and further training for their children). By the standards of developed countries, all these categories except for the well-off would be defined as poor. The interviewers judged that 13 percent of the women interviewed were very poor, living in real hardship; 31 percent were poor but living adequately; 33 percent were of middle level; and 23 percent were well-off.

Introductory Profiles

The profiles presented here – like the ones in later chapters – were chosen to give a more human face to selected members of our district sample and to illustrate some characteristic patterns in the lives of the larger group. They provide an introduction to many of the themes of our study, based upon its central questions, while at the same time demonstrating the range of responses we received. The key questions include:

- At what age and why did women decide to seek an income of their own?
- What factors influenced the kind of work they pursued? In particular, what was the role of education in shaping their options?
- How did they combine their domestic duties and care of children with income-generating activities?
- How did their work change over the course of their lives, and why?
- To what extent were their economic activities affected by broader developments in the country?
- How was their work related to other aspects of their lives, such as community involvement?
- How did their husbands or other male relatives feel about their work? Why did women's independent earnings cause tension in some families but not in others?
- How did other people in the community view their work?
- In what ways did working benefit women's lives, and what challenges did they confront?

The profiles also allow us to follow how women's experiences developed across the course of their lives, how their work and family relationships traversed the chronological periods into which our analysis in later chapters is divided. In conformity with privacy regulations, we use pseudonyms for these and subsequent profiles.[15]

Profile 2.1 A Pioneer Community Development Worker: 'Angela Akello'

Angela Akello entered community development work in 1965, one of the first women to do so.[16] Her work was especially unusual because she was living at that time in the Moroto District of Karamoja, a region of pastoral people with relatively few educated woman. A Protestant Lango, she was 57 years old at the time of the interview and separated from her husband. During the conversation, which took place at her home in a peri-urban setting outside Lira, she was welcoming, composed, and cheerful.

Angela was born in 1945 in a village in Lira District. Her father was a parish minister in the Church of Uganda; her mother prepared tea and pancakes for sale to pupils and staff at the local school and to vendors at the nearby market. Three other women in the area also sold pancakes, 'but my mother's were the best and would sell fast'. (As the wife of a minister, her mother had been trained how to cook new foods by white teachers sent by the CMS.) Angela went to primary school in the village and then to a secondary school in Soroti, continuing through S 3, the third year of secondary school. Her family's attitudes towards her education were mixed. 'My father wanted me to go to school, but my uncles discouraged him. They wanted me to get married and provide bridewealth to be used for my brothers' marriages. My mother was instrumental in my getting educated. She would ask a minister at the church to pay for my school fees.'

When Angela left school, she decided to go into community development work. She had studied Home Economics as a subject at school, so she had knowledge and skills she could impart to rural women in the villages. She was influenced by two women she knew who had been working as tailors but had recently been hired by the government to train other women. Angela went

---

through a course at Entebbe, paid for by the early Independence government, and at age 20 took her first job. The first community workers were generally men, and she was particularly unusual because she was young and unmarried. (The only women who had jobs in the Karamoja region at that time were a few teachers, ward maids in the hospital, and secretaries.) Her uncles did not approve of her work, a sentiment she suspects was shared by most people in the area. She worked from 8:00 a.m. to 5:00 p.m., earning Ush 200 monthly. That was a lot of money at the time, enabling her to support herself and provide assistance to her parents as well as sending her younger brother and sister to school.

She remained in that position until she was 33. In 1978, however, she became the second wife of a chief justice living in Kampala. She moved to the city to join him, and they had a daughter, who later graduated from the university. But tension developed between Angela and her co-wife, and her husband did not want her to work. When she insisted, he alternately resorted to violence or shunned her completely. She was especially worried about being economically dependent because of the instability of the Amin and Obote II years. People were being killed, and others went into exile. Yet women in the city were afraid to go into business because they might be looted, jailed, or killed by soldiers. So she decided to leave her husband and go back to the Lira area, where she had relatives and could continue with her own career more safely. After their separation her husband provided no financial assistance at all to her or their daughter.

In Lira, Angela went on with community development work. She was in 2003 a community development assistant focusing on women's groups at the local level, part of the country's decentralization policy. Riding her motorcycle (an uncommon form of transportation for Ugandan women!), she went out every day to the villages to sensitize and advise rural women. She talked with them about the importance of keeping water sources clean, ensuring domestic cleanliness and personal hygiene, and visiting a health center when they became pregnant or a family member fell sick. She was aware that although she had taken courses to upgrade her qualifications, her level of education did not match that of the university graduates who later entered her field.

Angela was also involved in business. During the NRM period, she explained, many women in Lira began to set up small income-generating activities. Even those who were family farmers started to dig additional gardens so that they could sell produce to gain their own incomes. She decided to try her hand at making and selling samosas (an Indian-style dough stuffed with meat or vegetables and then fried) in her spare time. Though her weekly earnings were modest (Ush 3–5,000, or US$1.50–2.50), they helped her to buy essential commodities. With this income plus her salary she could support her household, which included four dependants as well as a second child of her own; she also provided for the children of her late brother and sister, who were living elsewhere. Within five years after her interview, Angela would be required to retire from her government position because of her age. She was therefore constructing a permanent building that would include housing and a shop for her expanding business, allowing her to bring in more income.

Angela was active within the community. She was the chairperson of the local Mothers' Union (a women's group within the Church of Uganda), and she did voluntary advising for another group. She had in turn received various kinds of assistance during her lifetime. The National Association of Women's Organizations in Uganda trained her and other women in practical skills and leadership, through seminars and workshops. The Community HIV/AIDS Initiative helped her to provide for her nieces and nephews, and the Development Training and Research Centre (DETREC) in Lira taught her financial management. Because she knew how to keep records of income and expenditures, she could tell whether she was getting a profit from her business, and DETREC taught her to bank any extra money.

In reflecting upon her life, Angela stressed the financial benefit of her work. Most importantly, she had been able to provide an education for her own children and others. The problems she faced included the physical and emotional abuse she suffered while she was married and her low income, due in part to her husband's refusal to provide support for their child. Another difficulty was HIV/AIDS: she had lost her father, to whom she was closer than to her mother and who was her main advisor, as well as several siblings.

When asked to assess the NRM period, Angela gave a complex picture. She noted many positive features, including the fact that 'Women now love education, because the homes of those women who were educated earlier are examples of progress. Consequently, most mothers are very much concerned about their children's education, and they struggle to meet scholastic demands, sometimes going into business to do so.' But Lira had felt the impact of the problems that have unsettled the northern part of Uganda during the NRM years. Between 1987 and 1989, Karamajong rustlers from Moroto District took nearly all the cattle from Lango sub-region. This left farmers with no draft animals, so they had to do all the work by hand, using hoes. Angela was also keenly aware of the violence still going on just to the north of them. The fighting had brought great fear, for 'women are being raped and young children abducted'. Furthermore, the attacks were moving closer to Lira: 'Many families from rural areas are displaced and now starving in town.'

As she thought about what might help Ugandan women, Angela focused upon the poor. Noting that some women still slept on mats on the floor because they could not afford even a simple mattress, she described approvingly the informal saving groups that some poor women were forming on their own. Others earned small amounts of money by working together as a unit, digging in other people's gardens. Their pay was left in the keeping of the group's treasurer, to be handed out at Christmastime or distributed to members on a rotational basis. This allowed women to buy bigger items they could not otherwise afford, like bedding, clothes, and saucepans. The groups also tried to keep at least Ush 2,000 (US$1) on hand at all times, so that a woman could borrow if she faced an emergency like sickness or the death of a family member. At a slightly higher economic level, Angela believed that many women had good ideas on how they could go into business, but they lacked the capital with which to begin and the financial skills that would help them to succeed. Looking ahead, Angela thought it would be essential for whoever is elected in the Presidential elections of 2006 to continue supporting women's struggles. 'If he is not gender-sensitive, women's political and economic situation will deteriorate.'

Introduction

Profile 2.2 Running a Family Shop: 'Fatuma Kasirye'

Fatuma Kasirye's life shows how entry into marriage at a young age could be successfully combined with a long-term husband-and-wife business.[17] A Muslim Muganda, she was interviewed in 2003 at their photography shop in Jinja. She was dressed in a long maroon skirt and matching blouse, with a black scarf covering her head and neck. Aged 43 years and the mother of seven children, ranging from 9 to 22 years at the time of the interview, she had worked with her husband since the early years of their marriage, which took place when she was just 16. Her petite size, easy movements, and young-looking face explained why people addressed her by a nickname that means 'bride'.

Their shop was located on a busy street in the town and although it was small in size, it did a thriving business. During the interview customers came in and out to have their picture taken (in a studio behind the main room) or to buy cameras, frames, or photographic supplies. Her husband, addressed respectfully as 'Al Hadji' because he had made the pilgrimage to Mecca, sat at a desk overseeing the shop in general terms, while Fatuma, assisted by a son and daughter, attended to customers. On the street outside the shop another one of her children was in charge of a stool with a mobile phone, which passers-by could use for payment. A second room in the back was used as a storeroom and sleeping quarters for the boys who stayed in the shop at night to protect their valuable stock. Although normally a gentle person (though clearly also very competent), Fatuma was upset and angry on the day of the interview. That morning one of her husband's relatives had come into the shop to chat and then walked off with one of their professional quality, expensive cameras. She had spent much of the day contacting the police and local authorities and alerting other camera shops to the theft.

Fatuma was born in 1959 in Mbarara, where her father ran a hotel. Her mother and other women grew food for their own family's consumption. Despite her Muslim background, she went to a school run by missionaries, who 'were very good on discipline and academics'. Her father 'was interested in our education, but we were many and he could not afford the fees for us to complete our schooling'. Her mother was likewise supportive but had no income. Fatuma therefore had to leave school after S 2. Shortly after that, in 1976, she married. Although her husband was a good deal older, she was his only wife. At the time of their marriage, he was running a photography shop in Mbarara, but he became discouraged by the difficulties of trying to do business there, due to the disruptions caused by the Amin regime. He therefore decided to relocate to Jinja, choosing this destination because of the recent expulsion of the South Asians, many of whom had lived in this community. Although most large enterprises were given to Amin's friends, relatives, and army buddies, some smaller businesses went to less well-connected men.

Fatuma began to help in their shop as soon as they moved to Jinja and has continued to do so ever since. When asked why she took up that kind of work, she said simply, 'That's what I found my husband doing.' Her husband, who taught her how to use cameras and sell, was pleased to have her assistance. Although her husband was usually in the shop with her (he left mainly to go to the mosque), he trusted her to handle matters while he was away and did not object to her working there alone. While Fatuma was unusual in learning about photography and playing such an important role in the business, her work was well regarded in the community. Right from the start, she put in long days at the shop, from 7:30 a.m. to 9:00 p.m. Because they lived near the business, she could keep an eye on the children at the same time. Her husband allowed her to keep the cash she brought in herself, which she used not only for personal effects but also 'to start laying a basis for the family by making monthly savings and buying land'. With part of their shared income they were able to educate their children. The older boys had all completed S 6, the older girls were then in secondary school, and the younger children were in primary school.

At the time of the interview, Fatuma was functionally in charge of the shop. Her husband had developed diabetes and was not very strong: she had been trained by the nurse to give him regular injections of insulin, and she had to prepare special food for him. They had no paid employees, but the seven children all helped in the shop at various times, taking photos, developing and printing them, working at the cash register, and writing out receipts for customers. Their monthly earnings were in the range of Ush 600,000–700,000 (US$300–350), but their expenses were also high; they hoped to net around Ush 180,000 (US$90) per month. In addition, they had income from the large gardens Fatuma had bought. The farming was done by their children and some paid laborers, supervised by Fatuma. When asked who controlled the family's income, she said 'everything is a joint effort with my husband'. In 2003 their household included several grandchildren as well as their children, and Fatuma supported her mother, who lived elsewhere. A natural peacemaker, Fatuma was actively involved in the community, spending a good deal of time helping people to resolve their problems, though she held no formal offices.

Thinking back over her own lifetime, she commented that her work had been assisted by her husband and several microfinance lending institutions, such as FINCA. Whatever business skills she had were taught her by her husband. Her work had benefited her in several respects. She was able to educate her children, buy land, and build a house. Her major complaints were financial. She thought that the business taxes charged by the Uganda Revenue Authority were too high: 'women have failed to venture into business because the government taxes are too stiff. People are expected to pay even before the business picks up.' The interest rates charged by lending institutions also discouraged women. She concluded that many women 'are willing to work, but we often lack capital, working partners, and the necessary machinery for our work'.

As she looked into the future, Fatuma hoped to expand their business by injecting more capital into it. She thought that women were breaking into new kinds of work partly out of necessity. 'With the current economic situation and so much competition, we women must get into any available work in order to survive.' Yet most of the domestic responsibility still falls on their shoulders. 'The biggest burden of running the home rests on women. It is women who have to struggle with everything now, for the times are changing.' Compared with earlier generations, when women were looked after by their families, she believed they have to work harder now, especially those who have to support themselves and their children. But at the same time, they are more educated, and some can run businesses.

Profile 2.3 A Life of Limited Opportunities: 'Fulgencia Apio'

Fulgencia Apio was a childless woman in her early fifties whose life had been limited by lack of education, her family situation, and poverty.[18] Now aging, she supported herself in 2003 by piecing together several activities: working as a residential 'matron' in a boarding school (looking after the younger boys' living quarters), brewing and selling beer, and hiring out her labor in some seasons to farmers needing people to dig in their fields. When interviewed at the school, located in a village a few kilometers from Lira, she seemed unsure of herself and a little frightened at being asked questions about her life.

Fulgencia was born sometime around 1952, though she did not know her exact age. From a Catholic Lango family, she lived as a child in a village in Apac District where her parents were peasant farmers, growing food for their own consumption. Her father died when she was very young, and although her mother tried to send her to school, Fulgencia dropped out part way through the first year. This meant that she could not read or write in her own language, did not learn English, and could not do written arithmetic. She was married young, at around 15-17 years, to a parish chief who had multiple wives.

Fulgencia remembered Amin's regime, when she was still married, as a very difficult period. 'There was general suffering. People were killed or arrested for political reasons, and there was a major lack of essential commodities. When they were available, they were very expensive and people had to queue (stand in line) for long hours to buy them. Generally women and children would miss out. So people made local salt by drying and burning *kalanata* (a local plant), filtering it, and adding the filtrate to food. We made soap from local plants like *elila* and *iwele wele* (root fibers). You would get the roots, pound them, and soak them in water for washing clothes.'

In order to have some income for herself, she began to brew beer at home for sale. She learned the technique from older women in her community, many of whom brought in a little money that way. Her income was very low, but her husband did not like the idea of her controlling her own money and insisted that she give her earnings to him. This led to domestic violence, compounded by the fact that she was unable to bear children. When she was in her early thirties, her husband divorced her.

Because she had no way of supporting herself in the village, she moved to Kampala. There she took work as a housegirl, cooking, cleaning, and tending the children of other people. She received room and board, and though her cash wages were small, they were more than she had earned from brewing. Saving her meager income, she was able over time to buy two goats. One of them was later appropriated and sold by her brother-in-law, who needed money for taxes and the bridewealth for his son's marriage. Fulgencia continued as a housegirl in Kampala for many years before going back to Lira.

In 2003 she was living at the school, sharing her single room with a nephew, a boy in S 4. She received a small stipend there, she earned Ush 10,000–20,000 per week (US$5–10) from beer brewing, and at certain times of the year she brought in money from agricultural labor. She could not calculate what these sources of income came to in total, but she had enough money for basic food and clothing. Her major concern was that she did not know how she would be able to support herself as she got older. She regarded the NRM government as the most positive one she had known, because essential goods were now plentiful.

Profile 2.4 A Full and Satisfying Life: 'Mary Katushabe'

Mary Katushabe's life represents an ideal, one achieved by few Ugandan women.[19] This 65-year-old lady had successfully combined a socially useful and varied career with a rewarding family life, including a husband who accepted her work and helped to raise a large family of accomplished children. She was interviewed just outside the carpentry workshop on the edge of Kabale town that she had operated with her husband since they retired from their professional positions. During the conversation, four carpenters were making beds, chests, and other furniture in the big interior room of the shop. Mary had just returned from a meeting when she was interviewed, and was wearing a Western-style suit with matching skirt and jacket. Her manner was self-confident, and she seemed comfortable talking about her experiences. Her own comments were extended by those of her husband, who was interviewed separately.

Mary, a Mukiga member of the Church of Uganda, was born in 1937 in a village in Kigezi. Her father was a catechist, educating people in Christian belief, and her mother and other local women were peasant farmers, though sometimes they would sell off extra food. Her father was at first supportive of her education, 'but when he realized that my mother had borne only girls, he married another woman and left us to fend for ourselves'. Her mother was determined to keep Mary in school and came up with the money to do so. After primary school, Mary attended Hornby High School in Kabale, then as now a leading institution in the region, run by the Church of Uganda. From there she went on for teacher training at Bishop Stuart College in Kabale, with her expenses paid by the church. She chose this career 'because it was the most appropriate option' open to her: other girls at the time were becoming teachers, and such work was respected by her relatives and the community.

After qualifying as a Grade II primary school teacher in 1958, she took her first position, at a village school in Kabale district. She was then aged 21. As her husband commented in his interview, 'Educated ladies were then very few, so they could get jobs.' She worked 7 hours a day, at a starting salary of Ush 90 per month plus free housing. After two years she was promoted to headmistress of her school, and her pay gradually increased to Ush 300 per month. She used her earnings in part for her own personal expenses (like food and clothing) but also to pay school fees for her younger sisters.

When she was 24, she married, as his only wife, a man who was then the headmaster of a boys' primary school. Three years older than Mary, he too came from a rural community in the area, where his father was a chief. His mother would sometimes sell potatoes to men who came out from Kabale and took them to market, but she never sold directly to customers. After completing his secondary education, he went for teacher training, obtaining a certificate as a Grade II teacher. During the first 15 years of their marriage, while Mary continued to work, they had 9 children, who were aged 24–39 years in 2003.

In the early 1970s, circumstances worsened. Under Amin, Mary explained, 'There was a lot of insecurity and murder. The economy was destroyed, and people became poor. Education was not seen as important.' Although her husband had by then become headmaster at Hornby High School, where their family was living, they suffered economically because their salaries were supposed to have been paid in part by the government, which defaulted. Their position may have felt more precarious because her husband had previously

---

been active in a political party that was out of favor during Amin's regime.

In 1973, when she was 36, Mary changed careers. She accepted a position with the Mothers' Union, a job that would now be entitled an education officer. She was responsible for the entire Diocese of Kigezi, spanning the current districts of Kabale, Rukungiri, and Kisoro. The late bishop of the diocese, Festo Kivengere, persuaded her to take the position by showing her how it would help the women and children of her area. She had to travel a good deal, using the vehicle and driver provided by the Mothers' Union. Although she and her husband had a houseful of children at home, he accepted her absences. ('She was a very hard working woman, and even though she traveled a lot and left me with the children, it was not a problem for me.') Her husband noted, however, that other people in the community did not approve of her being away so much. Mary was able to pay for domestic help from her earnings, which rose in purchasing power despite the wild inflation of Amin's regime because British church officials paid her in pounds sterling. The rest of her income she used for 'family development', including school fees and buying land. She remained with the Mothers' Union until her retirement. Throughout her working life she controlled her own income. Her husband said, 'I knew she was committed to her family, she does not drink or go out, so all her money came back to the family.' Her husband meanwhile went into politics, becoming chairperson of the sub-county level of local government in their district.

In recent years, she and her husband had run their carpentry shop as a source of retirement income. Although Mary claimed they operated it together, she was apparently the dominant partner: her husband said he did not know the details of the business or how much they made from it. She explained that because they have a house of their own, their earnings from the shop of Ush 60,000 per week (US$30) plus her husband's pension are sufficient to cover most of their expenses. Their children provided the rest of the support for the household, which at the present time consisted only of her husband and herself, plus her husband's parents. Over the next few years, Mary and her husband wanted to stock the farm they had bought in a village with goats, pigs, and cattle. When it was ready, they would move to it.

Mary described the benefits of her work largely in terms of the schooling she had been able to provide for others. She educated all 9 of her own children up to the university level, as well as keeping 13 additional young relatives in school. In 2003 her children were doing extremely well: her daughters were among the leaders of the next generation of women. One was a member of the Ugandan Parliament, another held a key position in one of the European embassies in Kampala, and three had good jobs with a leading newspaper, one of the big banks, and a tourist agency. Mary's husband said that her work had benefited their family in economic terms and 'because it keeps her very busy. It has never led to problems between us.' Mary had also been able to travel. She went to England at least twice, in 1976 and 1982, and she spoke of how much she had learned during a recent trip to India about how the government there provides logistical support for working women and extended families.[20] A broader perspective was also demonstrated in her description of the NRM period. She went beyond the fact that her own situation was favorable, thanks to improved stability, to comment that, although the new government had started off well and had helped women's empowerment and advancement, HIV/AIDS had become a severe problem, poverty had worsened, and fighting in the north had continued.

Armed with this background information, we turn now to the stages in Uganda's history across which women's work developed.

Notes

1   U. Ministry of Finance, Planning and Economic Development, *An Overview of the National Economy*.
2   Foodstuffs for household consumption include sweet potatoes, finger millet, groundnuts, beans, maize, bananas, cowpeas, pigeon-peas, yams, and Irish potatoes.
3   See Appendix B for a listing of the 'Torchbearers' by the numbers used in subsequent chapters, together with information about where, when, and by whom they were interviewed. Further information about some of these groups is available on their websites.
4   See Appendix B for fuller information about the interviews. The actual numbers are displayed in Appendices C1-9.
5   See Appendix C1 for detailed figures.
6   See Appendix C2 for this and the following paragraph.
7   See Appendix C3.
8   See Appendix C4.
9   See Appendix C5.
10   See Appendix C6.
11   See Appendix C6.
12   See Appendix C7. The exchange rate with US dollars in 2003 was just under Ush 2,000 to US$1. A conversion rate of 2000:1 has therefore been used in this book.
13   The outliers were: in Hoima, a businesswoman and an NGO employee with incomes of Ush 600-700,000 per month (US$300-350); in Jinja, a deputy director of health services earning Ush 630,000 (US$315); and in Lira, a district nursing officer and retail trader earning Ush 800,000 (US$400).
14   The highest monthly incomes in Kabale were the Ush 320,000 (US$160) earned by a woman who owned a carpentry workshop and had a pension and by another who ran a shop and was the district coordinator for a national organization of women's associations. In Arua incomes of Ush 760,000, 800,000 and 950,000 (US$380, 400, and 475) were enjoyed by a woman who ran a bar and a retail shop, a senior labor officer, and a civil servant who directed a training center.
15   Pseudonyms were required by the University of Colorado's Human Research Committee for women interviewed as part of the district sample. The 'Torchbearers' could be named because they represented organizations.
16   She was interviewed by Sylvia Latigo-Otal on 16 February 2003, in Luo (tape: Lira10). The interviewer thought that her economic level was low but adequate.
17   She was interviewed by Anita Mago Sempa on 5 February 2003, in Luganda (tape: Jinja4). On 28 January 2003 Anita and Marjorie McIntosh had talked informally with her and her husband in the photoshop. Anita assessed Fatuma's economic situation as middle-level, not wealthy but comfortably off according to local standards.
18   Fulgencia was interviewed by Sylvia Latigo Olal on 17 February 2003, in Luo (tape: Lira12). The interviewer placed her in the lowest economic category: very poor, living in hardship, struggling to get by.
19   She was interviewed by Jean Kemitare on 4 February 2003, in Rukiga (tape: Kabale3). Marjorie McIntosh was present at the interview but does not understand Rukiga. Mary's husband was interviewed later that day, in English, again in McIntosh's presence. Each discussion occurred outside the hearing of the other spouse. The interviewer assessed their economic level, on the basis of local standards, as well-off.
20   UCU Mukono 1MU 38/3, a file of records from the Mothers' Union in Kigezi Diocese during her tenure with the organization.

Part II

The Generations
of Gradual Change
1900–71

Three

The Early Colonial World
1900–39

During the early colonial period, from around 1900 through the 1930s, the substructure of Ugandan life changed in many respects. Although the shifts were less pronounced than in many other parts of Africa, they had an impact upon both women and men. These general developments are described here, laying a foundation for our subsequent analyses. As a visual guide to the topics that will be considered in this and the following chapter, Figure 3.1 displays how the factors that affect women's participation in the cash-based economy operated during the 1930s. It makes clear (through broken lines with a bar at the end) that many of the pressures that were later to promote women's economic involvement had not yet developed: for example, rural women were rarely able to devote time to economic activities other than growing crops for their own family's consumption, few women moved into towns, and women's groups were limited to religious organizations.

The first section of this chapter traces economic, demographic, and political developments. We look next at the introduction of Christianity and a related area of great importance for women: Western-style education. Both Protestant and Catholic missionaries set up schools for the daughters of elite families and other girls. The schools assumed that girls would be wives and mothers and emphasized domestic skills as one component of their curricula, thereby consolidating certain features of what would become the Domestic Virtue model. A final section describes the limited opportunities for women to earn an income during the early colonial years, as well as the emergence of two new careers for educated women: teaching and nursing. It was the latter types of service work, especially when carried out by women from highly respected families, which forced the development of the first variation of the Domestic Virtue model. The next chapter will consider women's issues and Domestic Virtue more specifically.

The Economic, Political and Demographic Setting

To understand early colonial economic patterns, we must look first at the nineteenth-century background. The economies of all the ethnic groups that later

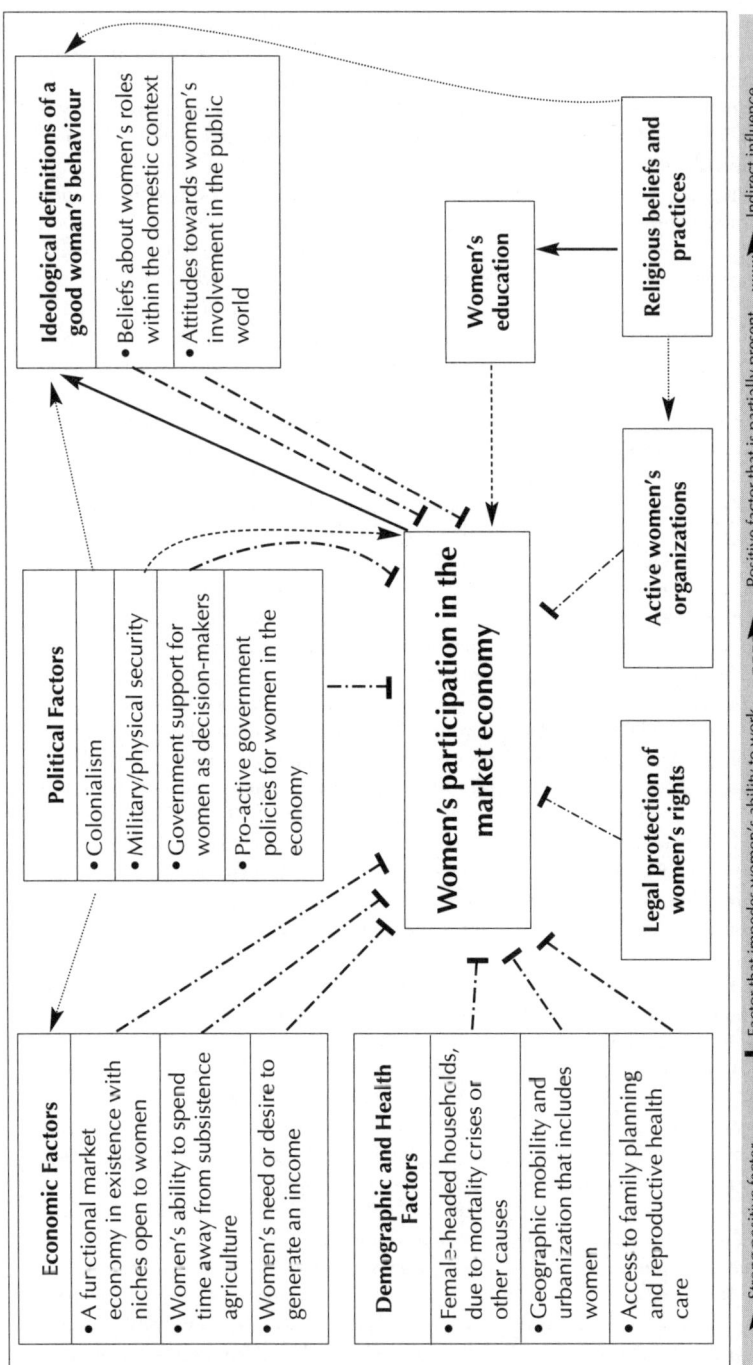

Figure 3.1 Ugandan women's participation in the market economy, 1930s

made up the state of Uganda were at that time based on subsistence agriculture and/or cattle raising. Evidence from oral histories and travelers' accounts makes clear that households grew all or most of the food they consumed and in many cases made simple craft items for their own use. Productive tasks were organized by type of work and gender. In Buganda, for example, men provided shelter, clothing, meat, and alcohol. In most ethnic groups men were responsible for the heavy work of clearing the bush before planting, and they attended to animals in pastoral economies. Women raised and processed the food staples (including root crops, bananas, and the vegetables used in sauces) and did the cooking. They also made mats, baskets, and other household goods, while men made bark cloth (using the bark of a fig tree which was soaked in water and pounded until it became thin and somewhat flexible), hunted, and in some areas fished. Because these responsibilities were seen as complementary and there were few slaves until the later nineteenth century, most work was done by members of the household.[1]

Patterns of trade in the nineteenth century differed in several respects from what has been described in parts of West Africa and many coastal areas of the continent. Markets existed but played a relatively small role in the weakly developed economies of Uganda's peoples: there was little demand for foodstuffs or craft items, since only a shiftless rural household was unable to provide for most of its own needs, and there were no towns. Nor was a uniform system of 'money' in use that could be accumulated or loaned. Informal markets, held periodically or even sporadically, were characterized by barter exchange of locally produced items among people living nearby. The only goods commonly traded among Ugandans themselves over a longer distance were salt and ironware (such as hoes and spears), joined sometimes by bark cloth. Salt was produced from natural deposits in some of the Rift Valley lakes in Bunyoro; ironware was made mainly in Bunyoro and the West Nile District. Until the mid-nineteenth century, contact with the East African coast was limited and focused initially upon ivory, supplemented later by guns and ammunition. As trade with the coast expanded after 1850, however, Uganda assumed a position on the margin of a wider commercial market that spanned much of East Africa and the areas bordering the Indian Ocean. Between the 1850s and 1880s, slaves became an increasingly important component of this long-distance trade, a different proposition from the types of slavery that had previously existed within Uganda.[2]

The nature and extent of trade varied between regions during the second half of the nineteenth century. In the West Nile area and Busoga, for example, most exchanges continued to be conducted informally, whereas a more organized system was developing in Bunyoro-Kitara and Ankole.[3] In Bunyoro-Kitara, local markets were joined by some trade over a wider area, with goods carried mainly by coastal merchants.[4] Ankole was connected with other kingdoms through two sets of networks. One focused on the salt lakes west/northwest of Ankole, while penetration of the region by 'Zanzibari' merchants starting in the 1870s led to an expansion of long-distance trade south around Lake Victoria and then on to the Indian Ocean. Among the Baganda, local trade flourished during the later nineteenth century and had probably done so for some time.[5] Markets were maintained by the *Kabaka* or local chiefs, who collected fees and dues. Along the western frontier, the Baganda traded bark cloth and bananas for Banyoro hoes and salt. Trade with the coast was originally controlled by the *Kabaka*, but gradually

Map 3.1 Ugandan provinces and districts during the colonial period

Baganda chiefs began to interact on their own with caravan traders. Although many exchanges were handled through barter, beads and later cowry shells were used as currency for more valuable sales. In 1903, the 'native market' at the foot of the royal compound in Kampala was four times its size twenty years before, and rupees from India were replacing earlier currencies.[6]

By the turn of the century, economic patterns were being influenced by British colonialism. Contact with Europeans had come late in this landlocked country. Explorers J. H. Speke and Captain Grant arrived in Buganda from the east coast in 1862, while Sir Samuel Baker reached Bunyoro from the north in 1864.[7] The first official representative of British-controlled Sudan arrived only in 1872. Because the area contained strong indigenous kingdoms, with clearly stratified social and political structures as well as more loosely defined groups, the British decided to designate Uganda a protectorate, not a colony. Creation of the protectorate in 1894 was followed by the Buganda Agreement of 1900, which established that kingdom as a privileged province within the larger territory (see Map 3.1.) The agreement also recognized the authority of the *Kabaka*, *Lukiiko*, and other Baganda officials, though the British monarch, acting through the governor, had the right to approve their appointment. Similar agreements were made with the kingdoms of Bunyoro, Toro, and Ankole. None of these gave any recognition or power to female members of the royal families (such as the queen mother and the official sister of the king) who had previously played designated political roles.

During the decades after 1900 the British devolved some of their authority to several layers of local chiefs.[8] This pattern was found to some extent throughout the protectorate but was especially marked in Buganda. The chiefs held greater power than their predecessors had enjoyed but were now appointed and supervised by the colonial government. In their courts, these Native Authorities were supposed to enforce 'customary law' concerning many issues that involved women, including marriages contracted in accordance with local definitions, landholding, and minor crimes. Customary laws, which were defined by the British as pertaining to individual ethnic groups (thereby promoting rigid tribal definitions), may not actually have been traditional and certainly were not static: they were influenced by the needs of the chiefs and the British above them to maintain social control. Over time colonial officials brought into the system of governance some members of the newly educated urban African elite, as chiefs and civil servants.

The impact of empire was profound but less obvious in Uganda than in many other parts of Africa. Because they ruled indirectly, administrators in Entebbe persuaded or forced African officials and institutions to act in accordance with British wishes. In Buganda and many other parts of the country, colonialism led to changes in authority and dependency relationships, the redefinition of chiefship, and new types of landholding, all of which destabilized existing economic and social patterns.[9] Because of women's subordinate position in society, they felt the effects of colonialism largely through their male relatives or the control of the chiefs and Native Courts.

In the years around 1900, a demographic crisis disrupted normal patterns in some regions of the country and weakened resistance to the introduction of British rule. A terrible epidemic of the parasitic disease known as sleeping sickness, carried by tse tse flies, broke out in eastern Uganda in the first half of the 1890s and then moved westward across the country. (It was associated with an outbreak of

Rinderpest, which killed millions of cattle throughout eastern and southern Africa: cattle had previously kept down the brush that harbored the flies.) Bishop Tucker wrote in 1909 that the population of Busoga was thought to have been about 1 million in the mid-1890s, but following the devastation wrought by sleeping sickness and the famine that resulted, it had dropped to about 400,000.[10] Dr Albert Cook, Medical Director of Mengo Hospital, estimated that sleeping sickness killed 200,000 of the 300,000 people living along the shores of Lake Victoria and on its many islands between 1900 and 1905.[11] In 1903 missionaries working in Ngogwe, located east of Kampala beside the lake, reported that on recent tours through their districts they had found that sleeping sickness had 'done away with whole populations'.

The destabilization caused by crisis mortality was intensified by British responses to sleeping sickness. In Busoga, the colonial government proposed that land that had been left uncultivated due to the deaths be confiscated and given to Indian immigrants.[12] Along the length of Lake Victoria and on its islands, British officials forced survivors of the disease to relocate to areas at least 10 miles away from the lake for a decade. A similar policy was implemented elsewhere. In 1912 a missionary in Hoima wrote, 'On account of the deadly sleeping-sickness having reached Bunyoro, the hundred miles of coast-line along Lake Albert has by orders of Government been completely cleared of its population and fisherfolk.'[13]

Colonialism was accompanied by economic change. In Buganda, the 1900 Agreement created a new system of landholding known as '*mailo*' (because the land was measured in miles), similar to what the British knew as freehold. *Mailo* tenure, whose implementation was facilitated by the deaths and forced resettlement that followed the outbreak of sleeping sickness, henceforth operated alongside previous forms of family or clan-based tenure. While the new form of landholding had administrative and economic merits in British eyes, it caused heated disputes during the 1920s involving kings and chiefs, the clan heads who controlled ancestral lands, and younger men who were excluded from ownership.[14]

Other economic developments were felt more widely. Each had consequences for women, requiring new kinds and additional amounts of physical labor, accentuating differences in gender roles, and increasing the responsibilities of women left temporarily as household heads. Tadria has suggested that the British, by appropriating but not destroying the land and labor of the indigenous system, created a dual economy.[15] The new capitalist cash economy, into which only men were recruited, was more highly valued and given special privileges; subsistence agricultural production, dominated by women, received little attention though most households were reliant upon it. The 'peasantization' of rural families also led over time to economic and social differentiation among rural families, with female-headed households concentrated in the ranks of the poor, not the middle class or rich.

Cash cropping in Uganda – the country's first step as a producer of goods within an international, capitalized economy – began with cotton, followed later by tea and coffee. Cotton was introduced into Uganda by the CMS in 1903. Production expanded over the following decade, supported by Buganda's *Lukiiko*, which apparently felt it offered economic potential to local landholders.[16] Prior to around 1920, African cultivators were joined by a few plantations established by Europeans, but thereafter almost all cotton was grown in little plots by Africans.

The limited presence of plantations was due to a combination of the collapse of cotton prices in 1921–2 and the colonial government's opposition to transfer of land from Africans to outsiders. By 1932, over a million acres of land held by local people were planted with cotton, almost as much as was devoted to bananas.[17] The processing and sale of cotton, however, were generally carried out by foreigners, at first Europeans, later South Asians. Women provided much of the labor for growing cotton, in addition to raising food for their own families. While it therefore increased their net workload, it did not cause extensive redefinition of gender roles because women had done most of the farming in Ugandan economies previously, and men normally took the cotton to be sold.[18] Some tea and coffee plantations were established in the 1920s and 1930s, but male migrants hired on short-term contracts did most of the work.[19]

Long-distance trade and formal markets likewise expanded after around 1900. To some extent, this stemmed from British encouragement of existing types of trade, but new forms of commerce were also appearing, promoted by the Mombasa-Nairobi-Kampala railway, started in 1896. Such trading focused on imported – usually manufactured or processed – items like cloth, umbrellas, lamps, tea, sugar, flour, and rice. In contrast to the basic foods that continued to be sold in local markets, the new commerce was concentrated in shops in urban areas and in trading centers or designated market places in smaller communities.[20] The availability of inexpensive foreign manufactured items undermined local production of such goods as metal wares and probably reduced trade between regions of Uganda, thereby promoting 'the growth of ethnic and insular nationalism because for nearly sixty years no Uganda ethnic group needed its neighbor for anything'.[21] Most of the early traders in imported goods were of South Asian background. At first some lived along the East African coast and came inland with caravans, but their numbers were later increased by the South Asians hired by the British to build the railway and by immigrant Indian wholesalers and shopkeepers. Africans rarely appeared as independent traders, though some worked for Indian employers. Insofar as there was capital to be accumulated through commerce, little of it came into African hands. In Lango, for example, where nearly all shopkeepers were South Asian in the late 1930s, only a few African men had saved up enough from their work as unskilled laborers or shop assistants to set up their own little businesses.[22]

Some form of paid employment – at least for a few months each year – became a necessity for many African men in the early twentieth century. Demand increased for money with which to buy the imported goods now becoming available, and bridewealth seems to have risen in many areas. In addition, the British system of taxation (hut taxes and poll taxes, both of which had to be paid in cash) deliberately forced Ugandan men to work for pay. These pressures were compounded by forced labor. In much of the country, men were required to work for the British as well as providing requisitioned and unpaid labor for the chiefs, kings, and sometimes the Christian churches.[23] In Buganda in 1912, men who did not own *mailo* land or have a craft were required to work for three or four months each year for the protectorate plus laboring for their own leaders for two months. This reduced the amount of time they could devote to work at home. Furthermore, slavery was outlawed by the British. Although the labor previously provided by male household heads and slaves was to some extent replaced by immigrants from other parts of Uganda, Rwanda, or Congo, heightened demands on the working abilities of the Baganda themselves may have led to a deterioration in people's standard of living and a decrease in craft production.[24] Women felt the double burden of increased responsibility within subsistence agriculture and their role in cash cropping.

The need for cash propelled most of the male rural-to-urban migration that began after 1900. Though African authorities and the British preferred to have men stay within rural settings, employment opportunities were limited. There were few European farms or large plantations, and no mines. South Asian traders and cotton ginners hired African men for unskilled labor, but only seasonally. In Masaka District, for example, 6 percent of the African male population gained some employment from Indian traders in 1914: 1,250 were employed as 'petty traders' working under Indian businessmen, joined by 270 workmen, 250 porters, and 90 cartmen.[25] Kampala and the other towns offered few kinds of paid work, because the British did not succeed in establishing artisanal or industrial development.[26] Men therefore moved into urban areas only for limited periods of time. Once they had earned enough cash to meet their needs, they returned again to the villages. Because colonial officials did not want to encourage permanent settlement of African town dwellers or 'detribalization,' they were content with this arrangement even though it meant an unstable urban labor force.[27]

A factor in the shortage of paid options for African men was the presence of competing foreign workers. Most were of South Asian background, and they were commonly given preferential treatment by the British in business and those kinds of employment that required some degree of education or direct personal contact with Europeans, like working as clerks, domestic servants, or hospital assistants. The colonial government itself relied mainly upon Indians for semi-skilled positions.[28] Although the governor wrote in 1920 that his ultimate goal was 'the substitution of natives of the Protectorate for the many aliens at present employed in the civil clerical staff and in all grades of skilled government employment,' on the grounds that African workers would be less expensive, this process did not in fact begin for another generation.[29] During the 1920s and 1930s the government made a deliberate effort to encourage Indians (as well as Europeans) to come to Uganda with their families. Retail trading licenses, for instance, which applied mainly to Indian shopkeepers, were set in 1927 at a much lower percentage of net income than were the market dues or street hawker's licenses paid primarily by Africans.[30] To cater for the needs of non-African families, the government provided advantages in the areas of education and healthcare. The special privileges granted by the British contributed to growing resentment on the part of many African Ugandans against South Asians, hostility that was to culminate in Idi Amin's expulsion of the Indians in 1972.

Yet despite these developments, Uganda remained overwhelmingly rural during the early colonial period, with little disruption of family patterns. In 1921, no town contained more than 6,000 people, except for Kampala and Lira.[31] Almost without exception, women remained in the rural areas, and they rarely headed households for extended periods. The lack of urbanization and the stability of most families stand in contrast to certain parts of West Africa and to areas heavily affected by plantation and mining economies, with their demand for ongoing male labor.[32]

Christianity and Female Education

Christianity played a vital part in the history of colonial women. Although Islam had been spreading in Uganda during the second half of the nineteenth century, with some success at upper political levels as well as among ordinary people, by the end of the century many of the country's leaders had accepted Christianity. The first evangelists to arrive in Uganda, in 1877, were two men from the CMS.[33] They were followed in 1879 by French missionaries from the Roman Catholic order of the White Fathers and later by Italian and British Catholics. The complicated political relationships between these groups, Arab and Baganda Muslims, and the *Kabaka* of Buganda, led to the burning of a number of early Christian converts in 1886. In subsequent years, however, the missionaries – backed in some cases by British military force – persuaded many of Buganda's leaders to convert to either the Protestant or the Catholic version of their faith. Particularly significant for African women and the emerging Domestic Virtue model was the (Protestant) Church of England and its CMS wing. Whereas in the late 1880s there were only ten CMS missionaries in Uganda, the number had grown to 40 by the later 1890s and to over 80 by 1903.[34] The early success of the CMS is suggested by the religious affiliations of Buganda's 112 chiefs around 1900: 62 were Protestants, 44 Roman Catholics, and six Muslims.[35] The Protestants were the most powerful in political and educational terms, and women from important Baganda families were key figures in Anglican 'women's work' from 1900 onward. Beginning in the early twentieth century, male British missionaries were commonly accompanied by their wives, and single women came as well. By around 1910 the CMS contingent was increasingly joined in formulating Christian policies by British-born leaders of the Church of Uganda, especially the bishops.

Members of the royal and chiefs' families of the other kingdoms – both men and women – were likewise turning to Christianity, in some cases becoming evangelists and teachers. In Toro, for example, four of the first ten female catechists licensed by the CMS were from the royal court and the rest were chiefs' wives.[36] Some women with spiritual authority under the previous system converted too. These included the favored spirit medium of the king of Toro and the leading female diviner of the king of Ankole. Because of the early involvement of many indigenous leaders, Christianity was regarded as a high-status religion in much of the country. Uganda thus experienced little of the tension seen in certain other parts of Africa during the early years of missionary activity between existing elites and the Christian converts who had access to new forms of Western-defined power.[37] Conversion in Uganda continued apace, and by 1938 it was estimated that about 25 percent of the country's inhabitants were Christian, with more Roman Catholics than Protestants.[38]

From the beginning, the Christian missionaries were committed to education. While both Roman Catholics and Protestants offered some degree of schooling for girls, CMS missionaries and the Anglican bishops were particularly attentive to female education.[39] Their concern stemmed in part from a conviction that both sexes had souls of equal spiritual value and that both should therefore be able to read the Bible. In addition, the early Protestant leaders were eager to ensure that their educated male converts would find well trained women to join them in their roles as leaders of the new faith. In consequence, the missionaries introduced several types of schools. At first most were 'catechist' schools for people who wished to be baptized or 'vernacular' schools that offered simple instruction in local languages; others, located in larger parishes or mission posts, offered up to six years of primary instruction.[40] While such schools have been criticized by some scholars for training their pupils to be subjects of the state, for ignoring or denying the validity of African cultures, and for treating young people with brutality, missionary education for girls in Uganda also contained some positive features.

Particularly influential were the high-status boarding schools founded in the decade after 1900 for daughters of chiefs and other local leaders. The Roman Catholics set up a school for girls from important families at Nsambya outside Kampala in 1903, while the CMS founded Gayaza High School in 1905 and Ngogwe the following year.[41] The CMS's Mengo School in Kampala and King's College, Budo were initially for boys only but later accepted girls as well. These schools were concentrated in Buganda, but a Christian education was made available to a limited number of girls from top families in some other regions as well. In 1912, when the CMS opened a boarding school for girls at Kabarole, the king of Toro enrolled one of his daughters and two other princesses; the prime minister sent two daughters and a niece; and the chiefs followed their example.[42] In these schools girls were taught that as adults they had a responsibility to be leaders in the church and their community, a lesson they implemented through participation in religious organizations, other women's groups, and sometimes their careers. The impact of the first few generations of women who attended Christian schools was magnified by the fact that many of them married influential men. These institutions continued to train many of Uganda's women leaders throughout the twentieth century.

But because Protestant missionaries felt that all Christians capable of learning had to be able to read the Bible, it was by no means only females of high status who were educated. In every district where the CMS established a church, it began to teach girls and adult women from many backgrounds. As early as 1909 the Namirembe area of Kampala, around the cathedral, included a girls' school and a women's school as well as a hall for training African teachers and a boy's primary school.[43] A missionary working in the Luwero area north of Kampala in 1903 reported that they had 3,091 boys and 3,078 girls attending the 200 schools associated with their churches. In Toro, a variety of classes were offered to adult women, in addition to those held for children.[44] Mature women received basic instruction in religion and reading; a more advanced class in writing had a membership of 120. The most proficient women, 'those promoted from a slate to a book, have ten minutes' daily instruction in geography before beginning their dictation'. In 1911 a missionary in Toro reported that their day schools had 480 boys and 823 girls on the roll, with an average attendance of 580.[45]

Female education took longer to introduce in some areas. In 1903 the two women missionaries working in Kooki, in the southern part of the country near the Tanganyika border, reported that their work with women was moving forward slowly. Only 40 youngsters came to their children's school, but one teacher was hopeful about an adult class she had recently introduced, meeting for an hour every morning, for 'some of our most earnest women'.[46] A missionary in Mbarara that same year was pleased with the attendance of women each morning at her newly built school. She commented upon their eagerness to learn but said they were slow to absorb new ideas and skills, not surprising since they had previously lived very secluded lives. Missionaries working in Busoga and Kamuli likewise attributed the difficulties facing girl and women readers to the substantial handicaps they faced as females.[47]

All the mission schools, whether run by Protestants or Roman Catholics, stressed 'domesticity' for girls. Domesticity, the idea that good women would remain in the home, concentrating on their husbands and children and utilizing their practical skills as housewives, was a bulwark of middle-class patriarchy in late Victorian Britain and on much of the European continent. When it was carried to Africa by missionaries and colonial officials, it was seen as a central component of 'the civilizing mission'. The early Christian schools and groups like the Catholic Women's Guild and the Protestant Mothers' Union taught that domestic work, including growing crops, was a virtue. Encouraging women to be diligent mistresses of efficient households, they instructed girls and adult members on how to keep their homes and children clean, how to feed their families in nutritious ways, and how to sew or do handicrafts.

Even the paramount girls' school in Uganda, an institution that later defined itself primarily in academic terms, had a strong domestic component. Gayaza High School was founded by the CMS in a village outside Kampala to prepare the daughters of Baganda chiefs and clergymen to become the wives of men from comparable backgrounds. As Musisi has shown, missionaries and chiefs agreed that education at Gayaza should not take girls away from their domestic roles.[48] An educational scheme for Uganda prepared by the CMS in 1909 stated that the primary function of Gayaza was to provide 'discipline and instruction in women's work and duties', including training in elementary hygiene and local handicrafts. Miss Allen, the first Headmistress at Gayaza, wrote in that year, 'Our aim is not so much to fill the girls' heads with knowledge, as to develop their character and make them good sensible women who are not afraid to work.'[49] (Here one sees the Protestant emphasis on labor as a virtue in its own right.) The school's goal of training not only 'good housewives' but also 'keen cultivators' was reflected in its schedule. The girls rose at 5:30 a.m. and dug in the fields for 2½ hours before preparing for school. Prayers and Bible lessons were joined by classes in English, geography, and arithmetic, interrupted by practical work like peeling bananas for the midday meal and fetching water. The missionaries realized that the girls' work might also have financial benefits: in 1912 the students planted about 1600 coffee trees, 'which ought to bring in a few rupees for the Church later'.[50]

Gayaza's approach was welcomed by Baganda leaders, who supported the school right from the start. In 1907 the *Kabaka*, prime minister, and other officials of the kingdom went to Gayaza to give prizes to the girls for good behavior, cleanliness, and character.[51] The *Lukiiko's* records note that the distinguished guests, who were greeted by 'a multitude of people who were filled with joy', then joined British school administrators for tea and bread. Four years later, the school held an exhibition for parents, at which examples of the girls' handwriting, mathematics work, sewing, and handicrafts were displayed.[52] The fifty chiefs who attended 'expressed the greatest delight at everything they saw', with some even commenting that 'their daughters would be quite useful in helping them with their accounts'. Whereas teachers at Gazaya had originally been told 'not to teach much English to the girls, in fact not to take it as a serious subject', some of the leading chiefs in 1911 'felt rather aggrieved and asked ... that it be considered a more important subject in the school's curriculum'. Gayaza's impact was magnified in two ways: it formed the basis for other girls' boarding schools founded later; and many of its graduates went on to play leadership roles, at first in the Mothers' Union and through their careers, and later as activists and politicians.

The CMS emphasized the merits of domestic labor in its schools in other parts of the country as well. In 1912 a female missionary stationed in the Toro kingdom described 'the democratic training' given to the 49 girls in their new boarding school, some of whom came from important families.[53] 'Regardless of their class', the girls took turns cooking food, sweeping, and cleaning. They washed their own clothes, fetched water from the river, and did at least an hour's digging in the fields every day. In addition, they learned sewing and either spinning or lacemaking. In 1911, the head of a school recently founded by the CMS in Busoga for the sons of chiefs asked the colonial government to support a parallel girls' school. His reasons for doing so are interesting: 'Those, who are interested in educational work, feel very strongly that it is absolutely necessary for the welfare of the country that the girls should also be educated to a degree suitable for their conditions in life. To teach the girls to lead pure, clean lives, and become industrious. To shew them the best methods for cultivating their gardens, and keeping their homes clean, and to teach them what I may call "Home Industries" e.g., mat making, basket making, sewing etc. is our wish.'[54] The government did not, however, share his enthusiasm for girls' education. Although the colonial authorities had awarded money for boys' education in Busoga, the education section of the Native Affairs division refused to provide any assistance for the girls' school.

Missionary women working in the Ankole kingdom saw practical labor as especially valuable in overcoming what they regarded – in implicitly racist terms – as the indolence and poor health of girls from the powerful cattle-raising Bahima group. Writing from the girls' school in Mbarara in 1911, one missionary noted that the teachers sent the girls into the fields to cultivate during the rainy season.[55] Useful physical activity was supported by the prime minister, who sent his daughter to the school, and by Queen Esita, who provided hoes for the girls. But manual labor proved difficult for 'the fat Bahima girls, who have been brought up to despise cultivation as the work of the Bairu or peasant class only, and to think that to drink plenty of milk and grow as fat as possible are their main duties in life'.[56] The school nevertheless hoped that exercise would 'in time make them stronger and healthier than their mothers have ever been'. Working in the fields was maintained as an element in the schedule in later years. A proposal in 1937 to link the girls' and boys' boarding schools in Mbarara stressed that fees could be kept low because 'the girls would continue to cultivate their own food to a great extent as at present'.[57]

Training in European-style domestic skills was offered by the CMS to adult women too. Already in 1903 female missionaries in Toro were offering a prize for the best kept house and garden, holding an exhibition of local crafts, and starting a sewing class.[58] By 1911 the newly established Toro spinnery was teaching girls and women to spin raw cotton and weave it into cloth. The Mothers' Union had more than 80 local branches by the late 1920s.[59] The MU linked domestic and personal purity, as seen in classes devoted to 'cleanliness of Speech, of Body, and of House'.

In some parts of Africa, Christian conceptions of domesticity led to a marked constriction of the economic and social independence that women had previously enjoyed. Among Yoruba women in southern Nigeria, for example, the expectation that Christian wives should remain at home, without engaging in commerce, was very different from earlier patterns.[60] Historians have therefore pointed to domesticity as a prime example of how foreign values were imposed by colonialism upon local people, inculcated mainly through educational institutions.[61] In Uganda, however, the Christian and colonial emphasis on women's domestic roles served to intensify values and patterns already in place in much of the country. In the eyes of the British, marriage, motherhood, and the domestic sphere were linked to notions of respectability and gentility, but these class-based definitions would not have been accepted so readily in Uganda had they not accorded with the existing social hierarchy and attitudes towards women's roles.

After around 1920 education for African boys – and to a lesser extent for girls – expanded due to increasing support from the colonial government.[62] The number of primary schools with six classes and trained teachers rose, joined now by a few technical schools. Junior and senior secondary schools were available in some areas, the latter usually boarding schools run by European missionary teachers. At Makerere College in Kampala, founded by the Protectorate government in 1922 and initially offering the equivalent of two years of secondary education, 76 male students were enrolled in 1925.[63] The annual report submitted by the Education Department in Entebbe in 1925 described improving facilities for boys at all levels but noted that there were no government-sponsored schools for girls above the primary level.[64] Although the CMS operated about 2,200 schools in that same year, it too was worried that the education of girls lagged far behind that of boys. The head of Ugandan operations therefore asked the London headquarters to increase its present staff of 37 women to 70.[65] In 1933, a few schools offered girls some intermediate-level education, but only two provided secondary training; as late as 1939, when 83 schools accepted girls, only 16 offered more than a lower primary education.[66]

Domesticity remained central to the gradually expanding system of female education, an emphasis promoted by the colonial government. The annual report on education for 1925 notes disapprovingly that girls' primary schools followed the same course as boys, a problem that would soon be corrected by a committee then at work to develop a separate syllabus for use with girls.[67] The 1933 report describes the new curriculum that had just been introduced. One of the ways in which it differed from the boys' syllabus was 'the emphasis laid on domestic economy, for which ten periods per week are reserved, while two periods weekly are devoted to hygiene and mothercraft'.[68] In addition, girls were henceforth to be taught in the local language, not in English. Colonial officers were running educational programs in maternal health, part of an effort to combat syphilis and prepare girls and women for marriage.[69] By the 1930s, European women in Kampala were offering classes for African women on sewing and knitting as well as reading and writing.

Women's Work

Very few women during the early colonial period pursued any income-generating activities. Most women were married when they were young, and once married it was not acceptable for them to mingle with other men. A historian of Baganda culture said that it was formerly taboo for a woman to go out of the home to a market or to trade.[70] It was the responsibility of the husband to provide for the family's cash needs, and widows were looked after by male relatives. Although women produced much of the food and sometimes the craft items that were taken for local exchange, it was their husbands or other male relatives who actually carried out the barter or selling process.[71] Women did not participate in trade involving manufactured items, nor were they involved in long-distance commerce, due to physical danger and cultural prohibitions against their travel.[72] The only partial exceptions were a few royal princesses early in the century who organized trading missions to the coast but did not join them in person. Here again we see a marked contrast with urbanized areas of West Africa during the early twentieth century, where most sellers in the large, regular markets were female and some women took part in longer-distance trade.[73]

After 1920, a small number of Ugandan women began to move into urban areas, but they found no socially approved ways to support themselves. Women were not employed to do unskilled physical labor, as were male immigrants. According to the gender definitions of most Ugandan cultures, women were strong enough to work with their hoes for long hours in the fields, but neither African nor British men thought it appropriate for them to do manual labor in the towns. Furthermore, authorities did not want them to compete with men in seeking paid employment, for the latter needed cash to pay their taxes. The semi-skilled jobs that were later to be seen as well suited to women (such as office work) were normally assigned at that time to South Asian men. Opportunities for producing and selling food or drink were restricted, for they required that a person have a little capital for equipment and supplies, a problem for most female migrants. In addition, Baganda and British authorities agreed that women should not be dealing in alcohol. Men therefore functioned as the primary brewers and sellers of alcohol; when liquor licenses were granted in Kampala, they went only to men.[74] A few women brewed illegally, but they faced the risk of punishment or extortion.

Domestic service in the households of wealthy European or South Asian families was not an option for women, for most servants in Uganda – as in other European colonies in Africa and India – were male, either Indian or African men and boys.[75] In 1932, Mrs Katherine Cook, an important early nursing missionary, founded a small school to train girls as domestic servants. Its opening was welcomed by the colonial administration: 'There is, without doubt, a great opening for girls in such a career, and the large number of boys at present in domestic service would be far better employed cultivating cotton or other economic crops. The opening of further careers to girls must have an important bearing on the future status of the African woman, and the vexed question of the present marriage system.'[76] In practice, however, Mrs. Cook's school proved unable to attract students. The sole domestic job open to a few women during the early colonial period was being an 'ayah' (the Indian term for women who looked after young children, later known as 'housegirls'). In the absence of legitimate employment, sex work might be the only way for a woman living in Kampala to generate some income.

A small number of women in Bunyoro were engaged in salt-making, perhaps not entirely voluntarily. A missionary stationed in Hoima in 1903 described her visit to Kibiro, on the eastern shore of Lake Albert.[77] Noting that 'all the salt that supplies Unyoro and Uganda comes from Kibero', she said the valley was filled with hot springs and the women who extracted salt from them. 'All the work is done by women who toil there from sunrise till sunset, many of them, I believe, being really slaves who have been raided from Bulega on the other side of the Lake. The men do absolutely no work . . . and they are as evil-looking a set of human beings as I have ever seen.' Her account seems more plausible than that offered by A. B. Fisher in a description of her travels in the Lake Albert region, published in 1911.[78] She too said that all the workers at the long-established salt 'mines' at Kibiro were women and described how they prepared salt from the briny water. She then commented, however, that they 'were able to earn a comfortable livelihood, supplying their husbands and family with all the necessities of life'; she emphasized the 'craven attitude' of their husbands towards these women, who were 'of powerful build and most quarrelsome nature.' Uzoigwe's research on precolonial markets in Bunyoro, based upon oral traditions, does not support Fisher's account, and he questions why women should have 'exercised this unusual commercial monopoly'.[79] Salt workers at Lake Katwe, south of Lake Albert, were evidently male in this period.

When one considers the limited educational opportunities for girls during the early colonial period and the extremely restricted niches in which women could work outside the home, it seems quite remarkable that two new occupations appeared that allowed a small number of educated women to generate their own income in highly respected ways. Because both school teaching and nursing required formal education, these positions were in practice open initially only to Christian women. The CMS in particular encouraged educated young women to go into socially needed work as teachers, midwives, and nurses.[80] The missionaries insisted, furthermore, that marriage and motherhood should not end a woman's career. The attitudes advocated by the CMS were readily accepted by the wellborn African women who constituted many of the first two generations of teachers and nurses. The number of these early professional women was not large, but their position carried great cultural weight.

The female missionaries provided energetic examples of women's ability to function in service roles. Married as well as unmarried women taught and ran medical dispensaries or worked in hospitals. This pattern continued even after an increasing number of the CMS missionaries had children with them in Uganda. A male missionary writing from a rural district north of Kampala in 1909 described his wife's activities.[81] In addition to looking after her own household and supervising the care of their young children, she taught the village school, with the boys coming in the morning and 120–130 girls coming in the afternoons. She also ran a class every day for 40 adult women. She was responsible for the work of the dispensary, to which over 9,000 visits were paid during the year, plus dealing occasionally with midwifery cases. Finally, she led the children's service on Sunday mornings, with an average of 150 present. Some of the missionary women took great pleasure in traveling around their districts to evangelize, in company either with another British female church worker or with an African Christian. Miss G. E. Bird, writing from Mengo in 1903, described with enthusiasm the trips she took every Monday to visit and hold services at village churches lying 10-12 miles from her base. In what must have been a startling sight, she rode a bicycle to get there.[82] Although we know less about the European Roman Catholic nuns who worked in Uganda, they evidently carried out many of the same activities.

These female missionaries, enjoying a degree of freedom that would not have been open to them in Britain or the European continent, demonstrated through their own behavior that Christian women could lead active and independent lives outside the home. Roman Catholic nuns showed that women did not need to marry, that they could play important roles without a husband. The married CMS missionaries proved that such activity could continue during marriage and mother-hood. While one may agree to some extent with Musisi's claim that the female missionaries contributed to an effort to restrain women's freedom by advocating ideas about marriage, sexuality, and morality based upon the patriarchal ideology of Victorian Christianity, that is only part of the picture.[83] The missionaries were at the same time undercutting patriarchal teachings through their encouragement of women's work outside the home and the behavioral models they presented.

African women were encouraged to teach from the early days of the CMS presence. They spread the word of God, primarily to other women, thereby helping to fill the urgent need for more Christian evangelists; but because all teachers had to be literate, they were also able to instruct children in basic educational skills. In 1899, a conference of CMS missionaries decided that the church in Uganda should define an office of Woman Teacher, whose duties would be 'to conduct such educational, evangelistic, and other work amongst women and children as does not necessarily fall within the duties of the [male] Clergy or Readers'.[84] In 1909 a proposed CMS educational scheme for Uganda stated that 'the principal aim in the educational work of the church should be to set before the most promising of our youth, both boys and girls, the work of teaching as a high calling, worthy of a life devotion'. The missionaries recognized, however, that married women teachers were obliged 'to stay with their husbands and can only give a limited amount of time to the work'; unmarried women were free to devote their full attention to teaching and could move to outlying areas.[85]

Many of the initial women teachers were from Buganda, but the range gradually expanded. As early as 1903 a missionary wrote from Mengo in Kampala that she was training two grades of Baganda women as certified teachers to work among women and children in her district. She noted that the exam taken by the women was similar to that of the Cambridge Junior Examination, though the candidates were still responding orally to the questions.[86] In that same year, a quarter of the African teachers in the CMS schools in the primarily Baganda Luwero district were women. In 1911, a mission in Luwero reported that they had started training 'girl pupil-teachers, with a view to sending them out into the villages to take charge of the girls in the day schools'.[87] A missionary assigned to Hoima in 1903, however, found only two women teachers at work, both Baganda. Although she at once set up a class for candidate teachers, attended by 15 women, most of them Banyoro, she thought that her area would be dependent upon teachers imported from Buganda for some time. Women in Toro moved quickly into teaching. By 1903 Kabarole had 49 female graduates who had passed their examination and were working as teachers.[88]

During the 1920s and 1930s the first formal teacher training colleges, for young African women as well as men, were set up by missionaries and the colonial government. These contained separate tracks for those preparing to teach in lower and upper sections of primary schools.[89] Gayaza was among the first to promote teacher training: a report in 1922 said that it included 'a High School for the daughters of Chiefs, many of whom take up the Teaching Profession'.[90] The number of African women who registered annually as elementary teachers in Uganda, a few of them nuns, rose from 26 a year in 1928 and 1930 to 90 in 1933. By the latter year missionaries had established five normal schools for women who would teach in primary schools; of the 453 students who were being trained that year throughout Uganda as the lowest grade of elementary teachers, 28 percent were women.[91] The few African teachers in intermediate schools, all male, had been trained at Makerere College. The government also began to offer support to teacher training programs for women at Nkokonjeru (Catholic) and Buloba (Anglican) Colleges, 'mainly to thwart wealthy chiefs' plans to send their daughters to England for further studies'.[92] By 1938, female students accounted for 42–47 percent of those enrolled in training colleges for vernacular (lower primary) and full-level primary school teachers.[93] At least an occasional Ugandan woman was hired on the staff at the teacher training colleges. In 1935, Mrs Lucy Bisereko of Bunyoro was offered a position as a needlework instructor at the Girls' Normal School at Buloba. She was described as 'a gifted expert' in that field.

In general, however, African women teachers did not play leadership roles during the 1920s and 1930s, nor were their particular concerns articulated. The education report for 1933, for example, referred only to men in discussing the remuneration given to African teachers in primary schools.[94] As teachers' organizations developed, African men took secondary place to foreigners, and women were generally invisible. The Uganda Education Association had 154 members in 1939, including 66 Europeans, 57 Africans, and 31 Indians or Goans.[95] Women were not mentioned.

The oldest woman interviewed for this project was one of the early trained teachers.[96] Born in 1911, her father did domestic work for British families in Buganda. Although her parents 'were not much bothered about education,' her uncle and grandparents wanted her to go to school and paid her fees. She went first to Namirembe Primary School, run by the CMS near the cathedral in Kampala, and later to Gayaza High School. Filled with admiration for her own teachers and encouraged by them to go into education, she was one of the second group of students who received certificates at Gayaza as trained teachers. In 1928, when she was 17 years old, she was hired as a primary teacher at Namirembe. At first she lived in a hostel at the school ('lady teachers were closely watched'), receiving a small but adequate salary; ten years later she married a man who was working in a bookshop, but she continued to teach. Together they had six children over the following twenty years, all of whom eventually received either post-secondary diplomas or university degrees. In 1940, she set up a school of her own in a rural area south of Kampala, 'because I wanted to do a service for the community'. She ran that school until her retirement, when it was taken over by her children. In

2003, aged 92 years and still strong, clear-headed, and erect, she reported that she continued to go to the school when needed 'to help out in teaching discipline and behavior' to the pupils.

Ugandan women moved into nursing even more gradually. Initially hospitals were staffed by a few European 'nursing sisters' at the top who supervised the work of male orderlies or assistants, most of them South Asian.[97] The first hospital in Uganda, founded by Dr (later Sir) Albert Cook in 1897 on Mengo Hill in Kampala, had nursing sisters from the CMS. They were overseen by Dr. Cook's wife Katherine, the first matron. In 1912, the medical workers in Uganda consisted of a handful of European doctors and nursing sisters, some Indian assistants, and an unenumerated group of 'native attendants'.[98] Five years later Albert Cook began to train African medical assistants. One reason for the reluctance to have female hospital nurses was that nearly all patients were men, and until at least the late 1920s it was thought appropriate that patients should be looked after by people of the same sex. During a smallpox epidemic in June, 1915, Buganda's *Lukiiko* appointed eight people to attend patients in a camp for infected people, four men for the male patients and four women for the female patients.[99]

Midwifery was the first medically related career to open to African women. Because local customs prohibited male involvement at births, Katherine Cook and the CMS started the Maternity Training School at Namirembe in 1918 to prepare Ugandan midwives and to educate mothers.[100] The first students were daughters of chiefs, which encouraged other girls to enter training. After qualification, the midwives were posted to the rural maternity centers being set up at that time under Mengo Hospital's supervision. By 1924 midwives were also being trained at Nsambya Maternity Training School by the Mill Hill Roman Catholic Mission. Between 1927 and 1933, 176 African women were examined and registered as midwives, compared with just 63 Europeans and South Asians.[101] In the latter year, the registry of active midwives included a total of 106 women trained at Namirembe and 47 trained at Nsambya.

Formal training of basic-level general nurses began in the second half of the 1920s, led again by Albert and Katherine Cook. The school they founded at Namulonge became, after a series of shifts in venue, the Mengo School of Nursing and Midwifery.[102] A three-year course for the higher certificate of enrolled nurse was instituted in 1930, its content based on the nursing syllabus from the United Kingdom, with some modifications to fit Uganda's conditions. The few women who undertook this course were qualified to assume administrative positions in the hospitals that were now multiplying throughout the country.

But women's movement into nursing was slowed by the ongoing preference for men in many hospital situations. In 1925, Uganda's medical personnel consisted of 76 Europeans, 53 Asians (all but two of whom were men), and an unspecified number of male African attendants.[103] The report for that year does, however, praise the great advances recently made at the training schools for midwives and mentions the living quarters for African nurses then under construction at Mulago Hospital. When it was decided in 1927-8 to establish a medical school at Mulago, the goal was not to train doctors or nurses but rather to prepare African men to take over the less skilled work then being performed by South Asian hospital assistants.[104] The government's aim was financial: correspondence from 1934 states explicitly that the students then being trained could be hired by the African Civil

Service for lower wages than were currently being paid to non-native (South Asian) workers.

With this discussion as a base, we now turn to the social and cultural uncertainties involving women that marked the early colonial years, leading to the emergence of the Domestic Virtue model and its first variation.

Notes

1 For domestic slaves elsewhere, see Robertson and Klein, *Women and Slavery in Africa*, and Coquery-Vidrovitch, *African Women*, ch. 2.
2 Reid, *Political Power*, pp. 160–67.
3 Middleton, *The Lugbara*, esp. pp. 12–5, and his 'Trade and Markets'; Jackson, *Essays on Rural Marketing*, pp. 1–5; Shiroya, 'Northwestern Uganda,' as described by Jackson, ed., *Essays on Rural Marketing*; Mukama, 'An Old Busoga Market.'
4 Uzoigwe, 'Precolonial Markets.' For below, see Good, *Rural Markets*, ch. 5.
5 Roscoe, *The Baganda*, pp. 452–7, and Hanson, 'Queen Mothers.'
6 Gutkind, 'Notes on the Kibuga.'
7 Karugire, *A Political History*, chs. 2–3, and Tripp, *Women and Politics*, p. 32.
8 See Mamdani, *Citizen and Subject*, chs. 4 and 5, and his *Politics and Class Formation*, p. 127, for this paragraph.
9 Hanson, *Landed Obligation*, esp. ch. 5.
10 CMS Birmingham G 3 A 7 O, 1909, #300. The previous year an official source had reported that over 60 percent of the population of Busoga was in danger of dying (UP, *Uganda Official Gazette, 1908*, 1 June, p. 88, PRO CO 612/1).
11 Hanson, 'Sleeping Sickness.' For below, see CMS, *Annual Letters, 1903*, pp. 161-3.
12 CMS Birmingham G 3 A 7 O, 1909, #300. For below, see Hanson, 'Sleeping Sickness.'
13 CMS, *Letters from the Front, 1912*, p. 89.
14 Mamdani, *Politics and Class Formation*, ch. 4, and Musisi, 'Transformations of Baganda Women,' ch. VI.
15 Tadria, 'Changing Economic and Gender Patterns,' ch. 3.
16 Ehrlich, 'Cotton and the Uganda Economy', in his 'The Marketing of Cotton,' Mamdani, *Politics and Class Formation*, ch. 2, and Lawrance, 'A History of Teso'; see also *Lukiiko* Transcripts, 12/8/1907, pp. 84–5; 16/12/1907, p. 94; 22/2/09, p. 108. Cf. Sheldon, *Pounders of Grain*, ch. 1.
17 UP, *Sessional Papers, 1932*, Agriculture (PRO CO 685/16).
18 For contrasting patterns in some parts of West Africa, see Afonja, 'Changing Modes of Production,' Ojo, 'Writing Yoruba Female Farmers,' Martin, *Palm Oil and Protest*, Shields, 'Palm Oil and Power,' Sudarkasa, *Where Women Work*, Guyer, 'Food, Cocoa,' A. Apter, 'Atinga Revised,' Allman and Tashjian, *"I Will Not Eat Stone,"* Clark, *Onions Are My Husband*, and Robertson, *Sharing the Same Bowl*.
19 Asowa-Okwe, 'Women Wage Workers,' and UNA New Series 3121.
20 E.g., Good, *Rural Markets*, pp. 180–91, and UNA A 46/1935. For older patterns, see Edel, *The Chiga*.
21 Karugire, *A Political History*, p. 128.
22 Steiger-Hayley, 'Wage Labour.'
23 Hanson, *Landed Obligation*, pp. 170–77, Hansen, *Mission, Church and State*, ch. 12, and UCU Mukono 02Bp 1/1, concerning *busulu*.
24 Hanson, *Landed Obligation*, pp. 175–7.
25 UNA A 46/1260.
26 UNA A 42/226, A 44/254, A 44/53, A 46/125, A 46/2661, and A 46/2457; 'Extracts from Mengo Notes: VIII'; Hanson, *Landed Obligation*, p. 190.
27 Obbo, *African Women*, pp. 21–3.
28 E.g., UNA A 44/243 and UNA A 46/1831; cf. A 46/1361.
29 Mamdani, *Politics and Class Formation*, p. 156, citing PRO CO 536/99.
30 Jamal, 'Taxation and Inequality.'

31 UP, *Census Returns, 1921*, Table 2.

32 See, e.g., note 18 above, Schmidt, *Peasants, Traders*, and Walker, 'Gender and the Development of the Migrant Labour System.'

33 Karugire, *A Political History*, chs. 2–3.

34 CMS Birmingham G 3 A 7 L 1, p. 341.

35 Dimock, 'The Silence of African Women?,' and 'Women's Leadership Roles.'

36 Dimock, 'Women's Leadership Roles,' for this and below.

37 See, e.g., for Yoruba regions, Peel, *Religious Encounter*, esp. ch. 8.

38 Oliver, *The Missionary Factor*, pp. 234–6. In 1922, the Roman Catholic missions claimed 69 percent of the 470,000 Ugandans who had converted to Christianity; by 1946, there were about 800,000 Catholics and 560,000 Protestants (UP, *Blue Book for 1922*, pp. 74–5 [PRO CO 613/22], and Oliver, *The Missionary Factor*, pp. 234–6).

39 Thus, although the Catholic missions claimed 69 percent of Uganda's Christians in 1922, only 36 percent of the girls then in school were taught by Catholics; the remainder were in CMS schools (UP, *Blue Book for 1922*, p. 79).

40 Ssekamwa, *History and Development of Education*, pp. 34–49 and 217–22.

41 Kwesiga, *Women's Access to Higher Education*, pp. 198–9, and Tourigny, *So Abundant a Harvest*, pp. 78–9.

42 CMS, *Letters from the Front, 1912*, p. 153.

43 CMS Birmingham G 3 A 7 0, #345. For below, see CMS, *Annual Letters, 1903*, p. 164

44 CMS, *Annual Letters, 1903*, pp. 180–82.

45 CMS, *Letters from the Front, 1911*, pp. 85–6.

46 CMS, *Annual Letters, 1903*, pp. 174–5. For below, see ibid., p. 178.

47 CMS, *Letters from the Front, 1911*, pp. 90–91.

48 'Colonial and Missionary Education,' and cf. Hughes, '"A Lighthouse".' For below, see CMS Birmingham G 3 A 7 0, 1909, #280.

49 Allen, Uganda Notes, May, 1909, p. 87, as cited in Musisi, 'Colonial and Missionary Education,' p. 172.

50 CMS, *Letters from the Front, 1912*, p. 140.

51 *Lukiiko* Transcripts, 25/3/1907, pp. 76–7.

52 CMS, *Letters from the Front, 1911*, pp. 76–7, for this and below.

53 CMS, *Letters from the Front, 1912*, p. 154.

54 UNA A 44/355. For below, see A 44/355, A 44/120, and CMS Birmingham G 3 A 7 0, 1909, #336.

55 CMS, *Letters from the Front, 1911*, p. 83.

56 The following year, another teacher at the school commented that although the girls' mothers approved of physical activity, some of their fathers objected, for 'the fatter and more inert their daughters are, the more beautiful they are in the eyes of the future husbands, who will pay ten cows for a very fat girl, and only one for a thin one' (ibid., *1912*, pp. 151–2).

57 UCU Mukono 02Bp 1/1.

58 CMS, *Annual Letters, 1903*, pp. 180–82. For below, see CMS, *Letters from the Front, 1911*, pp. 85–6.

59 Dimock, 'The Silence of African Women?'

60 E.g., Mann, 'The Dangers of Dependence' and her *Marrying Well*. For Igbo women, see Van Allen, 'Sitting on a Man.'

61 See, e.g., K. T. Hansen's introduction and the essays in *African Encounters with Domesticity*, esp. Musisi, 'Colonial and Missionary Education' and Denzer, 'Domestic Science Training' for this and below.

62 The annual contribution of the government to mission schools rose from around £10,000 in 1923 to about £400,000 in 1949 (Oliver, *The Missionary Factor*, p. 277). For below, see Ssekamwa, *History and Development of Education*, pp. 53–7 and 219.

63 Ssekamwa, *History and Development of Education*, pp. 41–2, and UP, *Annual Report of the Education Department for 1925*. By 1939 Makerere's enrollment had grown to 117, and manual courses, such as carpentry and mechanics, had been replaced by clerical training.

64 UP, *Annual Report of the Education Department for 1925*.

65 CMS Birmingham G 3 A 7 L 4, pp. 274–5.

66 UP, *Annual Report of the Education Department for 1933*; Kwesiga, *Women's Access to Higher Education*, Table 9.10, p. 205.

67 UP, *Annual Report of the Education Department for 1925,* and cf. UNA A 46/2128.

68 UP, *Annual Report of the Education Department for 1933.*

69 Summers, 'Intimate Colonialism'; for Tanganyika, see McCurdy, 'Urban Threats.' For below, see *Uganda Herald,* 19 June 1935

70 CultHist2 (App. B).

71 Prof. Uzoigwe ('Precolonial Markets') kindly checked his research notes on Bunyoro, looking expressly for references to women in trade, and found nothing (pers. comm.).

72 Mair, *An African People,* p. 130, 'Extracts from Lt.-Col. C. Delmé-Radcliffe's Diary,' Roscoe, *The Baganda,* pp. 452–55, and Nsimbi, 'Village Life and Customs.'

73 E.g., Ekechi, 'Gender and Economic Power,' Falola, 'Gender, Business, and Space Control,' and Robertson, *Sharing the Same Bowl.*

74 Willis, *Potent Brews,* ch. 5.

75 In the Mozambican town of Beira, for example, 8,600 men worked as domestic servants in 1940 but only 200 women (Sheldon, *Pounders of Grain,* p. 103).

76 UP, *Sessional Papers, 1932,* Education, p. 14 (PRO CO 685/16).

77 CMS, *Annual Letters, 1903,* pp. 186–7.

78 Fisher, *Twilight Tales,* pp. 30–31.

79 'Precolonial Markets,' p. 432, and cf. Syahuka-Muhindo, *Understanding Women's Participation,* esp. pp. 2–3 and 17–9. For below, see Barrett-Gaines, 'Katwe Salt.'

80 Dimock, 'Women's Leadership Roles.' For a contrasting pattern in the Belgian Congo, see Mianda, 'Colonialism, Education.'

81 CMS Birmingham G 3 A 7 0, #345a.

82 CMS, *Annual Letters, 1903,* pp. 147–8, and cf. Cox, *Imperial Fault Lines,* pp. 166–7. For below, see UP, *Blue Book, 1938,* pp. 126–7 (PRO CO 613/38). 213 nuns from the various European missions were then working in Uganda.

83 'Transformations of Baganda Women,' p. 192.

84 CMS Birmingham G 3 A 7L 1, #135/137, p. 4. For below, see G 3 A 7 0, 1909, #280.

85 CMS, *Annual Letters, 1903,* p. 162.

86 Ibid., pp. 147–8. For below, see ibid., p. 164.

87 CMS, *Letters from the Front, 1911,* p. 81. For below, see CMS, *Annual Letters, 1903,* p. 187.

88 CMS, *Annual Letters, 1903,* pp. 180–82.

89 Ssekamwa, *History and Development of Education,* pp. 53–7 and 219.

90 UP, *Blue Book for1922* (PRO CO 613/22), p. 77. For below, see ibid. and UP, *Uganda Official Gazette, 1933* (PRO CO 612/15), pp. 111–13.

91 UP, *Annual Report of the Education Department for 1933,* and CMS Birmingham G 3 A 7 L 6. In colonial Mozambique, as late as 1960 only 4 of 115 African primary school teachers and 31 of 191 African nurses were female (Sheldon, *Pounders of Grain,* p. 103).

92 Kwesiga, *Women's Access to Higher Education,* p. 204. For attempts by Sir Apolo Kagwa, the former prime minister of Buganda, to send his daughter and granddaughter out of the country for further study in 1928 and 1935, see PRO CO 536/149/5, CO 536/186/16, and CO 682/17, #40110.

93 UP, *Blue Book for 1938,* pp. 129–31. For below, see *Uganda Herald,* 19 June.

94 UP, *Annual Report of the Education Department for 1933.*

95 Uganda Education Association, *Bulletin,* Vol. I (1940), p. 7.

96 Kampala18.

97 E.g., UNA A 45/206 and A 45/207, and Holden, 'Colonial Sisters.' For below, see *Mengo Hospital Centenary Magazine.*

98 UP, *Annual Medical and Sanitary Report for 1912.* For below, see UNA A 42/265 and A 43/149.

99 *Lukiiko* Transcripts, 4 June 1915, pp. 171–2. For local fear of Western medicine, see L. White, '"They Could Make".'

100 *Mengo Hospital Centenary Magazine,* pp. 24 and 12. The MTS would later become part of the School of Nursing and Midwifery at Mengo Hospital. For the role of midwives from elite families in French West Africa, see Turrittin, 'Colonial Midwives'; for the difficult position of midwives in colonial Kenya, see Thomas, *Politics of the Womb.*

101 UP, *Uganda Official Gazette, 1933,* pp. 8–11, and see UNA A 46/2267 and A 46/2298.

102 *Mengo Hospital Centenary Magazine,* pp. 2 and 24, for this and below.

103 UP, *Annual Medical and Sanitary Report for 1925.*

104 UNA A 46/2629. For below, see UNA New Series 4319.

Four

*Women's Issues
& the Domestic Virtue Model*

The changes discussed in the previous chapter dislocated accepted patterns of life and thought concerning women during the years between 1900 and 1939. The practical impact of economic, political and demographic change was considerable, even if it was buffered by the indirect system of British control and the ongoing authority of local men. Christian teachings – backed in some decades by the colonial government – led to new definitions of marriage and inheritance, while altered economic patterns had an impact on female landholding. Whereas only a few African women had played public roles prior to European contact, the CMS missionaries promoted the participation of their female converts in decision-making. These changes led to vigorous debates between African men, colonial officials, Protestant leaders, and sometimes African and British women concerning three clusters of issues relevant to women: marriage and domestic relations, inheritance and landholding, and women's participation in the public world. Some women put words into action. By the 1920s and 1930s, most men in Uganda, of all races and positions, felt that women were escaping from appropriate male supervision, leading to shared efforts to regulate their behavior.

In response to these unsettled conditions, a model emerged that prescribed how a good woman should act, what her roles and duties were. This set of expectations defined an exclusively domestic focus for women's lives. Although it was based upon many features already present in Buganda and some other local cultures, the Domestic Virtue model gained its lasting force through the similarity of those values to the ones brought by British colonial administrators and, to a lesser extent, the missionaries. Yet at the same time the CMS undercut the model by promoting extended education for women and encouraging their work as teachers and nurses. This advocacy, when coupled with the activities of the early Ugandan career women, forced the development of the first variation of the Domestic Virtue model, one that allowed educated women to work in service positions while still maintaining an identity as respected women. The Ugandan situation was thus very different from what happened in parts of West Africa, like the Yoruba regions of Nigeria, where missionaries and colonial officials worked together in advocating a purely domestic life for women, in contrast to their previous involvement in the market economy.

In examining these issues, we give what may seem to be disproportionate attention to developments in Buganda and to the activities and concerns of Protestant missionaries and bishops. This weighting should not be taken as an indication that we regard Buganda or the Church of Uganda as more important than other regions of the country or other religions. Our focus derives in large part from the documentary evidence available. Colonial materials are richest for the ethnic groups with whom British officials had most regular contact, and the records of the CMS and Church of Uganda are exceptionally well preserved.[1] In addition, scholars are fortunate to have a transcript of the laws passed and the disputes adjudicated by the Buganda kingdom's *Lukiiko* during the late nineteenth and early twentieth centuries.[2] Formal legislation by the *Lukiiko* was subject to pressure from the British: Queen Victoria sent a representative to its sessions even before 1900, and after the Buganda Agreement, colonial officials clearly wielded some influence. But it is unlikely that the British played a significant role at the routine meetings held every few days at which some of the chiefs gathered to deal with complaints from individual people. The *Lukiiko* records are as close as we can come to hearing the voices of African male leaders in that period. Our emphasis on Buganda and Protestants stems also from the fact that disputes about women's issues and attempts to control female behavior were especially vigorous among those groups during the early colonial years. The Domestic Virtue model was heavily influenced by Baganda patterns, while its first variation was necessitated by the actions of Protestant women.

Disputed Issues Concerning Women

Dissention concerning women's proper place in a colonial and increasingly Christianized Uganda arose in three main areas. As was the case throughout Africa, Christianity advocated patterns of marriage and inheritance that conflicted with the polygamous practices accepted by most of Uganda's ethnic groups. The Christian assumption that marriage was a relationship primarily between two individuals likewise differed from the common African sense that it involved two families or clans.[3] The first area of debate therefore concerned what constituted a valid marriage, how to deal with the transition from one form of marriage to another, and questions about domestic relations and violence against women. The second cluster revolved around issues of inheritance, legitimacy, and landholding by women. The encouragement provided by the missionaries for women's participation in discussion of public issues led to a final set of disagreements. These thorny problems were not resolved during the early colonial period but instead remained contentious throughout the twentieth century. They were at the heart of three of the most bitter political disputes in 2003: the proposed Domestic Relations Bill; an amendment to the Land Act concerning women's inheritance and rights to family land; and the debate over reserved seats for women in Parliament and local government.

In the early colonial period, arguments over women's issues in Uganda involved three main groups: African leaders; colonial officials; and male and female Protestants, both African and British. Uganda provides a fine illustration of Jeater's observation that 'Far from there being a "patriarchal alliance" of white administrators and African elders conspiring to restrict African women, there was simply a mess of misunderstandings and colliding ideas about women and marriage throughout the African colonies during the early decades of the British Empire.'[4]

Conflicts over women formed part of a series of broader confrontations between the Church of Uganda and the colonial government in which outspoken Anglicans generally sided with African Ugandans in opposing policies of Protectorate officials. In 1909, for example, Bishop Tucker was violently opposed to the government's proposal to confiscate uncultivated land in Busoga and give it to Indian immigrants. Pleading that advantage should not be taken of the Basoga's 'present condition of sorrow and distress to hand over their lands to an alien people,' he argued that 'any appropriation by the British Government of the lands of the Basoga for the settlement of Indian immigrants' would be seen 'as an act of spoliation, an act without any warrant of laws – simply the triumph of might over right'.[5] During the 1920s, correspondence between Bishop Willis and the *Kabaka* of Buganda about such issues as the Buganda Agreement and appointment of African officials reveals serious tension between the church and the Protectorate government, with the *Kabaka* appealing to the bishop against actions by the latter. In 1929 Bishop Willis intervened unsuccessfully with colonial administrators on behalf of the kingdoms of Toro and Ankole, charging that new policies being introduced by the protectorate concerning taxation and naming of officials violated the terms of the Agreements of 1900; in 1936, at the request of the king of Toro, Bishop Stuart protested again, but equally unavailingly.[6]

One also finds divergent opinions within these groups. Uganda's many cultures had different practices concerning domestic matters, and they were affected in different ways by the changes of the early twentieth century. African women sometimes conflicted openly with men with respect to issues of importance to them. British administrators in Entebbe might take a different stand from Colonial Office officials in London. CMS workers on the ground, the CMS headquarters in London, the Bishop of Uganda, and the church's legal officials did not always see problems in the same light. Any suggestion that 'the British' (including both colonial and church leaders) had a unified imperial agenda that dictated their response to women is quickly dispelled by this evidence.

As background for analysis of the breakdown in familiar gender patterns, we may summarize roles and definitions as found in Buganda during the late nineteenth and early twentieth centuries.[7] Other ethnic groups had different traditions, but the Baganda formulation was of particular importance to the British and the CMS. Women's place was shaped by the stratified nature of their society, divided along lines of social status, clan, age, and sex. Respect for authority was deeply ingrained and was to be displayed through physical gestures, including kneeling. With the exception of certain members of the royal family, a woman's primary identity was as wife and mother, a nurturer, the person who generated, fed, and cared for her family. Women were expected to stay within the domestic context, where they bore and raised children, grew food crops, attended to household tasks, and looked after their husband and his male relatives. Women also carried out many of the duties associated with maintenance of the family or clan's cultural traditions, including the ancestral burial places.

Although rank mattered (the wife of a chief had higher status than a male commoner), Baganda women were subordinate to men of their own group in both function and status. The process of marriage involved the exchange of the woman for gifts. A married woman was expected to kneel in front of her husband, to cook for and feed him, and to provide sex upon demand. She had to obtain his permission before leaving their homestead. A woman who did not carry out her marital and domestic duties properly could be beaten. But women were also allowed to leave their husbands if they were abusive or did not treat them properly as wives. If a woman divorced her husband, returning to her parents' or brother's house, her family would have to repay the bridewealth. Children belonged to their biological fathers, and widow inheritance was common. Because women had no legal identity apart from their male relatives and a woman was considered a minor in the eyes of the law, a man had to act as her guardian and plead on her behalf in court. Women's sexuality and reproductive powers were central aspects of their productive relations, and male control over women's bodies was tied to their economic dependence. Sex was therefore normally confined to married couples. Although both spouses were supposed to be faithful, a husband who suspected his wife of infidelity was allowed to tie her up and punish her until she confessed; even if he killed her, he would only be expected to pay a fine to her relatives. A man who had sex with a woman other than his wife might owe a fine to her parents or husband.

These patterns were intimately connected to definitions of the roles and responsibilities of Baganda men. Men were the heads of households and the decision-makers, though their exact status depended upon their age and their position within the clan and social hierarchy. As we have seen, men helped with clearing land before planting and sometimes carried out additional farming activities. As well as providing the supplies needed to maintain the family's living quarters, they hunted, fished, and made bark cloth. If the family had items to trade, men handled the exchanges. They were responsible for the physical protection of their families, and they fought or provided labor for the *Kabaka* or their chief when called upon. It was within the context of gendered patterns like these that the disagreements of the early colonial period occurred.

Marriage and domestic relations

The first set of issues focused on marriage and domestic relations. Many questions grew out of the complex situation in which a wide variety of local practices for constituting a marriage, most of which accepted polygamy at least for wealthier men, were joined and in some cases replaced by an unfamiliar Christian definition of marriage, one requiring monogamy.[8] Even if all parties tried to act in good faith, confusion and problems were bound to arise. The difficulties were compounded because a redefinition of marriage was an issue not only for missionaries and Christian church leaders but also for British colonial rulers. During the opening decades of the colonial period, as other scholars have noted, Christian marriages had the backing of political authority. H. B. Hansen comments, 'By giving priority to monogamous marriages in its legislation, the government was clearly expressing its belief that Christian values should be the norm in African society.'[9] Tadria argues that British attitudes towards marriage, including opposition to polygamy and bridewealth, stemmed primarily from economic concerns. Their policies created 'small, nuclear families more suitable to the capitalist economy in which men were being paid meager wages. Within these families, male responsibilities and authority increased beyond that typical in the pre-colonial situation.' Musisi, referring to 'the alliance between the missions and the colonial state in regard to family and marital legislation,' notes that 'The colonial officials had a vested interest in stabilizing domestic relations if this would create order and strengthen their hold on Buganda for economic and political purposes . . . . Marriage was thus considered of high priority to the early administration's program of legislation.' [10] But by the 1920s and 1930s, these authors suggest, the church and the protectorate disagreed over African marriages. The government's wish to maintain social control forced it to accept certain elements of pre-Christian marriage patterns that the missionaries refused to tolerate. Our own analysis shows that the conflicts were more complex than such statements acknowledge.

Church people confronted problems with marriage early and directly. CMS missionaries on the ground wrestled with how to deal with Africans who had married under traditional patterns but then accepted Christianity. What should be done about the 'surplus wives' of a polygamous man who converted to Christianity and could then marry only one of them in church?[11] How should the church respond to people who refused to accept the new faith because they were not prepared to give up polygamy, or who became Christians but then reverted to traditional practices in order to marry a non-believer?[12] How should missionaries handle powerful people who had nominally converted but continued to practise polygamy?

Such problems were not easily resolved. During the 1920s and 1930s Bishop Willis of the Church of Uganda advocated flexible positions and sensitivity to African patterns, a stance unlike that of many British church leaders elsewhere in Africa. Willis's papers include a file of questions sent by local clergymen and others asking for his opinion about whether particular marriages were valid.[13] Willis's responses were more tolerant than those of the divorce courts and some of the clergy, expressing sympathy for the plight of women caught in difficult marriage situations. In 1931, for example, the bishop of Mombasa asked whether Uganda had a ruling concerning the situation of a Christian wife who acquiesced in her husband's polygamy. The Kenyan bishop thought such women should be debarred from receiving communion but wanted Willis's opinion. The latter said that Uganda had no policy, but 'in the great majority of cases the woman is the sufferer. In that case, it seems to me hard to penalize her for that for which she is in no way responsible. Unless, therefore, there is any direct charge against the woman she is always allowed to come to the communion.' In 1935, Willis answered a query about whether a man could be baptized if he had been married in accordance with tribal customs. After emphasizing that the same rules should be applied to both women and men, Willis said that it was the practice in some parts of the diocese for women to be baptized 'irrespective of their husbands being heathen or polygamists. This seems to me to be in accordance with what Our Lord would wish, and I would recommend you to continue it.'[14] Willis was also sensitive to the problem of 'surplus households'. In a written message to the clergy in 1934, he emphasized that although a polygamous man who accepts Christianity must send away his second wife, 'he must always support the woman and her children, and an agreement must be signed by him to that effect.'

The problems inherent in the co-existence of contradictory marriage systems were compounded by legislation passed by Buganda's *Lukiiko* and the colonial government. The policies of these two bodies were quite similar, probably due to the influence of Christian chiefs and British officials over Buganda's parliament. In 1895, for example, the *Lukiiko* prohibited wife beating, in 1901 it passed a resolution designed to control the movement of women, and in 1902 it virtually ruled out divorce in the case of Christian marriages.[15] Bridewealth rates were fixed at a high level in 1899, in an effort to limit customary marriages and encourage more people to marry in church. This measure made it difficult for young men to afford to marry and increased the control of wealthy men over their wives. In 1920 the *Lukiiko*, aware of these problems and eager to reduce the number of independent and unmarried women, abandoned its efforts to control bridewealth. The colonial government introduced its own regulations concerning marriage and divorce in 1902, 1903, and 1904.[16] These were based upon British law and practice, including differential rules for the two sexes. Thus, if a man were petitioning for a divorce, he could show simply that his wife had committed adultery, whereas a woman had to prove physical cruelty or desertion by her husband as well as his adultery.

Protestant leaders opposed some of these policies, beginning with the regulations passed by the protectorate early in the century.[17] In 1925 Bishop Willis was reproved by the head of the British Crown Law Office for contending that the protectorate's marriage ordinance could be interpreted to mean that 'a native professing Christianity can contract a valid marriage by native custom'. Whereas the bishop had argued that 'the Church has always acted on the assumption that a native marriage is a true marriage,' the lawyer said that 'a person professing Christianity abjures marriage according to native custom. He cannot have it both ways.'

At those sessions of the *Lukiiko* when smaller groups of chiefs met informally to settle disputes, older Baganda values and practices at first remained strong. Women's position within marriage was subordinate, but the chiefs were willing to protect their customary rights. Hanson has suggested that 'At the turn of the century, before the society had experienced the dislocations of incorporation into a cash economy, British colonial overrule, and the extreme population loss of sleeping sickness, women in Buganda could turn to their clans and their immediate relatives, and to their rulers, to force husbands to treat them within certain bounds.'[18]

These patterns may be illustrated by the cases related to marriage and family heard in 1905, the first year of surviving *Lukiiko* court records. One woman alleged that her husband had deserted her, and another complained against her estranged husband concerning rights to her children.[19] A man was found guilty of attacking his wife and biting off her ear when she prepared food to give to her lover, but the wife and her lover were found guilty of illicit intercourse. The *Lukiiko* convicted a man who had paid only part of the bridewealth for a woman and not completed a formal marriage ceremony before impregnating her. Another was charged with binding his wife with ropes, without official authority to do so, after he returned from a trading expedition and thought she had deliberately aborted a pregnancy during his absence; a week later it was ruled that he had falsely accused her of pregnancy, whereas in fact she was suffering from 'syphilitic infections', and he was ordered to pay her the considerable sum of 10 rupees in compensation.[20] The *Lukiiko* found a man guilty of allowing a married woman who had left her home and young child to stay with him and abort a pregnancy, and they ordered the woman to return to her husband.

Concern about marital issues was also visible in the Baganda Catholic news-paper *Munno* and its Protestant equivalent, *Ebifa*. The topics addressed between 1915 and 1935, usually in letters sent to the editor by African Christians, included bridewealth, monogamy vs. polygamy, 'surplus wives', relations between husbands and wives, and divorce.[21] The letter writers were all male, however, and the papers rarely ran articles that reflected a woman's viewpoint. In 1920, for example, *Munno* described the Pope's instructions to a group of Italian women to dress suitably and behave properly; the article stressed that Ugandan women too should follow that advice, so as not to break God's commandments and cause marital problems.[22] In 1930, the sole references to women in *Munno* were several announcements by men searching for their runaway wives.

Violence within marriage was another contested area. During the 1910s, the Baganda chiefs responded in a fairly even-handed manner to complaints of physical abuse. A man was arrested in 1916 for lashing his wife 31 times, nearly killing her, and when the *Lukiiko* learned the next year that a servant of one of the royal women had beaten his wife, breaking her leg, he was arrested.[23] Women too might resort to violence. In 1916 a woman was accused of murder before the *Lukiiko*. The problem had started when her husband gave her 10 cts. to keep for him. One day he returned from work and asked for the money. 'Because she was feeling unwell, she did not wish to give it to him in a respectable manner (kneeling down on both knees). The woman later decided to throw it to her husband who was outside. This resulted in a quarrel between the parties for not respecting him. This compelled the neighbours to separate them.'[24] A little later, the woman picked up a stick and hit her husband on the head, afterwards rushing into the house and hiding behind the door. When her husband followed her in, she stabbed him through the chest with a knife. He later died, and the woman set fire to the house where his body was lying.

British Protestants in Uganda were strongly and consistently opposed to wife beating, but colonial officials preferred to leave such problems in the hands of the Native Authorities (chiefs) and their Native Courts. In the early 1930s Bishop Willis and his wife became involved in an emotional dispute with the government over the marital life of a prominent Baganda chief.[25] Their intervention was part of a wider joint effort by the Protestant and Roman Catholic missions to force colonial administrators to do something about 'the moral degradation of the chiefs'.[26] In the case at issue, the woman whom the chief had married in a Christian ceremony appealed to the High Court of Uganda for divorce on two grounds: he had treated her cruelly (beating her so severely that she had to spend three weeks in hospital and then confining her to an outbuilding for five months); and he had committed adultery, marrying other women according to African customs and bringing them to live in her house. After the court ruled in her favor, finding him guilty of both cruelty and adultery, Bishop Willis called upon the Governor to dismiss the man from his position as a chief. The Governor responded that the private life of the chiefs was not a factor in their appointment and that the *Kabaka* himself led an immoral life, so one could not be too demanding.

At that point, in January 1933, Mrs. B. M. Willis, the bishop's wife and head of the Mothers' Union, wrote a stinging letter to the Governor, asking him to reconsider this decision. She pointed out that Africans

> look to the British Government to uphold the right, as it does already in upholding honest dealings, and if a chief is convicted of fraud, I understand he is immediately

71

dismissed. If this chief goes unpunished for cruelty and immorality, I am sure the British Government will definitely lose prestige with the people of this country. I realize that this case unhappily is by no means unique, and that many nominally Christian chiefs have been guilty of the same offence, but in other cases no formal evidence has been forthcoming, and no others have been formally convicted in the Court. [27]

Fearing that the Governor would dismiss her protest out of hand because she was a woman, Mrs Willis concluded:

I hope your Excellency will believe that I have no wish to interfere in political matters, but that as President of the Mothers' Union in Uganda I feel it to be my duty to endeavour to uphold the principles of Christian marriage, and I cannot just look on at the women's suffering and do nothing to help them. If the British Government can take no steps to help the people in this respect, I should be grateful if you could give me a reason for its abstention so that I can explain it to the people when they approach me.

The Governor's response was brief and formal. He said it was not within the powers of the British Government to dismiss a chief unless he failed in his duties. 'If you are asked why the British Government can take no steps in the matter, the obvious answer is that it is not a case for the British Government but for the Native Administration.' With that curt dismissal, the matter was closed.

Inheritance and landholding

Another cluster of issues concerned the legitimacy of children born to various types of marriages, the right of children and widows to inherit land, and the freedom of women to hold land in their own names. In part these problems were again due to the confusion introduced by Christian marriage and inheritance patterns, but they were also affected by political and economic issues, including British colonial attempts to shape the nature of landholding in Buganda and the introduction of cotton as a cash crop. Such questions were generally handled by churchmen and the Native Authorities: the colonial government, after passing some regulations concerning wills, inheritance, and intestacy early in the century, stayed out of inheritance disputes thereafter.[28]

Christian officials grappled with these issues. A file preserved in Bishop Willis's papers consists of letters and legal actions between 1918 and 1937 concerning the definition of illegitimacy within the Ugandan context and whether illegitimate children should be baptized.[29] These demonstrate genuine uncertainty and some disagreement between local clergymen, the bishop, the religious and secular courts in Uganda, and the Archbishop of Canterbury. As with marriage, Bishop Willis commonly recommended a tolerant and flexible position, focusing on the spiritual needs of the children. Thus, in 1934, at Willis's urging, the Diocesan Council ruled that 'illegitimate children might be baptized in the Native Anglican Church if the parents were truly repentant', and the bishop wrote a short and simple letter to all clergy about how to enforce this ruling. On several occasions, however, he was overridden either by the Ugandan High Court or the Archbishop, who demanded a more rigorous stance.

The conflicting claims of older Baganda inheritance patterns vs. Christian definitions led to an appeal made to the *Lukiiko* in 1931 by a group of high-status African Protestant women from the Mengo branches of the Mothers' Union.[30]

Complaining against the decision in a recent legal action concerning a disputed inheritance, the women raised two issues. The first was whether a man's oldest son should inherit, as in traditional Baganda practice, regardless of the terms of his mother's marriage to his father, or whether the oldest son of the only wife married in a Christian wedding was the true heir. The second question involved the right of a Christian widow to her husband's property vis-à-vis his other, customary wives. In connection with their case the women prepared a detailed statement about how marriages had traditionally been formed in Buganda, including the role of the clans and parents, and how the new Christian definition of legitimacy affected the legal status of children born to Africans in customary marriages before they accepted Christianity.[31] Though the women persuaded the *Lukiiko* to accept the primacy of the Christian heir in this particular dispute, the chiefs did not proceed to generalize the policy in legislation as they had promised. The *Kabaka* supported the *Lukiiko's* non-action, and British colonial officials refused to interfere, despite further agitation by the Mothers' Union.

Another question concerned women's right to inherit land from their fathers or otherwise to acquire property and hold it in their own name. Here earlier Baganda patterns and colonial economic policies were at odds.[32] In the nineteenth century, Baganda women had not been allowed to hold land: they could only use land that had been granted to a male relative by the *Kabaka*, a chief, or his clan. Under the new rules established by the British in the Buganda Agreement of 1900 and a land law passed by the *Lukiiko* in 1908, women could hold *mailo* land, though not own it outright, and they could inherit, buy, and sell other kinds of land in their own name.[33] But the *Lukiiko* was apparently unsure about the wisdom of that policy. Although it supported inheritance of land by daughters under some circumstances in the 1910s, later it generally ruled against women.[34] Hanson suggests that this change was due to 'the commodification of social relationships which accompanied the imposition of taxation and cotton as a cash crop'.

Cotton was indeed a factor in altered attitudes towards female landholding. While much of the crop was grown on land held by men or families, during the 1910s some chiefs and landlords who profited from cotton began to grant plots of land to women who were not attached to men and they could therefore raise their own crop.[35] This tendency may have been accentuated by the disruption caused by sleeping sickness and the relocation of the survivors. By the 1920s, fear of female economic independence was certainly a factor in the increasingly negative response of Baganda men to women's ownership of land. *Lukiiko* records document frequent conflicts between men and women over land, and newspapers make clear that women farming on their own were seen as a threat by conservative men. In 1925 a writer to *Ebifa* complained that there were now as many independent women farmers in the villages as men; because women wanted to leave their husbands to grow cotton on their own behalf, he urged the authorities to prevent women from moving freely.[36] *Munno* blamed chiefs in 1927 for giving land to women, noting that women who left home to grow cotton were reluctant to return to their husbands or to accept the authority of their fathers or brothers. This period of female cultivation was, however, short-lived. From the 1930s onward, women rarely appear as landholders in their own right. Women frequently provided the labor for cotton raised on family- or male-owned land, but it was men who took it for sale and kept the profits.

Public participation by women

The final set of vexed questions concerned women's roles in public settings and as decision-makers. Should they participate in discussion of public issues, at least those that concerned them, and should they receive leadership training? In considering such issues, British administrators and CMS people differed strongly with each other, and they encountered a range of patterns within various ethnic groups.

Although our sources of information are limited, we know that during the precolonial and early colonial periods women's involvement in public activities varied by region. In some areas, including Teso and Acholi, women played essential though specifically defined roles in certain clan activities, religion, and healing.[37] In the kingdoms, they might have political functions too. In Ankole, female chiefs and spiritual diviners were common at the turn of the century, and a woman later served as a sub-county chief. In Bunyoro, the 'queen sister' was a confidential advisor to the king, had specific ritual functions, and played a designated role in settling political disputes. In Buganda, female members of the extended royal family had previously been assigned important ceremonial and practical duties. Prior to the mid-nineteenth century, the queen mother of Buganda had 'participated in a system of gendered political authority in which the mother of the king had autonomous authority, which she used to check his excesses and protect the nation', including the right 'to enthrone or depose a king and to restrain the actions of the king in power'.[38] But the wealth and authority of the queen mother and the *Kabaka*'s senior wife were already being weakened before the arrival of the British, due to the economic, political, and military changes of the second half of the nineteenth century. The ability of royal women to benefit from their own estates, chiefs, and courts and to influence policy was further reduced during the early colonial period. Some wives nevertheless continued to provide informal advice to their husbands, and women were among a large and diverse coalition of Baganda who protested to the government in 1924 about the distribution of *mailo* land.[39]

In their approach to women's public involvement, Protestant leaders and colonial officials once more took opposing stands. CMS people, especially missionary women, felt that the new female Christians should be aware of church issues as they affected women and should take part in the groups that made decisions about them. A plan for church organization in Uganda prepared in 1899 recommended that a women's conference be held every year, attended not only by missionaries but also by 'one representative from each settled congregation . . . , elected by the female registered communicants'. Although the conference was to 'deliberate upon women's work only', it provided African women with the opportunity to participate in a body that discussed and made recommendations about issues of immediate concern to themselves.[40] Topics considered by the annual women's conferences included domestic issues (marriage, adultery, and inheritance), the disruption caused by men leaving home to work in the towns, and payment of women teachers.

Within the parishes and districts as well, the missionaries were quick to involve women and deliberately furnished leadership training. In 1903 a 'native women's Church Council' was formed in Kabarole, consisting of 'the queen and sixteen other steady, trustworthy Christian women, elected by the whole body of women communicants'.[41] A year later the council was described as 'a great success', with its members 'realizing their responsibility towards their fellow-women'. When a female missionary arrived in Hoima in 1903 and found that there were only 25 Banyoro women communicants, plus some Baganda residents, she immediately set up an elected women's council, consisting of one Baganda and six Banyoro women.[42] These women were valuable because 'they know so much more intimately the surroundings and difficulties of their sisters . . . and also the capabilities and qualification of those whom we hope to employ as teachers'. In Gayaza district, a women's committee was created in 1912 to screen all women and girls in the district who wanted to prepare for baptism or confirmation. Each church chose one representative, and an African woman served as secretary.[43] By the 1930s African women had been sitting on church councils for a generation and were active in the synod and diocesan educational boards.

The local chapters of the Mothers' Union likewise provided women with training in how to run an organization led by elected officers. Annual meetings brought together MU representatives at a national level. In 1932, Sara Mukasa, wife of a powerful Baganda chief, made a two-week tour of the organization's branches in Mukono District, submitting a written report at the end.[44] Although her speeches to the seventeen chapters focused on domestic concerns, her literacy, poise in addressing a public audience, and independent travel through the district demonstrated that highly respected women could move beyond their own households to play leadership roles.

Under some circumstances African women were even allowed to preach, a practice not found in Anglican churches in Britain at the time. In 1903 and 1904 new female converts in Ngogwe and Rakai joined missionary women in going on tour through their districts, all of them taking turns preaching.[45] In one case the CMS representative commented, 'We Europeans acted only as a kind of draw-net to attract the people, and then when a good crowd of Heathen had collected, the young Native Christians led the meeting.' In 1934 a minister in Mbarara complained to the local CMS representative about a woman who had 'insisted on preaching in his church last Sunday morning notwithstanding his remonstrances'.[46] When the problem was forwarded to Bishop Willis, he responded with characteristic broadmindedness that there was no ruling against women preaching in church: they might 'do so if the local clergyman agrees'. In general, however, he felt that 'ladies should naturally speak to the Mothers' Union' and would 'not as a right' speak in church buildings at other times.

Colonial officials, by contrast, regarded women's political participation in totally negative terms. The fissure between the government and Protestant leaders is illustrated by the dispute over inheritance rights involving Baganda leaders of the Mothers' Union and the *Lukiiko* in 1931. Although the African women argued openly and in spirited fashion with the chiefs for two hours, the *Lukiiko* failed to implement a general policy that protected Christian inheritance.[47] At that point, sixty-one influential members of the Mothers' Union (one of them the wife of the Prime Minister of Buganda) signed a letter to the British Provincial Commissioner, asking him to meet with them. He refused. When Bishop Willis remonstrated with him, the Commissioner explained that he had no intention of interfering on the women's behalf: he felt that 'the country was in no way ready for women to take such a part in framing the policy of the country'. To Mrs Willis, who had expressed her support for the women, he expressed his gender views even more explicitly: 'In my opinion the time is not ripe for Baganda women to constitute themselves as political reformers. ... Their normal function [should be] to improve their homes and leave the question of any political pressure, however desirable, to their husbands.' Bishop Willis defended the women, arguing in his response to the Commissioner that 'They can hardly be accused of "constituting themselves as political reformers" because they protest on a moral and social issue which vitally concerns themselves and their children.'

Some historians have seen a weakening of African women's public involvement as a characteristic feature of colonialism: they were 'excluded from the public politics and public discourses of colonial rule' at the same time as they 'struggled to retain control over their productive and reproductive labor in monetized colonial economies'.[48] With variations depending upon rank, status, and location, women 'used and adapted pre-existing forms of collective mobilization as they challenged the legitimacy of colonial rule and contested new configurations of patriarchy'. Within Uganda, this formulation cannot be applied in any simple way due to the diverse patterns previously found among the country's ethnic groups and the support given by Protestant leaders to African women's public participation.

Attempts to Control Female Behavior

Although African leaders, British government administrators, and missionaries held conflicting views about many issues involving women, they agreed that some women were engaging in inappropriate kinds of behavior. The areas of concern included women who offered sex for money, migration by women from villages to towns, alcohol production, especially by women, and women's declining ability to bear children.[49] Unmarried women who lived independently were a particular threat to the assumption that all women must be subject to a husband's control. These sentiments, which are most visible in Buganda due to better records, emerged in the 1910s, and gained intensity during the 1920s and 1930s. As was true in other parts of colonial Africa, maintaining control over women was a highly charged issue, commonly addressed through revisions of 'customary' law that gave senior African men more authority over women.[50] In Uganda, African and British leaders, joined in some cases by missionaries, worked together in attempting to control female misbehavior, acting with considerable unanimity across the racial divide.[51]

Prostitution was a major concern, though there is little evidence that it was widely practised. (Here as in later periods, attitudes towards sex workers serve as a convenient gauge of broader concerns about women.) Unlike the British, the Baganda acknowledged female sexuality and women's legitimate sexual needs. The *Lukiiko* heard a case in 1915 brought by a woman seeking divorce from her husband on the grounds that he had failed to satisfy her sexual desires.[52] After the man denied the charge, the chiefs ordered that they should go back to their home and sleep together for a fortnight. If the husband failed to satisfy her then, they were to return to the *Lukiiko,* where the case would be resolved 'according to local custom'. But women's sexual activity with men other than their husbands, especially if they received pay or other material benefit from it, was intolerable. A letter to his people from *Kabaka* Daudi Chwa, probably written around 1910–11, stressed that, before the arrival of Western culture, extra-marital sex was almost unknown, and anyone who engaged in it was castigated by society.[53] He assigned the blame for a rise in prostitution and deteriorating relations between men and women in Buganda to the 'immense freedom of these days', promoted by Western education. The *Lukiiko* began to address prostitution in Kampala in the 1910s, joined by the CMS in the 1920s.[54] Pressure intensified in the late 1930s, and in 1941 the Buganda government, unhappy that colonial officials were not dealing more vigorously with the problem, enacted another prohibition of its own.

All three groups opposed female migration into Kampala, believing that they could only control women's sexuality if they controlled their freedom of movement. From the turn of the century, the *Lukiiko* attempted to prohibit married women from moving to or even through urban areas where foreigners lived. The goal was to prevent sexual liaisons with traders, soldiers, and other outsiders as well as to keep women under closer supervision within the villages.[55] Between 1920 and 1940 a few women moved into Kampala, heightening the generic sense that the urban community transgressed the proper moral order. Uneasiness about the presence of African women in the town was intensified by fear of cross-racial liaisons, which both Ugandan and British men opposed. In 1936, ministers of the Buganda government joined missionaries in asking the colonial authorities to clamp down on village girls who had moved into sections of Kampala near the area reserved for the British and were working as prostitutes. Kampala's white authorities likewise expressed concern about excessively close contact between Africans and 'non-natives'.[56] Municipal ordinances banned European and Asian settlement outside the town itself, prohibited foreigners from living among African areas, and tried to bar African women from marrying foreign men.[57]

British government officers and church people were also worried by excessive drinking among Africans, a problem they felt was increasing in the early twentieth century. Missionaries preached against alcohol in their churches, schools, and women's groups; colonial administrators talked about introducing brewing licenses in an effort to curtail sales.[58] The government recognized, however, that because the traditional kinds of beer brewed by every ethnic group in Uganda were made from grains and fruits that formed a part of local diets, it would be virtually impossible to curb production. As one despairing official acknowledged in 1930, all village women knew how to brew, and 'every hut is a potential brewery, with its materials ready to hand'.[59] In Kampala, where the growth of a male population increased demand for liquor beyond its customary ceremonial and social purposes, attention was directed primarily at *waragi*, a locally distilled drink like gin that was apparently introduced by Nubian soldiers.[60] When women produced and sold alcohol, it was especially troubling. The underlying issue was evidently the independence they gained from having their own income.[61] Due to shared male opposition, the few women brewing drink in Kampala during the 1930s were far from being able to organize and confront colonial officers, as happened in Dar es Salaam.

Anxiety about female morality and weakening male control over women was related to fears about biological reproduction. A decreasing birthrate troubled both African and British leaders. Medical missionaries and colonial administrators attributed what they saw as an alarming population decline not only to sleeping sickness but also to venereal disease, stemming from sexual laxity.[62] White concern with the reproductive capacities of Baganda women, tied to worry about their sexual conduct, has been described as an example of colonial misperceptions of African women and as part of a broader colonial attempt to control female reproduction. British reactions were triggered also by a shortage of agricultural labor, especially for the new export crops. But Baganda leaders shared many of these concerns. In 1920, for example, the *Lukiiko* passed measures that attempted to curb the spread of venereal disease, combat the declining numbers of marriages and births, fight emigration from Buganda, and prevent the escape of wives from their husbands.[63]

In other parts of the country too, African leaders, colonial officials, and missionaries worried about what they perceived as an inappropriate increase in female independence and a breakdown in morality. In Toro, Christian marriages weakened earlier customs.[64] By the 1930s, 'concubinage' (cohabiting without marriage) was expanding, due in part to the rising number of men who went to Buganda in search of temporary employment; a higher proportion of children were born out of wedlock. The legal status of women rose, thanks largely to the progressive views of King Kasagama, and more women – especially those who had received a Christian education – were initiating cases in the courts to defend their right to land or cattle they had inherited. Husbands no longer controlled their wives so firmly, and mistrust and suspicion between them rose. In Bunyoro during the 1930s, tax demands similarly led many men to go to Buganda to seek work.[65] Their absence and the ability of some women to earn their own money by selling food led to a destabilization of gender relations. In one instance, a woman who wanted to free herself from her husband asked her father to return her bridewealth; when he refused, she raised and sold enough beans and cassava to repay the gifts herself.

Concern about what was regarded as the growing inability of husbands to control their wives underlay the opposition encountered by the colonial government to the ban it imposed in 1905 on corporal punishment of women who had been found guilty of offences by the Native Courts. Though the order was accepted in some parts of the protectorate, African and British officials in other regions believed that it was contributing to the mounting problem of wives who refused to accept their husband's authority.[66]

In 1927, the Entebbe government was asked to submit a report to the Colonial Office in London concerning the impact of this ban.[67] The Governor's lengthy response, based upon reports from his district officers, offers an unusually explicit justification of British support for African men's attempts to discipline women within marriage, including the use of physical violence. In Buganda, Bunyoro, and Busoga, the Governor said, 'native public opinion does not tolerate the beating of women', because these tribes have 'advanced beyond the stage when this form of punishment is regarded as suitable'. Therefore the order abolishing judicial whipping had had 'no deleterious effects on tribal life'. In much of the rest of Uganda, however, where 'civilization is at a much lower level, and the rule of law and order is of comparatively recent growth', the impact of the prohibition was negative. Women were becoming less active as cultivators and sometimes questioned the authority of their husbands, including their use of violence. If insubordinate wives could not be beaten by order of the court, how were they to be controlled? Husbands were complaining that they received no assistance from local authorities 'owing to the impossibility of devising a suitable penalty for disobedience and the non-fulfilment of conjugal duties'. When a man attempted to enforce his authority, it might lead to his conviction by the Native Courts for assault. In Gulu District, the Governor noted disapprovingly, 65 cases of 'excessive beating of wives' had recently been filed by women and tried by the Native Courts. The District Commissioner there believed that the combination of the abolition of corporal punishment by the courts 'coupled with the free exercise of the right of the women to complain to the Courts in cases of marital punishment has had a deleterious effect on domestic life for the reason that the women are beginning to realise that they can misconduct themselves with comparative impunity'. When this report circulated within the Colonial Office in London, one official suggested that the best solution would be to 'let the Native Courts hand over the offending wife to her husband for chastisement, she to be presented to the village chief afterwards as an assurance that the beating would not be excessive'.

The Domestic Virtue Model and its Service Career Variation

In an attempt to resolve the uncertainties surrounding the proper roles and duties of women in Uganda's changing world and to provide a justification for clamping down on what was seen as their undue freedom, African and British male leaders during the early decades of the twentieth century formulated a shared definition of a 'good woman'. This set of expectations was not laid out explicitly but can be pulled together from a variety of other statements and policies. We label it a model of Domestic Virtue, since it stressed women's contributions and responsibilities within the home setting. Because male leaders hoped the definition would promote a return to a stable if somewhat altered form of patriarchy, they formulated an ideal of female domesticity and submissiveness that may have been more restrictive than was found in actual practice. The model began to emerge in the opening decades of the century, becoming more clearly defined – and with a more negative tone – during the 1920s and 1930s. It then remained a dominant cultural influence right through the twentieth century.[68]

The Domestic Virtue paradigm defined how a good woman, one respected by her male and female peers, should behave.[69] Its basic components, closely inter-twined in practice, were the following:

- All women should marry. As wives they provide services for their husbands, including sex.
- Women are mothers. They provide for and care for their children, as well as socializing them into their culture's traditions.
- Women have practical duties within the household. They grow food for their family and do necessary work such as gathering fuel and water, cooking, and cleaning.
- Women's work occurs within the homestead and its fields, except when going to get wood or water.
- Women are subject to male authority. A woman should be submissive and deferential to her husband, his male relatives, and other men in the community.

This requirement is part of a broader tradition of respect for authority and hierarchy.

- Women are not decision-makers. In the family, a woman may discuss issues with her husband but does not decide on her own, with the exception of minor domestic issues. In the clan, women maintain certain traditions but do not participate in such issues as allocating clan land. In the community they are not involved in such decisions as where to put a well.
- Women may use resources, such as land and domestic property, but they do not control them.

A corollary was that women who were voluntarily away from the domestic context, especially if they were not married, were labeled as bad. Hence they were legitimate targets of male sexual interest.

This model was based upon social patterns and attitudes found within some of Uganda's own cultures. The most influential were expectations of women among the Baganda, which were similar in some respects to those of the other kingdoms. For the non-hierarchical ethnic groups, we have less information about the position of women, but it is likely that the Domestic Virtue definition constituted a greater change away from existing practices. Even for the Baganda, some components of the Domestic Virtue model restricted the position women had held in the past. There was little new about its assumption that a woman's identity was derived from her position within the family. Control over women by fathers and husbands, clan heads, and chiefs, including restriction of female sexuality and mobility, had likewise been present previously. But the model intensified the requirement that women confine their activities to the home and remain submissive to men. It implicitly limited certain traditional forms of protection for women within marriage, such as the ability to leave an abusive husband, and it removed the right of a small number of women to play public roles in governance, religion, and healing.

These tenets were shared and reinforced by British colonial officials. Most of the patriarchal, late Victorian assumptions with which government officials had grown up at home and which they carried with them to Uganda could be applied with only slight modification to African women. The British were particularly interested in two implications of the model. The first was how it reinforced the emerging economic system that accompanied colonialism, principally waged labor and commercial agriculture. Although the government wanted African *men* to work for pay at least on a part-time basis, they wanted *women* to remain at home, growing the foodstuffs consumed by their households and providing much of the labor for cash crops. Government officials also hoped to strengthen social regulation, lessening the problems caused by women who were unduly free from male authority.

The relation of European missionaries and church leaders to the model was more complex. In several key respects, their teachings and practices supported Domestic Virtue expectations. These included a primary definition of women as wives and mothers and an emphasis on domesticity, their roles at home. Because the model did not specify the nature of marriage, it could accommodate a Christian belief in monogamy as well as older polygamous practices. But at the same time CMS missionaries and the Protestant bishops of Uganda preached other messages that undermined certain features of the ideal.

The Domestic Virtue model acquired its practical force and surprising longevity because it formed the basis for the policies and laws of governments. It was applied to the entire protectorate by the British, including communities in which women had previously had a more independent position. Buganda's *Lukiiko* likewise implemented its expectations. It was probably welcomed by many chiefs and their Native Courts in all parts of Uganda, because it helped them to maintain control. Pressure to accept the assumptions of the Domestic Virtue model may have been increased by the government's decision to send Baganda men to other parts of the country as chiefs: for them, the model was close to the patterns with which they had been raised. We do not know whether this definition was resisted outside Buganda during the early colonial years, but certainly by the 1950s women in the Western Province were objecting to some of its features (see Chapter 5).

The model was not, however, rigid. Arising initially out of the specific problems that confronted male leaders during the early twentieth century, it proved itself able to adapt to changes in the experiences and practical needs of women. Over the course of the following century three variations of the Domestic Virtue model were to emerge, all of which responded to the lack of congruity between the basic model's expectation that women would remain at home and the opportunities that arose for them to earn money by participation in the public domain. Each modification re-defined or dropped certain features of the basic model while continuing to emphasize the importance of the rest, thereby making it possible for a certain group of women to engage in income-generating activities outside the home while still retaining their identity and status as respectable women. We thus observe an ideological formulation responding to the altered practical circumstances of women's lives. For women who were not directly engaged in the market economy, however, including the great majority who remained in rural communities, the original model retained its full force.

The first alternative version of the Domestic Virtue paradigm began to develop during the 1920s and 1930s, becoming increasingly important over the rest of the century. It was required by the presence of educated women working in highly respected service careers. Pressure came initially from Christian missionaries, for the move to educate women was in itself potentially subversive of the Domestic Virtue definition. Education threatened male dominance.[70] Girls and women who left home to spend time in the company of their peers were already moving away from the complete control of their fathers or husbands. Women who could read and do arithmetic might well have skills that were highly regarded in the new colonial world and that none of the men in their families possessed. Their teachers were British or educated African women who offered very different role models from what these pupils had encountered before. It is therefore not surprising that, although some African men, especially the Baganda and the rulers and chiefs of the other kingdoms, encouraged their wives and daughters to acquire a Christian education, others objected. A missionary working in Busoga in 1909 wrote that many local chiefs 'do not allow their women to attend reading classes for they have an idea that when the women are able to read and write, they will leave them.'[71] From Kamuli another missionary complained in 1911 that 'most husbands object to their wives reading, and those whom they have paid dowry for, however young, they call their wives, being afraid that if they become Christians they will be less subservient to their wishes.

I have known them to be beaten severely, almost to death, because they dared to venture near a school.'

The second way in which the policies of the CMS challenged aspects of the basic Domestic Virtue model concerned women's work outside the home. Its missionaries – joined to a lesser extent by the Catholic missions – taught that educated women could continue to carry out their responsibilities at home, maintaining their status as good wives, mothers, and supervisors of the household, while also gaining advanced training and taking on paid work as teachers or nurses. They could remain in such employment, which was presented as a valuable service to the church and their community, throughout their lives. This definition of good womanhood was illustrated by the female missionary's own activities.

Opportunities for further education and work as teachers and nurses were quickly taken up by African women. Although the initial numbers were small, the fact that many of them came from royal or chiefly families meant that they were inherently respectable. They did not earn large salaries, but they had the freedom conferred by their income to delegate domestic duties to others. They also worked closely with whites, in settings – schools, dispensaries, and hospitals – that were regarded by others as strange but high-status places. Serving as role models for others, they demonstrated that educated women who were contributing through their careers could nonetheless ensure that their families received good food and care, maintain the home, behave appropriately, and – a new virtue – pay for the education of their children. The impact of these women, who were active in the 'women's work' of the emerging Christian churches in Uganda, was extended by the prestige of the men they married, who were usually from similar backgrounds and well educated. The respect given to these professions continued in subsequent generations, even though many later teachers and nurses came from less elevated families.

Because the early working women did not conform to all the expectations of the basic model yet certainly could not be classified as bad women, the Domestic Virtue model was forced to respond. We label the resulting modification the 'Service Career' variation. Unlike the basic model, shaped by *male* concerns, this version was made necessary by the actions of British and educated African *women*. To allow the new teachers and nurses to be defined as proper women, the variation adjusted four features of the initial set of expectations.

- An educated woman who did salaried work that served the community was allowed to leave home during working hours so long as her behavior remained appropriate. She was to be submissive to her husband and other male relatives within the family context and to display suitable deference to men at work. Respect for authority and hierarchy thus continued unabated.
- While she was still expected to provide food for her family, she might buy it or hire someone else to dig in her fields rather than growing it herself.
- She was allowed to find another woman to carry out the daily work within her home, though she was responsible for the smooth running of the household.
- She could exercise authority over her pupils or patients and might be able to choose how to spend her own earnings, but she was not to make higher-level decisions at home.

Although this formulation was extended over time to a wider range of service and professional occupations, its requirements concerning domestic duties and proper deference remained in place.

It must be emphasized that the Service Career variation contained inherent strains and contradictions that would lead to tension in the future. It did not question the gendered division of labor that lay at the heart of the Domestic Virtue model: it accepted that obtaining and cooking food and carrying out other domestic tasks were women's duties. There was no suggestion that a working woman's husband would assume some of her tasks at home. Because professional women were still responsible for their families and households while also devoting time and energy to their salaried work, the system placed a considerable physical and emotional burden upon them. The Service Career version was implicitly class-based in several respects. It was limited to those women whose parents had been able to pay for their education and whose labor was not needed at home. No one argued that peasant women too should be free to earn their own incomes. Further-more, the ability of educated women to work relied upon cheap, unskilled female workers to take their place within the household. In some cases, the extended family system provided a relative who could help, but if this was not possible, another woman had to be hired to do domestic work. Moreover, though women might have considerable social and economic freedom at work, they were still expected to be deferential within the family context. This dichotomy could lead to severe tension. Lastly, the fact that some women now had their own salaries posed a potential threat to the emerging role for men as the income-earner for their family. In the short run this was not a problem, for most of the early teachers and nurses married men who had adequate sources of wealth and/or power. Over time, however, the ability of women to generate their own incomes was to cause conflict.

By 1939, the foundations had been laid for Uganda women's history through-out the rest of the century. Nearly all women were still occupied with their own rural households, a position now reinforced by the basic Domestic Virtue model. Yet gradual changes in the economic and political context, the introduction of Christianity and Western education, and the emergence of acceptable careers in teaching and nursing had destabilized familiar patterns. Disputes over marriage, inheritance and landholding, and women's participation in public settings, together with attempts to limit the inappropriate behavior of some women, underlay the formulation of the original Domestic Virtue definition and its implementation through government policies. The ability of the model to adapt to practical realities – in this case the participation of educated women in careers of their own – was illustrated by the emergence of the Service Career variation. The following chapter traces how these developments played out during the later colonial period.

Notes

1 Now at the University of Birmingham Library, UK, and the Bishop Tucker Campus of Uganda Christian University in Mukono. By contrast, Tourigny laments that so little of the work of the Catholic missions was documented (*So Abundant A Harvest*, pp. 91–2).
2 *Lukiiko* Transcripts, 1894–1917, on deposit in the Africana section of Makerere

The Generations of Gradual Change

University Library. This transcript was produced for Dr Lloyd Fallers (then at the East Africa Institute for Social Research) in the 1950s. After the destruction of the original documents in 1966, Dr John Rowe kept a copy of the transcript, which he later shared with Prof. Holly Hanson. She generously deposited this copy at Makerere in 2003.

3 E.g., Jeater, *Marriage, Perversion, and Power*, Chanock, *Law, Custom and Social Order*, Hawkins, "The Woman in Question," and his *Writing and Colonialism*.
4 Jeater, 'The British Empire and African Women', p. 240.
5 CMS Birmingham G 3 A 7 0, 1909, #300. For below, see UCU Mukono 02Bp 218/27.
6 UCU Mukono 02Bp 1/1 and 22/1; cf. CMS Birmingham G 3 A 7 L 5, p. 185.
7 Musisi, 'Transformations of Baganda Women,' esp. chs. III–IV, and her 'Gender and the Cultural Construction', Schiller, 'The Royal Women', Lusembo, *Transformation of the Status*, ch. 3, Tadria, 'Changing Economic and Gender Patterns,' ch. 2, and CultHist3 (see Appendix B).
8 Hansen, *Mission, Church and State*, pp. 260–79, and Musisi, 'Transformations of Baganda Women,' ch. 8.
9 *Mission, Church and State*, p. 266. For below, see Tadria, 'Changing Economic and Gender Patterns,' p. 59.
10 Musisi, 'Transformations of Baganda Women,' pp. 202–3 and 233–4.
11 CMS, *Annual Letters, 1904*, p. 520.
12 Ibid., p. 518, and CMS Birmingham G 3 A 7 0, 1909, #336 and 350. For below, see CMS Birmingham G 3 A 7 0, 1898, #173.
13 UCU Mukono 02Bp 177/79, for this and below.
14 UCU Mukono 02Bp 1/1, letter from A. E. Clarke in Mbarara. For below, see UCU Mukono 02Bp 9/1, in which he also defends the baptism of illegitimate children.
15 *Lukiiko* Transcripts, Buganda Laws, pp. 1–2, and Musisi, 'Transformations of Baganda Women', pp. 211–13. The 1902 measure abolished Baganda customs concerning how a marriage could be terminated, through an agreement between the husband's and wife's families, including the provision that women could return to their parents or brothers in the case of broken marriages.
16 PRO CO 457/6, pp. 248–51.
17 CMS, *Annual Letters, 1904*, p. 517 (two letters), and CMS Birmingham G 3 A 7 L 1, p. 336. For below, see UCU Mukono 02Bp 77/5.
18 Hanson, 'Sleeping Sickness,' esp. pp. 6–7.
19 *Lukiiko* Transcripts, 15 May 1905, pp. 3–4. For the two cases below, see 12 June 1905, pp. 18–19, and 21 August 1905, p. 55.
20 Ibid., 17 July 1905, p. 44; 24 July 1905, p. 48. For below, see 17 July 1905, pp. 46–7.
21 Musisi, 'Transformations of Baganda Women,' pp. 194–8.
22 February 1920. For below, see April and October 1930 (see Appendix A).
23 *Lukiiko* Transcripts, 13 March 1916, p. 205, and 3 September 1917, p. 281.
24 Ibid., 8 January 1916, pp. 188–9.
25 UCU Mukono 02Bp 177/79.
26 See, e.g., a joint memorandum sent to the Governor in 1934 by representatives of both missions: Musisi, 'Transformations of Baganda Women,' pp. 252–5, citing Secretariat Minute Papers, Entebbe, C 2042.
27 UCU Mukono 02Bp 177/79, for this and below.
28 UP, *Uganda Government Gazette for 1905–6* (PRO CO 457/6), esp. 1906, p. 48.
29 See UCU Mukono 02Bp 9/1 for the rest of this paragraph.
30 Dimock, 'The Silence of African Women?,' based upon UCU Mukono 02Bp 268/34. The action of these women, although an unusually strong step in Baganda terms, seems far removed from the aggressive uprisings of Nigerian Igbo women, many of them market traders or producers of cash crops, against British taxation in 1929 (Van Allen, '"Aba Riots"' and Bastian, '"Vultures of the Marketplace"').
31 UCU Mukono 02Bp 268/34.
32 Sebina-Zziwa, 'The Paradox of Tradition,' ch. 2.
33 Musisi, 'Transformations of Baganda Women,' p. 157, and *Lukiiko* Transcripts, e.g., 27 March 1908, p. 100, 1 September 1914, p. 117, 2 October 1914, p. 126, and 22 February 1916, p. 196.
34 *Lukiiko* Transcripts, 25 January 1915, p. 153; 14 July 1915, pp. 177–8; and 18 April 1916, p. 218. For below, see Hanson, 'Sleeping Sickness,' p. 7. For the contrasting

situation in colonial Lagos, see Mann, 'Women, Landed Property.'

35   Hanson, *Landed Obligation*, pp. 177–81.
36   Ibid., for this and below.
37   For this and below, see Tripp, *Women and Politics*, pp. 29–33, Tamale, *When Hens Begin to Crow*, pp. 4–8, Sebina-Zziwa, *The Paradox of Tradition*, Ch. 2, Perlman, 'The Changing Status and Role of Women,' Tikasiimire, 'Women's Contributions,' *Encyclopedia of World Cultures, Supplement*, sections on the Banyankole, Banyoro, and Basoga, and Schiller, 'The Royal Women'.
38   Hanson, 'Queen Mothers,' esp. p. 220, her *Landed Obligations*, Musisi, 'Women, '"Elite Polygyny"',' and Schiller, 'The Royal Women.' See also Kaggwa, *The Kings of Buganda*, passim, and Musisi, 'Transformations of Baganda Women,' chs. III–IV.
39   Hanson, *Landed Obligations*, ch. 7, discussing the *Bataka* controversy.
40   CMS Birmingham G3 A 7 L1, 135/137, p. 4. For below, see Dimock, 'Women's Leadership Roles.'
41   CMS, *Annual Letters, 1904*, p. 534.
42   CMS, *Annual Letters, 1903*, pp. 186–7.
43   CMS, *Letters from the Front, 1912*, p.141. For below, see Allen, 'The Women and Girls of Uganda,' as cited by Tripp, *Women and Politics*, p. 34.
44   UCU Mukono 02Bp 268/34, and Dimock, 'Women's Leadership Roles.'
45   CMS, *Annual Letters, 1903*, p. 162, and ibid., *1904*, p. 521, for the quotation below.
46   UCU Mukono 02Bp 1/1, letter from A. E. Clarke.
47   Dimock, 'The Silence of African Women?'
48   Allman, Geiger, and Musisi, section introduction, *Women in African Colonial Histories*, p. 217.
49   Musisi, 'Gender and the Cultural Construction,' and her 'Transformations of Baganda Women,' ch. IX.
50   Schmidt, *Peasants, Traders*, pp. 7–8, Lovett, 'Gender Relations, Class Formation,' Sheldon, 'Urban African Women,' and Jeater, 'The British Empire.'
51   Our argument differs from Mama's exclusive emphasis on British Victorian attitudes in shaping policies towards women in the colonies: 'Sheroes and Villains.'
52   *Lukiiko* Transcripts, 8 July 1915, p. 177.
53   Mutyaba and Numukadde, *Chwa II ne Muteesa II*, pp. 103–8, as translated for this study by Deus Mukalazi.
54   Musisi, 'Gender and the Cultural Construction'. Cf. Jeater, 'The British Empire'.
55   Musisi, 'Gender and the Cultural Construction'.
56   UNA A 46/10.
57   The level of female urban migration prior to 1940 was far lower than seen in Nairobi or South African cities (Robertson, 'Transitions in Kenyan Patriarchy' and her *Trouble Showed The Way*; Barnes, 'Virgin Territory,' Walker, 'Gender and the Development of the Migrant Labour System,' and Redding, 'South African Women'). Cf Schmidt, *Peasants, Traders*, pp. 7–8.
58   E.g., CMS, *Annual Letters, 1904*, p. 521, CMS Birmingham G 3 A 7 0, 1909, #349 and #350, CMS, *Letters from the Front, 1911*, p. 86, UCU Mukono 02Bp 260/33, and UP, *Uganda Official Gazette, 1920*, 30 June.
59   PRO CO 536/162/2.
60   Willis, 'The Only Money,' and *Lukiiko* Transcripts, 14 January 1907, pp. 72–3; 9/10/14, p. 130.
61   E.g., a letter to *Uganda Herald*, 21 August 1935, and cf. Allman, 'Rounding Up Spinsters.' For below, see Mbilinyi, 'This is an Unforgettable Business.'
62   Summers, 'Intimate Colonialism.' For below, see ibid. and Musisi, 'The Politics of Perception,' and her 'Gender and the Cultural Construction.' For a more complex analysis, see Thomas, *Politics of the Womb*.
63   Musisi, 'Transformations of Baganda Women,' p. 225, citing *Lukiiko* Resolution, 5 January 1920, Entebbe Secretariat Archives File 46621.
64   Perlman, 'The Changing Status and Role of Women.' For the wider concern with morality, see Hansen, *Mission, Church and State*, pp. 279–98, and Musisi, 'Transformations of Baganda Women,' ch. VII.
65   Willis, *Potent Brews*, pp. 106–7 for this and below.
66   For husbands' power elsewhere, see Jeater, *Marriage, Perversion, and Power*, esp. ch. 9,

Chanock, *Law, Custom and Social Order*, esp. ch. 11, Hawkins, "The Woman in Question" and his *Writing and Colonialism*, esp. ch. 7.

67 PRO CO 536/147/15 for the following discussion. The act stipulated that judicial whipping should not be inflicted on adult women, though children might receive as much as 12 strokes with a birch rod, and adult men could be given up to 24 lashes with a whip: UP, *Uganda Government Gazette for 1905–6* (PRO CO 457/6), 1905, pp. 208 and 391.

68 The longevity of the Domestic Virtue model was influenced by the limited and late role of waged employment for both men and women in Uganda, lessening the challenges to accepted gender definitions that derive from new types of work. See, e.g., Lindsay, *Working with Gender*.

69 For construction of gender identities, see Lovett, "'She Thinks She's Like a Man",' and Moore, Sanders, and Kaare, eds., *Those who Play with Fire*.

70 This differs from Okeke-Ihejirika's assessment for Igbo women: 'Christian values that spread through schooling aborted women's social autonomy both within and outside the domestic sphere' (*Negotiating Power and Privilege*, p. 16). See Chapter 3.

71 CMS Birmingham G 3 A 7 0, 1909, #336. For below, see CMS, *Letters from the Front, 1911*, p. 91.

Five

The Late Colonial Period
1940–62

Between 1940 and the gaining of Ugandan political independence in 1962, the lives of most women – those who remained in the villages growing food for their families – changed relatively little. The economy was marked by some expansion of cash crops, an increase in trade and marketing, and the entry of some Ugandan men into shopkeeping. But women's ability to earn money from such activities was limited, apart from those rural women who sold extra food occasionally if they needed cash. New patterns were, however, seen in some areas. Migration increased, including male agricultural workers and people moving from rural areas into the towns, especially Kampala. A few of the latter were women. In households affected by migration, male dominance was weakened. African opposition to colonial rule became visible, though it did not take the violent form seen in Kenya and some other settings. Political parties appeared, and British colonial officials began to think about preparing Ugandan men to move into positions of leadership, especially as Independence loomed. More women were gaining an education, and they were forming clubs and community groups, but they were almost entirely excluded from involvement in government and politics.

The basic Domestic Virtue model that had emerged during the earlier colonial period remained strong, as did the Service Career variant that permitted educated women to work in positions outside the home if they were serving the community. Women were still taught to be wives and mothers, to take care of their homes and families and be submissive to men. They were either to grow the food for their own families or to make alternative arrangements if they were employed elsewhere. This definition of a good woman was accepted by most African men and women throughout the country as well as by British colonial and Christian officials. The Service Career variation was becoming broader, applying to more women and some new occupations, such as community development workers. Neither version approved of the small number of women now living in towns, often unmarried, who supported themselves through sale of food, alcohol, or sex. Women's issues continued to be contentious, with severe disagreements separating the various segments of African male opinion, British colonial administrators, church leaders, and women's groups. Local-language newspapers published during these decades show that attitudes toward women, and the ability of women to express their views in public media, varied considerably by ethnic group, religion, and region.

In this chapter we look first at the underlying economic, demographic, and political changes that affected women and at their education, organizations, and political involvement. After examining women's work, we explore what happened to the paradigm for good women and how women's issues were discussed. Information comes not only from written sources but also from interviews with the older women in our district sample. Thirty-seven women were at least eight years old prior to Independence and thus had some recollections of the colonial period.[1] Of them, 23 were no older than 18 during the colonial period, so their comments pertain mainly to the 1950s and very early 1960s. The 14 women who were in their sixties or older experienced the colonial period as both children and adults, with comments stretching back into the 1940s and in several cases even earlier.[2] Most of these women grew up in villages (78 percent), but only about a quarter of their fathers were engaged in subsistence agriculture. Another quarter were catechists, primary school teachers, or ministers or priests; two worked in professions other than teaching; and five were in government service or were chiefs of a sub-county, parish, or sub-parish. Seven fathers did unskilled or semi-skilled work, with the largest cluster in the army or police. Only three were in business or trade. When compared with the total male population during the late colonial period, these figures underrepresent the proportion of subsistence farmers and exaggerate the number with higher-status or paid occupations. These distortions probably emerged because better educated and/or influential fathers were more likely to send their daughters to school or to help them start some kind of business as adults, leading them into the kinds of long-term work that made them eligible for our sample. The limited involvement of the fathers in business was, however, characteristic of African men in that period.

A Gradually Changing Context

Although the Ugandan economy developed in this period, the changes had relatively little direct impact upon women. Spurred by the British government's goal of making the colonies self-supporting and by growth in international trade, commercial production of cash crops for export increased (cotton, coffee, and tea, joined now by tobacco). Despite a call by a British Parliamentary committee to open up East Africa's economic system, most cash crops were sold by producers to government-run Marketing Boards, which set prices for the entire country and year.[3] Prices for cotton and coffee boomed in the early 1950s. In 1957, cotton exports reached $60 million and coffee $42 million.[4] By the end of that decade, however, prices had declined markedly, leading to a slowdown if the economy. The government also began developing mining, on a very limited basis, and a few secondary industries, the latter based in Jinja where they could get hydro-electric power from the newly built Owen Falls dam on the Nile River. Capital development in the form of roads, water, housing, and electricity was promoted to support the new industrial enterprises. But waged labor remained an unimportant part of the Ugandan economy, with only around 250,000 Africans employed for wages of any kind in 1952.[5] Hence the image of the male 'breadwinner' who provided for his wife and children was muted here. Few of the manufactures now being established provided any employment for women, nor was there a demand for female labor in semi-skilled and skilled trades.[6]

The most visible economic development was an expansion of trade and markets, though demand for imported goods remained low. Wholesaling and larger retail establishments usually remained in the hands of South Asians, but at the bottom of the distribution system African men – but not African women – were beginning to find a place as shopkeepers. In Ankole, where a rapid increase in the founding of new markets was tied to growing demand for meat, African men were only gradually becoming active.[7] A survey of licensed traders and shopkeepers in Ankole during the 1950s found that, of 164 licenses to trade within the townships and formal trading centers, only 7 percent were held by Africans; the rest of the licensees were Indians. Among those who traded at a lower level, however, African men were somewhat better represented. In Toro, trade was organized by South Asian or European middlemen but some local shops were run by Africans.[8] Most of these sold a few basic household goods plus a small amount of food. African shopkeepers, who obtained their stocks from Asian suppliers in Fort Portal, normally carried their goods home on foot or by bicycle. The predominance of South Asian wholesalers, perceived to be working together with the wealthy Indians who imported goods or ran cotton ginneries, led to mounting hostility against Indians during the later 1950s and 1960s.

These agricultural and trading patterns are reflected in the comments of the women in our sample about the late colonial period. Cash crops were a feature of the period, and prices for cotton and coffee were remembered as being high, unlike the present time. About a third of the group commented that, although there was little money and people had to work hard for it, cash had value and consumer goods were available. Rarely, however, were women involved in business. One woman, whose father was a soldier in the Karamojo area and whose mother brewed local beer illegally in the barracks at night, noted that all trading was in the hands of men, especially Indians.[9] A 67-year-old woman who grew up in a village in Lira District said, 'There were no women in business. Women assisted on their husbands' farms, but the money after the sale of produce would be controlled by the husband.'[10] The daughter of a wealthy family in Hoima explained, 'Women at the time did not go to work. Many of them did not even go to the market or to a shop. Instead, the husband went and bought the stuff and brought it home. A lot of times my father would bring the tailor with different pieces of cloth, and my mother would choose. The tailor would measure her and the clothes would be made up and brought home.'

Migration became a more important feature during the late colonial years. Men now moved between different regions of Uganda as the demand for labor in commercial agriculture grew, affecting the many women who remained at home and those few who accompanied their husbands. In 1951, for example, 12-27 percent of the adult male laborers in the Lugbara counties of the West Nile region were absent from their home area for at least part of the year, working for wages in Bunyoro or other parts of the country.[11] Labor migrants in this period usually returned within a year or two, bringing money and such goods as cloth and blankets. In a different pattern, Alur migrants from the north moved primarily to Buganda to work as tenant cotton growers.[12] By 1951, some Alur women were accompanying their husbands: one of every four or five men may have had his wife with him. For the unmarried women left at home, the greatest problem was a surplus of marriageable girls; for married women, the absence of their husbands intensified demands upon their labor in domestic agriculture and forced them to assume responsibility as household heads.

Rural–urban migration also increased, involving mainly men but a small number of women as well. Some men now stayed in Kampala or smaller towns for years on end, rather than working only long enough to earn money for taxes. In rural areas, male control over women was threatened when men migrated, leaving their wives in charge of the household. When Eunice Kyamanya (Profile 6.1) was a child in Fort Portal, her father was away from home most of the time, doing unskilled work for the Post Office in Kampala. Although he came home on occasion, bringing money, Eunice's mother was the functional head of the family, making all the day-to-day decisions. To keep the family going between his visits, she grew food for their own consumption and made and sold mats and baskets.

More dislocating in social terms was the movement of even a few unmarried women into urban areas, a process that violated several of the precepts of the Domestic Virtue model. It has been argued more generally that migration of African women away from their home villages into the anonymity and independence offered by an urban environment 'not only directly challenged the authority of state-appointed chiefs over their people, but, perhaps more disturbing to the state and capital, it presaged the creation of a fully urbanized, proletarianized generation of families, with attendant problems of social control and the demand for social services'.[13] Because women had difficulty in finding legitimate waged work in African cities and towns, they commonly resorted to proscribed activities like alcohol brewing or prostitution. The colonial state, capitalist employers, patriarchal African rulers, and ordinary men therefore worked in parallel to impede the movement of women into towns.

In Uganda, migration of women into towns – opposed by all male authorities – was relatively unimportant in this period. A scattering of young women from Toro, for example, moved into Kampala during the 1950s.[14] Sex ratios within African areas of the city and its suburbs became somewhat more even. In 1953-5, Kampala's poor and densely settled area of Kisenyi had only 2.5 men for every woman, while the suburb of Mulago, near the hospital, had just 1.4 men per woman.[15] Even Jinja, whose population more than tripled between 1948 and 1951 due largely to demand for construction workers at the Owen Falls Dam, had only 2 adult men per woman.

As conservatives feared, female mobility weakened traditional domestic arrangements. For village women, the impact of freedom to move was magnified by expanding opportunities for education and economic independence. In Toro, where some rural women went into towns during the 1950s to get training as teachers, nurses, tailors, or clerks, their ability to bring in their own income after marriage challenged the expectation that wives would be economically dependent and subordinate to their husbands.[16] In Kampala, the breakdown of customary household and marriage patterns due to female migration was especially visible. In Kisenyi, 23 percent of all households were headed by women in 1953-5.[17] Few of the women had ever undergone Christian marriages and fewer still were actually living in such marriages while in Kampala. In Mulago, more than a third of all households were headed by women.[18] Various kinds of sexual unions were found, including commercial agreements, non-traditional temporary unions, simple 'friendships', customary marriages, and a few Christian marriages.

Yet the extent of urban migration and its impact during the late colonial period should not be exaggerated: the country remained almost entirely rural. As late as 1959, when the total population was estimated at 6.5 million, even Kampala had only about 47,000 residents (24,000 Africans, 20,000 South Asians, and 3,000 Europeans); another 70,000 people, nearly all African, lived in peri-urban areas outside Kampala.[19] Central Jinja had 30,000 (of whom 20,000 were African), with another 9,000 Africans in its peri-urban area. Mbale, Entebbe, and Kabale had 11,000–14,000 residents each, and four other towns had between 5,000 and 10,000.

Overt opposition to colonial rule and pressure for independence were relatively limited and generally non-violent in Uganda. The weight of colonial rule was not felt as heavily in this protectorate as in many other imperial settings, and Uganda's ethnic groups were too divided – both within communities and between them – to mount an effective campaign against the British presence. At only a few times did Ugandan nationalist movements successfully link middle-class, educated 'urban protest against racial exclusion in civil society to rural movements against the uncustomary powers of Native Authority chiefs'.[20] The most important were the general strike and rural violence of January 1945, followed by the assassination of Buganda's prime minister Nsibirwa later that year, and another wave of rural violence in Buganda in 1949.[21] Both grew out of disputes between the protectorate government and Baganda nationalists, but they were also deeply intertwined with power conflicts within Buganda's leadership and resistance by other ethnic groups to Bagandan control. Independence came in part because the British concluded that they could never recoup the expense of running a government in the protectorate and that an independent Kenya could not be created without an independent Uganda.

The 1950s witnessed the entry of the Ugandan male elite into electoral politics, as the British expanded African participation in its organs of rule. The first political party to claim nationwide support, the Ugandan National Congress, was founded in 1952 by younger men who had attended the top boarding schools.[22] Although the UNC advocated democracy, it excluded peasants and women from its ranks. The other parties formed during the 1950s were composed of influential men who committed their movements to fairly narrow religious or ethnic goals. Women and issues were not central to any of these groups. As the author of a study of women in Ugandan politics concludes, 'colonialism had systematically alienated them from the redefined political structure. Such alienation was maintained by the nationalist parties, with women playing only marginal roles in decision-making processes and in the designation of political priorities at the time.'[23] This exclusion contrasted with some other African regions where women – many of them uneducated – were active in nationalist movements and military struggles against colonial rule.[24]

In a change that would have longer-term if not immediate consequences for women, the colonial government began to support the higher education and employment of African men in professional and administrative positions.[25] After India became independent in 1947, a growing number of British colonial officials believed that the African colonies too would inevitably move towards political freedom. Although administrators in Uganda appear to have assumed that independence would not occur until the later 1970s or 1980s, they began to reassess their current policies in light of the need to prepare Ugandan men for positions of leadership. This led to a series of measures that promoted advanced training for a limited number of men and attempted to raise the standing and rewards of professionals. Thus, when two scholarships in clinical medical research at Mulago Hospital were proposed in 1946, one was intended for a white medical officer and the other for an African assistant medical officer, open to men working in the local Civil Service.[26] In 1953 government officials considered a proposal to set up a training program for African men as incorporated accountants, and the following year the Legislative Council discussed the training of African men in the law and what posts they were likely to take.[27] A series of measures during the 1950s improved pensions and other gratuities for teachers. The government was also attempting to bring more African men into the middle ranks of its own service, replacing at least some of the Indians who had previously constituted the bulk of its employees.[28] The movement of some African men into the professions and government service helped to pave the way for African women in subsequent decades.

It is interesting that descriptions by the women in our sample of political conditions during the late colonial years were almost uniformly favorable. To some extent their approbation stemmed from a negative comparison with the early post-Independence and Amin/Obote II periods: the quality most often mentioned about the pre-1962 decades was the security and stability of life. As an elderly nurse in Kampala noted, 'The level of trust was high, people were peaceful and OK, all of my relatives were alive.'[29] Several women associated this stability with the continuation of the Bunyoro, Buganda, or Butoro kingdoms. A few women commented that the colonialists provided good social services (though they kept control over them in their own hands) and encouraged the education of girls.

These women said little about pressure for independence in Uganda. A woman whose father was a judge in the Bunyoro kingdom remembers hearing her parents talk about 'the chance for Ugandans to govern themselves', and she remembers being left behind at home when her parents went to Entebbe for Independence Day.[30] But, she explained, 'Really in Uganda, we had no experience of colonialism. We were under a protectorate, the British came, they were district officers, assistant district officers, they were administrators. The other white people were the nuns. So when people talk about the struggle for independence, our experience is not the same as places where people were oppressed, where there were liberation wars.' Rather surprisingly, Grace Ssembatia (Profile 5.1) said that during the colonial period 'the spirit of nationalism was high. People were proud of the Union Jack, and we learned to love our country.' She contrasted that situation with the situation in 2003, when she felt that national feeling was missing.

Women's Education, Organizations and Political Involvement

A development of profound importance for women was the expansion of girls' education. This led more women into the cash-based economy: some mothers needed to earn money to pay for their daughters' school fees, and educated girls were more likely to work outside the home as they got older. Between 1939 and 1947, the number of girls in primary schools trebled.[31] Some schools were still run by religious groups, but the involvement of the state was increasing. By 1959, 172,000 girls aged 6-15 had received at least a little primary education (28 percent of all girls in that age range and 34 percent of all primary school attenders), though only 22,000 girls had received five or more years of schooling, as compared with 63,000 boys (26 percent).[32] At this level progress halted for the time being, since the colonial government said that it could not afford to set up any additional schools for girls. Female education continued to emphasize domesticity. During the 1950s, for example, the government set up 20 'homecraft centres' designed to teach girls 'all skills necessary in home management and motherhood and wifery'.[33]

At secondary level, opportunities remained very limited. Just six secondary schools in the early 1950s took girls, three of them single-sex, three co-educational.[34] All but one of these schools were located within Buganda and all catered for Christian children. In 1959, 295 African girls (including some non-Ugandans) were enrolled in senior secondary schools, as compared with 2,819 boys (9 percent). Expansion of secondary education was held back in part by lack of qualified teachers. The slow rate at which African teachers were trained by the government was the topic of heated exchanges in 1945–6 between Bishop Stuart and various colonial officials, including the Director of Education and the Governor.[35] Stuart advocated rapid expansion of teacher training, including at the new program at Makerere, while the government claimed that its budget could not cover it. The bishop became so incensed that he wrote intemperately to the colonial authorities; he was then forced to withdraw some of his statements and apologize. The bishop and the government were still fighting over this issue in 1949–50, when Stuart again sent insulting comments to the education department.

By the late 1950s, a few young women were beginning to move beyond secondary education. Higher training for their daughters was desired by high-status African families and was accepted – on a limited scale – by British officials who felt that African men trained for professional and government work needed suitably educated wives. Lady Cohen, the wife of Uganda's liberal Governor, said in a 1955 article in the London *Times*, 'Modern Africa expects to produce educated Chiefs, doctors, teachers, clergy, agricultural officers, police officers, and many other callings. There is nothing sadder than the keen, well-educated African young man, unable to find among his own Tribe a girl who can share his interests and aspirations.'[36] Most of these female educational pioneers went to Britain to study. A report in 1958 notes that a total of 576 East Africans were then studying in the United Kingdom, whereas just two years before the total had been only 328.[37] The report does not give the sexes of the students, but it is likely that women predominated among 31 Ugandans studying nursing and 11 studying dressmaking. Others may have been

Profile 5.1 A Member of the Early Educated Elite: 'Grace Ssembatia'[38]

Grace Ssembatia provides a glimpse into the experiences of those few women from leading families who were sent to Britain during the late colonial period to train for careers and prepare for good marriages.[39] A Muganda who belonged to the Church of Uganda, Grace was 71 years old and married at the time of the interview. The conversation took place at the highly regarded school on the edge of Kampala of which she was a co-founder/co-owner and head of the primary section. A self-confident lady, she was dressed in formal European-style clothes and dealt in a pleasant but firm manner with the teachers and other staff members who came into her office to ask for advice about school issues as the interview proceeded.

Born in 1932, Grace was the daughter of the prime minister of the Buganda kingdom. Her family lived on Mengo Hill in Kampala, the kingdom's headquarters, and Grace was sent to King's College, Budo, one of the early schools founded by the CMS for well-born children. Both her parents wanted her to have good schooling. As she said, 'My father believed in education and made sacrifices for it.'[40]

Atypically even for elite women of her generation, Grace continued her education beyond secondary school. After doing her O-level exams, she worked briefly at the library at Makerere University. She then decided to become a teacher, but because there was no formal training course open to girls at the time, she went to Gayaza High School as an apprentice. Later, when a teacher training college opened at Buloba, she enrolled there, supported by the colonial government, and earned a certificate as a Grade III teacher. At that point, thanks to a scholarship from the Buganda kingdom, she went to Britain, where she did a diploma in education at the University of Hull. Upon her return to Uganda in 1953, when she was 21, she began teaching at Budo. Living at the school, she earned Ush 75 a month at first, a sum that eventually rose to Ush 200. That was a good deal of money at the time, enough for her to take care of her own clothing and other personal expenses and still give some to her mother, who was by then a widow and growing cotton and food for sale. Grace felt that she was greatly admired and respected within her family and in the community for teaching at Budo.

In 1956, when she was 24, Grace married a lawyer from a comparable background who would later become the chief justice of the Ugandan high court. They had four children over the following eight years, all of whom subsequently graduated from university. Because Grace was working while the children were small (as she did throughout her life), she relied on the care provided by housegirls and members of her extended family who were living with them. 'My husband and I would only go for outings at night, after the children were sleeping.'

Grace's history in subsequent periods: Forced into exile during the Amin period, she and her family went to Kenya. Upon their return in 1979, she went back into teaching. With the restoration of peace by the NRM, she and two other women decided to set up their own school. As a major shareholder and co-director, she was supervising a staff of 56 in 2003, including teachers, librarians, and cleaners. She also continued to teach social studies, English, and mathematics. At the time of her interview, Grace expected to go on teaching 'so long as I am in good health and still have my memory'. She believed that, because women have demonstrated they can work just as well as men, it would be easier for them to succeed in the future. She was not concerned about the impact of the 2006 elections: 'Women's work will continue to advance regardless of the political situation. Women will move on and retain their dignity.'

included among the 40 studying education, probably joined by a few in other fields.

Higher education for women within Uganda itself began at the end of World War II. In 1945, the first six women entered Makerere College, thanks in large part to the efforts of Mary Stuart, wife of the bishop of the Church of Uganda. As Kwesiga describes, 'The first warden of the women's hall of residence traveled all over East Africa to search for qualified women. Only two were found, and the other four were serving teachers who had to be persuaded to try.'[41] Progress was slow: with a single exception, the number of East African girls admitted to Makerere did not exceed nine per year until 1963.

The older women in our district sample described some of the factors that affected girls' education in this period. In assessing their comments, we must recognize the skewed nature of this early sample. Only three of the 37 women had no formal education at all, a figure far lower than was true of the whole population of girls in the late colonial years. Just under half had some primary or secondary education, while more than a third had received a certificate or diploma as well. Four of the women eventually received university degrees, among the first or second generation to do so.

The fact that so many of these women were able to get a good education derived from the willingness of one or both parents to send their girl children to school at a time when it was still not common. While two-thirds said that their father had been generally supportive or positive about their education, other responses indicate considerable male uncertainty about the value of educating girls. A woman who grew up in a rural area outside Kabale said that her father, a small subsistence farmer, 'liked education for his daughters, but he would sometimes get discouraged. People would tell him that if he sends his girl children to school, they will get promiscuous! However he would insist, saying that by educating his children he was banking for the future.'[42] Only three of the fathers were said to be negative or indifferent, due at least in part to financial constraints. A woman who lived as a child in the outskirts of Kampala, where her father was a builder, recalled: 'Although my father personally did not object to my going to school, he was influenced and discouraged by his friends while having drinks. When it came to paying the fees, he said he had no money, though he used to visit me in school. He felt a girl has to get married, and he did not see the purpose of going to school.'[43]

A quarter of the women said their father's attitude changed over time. In some cases, he became less willing to support the girl's education as she grew older, due largely to concerns about her marriage. The daughter of a catechist for the Catholic church in a village outside Kabale remembered, 'My father liked it at first but then was discouraged by friends and even stopped me. He argued that since women were not appointed to positions of authority, educating them was a waste of time and money. I was rescued by a seminarian social worker.'[44] In a few cases, however, the father became more willing to support his daughter. The daughter of a subsistence farmer outside Lira said, 'My father initially thought I was wasting time in school, so my uncle [with whom she was living at the time] kept me away from him. Later his attitude changed when I wanted to become a teacher, and eventually he became proud of me.'[45]

The most determined effort to obtain an education against the wishes of her older male relatives was made by a woman living in a trading center in Arua district, where her father was a health assistant. 'My father's attitudes towards my education were very positive. He wanted all his children to study, irrespective of the sex of the child. Our home was exemplary in the village. But when I was to go to Senior One, my father was in prison and my uncles stopped me from going to school. They insisted that I was too old for school and ripe for marriage. They also claimed that there was no money for fees. I cried and refused to eat food for three days until my aunt's husband took me away to school and paid my first fees. After that, luckily enough, the district decided to give me a bursary since I was the best girl in the district.'[46] During her secondary school vacations she worked as an unlicensed teacher in primary schools in Rhino Camp to support herself. She then went on to study sociology and political science at Makerere University and taught in a secondary school before becoming a labor and gender officer in a district.

The mothers of these women were slightly more supportive of their education (84 percent) than the fathers, though in many cases they could contribute little to the school fees. Their daughters recalled with gratitude their mothers' efforts to assist with their schooling: preparing breakfast for the children before they went off to school, selling sorghum to pay for fees, or brewing and selling *waragi* to supplement what the father was paying.[47] Several mothers were said to have intervened with less supportive fathers or to have sought help from a priest or someone else. The mother of a girl living in a village in Lira District personally escorted her daughter to primary school. 'My mother was eager that I should study. She would supplement my father's money by selling foodstuffs. She used to accompany me to Aloi Primary School [a boarding school] on foot, and when holidays came she would again walk to collect me from school.'[48] Only a few of the mothers were said to have been negative or indifferent. The daughter of a soldier stationed in Moroto said, 'It was difficult to know my mother's attitudes, as she did not show any concern with such issues. She was completely uneducated herself.'[49]

The majority of these women said that their teachers had had a positive impact upon their lives or the kinds of work they had done. Five said that their teachers, several of whom were white women, had encouraged them to train for a career as a teacher or nurse or had acted as role models because of their intelligence and professional appearance.[50] For some women, the value of school was assessed in terms of personal qualities. Five said their teachers had taught them hard work, patience, humility, or good manners, suggesting that Domestic Virtue values were being advocated at school. A woman who grew up in Hoima thought she obtained a sense of fairness, of giving, from the nuns at her school: 'You didn't always have to do things for profit.'[51] A few mentioned gaining useful practical skills.

The late colonial period also saw the growth of women's organizations. These constituted a potential threat to the Domestic Virtue model because they brought women out of their own homes and joined them into groups for training and discussion of shared problems. For this reason they were opposed by some African men, even though most of the associations had a strongly domestic focus. Some of the groups were run by religious bodies or European women to teach Africans what they regarded as superior skills in child-rearing, hygiene, care of the house, nutrition, and other domestic activities. Although most recent literature has criticized this approach as attempting to 'domesticate, sanitize, and civilize' African women and as perpetuating colonial and patriarchal values, a few authors point out that these early organizations served as stepping stones to women's advancement.[52] During the 1940s and 1950s, church-related and secular groups like the Mothers' Union, the Catholic Women's Guild, and the Uganda Women's League gradually expanded throughout the country. The Young Women's Christian Association (YWCA), founded in 1952, focused on assisting young women who were moving into urban centers. Years later Sarah Nyedwoha Ntiro, then a leading women's activist and politician, commented on the importance of her involvement with the Mothers' Union and the YWCA during the 1950s.[53]

The expansion of voluntary women's organizations was assisted by the decision of the colonial Ministry for Social Development in 1946 to work with women in creating community clubs. The government then began to hire community development assistants to teach domestic science and child welfare and to organize women's courses and groups. By 1957, when the government signed an agreement with the United Nations Children's Fund (UNICEF) to train over 3,500 women leaders of community clubs, these organizations had become important in several respects. Their original, domestically oriented, functions were still present, but now they also promoted discussion of educational, political and legal issues, encouraged women to gain leadership skills, and developed women's talents in such areas as writing and acting in plays.

The significance of women's clubs varied by ethnic group and region of the country. While organizations of women in Ankole and of educated women in Buganda appear to have been particularly advanced, even those with more limited functions were able to play vital roles within their communities. A description of the status of women in Toro during the 1950s drew attention to the importance of women's clubs, credited with important gains for women, alongside improvements in the education of girls.[54] Eunice Kyamanya (Profile 6.1), who lived as a child in Toro, commented: 'During the 1950s, when I was growing up, you would see women coming together in groups under missionaries. Whenever you met them you would feel, "Here is someone who has a bit of concern for our community and for girls like me".' In 1955 ten members of local women's clubs in Busoga, ranging in age from an elderly woman to a girl of 12, were brought into Kampala by the Community Development Ministry. Their visit featured a 15-minute live broadcast on the radio, with a program that 'included singing [in their local language] as well as a discussion of women's clubs and community development'.[55]

In Buganda, some educated women began to organize to express support for a loyalist (traditionalist) approach to kingdom affairs. Two women joined eight men in presenting a list of concerns to the *Kabaka* in 1949, and in 1953 women were involved in protests against the deportation and exile of the *Kabaka* by the British.[56] Two busloads of women went to the office of Buganda's prime minister in January 1954 to demand news of the *Kabaka*; a group of influential women mounted a campaign to raise money for his support while in England; and in June a large delegation went to Entebbe to tell the Governor that 'as mothers, wives, and obedient citizens of Buganda' they objected to his policies.[57] Musisi argues that women's contributions to the successful effort to obtain the *Kabaka*'s return to Uganda in 1955 were a turning point in Bagandan women's history. The protests 'gave women experience, courage, confidence, organisational skills and contacts that were to prove increasingly useful in their future struggle'.[58]

During the 1950s a few Baganda women also tried to participate in politics or at least to influence policy, though they were not allowed to vote or hold formal office. In agitating against the restrictions that promoted female 'passivity, submissiveness and subjugation', they formed part of a broader populist movement.[59] Eight women stood unsuccessfully for seats in the *Lukiiko* in 1957; their attempts to win chieftancies from the *Kabaka* also failed, leaving them with no political involvement apart from minor positions within municipal governments.[60] As Independence neared, women put pressure on the emerging political parties to name women to offices and to include women's issues on their agendas. This effort achieved only partial success. When, for example, the Democratic Party published a policy statement in 1961, it assumed a high rhetorical stance about the importance of women to national advancement but ended with the lukewarm promise, 'We will appoint women as Ministers, if any are able and willing.'[61]

The first broader political organization for women, one that deliberately brought together people from diverse racial and ethnic backgrounds, was founded in 1946-7. Triggered by the injustices of the inheritance system, a group of British, South Asian, and African women formed the Uganda Council of Women (UCW).[62] Growing out of the Young Wives Group of the Mothers' Union, the UCW was dedicated to fighting for women's rights. By 1957, it had nine chapters across the country and a membership of 2,000. It was later accused of being a useless, elitist organization. It is true that most of its membership was English-speaking and that its African participants were mainly educated Baganda women employed as teachers or community development workers. But the UCW had a political agenda and educated its membership about women's issues. During the later 1950s and 1960s, for example, the group pushed for reform of laws concerning marriage, divorce, and inheritance, writing booklets in English and local languages, and holding conferences on domestic and property laws.

Women also began to move into a few limited roles in the colonial government. Within the Legislative Council, the first African woman was named to an appointed seat in 1956, and by 1962, five African women had been chosen by the government, though none was elected to one of the open seats.[63] Nor were most African women eligible to vote in colonial elections, due to the way the qualifications for suffrage were defined. In 1957, colonial administrators in East Africa were corresponding about how voting by women might be accepted or opposed by various ethnic groups within the region, and Uganda's first Constitution granted them full suffrage.[64]

Women's Work

Women's economic roles were expanding during the late colonial years, but only to a limited extent and very slowly: most women still had little involvement with the extra-domestic economy. Although we lack statistical information, the overwhelming majority remained subsistence farmers, producing food for consumption by their own families. As a historian of Bakiga culture commented, 'We only knew that our role was to cultivate.'[65] If a woman needed to generate cash for some special purpose, she might sell excess produce, but in most regions women did not regularly engage in agriculture for market sale. Bakiga women, for example, sold food to Indian traders when the family needed salt or clothing. Only in rural areas influenced by urban demand were women engaged in the production of food specifically for market sale. Women living in villages near Jinja were said to grow food crops for the market in 1950-51, and in the vicinity of Kampala, commercial agriculture focused on such items as bananas, sweet potatoes, and vegetables.[66]

Cash crops did not generally benefit women. In some settings they provided much of the labor for cotton, coffee, or tea, but they had little control over how the crops were grown and sold. The earlier experiment in Buganda of granting land to women on which to grow cotton had come to an end. In Bunyoro, as profits from cotton increased during the later 1940s and 1950s, local legislation banned women from gaining any of the returns from cash crops, stipulating instead that they should stay at home to grow food for their families.[67] In Bugisu, although women participated in the cultivation and transport of coffee, it was men who controlled the disposal of the crop because it was they who held the land. At meetings of the [Coffee] Growers' Cooperative Societies, 1940-55, women were present but played no role in decision-making. A detailed study of tobacco growing in Uganda in 1951 suggests that this was an exclusively male operation.[68] Women are not mentioned in any stage of the production, and the photographs show only men working in the fields, harvesting, and carrying the leaf to the curing barn.

In rural areas, the expansion of trade in the late colonial period almost entirely passed women by. In Toro around 1950, for example, though trade was increasing and cash was more commonly used, local people did not buy or sell food for their own use.[69] Trade in such items as cattle, fish, salt, and copper was organized by Asian or European middlemen. Nor did women run shops on their own, though they might assist in a male relative's business, at least behind the scenes. Likewise in Lugbara communities in West Nile, 1949-53, many of the vendors who brought foodstuffs to the informal, periodic markets held at sub-county chiefs' headquarters were women, but they came only occasionally.[70] Seated on mats on the ground in an open place, they offered surplus food or the maize used for beer brewing. But trade in imported items, like soap, tobacco, and kerosene, was conducted in stalls or shops run by African men in the smaller townships and at Indian or Arab stores in the few larger centers.

In Kampala and its suburbs, however, new patterns were starting to emerge despite the ongoing reservation of many residential areas of the city for whites or South Asians. A few women now joined the many men who sold vegetables, fruit, and other food that was brought into the city by middlemen. Because non-Africans played no part in the provision of staple foods in Kampala, the gradual entry of women has been seen as a purely African response to the growth of an urban market.[71] In Katwe market, for example, 12 of 140 sellers (9 percent) in 1955 were women. All offered vegetables and other basic foodstuffs, not the more profitable meat, fish, or manufactured goods. Other women worked in Kampala's smaller markets or hawked food on the streets. A study of Mulago noted a sexual division of commercial activity in 1953–5 among the many small independent retailers, most of whom 'scrape by with a rather miserable existence'.[72] The sellers of bananas, charcoal, and firewood were likely to be older women, many of them Baganda who were separated from their husbands. A few women were also engaged in the somewhat more profitable trade in beer, but men generally sold higher-value goods. Small shopkeepers in Mulago were generally male, but it was common for their wives to look after the business while the men worked in other jobs. Indeed, although men in Mulago did not expect their wives to grow food crops, they commonly asked them to take part in some kind of production or sale, working either on their own or with their husband. In such cases, 'the woman assumes a position of considerable authority, and greater co-operation in daily life is called for'.[73]

Making and selling cooked food was beginning to appear as a way for women living in or near the large centers to make money. This opportunity was due both to demand (Kampala and Jinja contained many men who were there alone, without women to cook for them) and to supply (women with no other skills could extend what they had learned at home into a for-pay context). In 1950–51, some of the women living in the villages around Jinja were said to earn money from preparing and selling food and drink.[74] In Kampala, a Bahima woman from Ankole described how she happened to enter this kind of work.[75] Leaving her husband in 1948, having borne no children, she first lived for three years with a brother outside Kampala. Using money he gave her, she then moved into the town and rented a room. She noticed that many men had no one to cook for them, so she bought an empty paraffin tin, a little firewood, and a small bunch of plantain bananas. Cooking during the daytime, she sold bananas by the plate in the evening to poor porters as they returned from work. Because she did not have enough money to buy meat, fish, or relish, her customers had to do without these things or provide them themselves. Other women in Kampala hawked fried bread, rolls, or roasted groundnuts or sold them while seated beside the roads, working without licenses and hence vulnerable to police harassment. Market vending and small-scale sale of cooked food would become more important to urban women after 1962.

In an extension of an earlier pattern, more women were now brewing and selling beer, *waragi*, and other kinds of alcoholic beverages, both in towns and in rural areas. By the later 1950s, most alcohol was brewed for sale, not for use within households or as gifts, and it had become a part of the economic strategies of people of both sexes.[76] Since brewing unlicensed alcohol was illegal, we generally hear about it only indirectly. A court case in 1957, for example, involved a 'witchdoctor' who killed his girlfriend after they had been drinking *mwenge* (a Baganda beer made of bananas) in a beer-shop.[77] This informal establishment, located in Mityana, was run by a woman who had evidently brewed as well as sold the beer. In Bunyoro, women were attracted to brewing during the 1950s in part because the king had just ordered that women were not permitted to grow cash crops, or even to be present where they were grown.[78] Alcohol was one of the few other ways they could earn money. But they were only allowed to make beer if they paid for a permit, and under no circumstances were they allowed to run a drinking house or club in which it was sold.

In Kampala's poor neighborhood of Kisenyi, three-quarters of the 60–72 beer sellers in 1953–5 were women.[79] Such work, together with prostitution, was identified by foreign anthropologists as 'one of the main foundations of the newfound economic independence of African women'. It was especially common among landless women divorced from their husbands and for girls who had failed to marry and saw no future for themselves in their rural villages. Although a few female brewers and sellers were later able to build houses of their own, renting out rooms to lodgers, most remained in poverty. Indeed, the profitability of offering alcohol on a small scale was probably declining due to the development of more formalized structures of retailing.

One should not, however, overstate the extent to which women were engaged in food and drink work during this period. Even in Kampala, which had the greatest concentration of women trying to support themselves, 65 percent of all adult women living in Kisenyi in 1953-5 had no income-generating activities at all.[80] Only 14 percent of the female population were engaged in any kind of unskilled, self-employed work, which included provision of food and drink as well as prostitution and some miscellaneous occupations. Because most food and drink sellers were men, the few women engaged in such work did not trigger vigorous efforts to regulate their mobility and trading as occurred in Nairobi in these years.[81]

Opportunities for educated women as salaried workers – including teachers, nurses, and community development officers – were limited. Only 3–4,000 women were employed for wages of any kind throughout Uganda in 1952 (1–2 percent of all such workers).[82] Of these, 1,176 worked in education or medicine/health, with another 1,100 in commercial agriculture and forestry. Teachers almost certainly constituted the largest group of salaried employees. The number but not the percentage of female primary school teachers rose after 1940.[83] In 1958, 270 women graduated from teacher training colleges, and many others taught without formal preparation. At the secondary level, virtually all teachers were still either Europeans or African men.

Although teaching had become more professionalized, women's status within the field was low. Articles in *The Uganda Teachers' Journal* of 1940 were written almost entirely by Europeans, and when there was something about 'African teachers,' they were assumed to be male.[84] The sole reference to African women teachers in *The Uganda Teachers' Journal* for 1941 was an account of a 'homecraft vacation course' offered in the domestic science department of Mengo Girls' School, sponsored by the CMS and attended by 36 teachers. Of these, a third were said to be Africans, with most of the rest Europeans who taught in boarding schools or at teacher training centers. A photograph shows that four of the African women were nuns, joined by eight in lay clothing. Both female and male teachers were expected to maintain high standards of personal behavior. In 1953-5, 44 women teachers working for the Native Anglican Church in the Diocese of the Upper Nile were suspended for sexual immorality, as were 71 men.[85]

The number of Ugandan nurses likewise remained small, in part because many of the tasks later assigned to them were still being carried out by male hospital attendants (now Ugandans as well as Indians). Among the bottom tier of nurses, the 'enrolled nurses' who received a certificate in general nursing, relatively few Africans were trained prior to the late 1950s. For the 25 years between 1933 and 1958, the first period covered in the Register of Enrolled Nurses kept by the Uganda Nurses and Midwives Council, a total of only 517 nurses were listed.[86] They appear to have been mainly unmarried African women. During the 1940s and 1950s Mulago Hospital in Kampala, the main government facility for Africans, made a deliberate effort to find 'the right type of girl' for training; it complained that the mission hospitals had previously had the pick of the crop, with only poorly educated girls applying to the government hospitals.[87] In 1955, the newly opened School of Nursing at Mulago Hospital issued a call for women with a secondary school education to enter their program. Hospital training schools expanded hostels for the girls, where they could be introduced into a Western-defined professional world and their leisure time supervised. The respect given to nurses is suggested by the composition of the group that stood on stage at the ceremony held in Kampala to celebrate victory in World War II. Nurses were the only Africans to appear together with colonial government and legal officials, Boy and Girl Guides (all white or South Asian), and Bishop Stuart of the Church of Uganda.[88]

In more specialized kinds of health work, most of the nursing sisters at the hospitals and the nurse tutors at the nursing schools remained European throughout the 1950s.[89] In 1951, however, the first two Ugandan nurses returned from a two-year course in Britain leading to the state-certified midwifery award and became midwifery nursing sisters at Mengo Hospital. Registered nurses (who met the UK's higher 'registrable qualifications') were entirely foreign until the very late 1950s.[90] But between 1959 and 1965, ten African women – all of whom had obtained their qualifications in England or Ireland – were registered alongside eleven foreigners.[91] A few young women moved into other types of medically related work. In 1955, for example, the Buganda government provided a scholarship for a recent graduate of King's College, Budo to go to London to study pharmacy.[92]

Industrial employment, clerical work, and unskilled labor offered few opportunities for women. To explain the almost complete absence of women from the labor force in Kampala, Jinja, and Mbale during the first half of the 1950s, Elkan pointed to cultural factors as well as to the types of jobs available.[93] Work in heavy industries like those dealing with brick and stone was not seen as suitable for women. Nor could they be hired in building and construction work, which employed 43 percent of the 14,400 African men in Jinja in 1950–51.[94] Jinja did, however, provide a little employment for women in the nascent textile industry and processing plants for tea, tobacco, and certain foodstuffs. In an industrial accident in 1955, 18 women were injured when a large stack of bagged groundnuts, each weighing 180 lb, collapsed onto a group of people working alongside it.[95] In offices, skilled stenographers were usually European women, while most other clerical workers were South Asian men.

Within the tobacco factory studied by Elkan in Jinja, where, atypically, 250 women were hired, female employment had started only in 1950, 21 years after the factory's opening.[96] The management's decision to take on some women in addition to the larger number of male workers resulted from three considerations: an attempt to forestall possible labor shortages; a sense that women were more docile than men and hence provided insurance against industrial unrest; and the hope that they would be more reliable workers than men, lessening the high turnover and high absenteeism of previous employees. A study undertaken a year after the first hiring of women in the tobacco factories commented that 'this move has met with considerable African opposition. It is said that it encourages women to leave their husbands and undermines the customary authority of father or husband in that it enables the woman to support herself and encourages "immoral" living in the town.'[97] This fear might appear to be justified by the observation that 36 percent of the African women living in Jinja in 1950–51 were separated from their husbands, and some of the female factory workers had 'been in trouble' sexually. But in fact the directionality probably worked the opposite way: women came to Jinja and took employment *because* their marriage had failed or they had been ostracized by their families and hence needed to support themselves. In part because of the very small number of women workers, female involvement in the trade unions formed during the later 1940s and 1950s, which were themselves weak, 'remained elusive and passive'.[98]

Due to the ongoing preference for male domestic servants among the whites and South Asians who constituted the majority of those able to afford such help, few women found employment in that area.[99] But the pattern was beginning to change. In Toro during the 1950s some uneducated rural women were moving into Fort Portal to work as ayahs or housegirls.[100] The prime minister of Toro wrote to the prime minister of Buganda in 1955, asking him to help ensure the return of all Batoro girls under the age of 14 who were then living in Buganda, some employed as ayahs.

Because housegirls lived with the family for whom they worked, they were vulnerable to economic and sometimes sexual exploitation. In 1945 a British 'Arabella', writing in her 'For Women Only!' column in the *Uganda Herald*, complained that, unlike the competent and imaginative nannies of their own childhoods at home, Ugandan ayahs were 'well meaning but ignorant women'.[101] 'The average ayah without supervision mostly muddles through the day. She keeps the children out of serious harm and that is that.' Although Arabella had been warned that African girls 'do not like [such work] and are unwilling to take it up', she supported the idea that they be given formal preparation as children's nurses. The following week, when reporting on a proposal for training ayahs that was then under discussion by a government committee, she suggested magnanimously that ayahs might even be paid some kind of cash wage, not merely a food allowance plus housing as was then common.[102]

Exchange of sex for money or other benefits helped some urban women get by. A few sold sex openly to strangers; others worked in bars where they might have sex with customers on the side; and a final group had flexible temporary unions or 'friendly arrangements' with men.[103] In the mid-1950s a 32-year-old beer seller who had been living in the Kisenyi district of Kampala after separating from her husband three years before said, 'I just have a lover who keeps me . . . . I have had only one for a long time. He gives me clothes and buys me food. He only visits me, I do not visit him, because he has got his "legal" wife.' Another woman, who had left her children behind in the village, said that her lover in Kampala gave her food and was trying to find her a job. Musisi has pointed out that at least a few 'bad women' who lived with men in Kampala defended their right to do so.[104] Believing that it was better not to be committed to a single man whose economic situation was uncertain, they manipulated culture 'as a tool for their own liberation', forcing men to associate with them on their own terms and thus asserting their autonomy. Sex workers who were streetwalkers or received men in their rooms do not appear to have experienced the harassment faced by prostitutes in Nairobi, but neither is there any indication that wealthy prostitutes bought urban property and became semi-respectable landlords in Kampala as they did in Nairobi.[105]

A small number of women brought in some income in other, miscellaneous ways. Craftwork might be an option, selling items similar to those women made for their own family's use.[106] Generally, however, the craftware made by some women in a community could be made by others too, so there was little demand. Though tailors were still generally male, Florence Kabula, who had joined her husband in Kampala, was making wedding dresses for sale during the 1940s.[107] Her success led to conflict within the marriage. Kabula finally left her husband in a dispute over his second wife, taking with her the items necessary to her work that she claimed she had bought with her own profits, including a sewing machine and a bicycle. Her husband took her to court for stealing 'household property', and judgment was made in his favor. A few women were employed as sales people in the larger urban shops, and a very few wealthy Baganda women, profiting from their ability to hold *mailo* land in their own names, bought large houses in Mulago, rented out rooms, and lived on the proceeds of the rent they collected.[108] At Lake Katwe, most producers of salt were women during these years, as were some of the salt-pan owners.

Further information about women's work during these years comes from our district sample. We asked whether the mothers or aunts of these women were engaged in any income-generating activities. Just over a third said their mothers had no source of cash income at all, while just under a third worked primarily in subsistence agriculture but sometimes had excess produce that could be sold or exchanged. Several of the interviewees emphasized, however, that it was their father who would take the food to market and decide how the money was spent. Only two of the mothers, both living in rural areas outside Kampala, raised food or poultry expressly for market sale. Five mothers made and sold local beer or other types of alcohol on a part-time basis, while two sold tea and/or small cooked food items. A few did craftwork, producing items like mats and baskets. Eunice Kyamanya (Profile 6.1), who grew up in the Kabarole area, noted that in her mother's generation the missionaries encouraged women to learn handicrafts, mainly to improve their own homes but in some cases for sale. Since the Toro royal women had traditionally done beadwork and worked with animal hides, such activities carried high status. Only two of the mothers had a salaried income, a primary school teacher and a nurse.

Eight of the women interviewed began their own work prior to Independence.[109] Six were primary school teachers, one was a nurse, and the last assisted her husband by selling goods in his small shop in a rural area near Arua. Two of the teachers were living in Kampala at the time, the nurse and another teacher lived in district headquarters or peri-urban settings, and the remainder were in villages. These women were young when they began working: four were aged 17–19, and the rest 20–23. Only one teacher and the woman working in the shop were married at the time, each with a single child. A primary school teacher in Lira was soon dismissed from her position when she became pregnant outside of marriage.[110]

All chose their occupations for generally positive reasons: because these fields were respected and seen as appropriate for women, or because they liked the nature of the work. A woman who started teaching Home Economics in Hoima commented, 'At that time teachers were greatly admired and respected', while a nurse who began at Nsambya Hospital in Kampala said, 'I liked to care for people.'[111] Grace Ssembatia (Profile 5.1) said she became a teacher 'because there was a belief that the only jobs for decent women were teaching and nursing. I had wanted to be a pharmacist but was told I would be looked on as a bad girl.' Paying for their training was less difficult than for later women, because the colonial government covered the costs.

When asked if the work they did was common for women at the time, four of the teachers and the nurse said that at least a few other women were engaged in these occupations; the other two teachers and the woman who helped in the shop said they were unusual. Their work was in nearly all cases viewed with approval by their relatives, or at least greeted with a mixed response. Within the community too, their occupations were seen positively. Even the woman who worked in the shop said that 'the villagers appreciated my exemplary move' (as did her husband, because 'I knew good business language as a lady to convince the customers').'[112]

Public Discussion of Women's Issues

During the late colonial period, both the basic Domestic Virtue model and its Service Career variation remained powerful. The core version was supported by many African men and women in many parts of the country, including the chiefs acting as Native Authorities, by British colonial officials, and by some church people. Increased education, the growth of teaching and nursing, and the rise of some new professional positions led to expansion of the variant form. But the most interesting feature of the period between 1940 and 1962 is the wide disparity of beliefs concerning the three issues of concern to women that were visible during the earlier colonial period: marriage, inheritance and landholding, and public participation. Here we find marked divergences between the ideas of conservatives (including most British government administrators, many Baganda, and some other African men and women) and a more progressive position (advocated by some educated Baganda women and many more women in Ankole, joined by a few whites concerned with Africa's economic development and some Christian leaders). The divisions visible among the British stemmed in part from a broader shift in colonial policy after World War II designed to promote a more stable group of middle- and working-class Africans in urban settings.[113] As part of this effort, British administrators, joined by some Africans, felt it necessary to distinguish between 'respectable' women and 'disreputable' ones. In Uganda, government authorities could draw upon the existing contrast built into the Domestic Virtue model between good and bad women, cracking down on those they perceived as economically or sexually uncontrolled. At the same time, however, more thoughtful British people and Africans began to explore ways of legitimating further working roles for women and of lessening the obstacles that stood in their way.

From the later colonial period we begin to have abundant information from newspapers, some published in English and others (most of them newly founded) in local languages.[114] In working with papers we must remember that the press's portrayal of women was influenced by multiple factors: women's actual roles and behavior, attitudes toward women held by the people who were writing letters to the paper or reading it, the political stance of the region's or country's leadership, and what the editors of the paper thought would sell. While representations of women in the press are thus not a direct reflection of reality, they are an invaluable source for the concerns of literate people. What is particularly striking about the newspapers of this period is their divergent outlooks, with marked variations between papers published in different regions of the country and different languages, and between traditionalists and progressives.

The basic elements of the Domestic Virtue model continued to shape the attitudes seen in some of the Luganda-language and both of the English-language newspapers of this period. For example, in *Munno*, the long-standing but fairly moderate Baganda Catholic paper, one finds as late as 1950 few articles for or about women. By 1960, however, women were central topics and sometimes contributors. In many respects the paper's focus was conservatively domestic. Women should work very hard, not to advance themselves but so that their children could lead healthy lives.[115] Rural women should plan their time well in order to carry on their agricultural and household work and look after their husbands and children well even if they had other employment such as working on cotton or coffee plantations. But there were signs of a more positive valuation of women's role within the agricultural economy. One letter commented that married women who helped their husbands raise cash crops, the proceeds of which were used to pay taxes or school fees for their children, should be regarded as contributors to national development.[116]

A domestic emphasis was seen likewise in the two English-language newspapers, *Uganda Argus* and *Uganda Herald*. These were aimed at a readership of British and European residents, South Asians, and educated, Westernized Ugandans. Neither paid much attention to women in the earlier 1950s, but in 1955, a third correspondent was added to the 'Mainly for Women' column in Saturday editions of the *Herald*.[117] Joining the existing correspondents for British and South Asian women, 'Nadia' was described as a Ugandan. In her first column, she chose to discuss the training center that had just opened in Entebbe. At the center, Nadia noted approvingly, women 'are given useful lessons in many things, which are combined with their housework'. They learned how to look after and feed their children properly 'in order that they may become future healthy citizens of Uganda . . . . Any man who will set a high standard of leadership in our country must be a man who has been brought up by a good, well trained mother . . . . This country must progress, but it will never do so if women are left behind.'

In her next column, Nadia discussed several issues associated with food.[118] Noting that food had become very expensive, with prices going up all the time, she talked first about the need for women to work hard to produce more crops. In that context she proposed that the Ugandan government should offer farming courses for African girls and women. Practical instruction in such areas as vegetable growing and poultry-keeping 'would be much more useful to African women than trying to improve their culture by teaching them alien "arty-crafts"'. She suggested that some Ugandan women be given the opportunity to travel to England or other countries, 'not for university courses, but to learn how people there improve their land and how hard they work in cultivating it'. She ended by warning young wives in semi-jest that it was not enough to look attractive: 'you must feed your husband properly and never forget to include with the *matoke* [steamed bananas] a good, green vegetable sauce' of the kind his grandmother used to make.

Even women who were pursuing university education might think in gendered terms associated with the Domestic Virtue model. A young woman studying at Makerere in 1955 was quoted by the Governor's wife as saying, 'We shall get nowhere until our fathers receive a higher Bride Price for us if we have a School Certificate and an even higher one if we have been to Makerere.'[119] Occasions to honor women had a highly domestic tone. An article in *Uganda Herald* describes the tea party held in Hoima in 1955 to welcome back Miss Sarah Nyedwoha, returning to Uganda after four years in England.[120] Only gradually does it emerge that she was the first Ugandan woman to receive an undergraduate degree from Oxford University. After summarizing the speeches of congratulation given by the king of Bunyoro, a colonial official, and Mrs. Ridsdale, the head of Sarah's former school, the article continued: 'Miss Sarah Nyedwoha then spoke herself, and thanked those present for the honour they had done her, and hoped that she was but the first to tread this road that they might help their country.' Noting that Miss Nyedwoha would shortly be taking up a teaching position at Gayaza High School, the article warmed to its conclusion, 'She then cut a beautiful iced cake, which was much enjoyed by those present.'

Domestic Virtue expectations took a more negative form in concern about female mobility and sexuality, especially about women who had moved into Kampala and were supporting themselves by selling liquor or sex. *Uganda Empya*, published in Luganda by strong loyalists to the Buganda kingdom who held traditional views about women as well, printed a number of disapproving reports concerning women who made and sold *waragi* or worked in bars.[121] It printed letters complaining about prostitution and described a major crackdown on prostitutes in Kampala, claiming that the women also sold alcohol and were all from Toro.[122] A letter from a former mayor of Kampala explained his reasons for chasing idle women away from the city and congratulated his successor for continuing the fight against prostitution. At a press conference the current mayor justified his actions on the grounds that prostitutes were thieves (because they came to Kampala but had no jobs) and noted that the *Lukiiko* had also legislated against prostitution.

The Service Career variation of the basic model was clearly gaining ground in the later colonial period. More people subscribed to it, and the range of service occupations that were considered respectable was expanding. *Munno* reported favorably in 1960 upon the kinds of work done by educated women. It published a letter saying that, although women should be respected as 'the mothers of the nation', they were also contributing to the country as teachers.[123] (The vaguely defined but emotionally powerful term 'mother of the nation' could potentially be used to justify either women's active participation in nationalist movements or their place within the home, producing and caring for the men who would lead the nation.) *Munno* covered a speech day presided over by the queen of Buganda at a domestic science school, the only one in Uganda owned and operated by a woman.[124] Other reports described a woman who had graduated from nursing school in Uganda, one who had finished a course in Holland and was now working at Rubaga Hospital 'to serve her nation', and a married woman who was going to England to study law, with a scholarship from the Buganda government. Nuns too played an important part, in spiritual and moral terms. Several articles told of nuns who had completed their theological training or were going abroad to study, and the bishop of Masaka was quoted as expressing his gratitude for the increasing number of Ugandan women who were choosing to serve the Catholic Church.[125]

Even those people who supported expanded opportunities for working women agreed that their conduct at work should remain chaste, modest, and deferential to men, regardless of their background or the type of job. When the African Art Studio advertised a job in the generally conservative *Uganda Empya* for a female employee, it said she should be well behaved in her personal life as well as hardworking, able to speak some English, and beautiful.[126] An article in *Munno* advised all employed women to appreciate their jobs, maintain proper behavior and self-respect, respect their bosses, stay out of conflict, and avoid 'shameful acts' that could jeopardize their success. This message was directed both at educated women (like nurses, nuns, secretaries, and lawyers) and at those selling food or working as bar attendants, types of work not normally included within the 'respectable' category at the time.

The only direct challenges to the Domestic Virtue definition came in the Runyankore newspaper *Ageteraine*, published in Mbarara, the center of the Ankole area of the Western Province. Articles written by and about women and letters to the paper in 1960 suggest that women in the western region were thinking more actively about gender issues, were more resistant to the dominant model, and were more outspoken than was generally the case in Buganda. One young female author encouraged leaders not to neglect the schooling of girls.[127] She chastised a parish chief who refused to allow a man to sell cows to get money to send his daughters to school. (The chief instead advised the father to pull the girls out of school and not waste his money, since they would become impregnated before they could get married.) Several articles emphasized women's importance in development. Urging men to respect women, one male author asked how Ankole could progress and Uganda develop if women were not treated as human beings.[128] If Ugandan men have decided to adopt a Western lifestyle, they should treat women well, as Europeans do. *Ageteraine* also presented an appeal for broader female employment. An unmarried woman began her letter, 'I hear you want to get Independence tomorrow. I am happy to hear that, but if I may ask, are all the jobs for you men? Where are the jobs for us women?'[129] Men have a wide range of jobs, she said, but women can enter only two fields, teaching and nursing, and these positions are open to only a few.

Because women were starting to work for wages, it raised the question of whether they should be taxed. This issue came under discussion in the later 1950s, with some men claiming that if women earned their own money like men, they too should pay tax.[130] In response, Baganda women in particular argued that women's salaries and conditions of work should be improved before they were taxed. One female letter-writer to *Munno* said in 1957, 'If women are seen seated on the verandas of the Indian men's shops sewing a garment for 15 cents, or are seen at Mulago peeling bananas for the patients or even seen in Jinja as nannies for the white people; is this what one would call good employment for women and want to tax it?' A few women went further, arguing that if women were to pay taxes, they should have access to all offices, and be able to become even the *Kabaka*.

Other regions too considered taxation. *Ageteraine* reported in 1960 that the Kigezi District Council had discussed a proposal to tax women who earned their own salary.[131] One married woman supported the measure, saying that if women had similar incomes, why should they not be taxed? Women themselves had to contribute materially in order for the dream of girls' education to be realized. A devastating argument was put forward on the other side by a radical young woman who said that if women were to be taxed in their own right, they could no longer be regarded as property. This would mean that brideprice would have to be abolished. This comment was said to have 'mesmerized' the meeting and was followed by applause. The taxation proposal was then defeated by 49 votes to 2. In Toro the following year, the Legislative Council introduced a tax for 'enlightened' women, to be imposed on educated women working in the modern sector but not on women earning an income from the sale of crops or in other ways.[132]

Female domestic help came under discussion in the 1950s. Although it was still assumed that employers of domestic servants would be British, European, or Indian, people were questioning the wisdom of using males (either Indian or African) as domestic employees. Discussion of proposals that African women might be hired in their place revealed disagreement among the British. Conflicting values were at odds in this debate: ideas about the gender division of labor as related to Africa's ability to grow in economic terms; the desirability of promoting the training and employment of African women; and fear of sexual relationships between white employers and African female servants.

As *Uganda Argus* reported in 1955, several white male speakers at a conference about urban development in East Africa stressed that African women needed to learn to work for wages, ideally within a domestic context. Echoing the Ugandan government's support for Katherine Cook's school from two decades before, they said, 'It is ridiculous for strong, strapping men to be making beds and sweeping floors. This is women's work. If women could be taught to work there would not be so many problems of financing African housing.'[133] Domestic work for Ugandan women was advocated for very different reasons by Mary Stuart, wife of the bishop and promoter of women's education at Makerere University.[134] Writing in 1950 as president of the Uganda Council of Women, Mrs Stuart asked the colonial government's town planner in Kampala to provide suitable accommodation within government quarters for female servants, as was currently done for male servants. She argued that this would not only assist employers in finding help but would also encourage 'self-respecting [Ugandan] women . . . to take up the vocations of children's nurses and domestic servants'.

But when her proposal was forwarded to the Director of Public Works, he trounced the idea. He first pointed out that it would be disruptive and improper for British officials to have female servants living in the same compound with them. Moreover, during his 20 years of colonial service in Africa, he had not observed 'any tendency for African women willingly to take up domestic work, and I do not believe that they will be prepared to do so here'. In a clinching argument, he noted that even if 'domestic servants of the type visualised, that is to say, the daughters of respectable African families, were to become available, they would require higher salaries than those now paid to the "common" or "garden" ayah'. The question of domestic help would become important to African women as employers in subsequent decades: as more Ugandan women began to work outside the home, they were reliant upon female assistance to keep their households running smoothly, one of the requirements of the Domestic Virtue model.

Debate continued over the issues of marriage/domestic relations, inheritance/landholding, and women's political participation. Buganda was rocked by a highly publicized and controversial marriage case during the early 1940s. 'The Namasole (Queen Mother) affair' revealed considerable opposition among conservative Baganda to disruption of traditional marriage patterns and the growing freedom of women. In 1940, Irene Namaganda, the widow of the former *Kabaka* and mother of the young new king, decided to remarry.[135] This was in itself against tradition, and to compound the problem, she planned to marry a commoner. When Namaganda, the daughter of one of the first African priests in the Anglican church and herself a graduate of Gayaza High School, announced her intention to the *Lukiiko*, they refused to approve her plan. After she became pregnant, and with backing from the Church of Uganda and Buganda's prime minister, Namaganda proceeded with her marriage. At this point the issue became a useful weapon for neo-traditional Baganda loyalists who were fighting against reform. The *Lukiiko's* chiefs brought a legal action against Namaganda and her husband in a Native Court in 1941, which found them guilty of breaking the customs of Buganda. Her husband was banished from the capital for four years, and she was stripped of her title and the benefits associated with it. When Namaganda's husband appealed against the judgement to the protectorate's high court, it refused to alter the judgment of the lower court. Its justification for doing so made clear that the British were still not prepared to interfere with what it defined as customary law with respect to women. 'Where a Native Court has held that a certain act is contrary to custom, an appellant court should be reluctant to hold otherwise except upon substantial grounds and should, unless it be repugnant to natural justice, give effect to the custom in its judgment.'[136]

The only newspaper to tackle marriage relations was *Ageteraine*. In 1960 a number of women in Ankole were questioning the expectation that women should be subordinate to their husbands. One married woman wrote that some men are still 'so primitive and foolish' that they undervalue women.[137] After summarizing the main grounds on which women are criticized by husbands (including that they cannot keep secrets), she answered each point carefully and pointed out the distinctive contributions of women. If she were God, she would not allow men who underrate women to marry at all! She closed this powerful letter by wondering how Africans could be pushing for political independence from the British when a wife and husband could not sit down together as equals to discuss issues in the family. Men wanted to keep their wives subordinate, which was why they refused to allow them to join women's clubs where they could learn things like reading, writing, and tailoring. 'This is the time for men to stop trampling on women's self-respect.'

Bridewealth was challenged in several of *Ageteraine's* articles and letters. One unmarried woman lamented the high brideprice demanded by parents: rather than considering whether two people love each other, parents think only about how much a man can pay for their daughter.[138] In forceful terms, she concluded that insisting that your daughter marry a rich man is tantamount to selling her. Even a conservative male letter-writer argued that parents were requiring unreasonably high bridewealth, forcing some girls into prostitution in the towns.[139] When, he said, a man sees that his wife is not doing what he wants and thinks about all those cows he had to pay for her, maltreatment naturally results. The evil practice of demanding bridewealth should be abandoned. At least some daughters were prepared to resist pressure to marry. One story described a father who was forced to sell his shop to pay back the bridewealth he had received for his daughter after she twice refused to marry the man with whom the father had made an agreement.[140]

Issues associated with female inheritance and landholding were occasionally discussed in the papers in 1960. *Uganda Empya* published a letter objecting to a proposal by the Uganda Council of Women that would have given a woman the right to know what was in her husband's will and to claim family property after his death.[141] The male writer suggested that women should have been married for a minimum of 10 years before gaining inheritance rights. *Munno* was willing to print letters advocating a more progressive stance. One said that women should share property with their husbands and be given a share of the man's property in the case of death.[142] It was unfair for a widow who had worked hand-in-hand with her husband in raising the family's economic level to be chased away from the home by his male relatives after his death.

The papers reacted in differing ways to women's increased participation in public institutions, through women's organizations and politics. All felt that women's clubs were fine so long as they focused on domestic, cultural, or religious activities. *Uganda Empya* reported approvingly on a concert performed by twenty women's clubs in Kampala (though the focus of the article was the queen of Buganda, who opened the performance).[143] *Munno* was supportive of Catholic women's clubs. Reporting on a tea party organized by one of these groups for religious and colonial educational officials, it talked about the important role played by such organizations in promoting community development.[144] *Ageteraine* showed that women's clubs in the western region were trying to improve their effectiveness and leadership strengths. A residential training workshop was held in 1960 to improve the leadership skills of club heads.[145] Presidents of the clubs in one area, sometimes joined by parish or county chiefs, were visiting each others' organizations to share experiences, offer positive critiques, and copy best practices.

What part women should play in politics was a vexed question. A male member of the Uganda National Congress wrote an article for *Munno* in 1960 arguing that women should never stand for elections.[146] Yet the paper also printed a response by a woman who said that women were not just voters and members of political parties, they should also seek elected office. She stressed, however, that it was only women with education and money who should put themselves forward in their constituencies. (The elitist assumptions that surrounded women's entry into teaching and nursing in the earlier colonial period were thus carried forward into another expansion of women's roles.) In the western region, some women were already heavily involved in politics. A photograph published by *Ageteraine* showed a Kabale couple where the wife was not only a teacher and member of the Kigezi Local Education Authority but also president of the Uganda Council of Women in Kigezi District and an executive committee member of the Democratic Party in Kigezi.[147] Well in advance of most Ugandans, a married woman wrote to *Ageteraine* in 1960 advocating 'affirmative action' for women in politics, assigning some seats to women and ensuring their say in meetings. Women were being pushed to vote, so why should they not participate more fully in the political life of their areas? In a veiled threat used by later women as well, she reminded men that there are a great many women, and if they all decided to vote for someone, that person would win the election.

By the time of Ugandan independence in 1962, the foundations for more extensive female involvement in the country's economy and public life had been laid. Even some women primarily engaged in subsistence farming were selling foodstuffs on occasion, women were beginning to market food and drink in urban settings, and well respected teachers, nurses, and community development workers were leading the way into a wider range of careers, building upon an expansion in female education. Although questions remained about such issues as marriage, inheritance, and women's public participation, the basic Domestic Virtue model remained strong for most women, and its Career Women variation was growing. The question now was how much and in what ways Uganda's Independence would affect women and their work.

Notes

1 For the ethnic and religious affiliations of these women, the nature of their current work, and their current marital status, see Appendices C8-9. The occupations of the mothers are described in a later section of this chapter.

2 The oldest woman, whose career as a teacher is mentioned in the previous chapter, is included in this period.

3 East Africa Royal Commission, *Report, 1953–1955*, as discussed by Elkan, 'Review.'

4 See Ellyne, 'Economic History,' for this paragraph unless otherwise noted.

5 Elkan, *An African Labour Force*, ch. V, his 'The Employment of Women,' and his *Migrants and Proletarians*, e.g., pp. 32 and 126. For below, see Lindsay, *Working with Gender*, esp. ch. 5.

6 Elkan, *Migrants and Proletarians*, pp. 32 and 95.

7 Good, *Rural Markets*, pp. 213–25. For below, see Elkan, 'Trade in Ankole.'

8 Taylor, *Tropical Toro*, pp. 174–81.

9 Arua11.

10 Lira4. For below, see Kampala17.

11 Middleton, 'Trade and Markets'.

12 Southall, 'Alur Migrants'.

13 Lovett, 'Gender Relations'.

14 Perlman, 'The Changing Status and Role of Women'.

15 Southall and Gutkind, *Townsmen in the Making*, Table XII and p. 108, and Gutkind, 'Town Life in Buganda'. For below, see Sofer and Sofer, 'Recent Population Growth in Jinja'.

16 Perlman, 'The Changing Status and Role of Women'.

17 Southall, 'Kinship, Friendship,' and his and Gutkind's *Townsmen in the Making*, pp. 28 and 69.

18 Gutkind, 'Town Life in Buganda,' and Southall and Gutkind, *Townsmen in the Making*, ch. IX.

19 UP, *Uganda Census, 1959: African Population*, p. 91, and *Non-African Population*, pp. 73–9. See also *Report of the Constitutional Committee*, p. 52, as cited by D. Apter, *The Political Kingdom*, p. 38.

20 Mamdani, *Citizen and Subject*, pp. 102–3.

21 Mamdani, *Politics and Class Formation*, pp. 178–83.

22 Tamale, *When Hens Begin to Crow*, pp. 13–14.

23 Ibid., p. 14.

24 E.g., Schmidt, '"Emancipate Your Husbands",' Geiger, *TANU Women*, Presley, *Kikuyu Women*, White, *The Comforts of Home*, ch. 8, and Sheldon, *Pounders of Grain*, ch. 4.

25 Mamdani sees this as part of a wider reform by the colonial powers of the system of indirect rule, an attempt 'to broaden the social base of rule by incorporating into the governing alliance the new social force on the colonial horizon: the native middle class' (*Citizen and Subject*, p. 103).

26 UNA New Series 4,319. Improvement did not mean equality, however: the medical officer was to live in a European-style house valued at £2000, while the assistant received an African-style house worth £800.

27 UNA New Series 7,203 and 15,287. For below, see UNA New Series 19,145.

28 E.g., UNA New Series 17,991 and New Series 15,509, and UP, *Official Bulletin*, Vol. 5, no. 9, September, 1954.

29 Kampala19.

30 Kampala17.

31 Kwesiga, *Women's Access to Higher Education*, Table 9.11, p. 206.

32 UP, *Uganda Census 1959: African Population*, p. 32.

33 Ssekamwa, *History and Development of Education*, p. 150.

34 UP, *Development of African Teacher Training*.

35 See UCU Mukono 02Bp 77/5, for this and below.

36 As quoted in *Uganda Herald*, 23 March 1955.

37 East African Governments, *Report of the Working Party on Higher Education*, p. 41.

38 For the use of pseudonyms, see Ch. 2, note 15.
39 She was interviewed on 23 May 2003 by Jean Kemitare, in English (tape: Kampala22). The interviewer described her economic level as high.
40 Her claim was indeed true, for her father was embroiled in the controversy concerning land for Makerere College in 1944–5. When the school needed more space after its initial foundation in the early 1920s, colonial officials put pressure on Baganda landholders to give up another 200 acres on Makerere Hill. Many Baganda objected, arguing that the British should use land reserved for their own use by the Buganda Agreement of 1900. Grace's father had been removed as prime minister in 1941, due to pressure from more militant Baganda who felt he was cooperating too closely with the British, but after the riots of January 1945, the colonial government returned him to office. He and the British then forced the current holders of land at Makerere to give up their property, and this became one of the issues that led to his assassination later that year. One of the residence halls at Makerere University is named after him. See Mutyaba and Namukadde, *Chwa II ne Muteesa II*, p. 24, Apter, *The Political Kingdom in Uganda*, esp. pp. 226–33, and Thompson, *Governing Uganda*, chs. 11 and 14. For the *Namasole* incident that led to his being forced out of office, see a later section of this chapter.
41 *Women's Access to Higher Education*, p. 207. *Uganda Herald* (8 August 1945) reported that one girl had taken the entrance exams on the same basis as male students; the other new entrants were older women who had shown their quality by doing valuable work in some particular field since leaving school.
42 Kabale15.
43 Kampala20.
44 Kabale14
45 Lira2.
46 Arua5.
47 Arua3, Kabale3, and Arua5.
48 Lira17.
49 Arua11.
50 E.g., Lira2 and Kabale1.
51 Kampala17.
52 Tripp with Ntiro, 'Women's Activism,' Tripp, *Women and Politics*, pp. 34–6, and Kisubika, 'Contributions of Pre-Independence Women's Organizations'.
53 *Monitor*, 8 March 2002.
54 Perlman, 'The Changing Status and Role of Women'.
55 *Uganda Argus*, 21 August 1955.
56 Musisi, 'Transformations of Baganda Women,' p. 168.
57 Ibid., p. 297, citing a personal communication from Rebecca Mulira.
58 Ibid., pp. 299–300.
59 Ibid., p. 290 and ch. XI.
60 Tamale, *When Hens Begin to Crow*, pp. 10–11.
61 Musisi, 'Transformations of Baganda Women,' p. 305.
62 Brown, *Marriage, Divorce*, Tamale, *When Hens Begin to Crow*, pp. 9–10, Tripp with Ntiro, 'Women's Activism,' and Tripp, *Women and Politics*, pp. 36–40, for this paragraph.
63 Tamale, *When Hens Begin to Crow*, pp. 10–11.
64 UNA New Series 18,283. A UN Convention on the Political Rights of Women in 1952 had stipulated that women should be allowed to vote on the same basis as men.
65 CultHist1 (see Appendix B), for this and below.
66 Sofer and Sofer, *Jinja Transformed*, p. 40, and Mukwaya, 'The Marketing of Staple Foods'.
67 Willis, *Potent Brews*, p. 107. For below, see Bunker, *Peasants against the State*, esp. pp. 66–7.
68 Purseglove, *Tobacco in Uganda*.
69 Taylor, *Tropical Toro*, pp. 171–81.
70 Middleton, *The Lugbara*, pp. 13–15.
71 Mukwaya, 'The Marketing of Staple Foods'. For below, see his 'Katwe Markets'.
72 Gutkind, 'Town Life in Buganda,' and Southall and Gutkind, *Townsmen in the Making*, pp. 137–43, for this and below.
73 Southall and Gutkind, *Townsmen in the Making*, p. 176.

74 Sofer and Sofer, *Jinja Transformed*, p. 40.
75 Southall and Gutkind, *Townsmen in the Making*, pp. 55 and 105, for this and below.
76 Willis, *Potent Brews*, p. 117 and ch. 11.
77 Few, 'On Avoiding Detection'.
78 Willis, 'The Only Money'.
79 See Southall and Gutkind, *Townsmen in the Making*, pp. 60–62, for this paragraph.
80 Southall and Gutkind, *Townsmen in the Making*, Table XII and the note to Table XIII.
81 Robertson, 'Traders and Urban Struggle,' her 'Transitions in Kenyan Patriarchy,' and her *Trouble Showed the Way*, ch. 4.
82 Elkan, *An African Labour Force*, ch. V, his 'The Employment of Women in Uganda,' and his *Migrants and Proletarians*, e.g., pp. 32 and 126.
83 In 1951, for example, a total of 183 women (31 percent) joined the 403 men who graduated from Uganda's teacher training colleges. Eighty percent of the women, however, were trained as Grade I teachers, the lowest level, and none as Grade III teachers (UP, *Education in Uganda, 1958/59*, p. 41, for this and below). By 1958, Grade I training was being phased out. Of the 880 people who completed their training as Grade II teachers, 260 were women (30 percent), but women constituted only 12 percent of the 77 Grade III teachers. See also Profile 5.1.
84 Vol. II (1940). For below, see ibid., Vol. III (1941).
85 UCU Mukono 02 ESG 234/17.
86 UNMC, 'Register of Enrolled Nurses,' Book I. I am grateful to the Council for allowing me to use these invaluable records. Enrolled nurses were trained exclusively at Mengo Hospital in Kampala until 1955, when Mulago School of Nursing opened.
87 Holden, 'Colonial Sisters'. For below, see *Uganda Argus*, 29 July 1955.
88 *Uganda Herald*, 16 May 1945.
89 UNA New Series 19,141. For below, see *Mengo Hospital Centenary Magazine*, p. 16.
90 A sample of registered nurses in the earliest registry book of the UNMC, for the period 1929–1958, includes 54 European or North American women and 1 Indian woman, but no Ugandans (UNMC, *Register Book of Registered Nurses*, Book I). The sample consisted of surnames beginning with the letters C, D, and M.
91 The other nurses included 99 Europeans/North Americans and 12 described as Indian, Goan, or Pakistani but perhaps in some cases Ugandan-born.
92 *Uganda Argus*, 3 September 1955, and see *Obugagga Bwa Uganda*, 6 January 1955, for work with a drug company.
93 See references in note 82.
94 Sofer and Sofer, *Jinja Transformed*, p. 38.
95 *Uganda Herald*, 5 January 1955.
96 See note 82.
97 Sofer and Sofer, *Jinja Transformed*, p. 40. For below, see ibid., p. 85; Elkan, 'The Employment of Women'.
98 Asowa-Okwe, *The Dynamics of Women Participation*, p. 16.
99 E.g., Sofer and Sofer, *Jinja Transformed*, pp. 38–40.
100 Perlman, 'The Changing Status and Role of Women,' and Taylor, *Tropical Toro*, pp. 171–2. For below, see *Uganda Argus*, 22 Dec.
101 6 June 1945.
102 *Uganda Herald*, 13 June 1945. For the 'pattern of coercion and oppressive control' that marked relationships between white and black women in the Cape eastern frontier in South Africa, see Cock, 'Domestic Service'; more generally, see Hansen, *African Encounters with Domesticity*.
103 Southall and Gutkind, *Townsmen in the Making*, pp. 70–71 and 79–88, for this and below.
104 Musisi, 'Gender and the Cultural Construction,' drawing upon descriptions in Southall and Gutkind, *Townsmen in the Making*, passim.
105 White, *The Comforts of Home*, esp. chs. 3–6 and 8.
106 E.g., Lugbara women in the West Nile region made pots from local clay and wove mats from papyrus they had collected; women living in the villages around Jinja sold handwork (Middleton, *The Lugbara*, pp. 12–13; Sofer and Sofer, *Jinja Transformed*, p. 40).
107 Hanson, 'Sleeping Sickness,' pp. 9–10.
108 E.g., Southall and Gutkind, *Townsmen in the Making*, pp. 144–5, and Gutkind, 'Town Life in Buganda'. For salesgirls, see Sofer and Sofer, *Jinja Transformed*, p. 40, Gutkind, 'Town

Life in Buganda,' and *Uganda Argus*, 29 November 1955. For below, see Barrett-Gaines, 'Katwe Salt,' ch. 7.
109 Throughout this study, a woman's first job is defined as that begun after completion of her education, as distinct from part-time work done to help pay her school fees.
110 Lira2.
111 Kabale15 and Kampala20.
112 Lira4.
113 Parpart, '"Wicked Women"'.
114 See Appendix A for the papers and years examined.
115 5 January. For below, see 14 January.
116 26 January 1960.
117 22 January 1955.
118 12 February 1955.
119 *Uganda Herald*, 23 March 1955.
120 Ibid., 23 February 1955. Sarah Nyedwoha Ntiro went on to a long and distinguished career in education and government.
121 E.g., 16 May, 6 June, and 23 March 1960.
122 27 April and 15 August 1960. Rather surprisingly, it also ran a letter from a housewife complaining that it is men who sustain prostitution but then turn the blame on women (27 July). For below, see 28 April and 5 March 1960.
123 24 March 1960.
124 6 December. For below, see 16 January, 13 February, and 11 February.
125 9 January, and see 13 October, and photo, 10 September 1960.
126 4 March 1960. For below, see 9 April 1960.
127 1 April 1960.
128 9 January 1960.
129 29 April. For an appeal to husbands to let their wives join clubs, see 9 January.
130 Musisi, 'Transformations of Baganda Women,' pp. 310–18, for this and below.
131 14 October 1960.
132 Musisi, 'Transformations of Baganda Women,' p. 313.
133 *Uganda Argus*, 20 December 1955.
134 See UNA New Series 5,021, for this paragraph and the next.
135 See Musisi, 'A Personal Journey,' her 'Transformations of Baganda Women,' pp. 241–2 and 291–6, and D. Apter, *The Political Kingdom*, chs. 10–13.
136 'Decisions of H. M. High Court of Uganda on cases originating from the Buganda courts, 1940–58, compiled by Haydon, 1958,' 7–9, as cited by Musisi, 'Transformations of Baganda Women,' p. 241, with no further information.
137 15 April 1960.
138 16 September 1960.
139 25 November 1960.
140 30 September 1960.
141 14 April 1960.
142 26 March 1960.
143 6 June 1960.
144 19 October.
145 2 September. For below, see 29 April.
146 7 January for this and below.
147 Mr and Mrs Mbire, 25 November 1960. For below, see 15 April.

Six

The Early Independence Years
1962–71

On 9 October 1962 Uganda gained its political independence from Britain, with Apolo Milton Obote as Prime Minister.[1] The following decade was marked by considerable continuity with the late colonial period. In Uganda one does not see the energetic efforts to remove all vestiges of imperial power found in many other newly independent nations. Even in 2003, such symbolically important locations as national parks, large lakes, district towns, and streets in the capital city bore the names of the British royal family or important colonial officials in Uganda. Uganda also forms Mamdani's principal example for his claim that political independence in Africa brought the end of racism in government but did not introduce democracy or bring an end to the forms of colonially created 'native' control that emphasized tribal or ethnic identities.[2] Gradual change did occur, however, in areas that affected women's work. Among these were economic development, more urban migration, improved educational opportunities for girls and young women, and greater participation in women's organizations. Women took up a slightly wider range of work in Kampala and other towns, though most of them still produced and/or sold food or drink, and they entered additional educated careers.

At the level of public discourse, the government and media advocated a different position with respect to women's involvement in the wider economy and community from that found during the colonial era. The new rhetoric, which encouraged women to participate in many aspects of the country's public life, including a wide range of income-generating activities, interacted in complex ways with the actual nature of women's work and with the older Domestic Virtue model and its Service Career variation. The government's position, as reflected in the press, did not extend its positive valuation of women's contributions to those engaged in subsistence farming or to political involvement. Nor did it acknowledge the tension between women's emergence into the public world, which it hailed, and the ongoing expectations of the Domestic Virtue model within the family, which it continued to accept. Women were therefore caught between two different set of norms: they were praised for their contributions to the economy, community, and nation while they were away from home, but when they came back into the domestic context they were still expected to fill the traditional roles.

In addition to written materials, our sources for this period include information from 72 women in our district sample. Of them, 37 were aged 17 or more during the early Independence years, while 35 were children aged 8–16.[3] The younger ones were living in the same types of communities as had the older women: four-fifths grew up in villages, one in Kampala, and the rest were divided between district headquarters and peri-urban settings. But their fathers' occupations reflect some of the changes that began when the British left. Just under a quarter were involved in business, concentrated in trades other than food or drink. Somewhat more than a quarter were primary school teachers, and nearly a fifth held other skilled or high-status positions, including being a local chief. Only a fifth were peasant farmers, continuing the under-representation of this kind of work that we noted in the interviews from the colonial period; 14 percent of the fathers were engaged in unskilled or semi-skilled labor.

Economics, Migration, Education and Public Activity

The early years of Ugandan Independence were marked by a sense of expansiveness, of new opportunities. As Eunice Kyamanya (Profile 6.1) noted, 'After Independence, people were finding avenues, leaving their home areas, moving around Buganda, Ankole, Bunyoro. The opportunities were there now. The whites were leaving, and people were coming to get jobs, even in Kampala. We now had our own people taking up positions.' Grace Ssembatia (Profile 5.1) likewise remembered those years warmly. (Married and with a young family, she had returned from England and was teaching at Budo.) 'This was the most favorable period I have known, due to the peace, stability, and development taking place then.' A historian of Baganda culture recalled that, during the early Independence years, women were coming up gradually in education, business, and government, encouraged by *Kabaka* Muteesa.[4] He believed that, if the kingdoms had not been abolished, change for Baganda women would have continued at a rate that allowed both men and women to adjust to greater female independence. Instead, women were pushed abruptly into new roles after 1971, leading to the gender tension visible in 2003.

In political terms, the first decade of Independence brought relatively few changes for women. A high degree of continuity between the years before and after 1962 is reflected in the fact that some of the women interviewed, especially those living in rural settings, could not remember anything that distinguished the late colonial and early Independence periods. Although some of the new male leaders and many intellectuals were influenced by socialist ideals, the government attempted to steer a middle road between the two superpowers.[5] Hostility between the political parties became acute. (The Uganda People's Congress was identified with the Church of Uganda, the Democratic Party was Catholic, and *Kabaka Yekka* was specifically Baganda.) The initial structure of government was changed in 1966-7 when Obote abolished the kingdoms, forced the *Kabaka* of Buganda into exile, unilaterally set aside the Constitution, forced the passage of a new one, and assumed the Presidency. Until 1971 and General Idi Amin's military coup, Uganda was ruled as a one-party state by Obote and his Uganda People's

Congress. Several women in our sample felt that Uganda's subsequent political problems arose from Obote's seizure of power in 1966–7 and conflict between the parties. A teacher living in a peri-urban area south of Kampala said that the removal of the *Kabaka* triggered instability: although she was 55 at the time, 'I went to the sub-county center to fight for the *Kabaka* with stones!'[6] Several emphasized that the emergence of political parties led to ill-will and sectarian violence. A woman who grew up in a politically active family in Hoima commented, 'The big change was political parties. People who had been friends before now did not greet each other any more. There was this division between DP and UPC – very, very strange. My dad was Catholic, and people who were UPC no longer even said hello to him.'[7]

The new government was committed to the process of replacing non-Africans in the civil service (mainly British and Indians) with Ugandans, but this took time to accomplish. A report from 1964 that lists names by rank shows that although many men in the middle ranks of government were then Ugandan, some of the top people still had British names and some of the lower ones were still Indian.[8] African women remained almost entirely absent.

The economy continued to develop well, following along the lines established prior to 1962. It remained dependent on subsistence farming plus the cash crops of coffee, cotton, tea, tobacco, and sugar (in decreasing order of importance).[9] The development strategy of the new government included both private and public participation, the former seen as necessary for rapid economic transformation. Many of the emerging industries were owned by South Asian or multinational corporations and relied on imported inputs and machinery. During the 1960s, the economy had a high annual rate of growth (averaging 4.5 percent), a modest level of inflation and low fiscal deficit, and comfortable foreign reserves. Male wage earners, including most urban workers, formed a labor aristocracy, faring better than farmers.

Limited industrial growth and continued dependence upon agriculture led the government to introduce a strategy of partial nationalization: in 1970 it bought 49 percent of most large industrial enterprises, companies and banks. Over the following years this policy distorted domestic prices, reduced the real incomes of farmers, and biased Ugandan consumption towards imports. International trade and finance continued to be dominated by Europeans, while the major outlet for Ugandan exports was the East African Community, founded in 1964. Domestic trade and imports were controlled by South Asians, people of Indian, Goan, or Pakistani background though some were citizens of Uganda. In 1968, however, it was reported that Uganda – like Kenya and Tanzania – was starting to force South Asians out of their jobs and out of the country by means of 'governmental regulations designed to break the Indians' grip on commerce and crafts and to move Africans into the resulting vacancies'.[10]

The new government tried but did not entirely succeed in regulating what was now expanding trade. It maintained the older Marketing Boards to handle cash crops and continued the distinction between trading centers, which offered manufactured goods like soap, matches, clothes, kerosene, lamps, and clocks and were run mainly by South Asians, and smaller local markets that handled mainly foodstuffs.[11] Eunice Kyamanya (Profile 6.1) was asked where people living in villages in Toro, where she grew up, bought salt or soap during the period just after

Independence. 'You would go to an Indian in the trading center. The villages did not have businesses yet. You had to take a day off to travel to town, buy whatever you needed, and take it back to stock the house. The selling of commodities deep in the villages came later.'

The women in our sample remembered these years in positive terms economically. Goods were plentiful, work was available, and money had considerable value. A woman whose childhood was spent in a village outside Arua recalled, 'My father, who was a primary school teacher, could afford a very decent life for us. Everything was available, nothing was lacking.'[12] 'Independence came with some privileges,' said a woman whose father was in the army. 'For example, charcoal had not been allowed to the Africans in the barracks, but as soon as the whites left, we started using charcoal. This reduced the kitchen workload on me and my mother, giving us extra time for making drink to sell.'

Independence changed demographic and migration patterns in several respects that were significant for women.[13] Kampala was now fully open to African residents. Members of the political, professional, and economic elites moved into the houses vacated by colonial administrators and other Europeans, while the rural poor flocked into the city in hope of finding work. The population of greater Kampala rose from about 147,000 in 1959 to 333,000 in 1969, despite the departure of most Europeans.[14] The post-Independence immigrants were increasingly female, and women now stayed for longer periods, contributing to a more settled population. Rather than marrying local Baganda people, however, migrants were likely to form close relationships with other newcomers.[15]

Kampala shared the experience of many other African countries after Independence, in that socio-economic differentiation was accelerated.[16] For urban immigrants, employment was becoming harder to find. A study of hiring patterns in Kampala and Jinja in 1964–7 noted that, whereas in the past men who moved into the towns had a good chance of finding employment, this was no longer the case.[17] The government, itself the largest single employer, was unable to meet the demands upon it, including from the relatives of its own members. Urban planners, hoping that the process of rural–urban migration could be reversed, introduced a policy of rural development to try to make village life more attractive, but this did little to correct 'the basic imbalance between the rapidly growing urban labour force swollen by rural–urban migrants, and the slower growth of job opportunities'.[18] Female immigrants were concentrated at the bottom of the system. A study of an unnamed poor neighborhood of Kampala in the late 1960s showed that households that contained only adult women, with no men, were far more likely to be poor than were those that included a man.[19] In these 'female-only' households, most of the women capable of some kind of work or trade were active, though some also received assistance from lovers or paying sexual partners.

The new government worked hard to improve education, building many new schools and devoting a rising proportion of public spending to education. By 1970, 720,000 children were in primary school, 39 percent of them girls.[20] Private Christian schools continued, and education was advancing among Muslims too. A woman in our sample from a Bagisu family living to the east of Kampala attended Bugembe Muslim Primary School, with the support of both her parents, and then trained as a Grade III teacher.[21] She is the only woman of all those interviewed who mentioned that her teachers encouraged her to develop her leadership skills.

Options for girls at the secondary level remained limited. In 1964, only 41 secondary schools accepted girls, and 17 of these were in Kampala or other parts of Buganda.[22] In the entire western region there were only seven such schools, and just eight in the north. Furthermore, within these schools girls were studying mainly at the lower level (Secondary 1–4) rather than in the Secondary 5–6 classes that prepared them to attend university. The 2,828 girls in the lower classes constituted 24 percent of the total enrolment of children, while the 160 girls in the upper two years formed just 17 percent.

Greater change was seen at Makerere University, where the number of women students admitted annually was rising quickly: from just three in 1961 and 1962 to 73–76 in 1967 and 1968.[23] By 1969–70, 22 percent of the 1,484 Ugandans enrolled at Makerere were women, but they were heavily concentrated in the liberal arts subjects, not in professional fields. They were not represented in Makerere's Guild Cabinet (student government), and when it was proposed in 1965 that they should be guaranteed a place, there was strong opposition from the male students.[24] Women graduates had an impact on girls in other regions of the country. Several women in our sample mentioned that they were aware when growing up that girls could now get a university education, and a woman from an influential family in Hoima said, 'We started seeing some very well educated women coming home, like Sarah [Nyendwoha] Ntiro, and talking about the university.'[25]

The educational experiences of the women in our district sample who were children during the early Independence period provide some additional information. The schooling they received reflects improving access for girls during the 1960s, though the sample is distorted because a disproportionate fraction of the group went into types of work requiring formal training. Only one of the 35 (3 percent) had no schooling at all, and only a quarter stopped with primary school. Forty-three percent had a secondary education and 11 percent later went on to obtain a university degree. Two of these women worked while in school to help pay their fees, one growing and selling food, the other picking coffee and cotton.

As was true of the older women, two-thirds of the fathers of these early Independence children supported their education and usually paid their fees. A woman who grew up in a rural community in Lira District said, 'My father had a positive attitude and sold cotton, red pepper, and millet to Gulu District to earn income for my fees.'[26] Jackie Asiimwe of UWONET described her grandfather's determination to keep his daughters in school during the 1960s. 'My mother,' she said,

> is still very appreciative of her father, because within their village, he was among the very few to send his girl children to school. His peers – her uncles and others – would come and say, 'Why are you wasting time on the girls? They are going to get married anyway.' But he just said, 'Leave me alone. This is my family, I'll do whatever I want.' So he continued to send his girls to school. Maybe he did this because he was a Christian, maybe through missionary teaching, they were telling him why it was important for girls to go to school.[27]

Despite widespread paternal backing, some women still faced problems. One noted that her father's other wives sabotaged her education; another said that, although her father wanted all his daughters to be educated and she had some years of training, she was not allowed to continue after she became pregnant.

Several women said their fathers were positive about girls' education but were unable to keep paying the fees. Some fathers were negative or at least indifferent to their daughters' education, attributed in several cases to an emphasis on marriage. A woman whose father was a subsistence farmer in Apac District said, 'He was a bit resistant. His attitude was that girls should be groomed for marriage and home management.'[28] A woman living in a rural area of Kabale, whose father earned cash by growing sorghum and making local alcohol from it, noted: 'My father was not bothered about my education until I was in Primary Five. Then one of my sisters became pregnant, and my father became disappointed. He removed all his girls from school, saying, "That is the trend they are going to follow. This would be a waste of my money".'[29] That woman, who now runs a carpentry workshop in Kabale, concluded, 'I am still bitter about it to this day.' The sole woman in this cohort to receive no formal education, whose father was a Muslim sub-county chief in a rural part of West Nile, said, 'My father never allowed me to go to school. He termed school a place for prostitutes.'[30]

Interestingly, the mothers of these girls were somewhat less positive about their education than the mothers of the late colonial girls. This suggests that enough fathers were now willing to pay school fees for girls to be educated even without active backing from their mothers. Only 59 percent of the mothers were supportive, while another 17 percent made qualified responses: they supported the idea of education but either had no income with which to pay for it or had no say in the family. A quarter of the mothers were negative or indifferent.

Women became more actively engaged in some aspects of community life during the early Independence years, due in part to a considerable expansion of women's organizations. These groups were more numerous and active, and they branched into new areas.[31] The skills women gained from church or community organizations were no longer concentrated within the domestic context but now included income-generating activities and leadership training that could be used in other contexts as well.[32] The Mothers' Union, for example, continued to provide courses in domestic matters for its members, but it also offered typing and other secretarial classes and provided a two-month training workshop in leadership and management skills. The latter included keeping accounts, running an office, doing program planning, and implementing social change. The YWCA offered courses on nutrition and agriculture, but it also introduced a course on simple car mechanics and maintenance.[33] The Uganda Association of University Women raised funds for bursaries (scholarships) for girls in senior secondary schools and awarded prizes to outstanding women students at Makerere. The government joined these efforts, sponsoring, for example, a three-month course for volunteer leaders of women's clubs.

Although such organizations were generally led by educated urban women, they made some effort to reach out to a broader constituency and to address issues of concern to all women. Paramount among these was family law. The Uganda Council of Women (UCW) published a short guide in simple English, called *Laws about Marriage in Uganda,* aimed at women who found themselves in marital difficulties.[34] It was part of an ongoing but unsuccessful campaign by the UCW to change the laws concerning bridewealth, ownership of property by married women, and inheritance. An apparently promising step was the establishment in 1963 of the Kalema Commission to study 'marriage, divorce, and the status of women', but when the issue of marriage was raised in Parliament shortly thereafter, 'it provoked roars of laughter and heated debate'.[35]

The Uganda Association of Women's Organizations (UAWO), which grew out of a conference held in 1965, was intended to serve as a conduit of ideas and experiences between various groups of women.[36] Quickly, however, the UAWO became little more than an arm of the UPC, with the President's wife, Miria Obote, named as its honorary president and the wife of the Minister of Finance as chair. Many of the lobbying efforts that had previously characterized the UCW's program were dropped by the UAWO. The government did, however, respond to one of the issues that had been advocated by the UCW since the 1950s: the terms of service for female civil servants. In new rules announced in 1968, married as well as unmarried women were allowed to apply for permanent employment and were to receive equal pay with men; they were also entitled to 120 days' maternity leave (a higher level than in 2003).

Ugandan women's organizations also began developing international ties. The UCW sent a delegation to an international conference of women in Washington, DC in 1963, and the next year Uganda was represented at the All Africa Women's Conference held in Liberia. Even in such contexts, however, women did not necessarily speak for themselves. The women's page of *Uganda Argus* in 1965 described a speech given at a recent meeting of the International Cultural Association of Black Women.[37] Rather surprisingly, it was a man who made an impassioned call for greater participation by African women, entitled 'The Lost Identity,' which quoted the now familiar statement by Dr Aggrey of Ghana: 'To educate women is to educate a nation.' In 1970, three women working with the Family Planning Association of Uganda went to Ghana for a meeting of African women, and the executive director of the Ugandan branch was named vice convener of one of the committees of the International Council of Women, based in Paris.[38]

In part because the independence of these women's organizations was compromised by their relationship with the government, they have received a bad press from later women's activists. Winnie Byanyima wrote in 1992 that the only women's groups able to survive during the years of what she regarded as the first dictatorship were those that insisted on their 'unpolitical' nature, like the Mothers' Union and the YWCA.[39] Although she was generally dismissive of such organizations, 'led by elite women (usually the wives of local notables) [who] taught Victorian and Christian values which reinforced male domination', she acknowledged that 'some women were able to develop leadership and organizations skills through participation in them'. Miria Obote has likewise been criticized for letting the UAWO be taken over by the UPC. In the newspapers, however, Miria appears as a strong backer of women's groups. Between April and November of 1970, for example, she was reported as having hosted or joined in ten events involving women's organizations.[40]

While participation in women's groups was common, participation in politics was not. Women were now allowed to vote, but only two women were members of the National Assemblies (Parliaments) chosen in 1962 and 1967, out of a total of 172 members. Moreover, both were part of the delegation appointed by the Buganda *Lukiiko*: no women at all were elected to open seats. Obote's own thinking about women's political roles was at best ambivalent. In a speech opening the national meeting of the UCW in November 1965, he emphasized that women's contribution to building the nation should occur through their roles as mothers.[41] Though he went on to say, 'Mothers must move away from the position where they are docile, receptive and uncritical. They are full-fledged citizens and their position is in no way inferior to men,' he did not encourage them to compete for elected office. After 1966–7 and Obote's abrogation of the Constitution, the UPC was increasingly at odds with the UCW and unwilling to promote women's entry into politics. When it was announced in 1970 that Parliamentary elections would be held the following year, the UPC denied a request by the UCW for help with speech writing, campaigning, and transportation, rejecting the UCW's claim that women needed an extra boost because they 'were late starters in this type of activity'.[42] In some regions, however, women were starting to move into local politics.

Nor were women generally allowed into the religious elite. Neither the Protestant nor the Roman Catholic Christian churches nor the leading Islamic denomination allowed women to preach. They had previously had more opportunities in the 'Balakole' (or born-again Christian) movement active between the late 1920s and the 1940s, where they could speak if possessed by the holy spirit. But the women who joined these groups lacked social status and were commonly regarded as disobedient wives, and the movement had died out by the 1960s.[43] In an atypical example, Hawa Namugenyi, who had been married to a sheikh at the age of 14, was ordained as a sheikat in 1966, the first Muslim woman in East and Central Africa to hold that position. She was thenceforth allowed to preach at weddings, funerals, and privately in people's homes, and she went on to found the first Muslim boarding school for girls in Uganda.

Women's Work

The scope of women's economic activities grew somewhat during these years, due mainly to two factors: the growth of Kampala and other urban areas, leading to expanded markets and greater demand for food and drink; and improved education for girls. But options nonetheless remained limited. When asked about women's work during the early years of Independence, the women in our district sample emphasized the narrow range of opportunities available. Margaret Birungi (Profile 9.1), who grew up in a village outside Hoima, said: 'When I was young, women were just housewives, looked after their kids, dug their gardens. A few women were nurses or schoolteachers, but women had no ability to work on their own in business like I do. They used to think everything is for men.'

Subsistence agriculture remained the primary economic activity for most Ugandan women, though such work is poorly documented. A study of young women living in villages in Buganda, Bugisu, and West Nile in 1970 noted that most of their time 'is spent in non-financial employment: digging the subsistence crops, assisting on the family shamba, working in the house, cooking, caring for siblings, and if they are married, for their own children'.[44] Some women assisted their husbands in growing cash crops, though they did not usually share in the profits. When asked how women earned money in the 1960s, Sarah Kitakule of UWEAL said, 'It was really only the cash crops that women were involved in, not selling things. Women remained at home, they went to farm, they waited for the harvest time, then together with their spouse they went to the Society [marketing organization for that crop] and sold. Those who had reasonable husbands shared the profits. Those who didn't have, the husbands took away the money and deployed it as they wished.'[45] A limited number of women found paid work as agricultural laborers. The earliest use of female employees on tea plantations in western Uganda apparently dates from this period, and young women sometimes worked in coffee farming in Bugisu and in tobacco growing in West Nile (for example, hauling water for young plants).[46] Toro was unusual in that a few women were growing cash crops of their own.

The cooperative movement, which flourished during these years due to the government's policy of Africanizing the economy, contained no significant female involvement.[47] In the coffee cooperatives, for example, which gained economic and political importance within some regions, women were not active in decision-making and did not normally share in the benefits. Peace Kyamureku of NAWOU explained, 'A woman joined the cooperative society because the husband was a member. She would grow the coffee, harvest the coffee, dry it. The husband and children would carry the coffee to the central place where it would be sold, and the man would get the money. The wife would go back home and wait for a piece of cloth.'[48] Attempts to unionize workers on the newly emerging sugar plantations in the later 1960s seem likewise to have bypassed women. In neither rural nor urban settings was there a labor movement anything like that found in Nigeria, which organized a general strike of 800,000 wage-earners in 1964.[49]

One of the most conspicuous changes in women's work was their more prominent role as sellers of food and drink in urban markets. A survey of greater Kampala's markets in 1964 showed that, of 1,664 vendors, 41 percent were women.[50] In Nakasero market, specializing in fruits and vegetables, 48-54 percent of the vendors in the two halves of the market were women.[51] A geographer noted that 'African control of [Nakasero] market has been made possible by the special nature of the trade: a start can be made here with very little capital, the turnover is probably small but rapid, [and] local contacts are valuable', including those between nearby growers and stallholders.[52] For those reasons, 'the otherwise ubiquitous Asian trading competition can be overcome'. Some female vendors were now present every day in Kampala's markets, usually offering food they had not grown themselves. Women were concentrated in low-profit items, like bananas, whereas male sellers focused on higher-value items like haberdashery, secondhand goods, craft items, meat, chicken, and fish. Women were increasingly active in other urban markets as well. Of the vendors at the daily market at Arua, West Nile, which had an average daily attendance of 5,500 people and offered mainly staple foods, 94 percent were women, though most came irregularly.[53]

Yet despite the growing presence of women, scholars who studied Uganda's markets during the 1960s commented on how minor women's roles were as compared with many West African settings, where women constituted virtually all the sellers and often had some control over how the market was run.[54] There is, however, no evidence of government policies in Uganda that discriminated against women traders on economic grounds, as has been described in Nairobi during this period.

Selling cooked food was a growing option for urban women, especially in or near to Kampala's markets.[55] Common types of food were cups of maize porridge, cooked or roasted ears of maize, and cassava which had not been sold raw during the day and was fried in oil and sold in the evening. These transactions often occurred on the periphery of the market, where the buyers were mainly poor people who could not go home for lunch or schoolchildren buying snacks. Women were also beginning to sell food and other small items along the streets in Kampala. Lydia Rugasira of UWFT recalled that, during her childhood in Kampala in the 1960s, 'Nubian women and police wives, who mainly came from West Nile and the north, were out there selling little, little things. They would sell groundnuts in little twists of paper, they would sell sweets, they would sell cigarettes. They were my first impression of women in commerce.'[56] The sale of cooked food was not limited to the capital. A letter to *Taifa Empya* from Kasese in 1970 called on the government to respect and assist the increasing number of women who were selling cooked food in town centers.[57]

Brewing and sale of local alcohol by women also expanded during these years, though the independent government looked upon these activities with no more favor than had its colonial predecessor.[58] In villages in Buganda and West Nile, girls and women had a monopoly over production of beer, *enguli* (a local gin), and other spirits, while in Bugisu they were joined by men.[59] In 1965, 100 female brewers in Aboke, Lango, inspired by a lecture given by the manager of the Cooperative Union, organized themselves into the 'Enguli Cooperative Society'. A government commission appointed in 1963 to study the *waragi* issue estimated that over 37 million liters of illegal gin were brewed every year and emphasized the importance of women in this production.[60] When women sold brew they had made themselves or worked as barmaids, their work was generally greeted with male disapproval. Fulgencia Apio's husband (Profile 2.3), an older parish chief, objected when she began to brew beer for sale after their marriage.

In most parts of the country, shopkeeping was not yet an option for women. In Kampala as in the smaller communities, although a few women helped in their husband's shop or were hired as salesgirls, they did not run their own.[61] Kitakule said of her small-town childhood, 'I don't remember seeing any women selling in the shops in my area. Women were not involved in business at all then, except for selling crops.' But in the Ankole area, traders of South Asian background were starting to be replaced by African Ugandans, including women. The town clerk of Mbarara reported in 1970 that nearly all the shops that had originally been run by Indians had been taken over by Ugandans.[62] Noting that some of the new traders were women, he thanked them for setting a good example to the whole of Uganda.

A rising level of wealth among successful Ugandan families had several implications for working women. Demand for domestic help increased, with African village girls now favored over Indian men. Girls in Buganda, Bugisu, West Nile, and Toro took positions as housegirls or ayahs, doing housework and looking after children.[63] The acquisition of more disposable cash and leisure time by middle-class Ugandan woman opened up a new occupation, one that was to become increasingly important over the following decades: hairdressing. Although this work was not explored in any of the research studies, a photograph from 1970 shows a Baganda woman dressing hair.[64]

In Jinja and Kampala, a small number of women worked in industry. British American Tobacco employed 197 women together with 283 men at its plants in these towns, but female workers were concentrated in the lowest ranks of skill and pay.[65] An article about a match factory in Jinja run by the Madhvani group (one of the largest Indian-operated conglomerates) stressed the large number of female workers there. 'At first, men were employed throughout the factory, but soon it was found that the women were able to concentrate better and were more dexterous, especially where the packeting and labelling was concerned.' Elsewhere in the Madhvani companies, however, the level of female workers was much lower.

Craftwork was actively promoted. Women's organizations encouraged it, in part as a way to earn money for their clubs, and so did the government, which sponsored handicraft exhibitions.[66] To people interested in development, craftwork has frequently seemed an ideal way for women to earn some money while still maintaining their normal domestic duties. But because most of the crafts required relatively little skill and could be made by many other people, and because there were no valuable raw materials in Uganda from which to make high priced goods, there was scant demand for craftwork and it brought little profit. This was to remain the case into the early twenty-first century.

Among educated women the most conspicuous growth of female activity came in teaching and nursing, at least at the lower levels of these occupations. They were now widely accepted as appropriate careers for women, even by men who opposed other kinds of female work. Kitakule said about her childhood during the 1960s, 'There were only two professions for the women. They were either nurses or teachers, but not very highly qualified teachers – either vernacular school or primary school teachers. The first women engineers and others came in a later generation.'[67] Because teaching and nursing were not well paid, some women began to augment their salaries in other ways. Grace Mukasa of ACFODE said that her mother, who was a teacher, also ran a shop. Every day after school, leaving Grace in charge of the nine boys at home, she would go to her shop. She also collected the rent for properties owned by her polygamous husband. 'It never even struck me that my father should pay my school fees, because for us, she was in control.'[68]

Not only did the system of education initiated after Independence expand the demand for teachers at all levels, the conditions of employment were also improving.[69] The Education Act of 1963 addressed the problem of teachers' pay, which had been lower than for other civil service workers, permitted married women to continue teaching, and relaxed the requirements for proper behavior on the part of teachers.[70] Female teachers who became pregnant outside wedlock were no longer forced to resign. The educational standard of teachers was likewise rising. In 1970, 309 students (24 percent of them female) were enrolled in advanced teacher training programs, and efforts to encourage university students – both men and women – to become teachers were bearing fruit.[71] The three-year course leading to the degree of Bachelor of Education at Makerere included 118 students in 1969-70, 28 percent of them female.

Uganda's women teachers did not usually play leadership roles. Of the heads of 21 new schools opened in 1965, for example, 11 were European men, 6 were Ugandan men, and 4 were European women.[72] Men also continued to dominate teachers' organizations. A paper about Ugandan teachers presented at a meeting in 1966 by the general secretary of the Uganda Teachers Association made no mention whatsoever of women or their concerns.[73] But a few Ugandan women were gaining influence within the profession. Mrs Margaret N. Nsereko was a graduate teacher and an education officer in the Ministry of Education when the 1963 Education Act was going through the National Assembly.[74] In 1965 she was appointed the first Ugandan headmistress of Trinity College, Nabbingo, one of the elite girls' boarding schools. A teacher in Batheleny Girls School in Mbale was elected president of the Uganda Teachers Association in 1970.[75]

Among nurses and midwives, more Ugandan girls were being trained within the country and some of them were married when they started their course, suggesting that mature women were entering the field. The earliest surviving register of nurses at Mulago School of Nursing, from 1968, shows that 145 of 151 enrolled nurses, the lower level, were Ugandan; of them 28 percent were listed as Mrs rather than Miss.[76] Mulago graduated its first class of registered nurses in 1965, but women trained in Uganda did not immediately take over this career.

During this decade we see the beginnings of African women's entry into certain clerical positions, particularly unskilled jobs such as copy typing. An advertisement for a manual typewriter in 1965, headed, 'Does the perfect secretary exist?', shows an attractive but simply dressed young Ugandan woman copying a hand-written document into her typewriter.[77] Female clerical workers were eligible for membership in the National Union of Clerical, Commercial, Professional and Technical Employees (NUCCPTE), formed in 1961.[78] Although NUCCPTE was one of the first genuinely multi-racial labor organizations, welcoming African and Asian Ugandans and immigrants from Kenya, women's participation was very limited. Married women 'found it extremely difficult to attend to union matters due to domestic commitments and the reluctance of their spouses to let them attend union meetings. The few women who found time to participate effectively in union affairs could rarely compete with their male counterparts for union positions.'

We gain some quantitative information about women's role in teaching, nursing, and clerical positions in 1967 from Uganda's first survey of 'High Level Manpower'.[79] Most progressively for this era, the detailed Appendix was broken down by sex as well as by nationality (Ugandans; Asians and non-Ugandan Africans; Europeans and others). Unfortunately, however, it does not provide sex within nationality, so we cannot determine how many people within each

Table 6.1. Ugandans and women employed in selected high-level occupations, 1967 [a]

Occupation	Number of people employed	% Ugandan	% women
Nurses	2,949	99	75
Nursing sisters	460	55	95
Grade II teachers	9,681	97	28
Grade III teachers	1,663	77	26
Grade IV-V teachers	943	39	34
'School teachers'	1,491	13	29
Typists	327	79	42
Personal secretaries	751	45	76
Book-keepers	1,390	70	12
Clerks	6,394	89	7

a) Figures calculated from U. Ministry of Planning and Economic Development, *High Level Manpower Survey, 1967*, App. I.

national/ethnic group were women. In a few occupations, it is nevertheless clear that Ugandan women were taking part. As shown in Table 6.1, by far the highest concentration occurred among nurses: 99 percent were Ugandan and 75 percent were women. Of the higher level nursing sisters, by contrast, though 95 percent were women, only 55 percent were Ugandan. Similarly among teachers, Ugandans (including some women) were concentrated at the lowest level: as one moves up through the grades, the proportion of Ugandans drops sharply. The other large clusters of Ugandans and women were found among the clerical workers. The 79 percent of typists who were Ugandan must have included some women, whereas many of the higher-status personal secretaries were European women. Among clerks, an occupation formerly dominated by Indian males, Ugandans now formed 89 percent, but it remained an overwhelmingly male job.

A few pioneer women entered other professions during the early Independence period. Princess Elizabeth (Bagaya) of Toro passed the final bar examinations at Gray's Inn, London in 1965, becoming the first East African woman barrister.[80] A graduate of Gayaza High School, she then attended a girls' secondary school in England and studied French in Paris for 6 months before doing her undergraduate degree in law at Girton College, Cambridge. Thereafter she pursued advanced legal training. When Miss Rose Mary Bagenda, daughter of a school teacher in Mbale, graduated as a medical doctor from Makerere in 1965, she was said to follow two other women who had become doctors within the past five years; one of them trained in Britain, the other at Makerere.[81] Later that year Dr. Juanita Kagwa, daughter of the former prime minister of Buganda, returned to Uganda after spending 11 years studying in Canada and the United States and receiving five degrees. A specialist in children's diseases, Dr. Kagwa joined the staff of Makerere University College as a lecturer in Paediatrics. Her sister, Dr. Mary Kagwa, was a dentist at Mulago Hospital.

The government offered additional opportunities. Community development was an expanding field. When Angela Akello (Profile 2.1) took a position in Karamoja in 1965, her decision was opposed by her uncles and – she suspected – most of the people with whom she was working, for the few other community development workers in that area were men. Asiimwe said that when her mother was young, during the 1960s, her grandfather had wanted her to teach.[82] But her mother insisted on going to the Veterinary School in Entebbe and became one of the first women veterinarians, working initially for the government. A woman who worked as a telephone operator at the district administrative headquarters in Busoga was elected president of her Employees Union in 1970.[83] The government also provided new kinds of employment at a lower level, recruiting women to work as wardresses in the prison service, cooks in rural schools, and semi-skilled assistants in medical dispensaries.[84]

The achievements of the early professional women encouraged younger women to widen their own horizons. Of a sample of girls in secondary schools interviewed in the late 1960s, 21 percent aspired to be doctors and 6 percent lawyers, though only 12 percent and 4 percent expected that they would actually succeed.[85] Another 20 percent expected to become teachers, 15 percent nurses, and 15 percent secretaries. More women were preparing to enter professional work. In 1969–70, Makerere reported that 9 of the 45 Ugandans studying law were women, as were 30 of 195 in medicine and 6 of 18 in social work.[86]

A few women were starting to enter the corporate world, though their activities were rare enough to be seen as noteworthy. In 1965 Eseza Makumbi was featured in *Uganda Argus* because she was about to leave for a study tour in Israel.[88] In the article that accompanied her photograph, she was described as a Director of the Mengo Coffee Company Ltd and Managing Director of the Sky Line Travel Bureau, as well as being a member of the Legislative Assembly. (Perhaps not coincidentally, her husband was Permanent Secretary of the Ministry of Commerce and Industry.) In 1970 the female general secretary of the Ugandan branch of a British insurance broking company was chosen to hand over a check to two men participating in the East African Safari Rally.[89] Juliet Bateyo, who had been active in drama while a student at Makerere and wrote poetry and novels, was named as sales promotion officer and drama editor of the East African Publishing House. Another Makerere graduate was given a scholarship by Esso Standard Uganda Ltd to pursue advanced secretarial studies in Nairobi; Shell Uganda Ltd offered scholarships to four young women to do the same.[90]

Profile 6.1 A Career in the Media World: 'Eunice Kyamanya'

Eunice Kyamanya, a Mutoro who worked for many years with Radio Uganda, was 59 at the time of her interviews in 2002–3.[87] A trim, well-dressed woman, she spoke quietly but with assurance and precision. She was born in 1943 outside Fort Portal, Kabarole, where her family lived on the lower slope of the hill where the palace of the king of Toro was located. Her father was away most of the time, doing casual labor for the Post Office in Kampala, so her mother was the effective head of the family. In addition to growing food for their own consumption, her mother wove and sold reed mats and baskets for millet. When Eunice's father returned home, which happened periodically, he would bring cash, used mainly for school fees. Although he did not like wasting money on educating girls, his wife insisted and for some time he grudgingly agreed. Eunice began at a Protestant school but after she changed to a less expensive Catholic one, she became interested in that religion and converted to it. When her father stopped providing money for her education, her teachers and the Catholic Church helped her to get a bursary (scholarship) that allowed her to continue up to 'O-levels'. This was a high qualification for a girl in her region at the time.

In 1962, when she was 19, Eunice moved to Kampala. Staying with a brother who was already working there, she began to look for a job. Shortly after her arrival she heard on the radio that the government was calling people to come to the Makerere campus to interview for positions. She went and was offered a job as a program assistant with Radio Uganda. After going back to Kabarole to gather money from relatives with which to buy clothes and household goods, she joined the civil service, four months before Independence. Her first assignment was to translate programs from English into the vernacular. She soon moved into broadcasting, however, 'because people loved my voice'. She began with a weekly children's program, going on to read the news in her local language. 'This was a privilege for me. My bosses used to wonder, "How can this young person move into news? We've been here for so long but nobody allows us to do that. She has just come!"'

Eunice's career continued to progress. In 1971 she was sent to the BBC in London for three months of intensive training, after which she was assigned to

English-language broadcasting at Radio Uganda. She inaugurated a popular program called 'News Hour' and by the time of her retirement had headed the Western Section and the News and Current Affairs unit. When she was in her mid-twenties, she became the only wife of an administrator in the civil service. He worked in the President's Office during the first Obote government and later became head of a department. They had three children, in their twenties at the time of the interviews, who had either graduated from or were then at Makerere University.

In 1966, when she was 23, Eunice initiated what must have been one of the very first legal actions stemming from sexual harassment. A few years after she joined Radio Uganda, her much older boss began to invite her out. 'You know here, our men, when they see that you are under them, they want to exploit you.' Despite the fact that he was married – and that his wife was related to Eunice's aunt – he put increasing pressure on her. 'One day I just told him off. I said, "Can't you see that I am not going to accept? You are an old man".' (Describing the scene later, she commented: 'Now I think that was not tactful. I could have found better words!') He became extremely angry and said in front of others, 'I must kill this girl.' These were not idle words, for he hired boys to break into the room where she was living to attack her, and he paid a man to try to run her over with his car. When Eunice complained to the Ministry, the under secretary – a British man – said it was her fault for tempting and provoking her boss.

Because she was determined not to be intimidated, even though she was young, female, and of a low rank within the civil service, Eunice decided to take her boss to court on charges of attempted assault and murder. Both her own family and his relatives were horrified at this plan. They told her she was making a terrible mistake and urged her to drop the allegation. But she persisted, and when testimony confirmed that he had indeed tried to harm her, she won her case. The law required that the man be sent to prison, but he was merely transferred to another position in the government. 'It was a bitter experience, but after that people knew they had to take me seriously. If those religious people at my school had not imparted to me a feeling of trusting in God, it would have been too much for my age, my position. When I look back on it, I suppose I was a pioneer in the women's struggle.'

Eunice's life in subsequent periods: During the Amin regime, she and her husband went into exile in Tanzania. When Obote came back to power, they returned to the country and she resumed her position at Radio Uganda. As discussed in Chapter 7 below, she participated actively in the women's movement in 1982–5 and in the Nairobi Conference of 1985. Looking back over her working life, Eunice felt that, although she had reaped relatively little financial benefit from her work (government employees were not well paid), she had gained experience and social confidence. She described with pride the events she had covered, in some cases meeting the people involved – the visits of Haile Selasse of Ethiopia and the Pope, the return of the *Kabaka* to Uganda. She felt also that the time she had devoted to women's organizations had been well spent. Even in retirement she continued to put her skills to use. She was the Director of the Association of Ageing and Retired Persons, and on the day of her first interview she had been at a workshop organized by the Uganda Media Women's Association to train women who were going to the north of Uganda to contribute to peace-building efforts there.

The arts and entertainment offered opportunities for other women. Theresa Nakacwa's play in Luganda, *Empologoma*, won first prize in the Uganda Drama Festival in 1964 and second place in an East African play-writing competition.[91] In 1970 'The Kampala Shining Stars,' a women-led drama club, wrote a Luganda-language play about marital relations called *Who Is the Owner of the Family?*, which was produced at the National Theatre and later broadcast on radio and television.[92] Women co-directed and performed in the first play to be staged at the National Theatre that contained a mixture of songs and dances. A report described Catholic singers who were going to France to study church music, and on several occasions female staff members at galleries in Kampala were shown preparing artwork for exhibitions.[93]

Women, even Muslim women, were found in more popular types of entertainment too. An article in 1970 discussed the singer Sarah Namagembe, 'a musician with great talent', who had been performing with the band 'Kampala City Six'.[94] She was now hoping to go international, thanks to the support she had received from Ugandans. The article concluded that Sarah 'has brought Uganda into the limelight in the new era of the music world'. Florence Maniasa and Christopher Kato demonstrated their dance style in Masaka, part of a country-wide tour with their band 'The Top Ten', and Hadijah Namale, 'Uganda's talented female artist', released a new end-of-year album with the same band in December, 1970.[95] A young woman was described in 1965 as the first African girl in Uganda to become a professional photographer, and another was hired as a regular journalist – not just as a columnist on women's matters – by *Taifa Empya* newspaper in 1970.[96] Women were also participating in beauty contests, and these were reported occasionally in the papers.

Further information about working women comes from our interview sample. The mothers of the women who were children during the early Independence period displayed economic patterns similar to those of mothers during the late colonial years. A third had no income-generating activities at all, while another 20 percent were primarily subsistence farmers who sold extra food if they had it. Only 10 percent grew foodstuffs or poultry expressly for market sale. Several of the mothers living in or near towns during the early Independence years engaged in trade: four made and sold craftwork or clothing ('my mother was a tailor, one of the first to make babies' dresses at the taxi park in Nsambya, a suburb of Kampala'[97]), and one had a market stall. The proportion of mothers who made or sold local alcohol had risen to more than a third, while another woman sold tea as part of a group of women at her church. A few of the mothers were primary school teachers.

Fifteen women began to earn an income of their own between 1962 and 1970. Five were nurses, three were primary school teachers, one was a community development worker, and one worked for Radio Uganda. A higher fraction were in business than had been the case before, with two making and selling food or drink and two in other kinds of trade. One woman sorted coffee in a factory. None of them worked with their husbands. Just over half lived in villages when they started work, a quarter were in Kampala, and the remainder were in district headquarters or peri-urban areas. These women were somewhat older than their predecessors at the time they began to gain an income. Only a quarter were now under 20, just over half were aged 20–24, two were in their later twenties, and one was in her thirties. Due to their older age, they were slightly more likely to be married and to have children than had been the case before. In deciding what kind of work to enter, these women were more heavily influenced by practical factors than earlier women had been. A third cited their need for money as the primary factor in their choice of job: they had to earn money to support their home and family, or they wanted to have their own earnings. Only a third now said they had an aptitude for such work or admired the people who did it.

When asked whether it was common for women to do the kind of work they began during the early Independence period, three-quarters said it was. This group included most of the nurses and teachers, all the women in business, and the factory worker. Two teachers working in Lira, however, said they were atypical. 'I was the only female teacher in that community. Afterwards other girls started emulating my good example.'[98] 'There were very few female teachers then, though the number gradually increased, especially in urban schools.'

While the majority of women who began work during the early years of Independence said that their husbands or other relatives approved of their work, a higher fraction than before mentioned some opposition. One of the women who encountered resistance to her work was a young hospital nurse married to a Muslim politician. 'Of course no man wants his wife to go for night duty because it means leaving the home and children, but it is part of a nurse's duty. My husband had to cooperate: there were sick people to be cared for.'[99] More serious problems were recounted by several women, but these stemmed less from the nature of the work than from the woman's economic independence or professional competence. A teacher working in Apac District reported, 'My husband cooperated with my work at the beginning of our marriage, but there was a dramatic twist when I had to upgrade my status to become a Grade II teacher. When I went away to the training college to upgrade, my husband brought in other women to my house. When I came back, I was on the same level of teaching as him, though his salary was slightly higher. Soon after, domestic violence ensued, and that later resulted in our divorce.'[100]

Three-quarters of these women reported that their first work was perceived in positive terms by the community. A woman who was making baskets and taking them to the bus park in Hoima to sell noted, 'The community looked at it as good work for a woman, because she does it from home while she also takes care of the home.'[101] A nurse from Moroto District, who had been sent to England to study nursing and midwifery thanks to a local government scholarship, said that when she returned to a supervisory position at a hospital in Lira, 'The community was happy to see me in that status. At that time not many girls had gone abroad for that type of training.' But some women faced public disapproval. One who was selling local brew and *waragi* in a trading center near Hoima said, 'People did not like to have that kind of work done by a woman.'[102] A nurse working at a hospital in Soroti reported, 'The community was upset about my work and feared me because of my education. Some talked ill of highly educated girls. I was attacked because of putting on trousers and was taken to be a prostitute.'

Public Attitudes and the Domestic Virtue Model

During the early Independence period, attitudes towards working women were shaped by three factors: the changes occurring in the actual nature of women's economic activities; the expectations of a good woman as defined by the Domestic

Virtue model and its Service Career variant; and the position taken by the government and the media. Whereas, during the colonial period, official attitudes towards women and their activities had been based upon Domestic Virtue expectations, in the 1960s a new rhetorical stance was adopted by the government and the press. Advocating qualified public participation for women, it stressed the importance of women's contributions to the economic development and public life of the newly independent nation. In emphasizing the need for women to work alongside men, this image was influenced by the desire of the country's leaders to portray Uganda to its own citizens and the world community as a modern nation in which women were full and active members. Uganda was shown as sharing basic values and practices with the Western world and – perhaps more importantly – the socialist world, with its emphasis on the equality of men and women. Official support for women's participation was, however, limited to rhetoric: the government did not take steps to assist women in entering the public domain. Furthermore, the scope of female involvement was qualified. While women were encouraged to enter careers and the public economy, they were not welcomed in electoral politics at the national level.

The impact of this new conception of women's roles and the way in which it interacted with the Domestic Virtue model depended upon the kind of work women were doing. The government's positive valuation did not extend to the labor of rural women who stayed at home and grew food for their own families. Their contributions were ignored or dismissed even if a husband had migrated to town in search of paid employment, leaving his wife responsible for feeding the household, or if a wife was providing the labor for cash crops raised on family land. Obbo has suggested that such women were devalued in several respects: they were 'on the one hand producing within a capitalist system for which they received no remuneration; and on the other hand subjected to an ideology that regarded land as a resource that belonged to men'.[103] Because subsistence farming was not perceived as augmenting the economy of the country, the great majority of the country's female population received no public acknowledgement of their work, and their lives continued to be shaped by the more restrictive definitions of the basic Domestic Virtue model. We do see a little flexibility, however, for rural women who grew and sold extra food or engaged in small income-generating activities in order to pay their children's school fees; they were accommodated within the model, now and in subsequent periods.

At the upper end of the socio-economic spectrum, the growing number of educated women who were working in an expanded range of professions or respectable clerical positions were praised in public discourse. Their work was presented as a contribution to the nation as well as to their own families. Because the government's stance emphasized especially those women who had attended the leading boarding schools, it retained the elitism of the early colonial formulation. The new group of educated working women could also fit within a slightly enlarged definition of the Service Career variation, thereby gaining a positive personal identity.

Uncertainty arose with respect to the women who were starting to sell in urban markets or to produce and sell cooked food or drink. These women were now receiving attention in the press, and their work could potentially be described as helping the country's economic development and hence commended within the public participation framework. But because they were not educated and were not working in salaried service positions, they did not qualify for inclusion under any form of Domestic Virtue thinking. It was therefore unclear whether they should be regarded as good women, or treated with the disapproval that had previously greeted sellers of alcohol and prostitutes. This ambiguity would not be resolved until the Amin/Obote II period, when a new variation of the Domestic Virtue model emerged to cover their situation.

Furthermore, although the government and the media's new definition advocated active female participation in most aspects of the nation's public life, it assumed that women would nonetheless marry and have children, continue to look after their family and household, and remain submissive to their husbands and other men. These Domestic Virtue expectations made it difficult for women to be fully involved in the broader world. If a woman worked for pay during the day but was expected to shoulder her traditional responsibilities when she returned home in the evening, she faced physical exhaustion and the risk that the quality of her performance in one or both settings would suffer. A woman who was educated and/or effective on the job might find it difficult to conform to the position of submissive deference that was still demanded of wives.

Yet the government did not call for an end to practices that restricted women's personal lives. Earlier laws concerning marriage and inheritance, for example, which greatly disadvantaged women, remained largely unchanged. Nor did the political parties take a stand on women's issues. In Uganda, one finds no parallel to FRELIMO's call in the early days of Mozambican independence, '*Abaixo com lobolo!* (Down with bridewealth!)'.[104] As Musisi has commented about the leaders of the Baganda women's movement of the 1960s, 'The fact that they were the "firsts" in an environment that still downgraded women and defined a "good woman" as subservient and dependent, created for many of these women an identity crisis. Were they really bad in challenging the establishment that denied them their rightful positions according to their qualifications? Or were they prepared to appear as rebellious women?'[105]

This tension has been noted in other post-colonial societies as well. Kandiyoti has stressed the ambiguity and paradox concerning women's place in many new nations.

> On the one hand, nationalist movements invite women to participate more fully in collective life by interpellating them as 'national' actors: mothers, educators, workers and even fighters. On the other hand, they reaffirm the boundaries of culturally acceptable feminine conduct and exert pressure on women to articulate their gender interests within the terms of reference set by nationalist discourse.[106]

Duara has made a similar point about patriarchy within decolonizing nations in Africa and Asia:

> The new woman was to be educated so that she could contribute to making the nation strong by rearing healthy children . . . . [Women] were to be mothers of the nation, protecting and cherishing its inner values especially within the home . . . . Women's questions, particularly relating to changes in gender relationships or to their desire to undertake roles equal or similar to men's, were subordinated to the overall needs of the nation as perceived by men.[107]

Analysis of how women and their work were portrayed in the media of the early

Independence period reveals some of the dissonances between the new official position regarding their public participation, the nature of their work, and the ongoing expectations embodied in the Domestic Virtue model. Local-language and English newspapers display several striking features.[108] The first is how positive a stance they all take – in their articles and the letters they chose to publish – with respect to women's involvement in public arenas. Although many people must have held more traditional views about women and their work, such opinions were rarely expressed in the papers. Instead, their attitudes resembled the progressive position defined by *Ageteraine* and, to a lesser extent, *Munno* during the previous decade. Another notable feature is how similar the representations of women in the various papers have become. Unlike the wide divergences seen during the late colonial years, the papers discussed the same kinds of topics and generally reflected shared views. Furthermore, the papers seem to have been making a deliberate effort to cover a wider range of religions, ethnic groups, and regions. Muslim women's activities were reported by Catholic papers, and *Taifa Empya*, though written in Luganda and based in Kampala, offered articles dealing with Mbarara and women in Ankole. Several letters about women's issues sent to Luganda papers in 1970 were written by people with British names, while many letters submitted to *Uganda Argus* in 1965 came from people with Ugandan names.

In some respects, representations of women and their issues continued along pathways visible prior to Independence. Higher education was promoted, with virtually every issue containing short reports and/or photographs of women who had completed training in Uganda or were going to Europe, North America, or Israel for further study or returning. The papers also described the projects of a wide range of women's organizations – frequently, fully, and positively – as well as the charitable activities that were becoming common among wealthy African women in Kampala.[109] *Uganda Argus* gave particularly full coverage to the national meeting of the UCW in 1965, whose theme was 'Uganda Women Build a Nation'.

Taxation of women remained a heated issue. When Buganda's *Lukiiko* introduced an income tax for working women in 1962, some women wrote to *Munno* to object. They claimed that they did not oppose the principle of paying taxes but were angry that an important issue for women had been decided by a body in which they had no representation and which had failed to address problems like bridewealth.[110] Other women argued in favor of the tax, on the grounds that women would then be recognized as independent wage earners and could seek improvements in working conditions. The topic was vigorously debated in letters to *Uganda Argus* and *East African Standard* in 1965.[111]

In addition, the papers now promoted female participation in the cash-based economy, seen as essential to national development. Rural women were encouraged to grow crops for the market and develop projects that would bring in an income for themselves and expand the country's economy. A wider range of paid occupations were accepted as legitimate for women, including some that would previously have been seen as undesirable. A set of photographs of Ugandan working women in *Taifa Empya* in 1970, for example, included, on an apparently equal footing, traditional healers, street vendors, tailors, hairdressers, farmers, city sweepers, local politicians, bar attendants, and secretaries.[112]

As part of the more positive valuation of working women, earlier objections to women's involvement with alcohol or sex work were partially replaced by more sympathetic attitudes. This is illustrated by the papers' treatment of bar girls, a type of employment condemned in the past. Bar employees were sometimes mentioned simply because they had done something newsworthy, the same kind of coverage given to other workers.[113] Some letters argued that bar attendants, often quite young girls, should be protected against exploitation by their bosses and customers. The author of a letter to *Uganda Argus* said that if bar girls – who were expected to work long hours, dress well, and live in miserable rooms in return for little if any pay – sometimes turned to prostitution or begging, they should not be blamed.[114] In socialist countries, he noted pointedly, prostitutes and beggars were not a major problem and the level of crime was very low. In *Taifa Empya*, a letter criticizing bar girls in 1970 started a string of correspondence.[115] Some letters complained that bar maids were rude to their customers, were lazy, did not give proper change, or fished money out of the pockets of drunken men. But only rarely were they attacked for wearing short skirts or acting like prostitutes.

Sex work too evoked a less uniformly negative response. Traditional views were still expressed, especially among members of the African elite. In 1965, for example, *Uganda Argus* published a letter by Jane Musoke of Kampala complaining that 'when one goes for a shopping expedition one faces the risk of bumping into several beggars, and when one goes out for an evening one is exposed to the sinews of prostitution'. Describing prostitution as a foreign institution, she said that such people 'make the place disgusting to stay in'.[116] In response, B. Chango Machyn wrote that many girls come into towns with high expectations of a better life but cannot find work. 'As long as we follow a capitalist mode of development and bourgeois social concepts, these problems are inevitable.' Other discussions of sex work attempted to understand its causes. *Ageteraine*, for example, published a collection of twelve articles and letters about prostitution.[117] Among the factors identified were polygamy (wives who are less loved or less well provided for may become prostitutes); inadequate inheritance rights for widows; high brideprice; men who leave home for long periods of time to work elsewhere (spending all their money on prostitutes and not helping their wives at home); and poor parenting (neglected children may become prostitutes or thieves). A married woman in Mengo wrote to *Taifa Empya* that the prostitutes on Kampala's streets were simply business people who had a service to exchange for economic gain.[118] A Muslim man from Kasese said that it was not fair to criticize women who have turned to prostitution 'as a means of survival in the absurd economic conditions of the present'. Since it is men who sustain their market, they too are to blame for this social evil.

The papers covered aspects of women's lives that had not appeared in the press before, including competitive sports. Of the 28 athletes selected by the Uganda National Council of Sports in 1970 to represent the country in the Commonwealth Games in Edinburgh, seven were women.[119] Runner Judith Ayaa was selected as 'Sports Woman of the Year' by the Uganda Amateur Athletics Association. Netball teams, a girls' sport introduced by the British, were organized into leagues and covered extensively. In 1970, the papers mentioned teams consisting of nurses from Masaka, Jinja, and Mulago Hospitals, employees of National and Grindlay's Bank, workers of the Coffee Marketing Board, members of Kampala Women's Club, and airport workers at Entebbe.[120]

Yet amidst this generally favorable portrayal of women's activity in the public domain, there was little support for the entry of women into politics. When women did stand for office, they faced criticism for venturing into areas where they did not belong. The male opponent of Ansuya Pandya, an unsuccessful candidate for the National Assembly in 1962, declared that 'the lady should be entered in beauty competitions – and forget about elections'.[121] *Uganda Argus* was unusual in publishing a letter from a male Ugandan in 1965 that followed its statement that 'a woman is the mother of the state' by appealing to 'highly educated ladies to bury their inferiority complex and wake up to join political parties. They should struggle for nomination to stand for the next general election.'[122] Reports in the papers from 1970 concerning women who were vying for political office suggest considerable discomfort about this role. When Mrs Florence Lubega, a serious women's activist, was chosen as chairperson of the Mubende central constituency of the UPC, the article about her election focused on how graciously she thanked the President for his support.[123] As elections for the National Assembly approached in 1970, a married woman employed by Nile Breweries who was the chairperson of the Jinja branch of the UPC was the first to declare her intention to stand. Noting that tension was rising, *Taifa Empya* sounded quite taken aback that she not only encouraged other women to come out as candidates in their own constituencies but also vowed to beat all the men who stood in her way.

Nor did the papers discuss the problems faced by working women in reconciling their employment with the reality of their lives at home, where the expectations of the Domestic Virtue model reigned supreme. Finding a husband could be difficult. Parents and prospective suitors were sometimes uneasy about the excessive independence of women who earned their own money, interacted with other men on the job, and sought a more equal relationship with their husbands. Highly educated women were commonly perceived as difficult to control. One of the women in our sample, whose father was chief justice for the Bunyoro kingdom, described her own mother's worries about how higher education would affect her daughters' marriage chances. 'My mother was telling us that it's good to be well educated, but she feared that men would not want to marry us if we were too educated. "I want my daughters to attain the highest education, but I also want them to get married. How is this going to be done?"'[124] Nor was her anxiety misplaced: her daughter observed that most of the first generation of educated women from her region either married foreigners or did not marry at all.

The domestic challenges that confronted women active in the public sphere were intensified by new standards for appearance and household management. These stemmed in part from the emergence of advertising directed at female African consumers: educated and prosperous urban women. Good examples come from *Uganda Argus* in 1965, published in English but aimed primarily at middle-class African readers in Kampala. One advertisement ('The Beauty Secret of a Popular Girl') shows an African girl with a fashionable Western hairstyle preparing for her wedding. Stressing the importance of being 'fresh and feminine', it promoted use of Bu-Tone Talc as a face powder in part because it 'lightens the tone of her complexion'.[125] An advertisement for Ovaltine emphasized the importance of running the household in accordance with Western standards so as to please one's husband (see Illustration 6.1.).

Surprisingly little opposition was expressed in the papers to the call for greater female participation in most aspects of the new country's public life. This silence is particularly interesting in light of evidence from other sources that documents the

Illustration 6.1 Advertisement for Ovaltine, Uganda Argus, 6 October 1965

changes in marital and family patterns that were occurring as the result of the greater economic freedom of women. Some young Toro women who were training as teachers or nurses refused to marry until after they had completed their certificate, so that if their marriages broke down, they would have a good job.[126] Rural women too were becoming more independent. A local chief instructed women 'who roam up and down Fort Portal township' looking for work to return to their homes.[127] In three Toro villages, where women were employed as teachers, nurses/midwives, community development assistants, bar owners or bar girls, and assistants in agriculture and poultry raising, 15 percent of the households were headed by women. An observer noted that women with their own income were less willing to put up with a husband who beat them, and more unmarried women were having children. Likewise in Busoga, the relatively small number of employed women 'often prefer establishing an own homestead and "illegal" love affairs to a marriage, because in these cases they maintain their right to dispose of their children and income'.[128] In Buganda, young women who went off to work before marriage might not be willing to accept the man chosen by their parents. They were becoming emancipated, recognizing that they could move freely and support themselves until they decided to marry.

Because traditionalists might well have pointed to the negative consequences of women's new economic activities and the consequent bending of familiar gender roles, the newspapers were obviously portraying only one side of a more complex situation. We cannot determine whether the press (perhaps encouraged by the government) deliberately chose to muffle resistance to the public participation of women or whether more conservative people did not commonly express their complaints through letters to the newspaper. Among the few overt objections were several letters to *Munno* in 1962 expressing anger against women who were taking jobs away from men and refusing to marry.[129] A letter sent to *Uganda Argus* in 1965 by a man with a South Asian name began, 'I feel spellbound [sic] to say that some firms, particularly those around Jinja, have taken to employing women workers instead of ambitious men who wait the whole day outside any concern. There are numerous such work seekers who seem ready to do any kind of job allotted for a wage. It is especially annoying to see women employed in some dangerous machine-work . . . or serving drivers with fuel.' If this trend continued, the world would one day be shocked to see 'women in Uganda climb up to put nails in wood, or repair an electricity connection over a high pole or do some mining or cane cutting. I am not really against our women, but I am wholly against the work for which they are not qualified.' In other cases conservative views appear only indirectly. *Uganda Argus* reported on a speech by the assistant district commissioner in Busoga in 1965 urging men to allow their wives to take part in women's clubs.[130] The article emphasized, however, that the speaker justified his recommendation on the grounds that in clubs women 'could be enlightened and trained not only to look after themselves, but also to look after their husbands and children properly'.

If the gradual changes that had marked the generations between 1900 and 1970 had continued, it seems likely that the tensions between the expanding participation by women in the public economy, the government and the media's stance regarding their activity, and the Domestic Virtue model would have slowly been resolved. Instead, women were plunged into radically different and often terribly difficult circumstances during the Amin and Obote II regimes.

Notes

1 For a summary of the political history, see Karugire, *A Political History*, ch. 6, and Jørgensen, *Uganda*, ch. 5, and, for photographs, Tumusiime, *Uganda 30 Years*, pp. 34–42.

2 Mamdani, *Citizen and Subject*.

3 See Appendices C8–9 for the ethnic and religious affiliations of these women, their current work, and marital status when interviewed in 2003. For their mothers' occupations, see a later section in this chapter.

4 CultHist3 (see Appendix B).

5 For the impact of socialist ideas upon independence movements, see Duara, 'Introduction' to his *Decolonization*.

6 Kampala18.

7 Kampala17.

8 UNA New Series 18,269. A study of 5,650 Civil Service workers carried out in 1965 does not provide gender-disaggregated figures, though the author says the sex of workers was listed. Women are mentioned only once, in a note to a table that provides information by age: 'A discreet veil is drawn over the age of all female officers' (Knight, 'The Determination of Wages,' p. 255).

9 Ellyne, 'Economic History,' Bigsten and Kayizzi-Mugerwa, *Crisis, Adjustment*, Ch. 2, Jamal, 'The Agrarian Context,' Lateef, 'Structural Adjustment,' and Edmonds, 'Crisis Management.' Exports of coffee, cotton, tea, and groundnuts all increased between 1965 and 1970, though exports of tobacco declined (World Bank, *Africa DataBase, 2003*).

10 *New York Times*, 6 February 1968, p. 2.

11 Jackson, *Essays in Rural Marketing*, p. 6.

12 Arua15. For below, see Arua11.

13 Obbo, *African Women*, pp. 23–9. For both males and females, life expectancy at birth rose by several years between 1965 and 1970, while the population growth rate dropped from 4.5 to 3.1 percent; the infant mortality rate (per 1000 live births) dropped from 122 to 109 (World Bank, *Africa DataBase, 2003*).

14 Oloya and Poleman, *Food Supply*, p. 8. The urban population as a percentage of the national total rose from 6.5 percent in 1965 to 8.0 percent in 1970, though urban households had an average of only 3.8 people in 1969, as compared with 4.9 in rural areas (World Bank, *Africa DataBase, 2003*; UN, *WISTAT, 1999*).

15 Parkin, *Neighbour and Nationals*, ch. 5.

16 Glazer, 'Alcohol and Politics.'

17 Hutton, 'Unemployment in Kampala and Jinja.' For below, see Oloya and Poleman, *Food Supply*, p. 9.

18 Oloya and Poleman, *Food Supply*, p. 24. Only 6 percent of Ugandan-born adult males were employed in the mid-1960s (Hutton, 'Unemployment in Kampala and Jinja').

19 Mandeville, 'Poverty, Work.'

20 Ssekamwa, *History and Development of Education*, ch. 12, World Bank, *Africa DataBase, 2003*, and UN, *WISTAT, 1999*.

21 Jinja10.

22 Kwesiga, *Women's Access to Higher Education*, p. 199. The proportion of girls varied markedly by region. Within upper secondary classes, girls formed 37 percent of the pupils in Buganda but only 1 percent in the west; no girls at all were enrolled in the upper classes in the north.

23 Ibid., p. 207. For below, see Makerere University College, *Report for the Year 1969–70*, p. 418, and UN, *WISTAT, 1999*.

24 *The Makererian*, 29 October 1965.

25 Kabale3 and Kampala17. Sarah Ntiro was the first East African woman to graduate from Oxford University, the first woman member of the Bunyoro-Kitara Council, and the second woman to sit on the East African Legislative Council: see Chapter 5 and Tripp and Kwesiga, *The Women's Movement*, p. 206.

26 Lira17.

27 TB3.

28 Lira3.

The Early Independence Years

29 Kabale10.
30 Arua8.
31 See Tamale, *When Hens Begin to Crow*, pp. 14–5, and Tripp, *Women and Politics*, pp. 38–48, for this paragraph and the next three, unless otherwise noted.
32 E.g., UCU Mukono IMU/WN/02, Minutes of Provincial Women's Consultation, April 1964. For below, see UCU Mukono IMU 111/6, April 1969; IMU 111/6, February 1971; and IMU/113/6, May–June 1967.
33 *Uganda Argus*, 18 August and 6 February 1965. For below, see ibid., 15 February, 21 October, and 3 September 1965.
34 Uganda Council of Women, *Laws about Marriage in Uganda*, reviewed in *Uganda Journal*, 26 (1962):220–21. See also Musisi, 'Transformations of Baganda Women,' pp. 318–24.
35 Tripp, *Women and Politics*, p. 44. The recommendations of the Commission were never implemented, though in 1972 a presidential decree improved the inheritance rights of widows and children.
36 *Uganda Argus*, 28 April 1965.
37 7 January 1965.
38 *Taifa Empya*, 19 November and 9 December. The executive director was also active in the UCW, YMCA, UAWO and Uganda Association of University Women.
39 'Women in Political Struggle,' esp. pp. 132–3.
40 *Munno*, 15 and 20 April, 1 and 5 May; *Taifa Empya*, 4 May; *Munno*, 26 May and 1 July; *Taifa Empya*, 29 July; *Munno*, 7 October; *Taifa Empya*, 9 October and 27 November.
41 *Uganda Argus*, 25 November 1965. For his response to the 1985 Nairobi Women's Conference, see Chapter 7 below.
42 Tamale, *When Hens Begin to Crow*, p. 15.
43 Musisi, 'Transformations of Baganda Women,' pp. 324–37 for this and below.
44 Wallace and Weeks, *Success or Failure*, p. 19.
45 TB7.
46 Asowa-Okwe, 'Women Wage Workers,' and Wallace and Weeks, *Success or Failure*, pp. 17–19. For below, see Perlman, 'Some Aspects of Marriage Stability'.
47 Okereke, 'The Role of the Co-operative Movement,' pp. ii–iii. For below, see Bunker, *Peasants against the State*, chs. 6–7.
48 TB2. For below, see Ahluwalia, *Plantations*.
49 Lindsay, *Working with Gender*, ch. 7.
50 Temple, 'Urban Markets.'
51 Temple, 'Nakasero Market.'
52 Ibid., p. 177.
53 Jackson, *Essays on Rural Marketing*.
54 Oloya and Poleman, *Food Supply*, p. 40, and Temple, 'Urban Markets,' p. 356; cf. Ekechi, 'Gender and Economic Power.' For below, see Robertson, 'Traders and Urban Struggle,' and *Trouble Showed the Way*, ch. 5.
55 Temple, 'Urban Markets'; Oloya and Poleman, *Food Supply*, p. 41.
56 TB8.
57 9 January 1970.
58 Willis, *Potent Brews*, chs. 10–11. For urban Zambia, see Glazer, 'Alcohol and Politics.'
59 Wallace and Weeks, *Success or Failure*, pp. 17–19. For below, see *Uganda Argus*, 15 April. 1965
60 Willis, 'The Only Money.' It was not until the 1970s that government control over brewing broke down completely.
61 TB8 and Wallace and Weeks, *Success or Failure*, pp. 17–19. For below, see TB7.
62 *Ageteraine*, 22 February 1970.
63 Wallace and Weeks, *Success or Failure*, p. 18, and Perlman, 'Some Aspects of Marriage Stability'.
64 Wallace and Weeks, *Success or Failure*, p. 18.
65 Baryaruha, *Factors Affecting Industrial Employment*, pp. 46–54. For below, see *Uganda Argus*, 14 June 1965.
66 Perlman, 'Some Aspects of Marriage Stability', Wallace and Weeks, *Success or Failure*, pp. 17–19, *Uganda Argus*, 14 and 28 July, and 8 September 1965.
67 TB7.
68 TB1.

69 Ssekamwa, *History and Development of Education*, pp. 165–72.
70 Ibid., pp. 175–6. This relaxation affected male teachers too, in more troubling ways. Whereas those who had 'befriended' their pupils in the past had been expelled, after 1963 there were many reports of male teachers who abused schoolgirls (ibid., p. 176).
71 UN, *WISTAT, 1999*. For below, see Makerere University College, *Report for the Year 1969–70*, p. 418.
72 *Uganda Argus*, 4 January 1965.
73 Kisaka, 'The Uganda Teachers Association.'
74 Ssekamwa, *History and Development of Education*, p. 174. In 1986 she wrote a book about education for parents and teachers in Uganda.
75 *Taifa Empya*, 16 June 1970.
76 Mulago School of Nursing, Kampala, *First Register of Enrolled Nurses*. For below, see *Uganda Argus*, 13 April 1965. In 1968, several of the Ugandan women who entered Mulago's course for registered nurses had obtained their first qualification in Britain; five of the 31 students were foreign women and one was an Asian male (Mulago School of Nursing, Kampala, *First Register*).
77 *Uganda Argus*, 31 May 1965.
78 Asowa-Okwe, 'The Dynamics of Women Participation,' pp. 21–3.
79 U. Ministry of Planning and Economic Development, *High Level Manpower Survey, 1967*, and *Analyses of Requirements, 1967–1981*, esp. Appendix I. The 'high level occupations,' which were estimated to include only 2 percent of the total labor force, are clustered in this survey into the categories of Professionals, Technical Workers, Artisans, Skilled Office Workers, and Others. The other occupations with concentrations of both women and Ugandans employed relatively few people, including librarians, pharmacists, X-Ray technicians, personnel/social workers, punch operators, calculating machine operators, housekeepers, and people in radio management.
80 *Uganda Argus*, 12 July 1965. Five years later she was featured in a film called 'The Bullfrog in the Sun,' concerning the atrocities committed during the civil war in Nigeria, and it was noted that she had put Uganda on the map through her fashion shows in London (*Taifa Empya*, 23 November 1970).
81 *Uganda Argus*, 31 March 1965. For below, see ibid., 23 June and 22 September 1965.
82 TB3.
83 *Munno*, 24 April 1970, and *Taifa Empya*, 10 June. She was also active in the Red Cross, Mothers' Union, Girl Guides, and YWCA, and she went on to become an executive member of the Uganda Labour Congress.
84 *Uganda Argus*, 15 April 1965, and Wallace and Weeks, *Success or Failure*, pp. 17–19.
85 Evans, 'Image and Reality.'
86 Makerere University College, *Report for the Year 1969–70*, p. 418.
87 She was first interviewed by Grace Bantebya and Marjorie McIntosh on 27 November 2002 and again by McIntosh on 27 January 2003 (tapes: InitInterv2 and Kampala6). Both interviews were in English. Her economic level was assessed as well-off, though she and her husband were living quite simply in their retirement.
88 31 March 1965.
89 *Munno*, 25 March, and *Taifa Empya*, 16 December 1970. For below, see *Munno*, 23 April.
90 *Munno*, 13 May 1970, and *Taifa Empya*, 13 January.
91 *Uganda Argus*, 6 February 1965.
92 *Taifa Empya*, 1 May 1970, and *Munno*, 5 May. For below, see *Taifa Empya*, 19 June, and *Munno*, 29 August.
93 *Munno*, 12 May, 26 June and 5 September 1970.
94 *Taifa Empya*, 6 March 1970.
95 Ibid., 23 October and 11 December 1970.
96 *Uganda Argus*, 13 April 1965, and *Taifa Empya*, 18 February 1970, p. 5. For below, see, e.g., *Taifa Empya*, 13 May, and *Munno*, 5 August 1970.
97 Jinja2.
98 Lira2. For below, see Lira11.
99 Lira17.
100 Lira11.
101 Hoima11. For below, see Lira17.
102 Hoima12. For below, see Lira6.

103 'Sexuality and Economic Domination,' esp. p. 84.
104 Sheldon, *Pounders of Grain*, p. xxiii.
105 'Transformations of Baganda Women,' p. 340.
106 In 'Identity and Its Discontents,' p. 380.
107 In his 'Introduction' to *Decolonization*, p. 10.
108 See Appendix A for the papers studied.
109 E.g., *Munno*, 30 April, 23 July, 14 February, and 23 June 1970. For below, see 23 November (several articles), 25 November, and 27 November.
110 Musisi, 'Transformations of Baganda Women,' pp. 313–18.
111 E.g., *Uganda Argus*, 31 March, 1 September, and 29 October; *East African Standard*, 4 February.
112 25 November.
113 *Munno*, 9 January and 9 April 1970, and *Taifa Empya*, 19 February, 9 April, and 26 May.
114 21 September 1965.
115 13 March, 7 April, 22 September, 21 October, and 14 December.
116 10 September. For below, see 21 September.
117 22 February 1970.
118 10 June. For below, see ibid., 9 January.
119 *Taifa Empya*, 2 January. For below, see *Munno*, 8 May, and *Taifa Empya*, 8 May, 9 June, and 19 November.
120 *Munno*, 9 June, 16 June, and 25 June; *Taifa Empya*, 1 September, several articles.
121 As cited by Tripp, *Women and Politics*, p. 40.
122 18 June 1965.
123 *Taifa Empya*, 23 November. For below, see ibid.
124 Kampala17. The daughter trained as a doctor and at the age of 24 married a Ugandan man working in another high-status profession. For below, see, e.g., the marriage of Eunice Lubega, the first woman to receive a degree from Makerere, to Merrick Posnansky, the British curator of the Uganda Museum (*Sunday Vision Magazine*, 14 March 2004), and that of Sarah Nyedwoha to Sam Ntiro, a Tanzanian artist.
125 1 January 1965. For below, see *Uganda Argus*, 6 October 1965. Cf. the earlier appearance of such advertising in Zimbabwe: Burke, '"Fork Up and Smile",' and his *Lifeboy Men, Lux Women*.
126 Perlman, 'Some Aspects of Marriage Stability'.
127 *Uganda Argus*, 7 August 1965. For below, see Hoover, 'Aspects of Village Structure'.
128 Gerken, 'Social Structure,' p. 366. For below, see CultHist2 (Appendix B).
129 Musisi, 'Transformations of Baganda Women,' pp. 317–18. For below, see 16 April.
130 1 July 1965.

Part III

Radical Transformations
for Uganda & its Women

1971–2003

Seven

The Amin/Obote II Period
1971–86

The years between 1971 and 1986 were deeply troubled, for Uganda as a nation and for women in particular. During Idi Amin's regime, the second government of Milton Obote, and the brief rule of Tito Okello, political and military violence and the resulting dislocations resulted in the loss of 800,000–1,000,000 lives and the migration of millions of people. The collapse of the formal economy, the departure of the South Asians, and the acute shortage of basic goods caused great hardship. Education and health care suffered. Problems were especially great for women, many of whom were left as heads of their households through the death or absence of their husbands and facing gender-based violence as well. Simply to enable their families to survive, many women were forced into the cash-based economy, trying to gain some income through whatever means they could find. Whereas the previous history of women and their work in Uganda was a story of gradual evolution, these were years of abrupt and forcible change.[1]

During the Amin period and to some extent under Obote II, the government undertook a campaign of repression against women, backed by the press. Women's appearance and behavior were controlled, their positive contributions to the economy and society were largely ignored, and their organizations were banned, rising up again only in the mid-1980s. This negative official stance towards women was based upon an exaggerated version of the Domestic Virtue model. At the same time, however, that model demonstrated its adaptability once again, this time responding to the work done by female migrants to Kampala and the towns. The Petty Urban Trade variation said that a poor woman who had to work to support her family, especially her children, could be accepted as a good and respected person even if she were engaged in activities like making and selling food and drink or providing unskilled services.

The major events of this period can be summarized briefly here.[2] On 25 January 1971, Amin led an army coup that ousted Obote and the initial post-Independence government, naming himself head of a military regime. Amin's rhetoric, if not always his actions, courted the favor of socialist countries, whom he portrayed as his supporters against imperialism. Among the actions of his erratic and brutal regime was the expulsion of South Asians from Uganda in 1972. In

1979 the Tanzanian army invaded Uganda, leading to Obote's return to power. The next two years were marked by a growing power struggle between the older politicians (backed by foreign sponsors) and the young and relatively unknown leadership of more radical nationalist movements. In 1981 the National Resistance Movement, led by Yoweri Kaguta Museveni, split from the government and declared a people's war on Obote's regime. For the next five years the National Resistance Army engaged in guerrilla fighting (known as 'the bush war') against government troops. Mortality was highest in the Luwero Triangle north of Kampala. In July 1985, Tito Okello led a military coup against the Obote government, followed by six months of even greater instability and violence. In January, 1986 the NRA took control of Kampala and Museveni was sworn in as President. Those 15 years brought decolonization with a vengeance, as many of the inherited institutions of government and law broke down, but they also witnessed the destruction of many earlier forms of informal social regulation that had existed within the country's various ethnic groups.

Although the Amin/Obote II period had a profound impact upon women, the topic has not been thoroughly examined, in part because of poor sources. Written materials are limited. Many official and private records were either not maintained or destroyed during the fighting, and newspapers were under tight government control. Furthermore, people who lived through these years were often reluctant to talk about such painful times. The NRM government's decision to give a blanket amnesty to everyone involved in the disruption, except for Amin and Obote themselves, and its emphasis on setting aside the past in order to create a new, united Uganda have also tended to obscure what happened during the troubled years. Nor were many academics studying social and economic patterns at the time, with the notable exception of Christine Obbo, a pioneering Ugandan urban anthropologist.[3]

The following discussion integrates information from written sources with material from our interviews. The latter include both the Torchbearers and our district sample. For this period we have material from 107 district women: 20 who were aged 40 or over in 1985, 61 who were aged 20–39 at that time, and 26 who were aged 8–19.[4] Among the women who were children during the Amin/Obote II period, more were living in urban areas than had previously been true, reflecting a broader movement into the towns. Whereas 78–80 percent of the older interviewees had grown up in rural areas, only 63 percent of these women did so. The fraction living in Kampala itself was 6 percent, with most of the growth seen in district headquarters (17 percent) and peri-urban areas (14 percent). There was also a slight decrease in the proportion of women whose fathers were subsistence farmers or unskilled or semi-skilled workers (with most of the latter in the army or police). Nearly a third of the fathers were now in business, mainly in shops that sold goods other than food or drink, an increase as compared with earlier periods. The fraction of fathers who were teachers had declined to just one-eighth, with a slight rise in the proportion working in other professions or high-status occupations, mainly government jobs.

In this chapter we look first at the instability and violence of the period and at the collapse of the formal economy. After considering women's mobility and education, we examine the repression of women by the government and the press. The chapter ends with an analysis of the kinds of work women did and the evolution of Domestic Virtue expectations. As a visual introduction to this

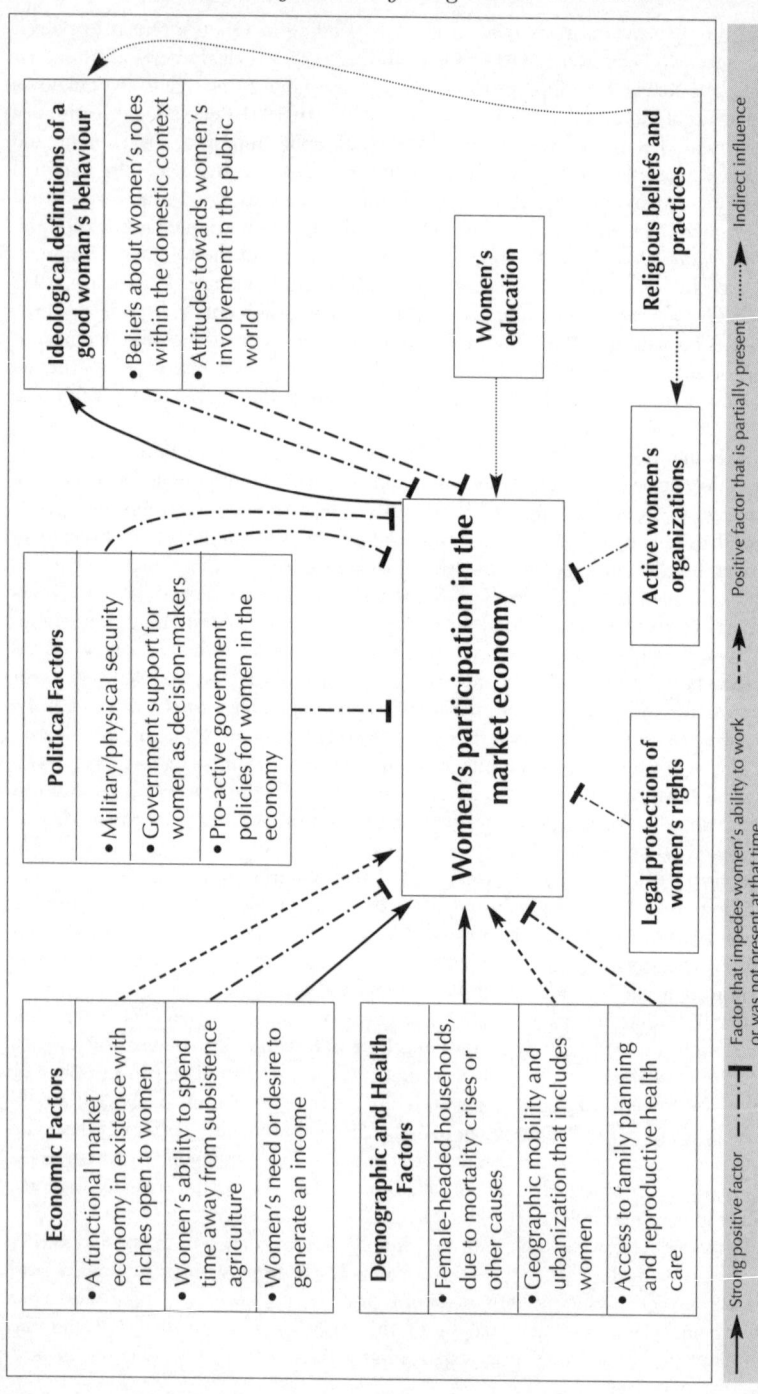

Ideological definitions of a good woman's behaviour

- Beliefs about women's roles within the domestic context
- Attitudes towards women's involvement in the public world

Women's education

Religious beliefs and practices

Political Factors

- Military/physical security
- Government support for women as decision-makers
- Pro-active government policies for women in the economy

Women's participation in the market economy

Active women's organizations

Legal protection of women's rights

Economic Factors

- A functional market economy in existence with niches open to women
- Women's ability to spend time away from subsistence agriculture
- Women's need or desire to generate an income

Demographic and Health Factors

- Female-headed households, due to mortality crises or other causes
- Geographic mobility and urbanization that includes women
- Access to family planning and reproductive health care

Strong positive factor

Factor that impedes women's ability to work or was not present at that time

Positive factor that is partially present

Indirect influence

Figure 7.1 Ugandan women's participation in the market economy, mid-1970s

discussion, Figure 7.1 summarizes the factors that promoted or stood in the way of women's economic participation during the mid-1970s.

Physical Violence and Economic Collapse

Violence stemming from political instability
Perhaps the single most disturbing feature of these years for women was the level of physical violence. Some of it came at the hands of individual soldiers, government agents, or paramilitary groups, while after 1979 many people were killed in fighting between government soldiers and the Tanzanian army or the NRA's forces. Although Amin's reign is better known among non-Ugandans, Obote – dogged by several guerrilla movements from the start of his second term of office – 'ruled with a ruthlessness that many believe was worse than Idi Amin's'.[5] While the exact number of men, women, and children killed under Amin and Obote will never be known, President Museveni estimated in the late 1980s that 300,000 people had died in 1971–9 and another 500,000 in 1980-86.[6] Byanyima believed that 500,000 were killed during the 1970s, which would raise the total to around one million people. Since the total population of Uganda was probably around 10 million at the start of Amin's rule, this is a very large fraction.[7] When one adds to mortality the hundreds of thousands of men who were fighting, hiding in the bush, or in exile, it becomes clear why so many women found themselves responsible for providing for their own families.

When the women in our district sample were asked about the Amin/Obote II period, two-thirds of them mentioned violence and insecurity. Especially in the north of Uganda, home to many men in the army, and in areas of aggressive fighting, women lost their husbands, fathers, brothers, or other relatives. Grace Ssembatia (Profile 5.1) said that her job as a teacher helped her to maintain her emotional stability, especially when her brother was killed in the Luwero area.[8] A young woman working as a library assistant in Lira town remembered that after battles, people 'were chased from their homes and everything was looted'. Some instances of violence were directed against political opponents. Thinking of her childhood along a road near Fort Portal, another woman said, 'During Obote II, most men were not sleeping in their homes at night. People falling under different political parties were always being hunted and killed.'[9] Thereza Kamugasa (Profile 8.1), recently married and living in a village outside Hoima, was left on her own with her young children for several months while her husband was carried away from home for political reasons.

More upsetting still were illegal murders and arrests by the government, army, or police with no reason given. Words like 'fear', 'terror', 'abduction', and 'harassment' abound in these accounts, as do statements that people were randomly arrested and then disappeared. A woman from Kabale said, 'My husband was kidnapped in Amin's regime and has never been seen to date.'[10] A woman living in Hoima explained that under Obote II, 'My husband was picked up by army men from his home and disappeared forever.' Another said of her childhood in a village outside Hoima, 'During Amin's time there was what they called "boarding the vehicle". Soldiers would move around with lorries or pickups and order people to board them. Most of the time they would be killed.'[11]

Eunice Kyamanya (Profile 6.1) described the violence and uncertainty of the Amin period. 'Men and women were picked up from their homes, their offices, the streets. They were beaten, imprisoned, or killed. No reason was given, and some who went into prison did not come back out. Every day you would hear about more people taken, in Kampala and in the villages too.' Her working environment was dangerous too. 'Radio Uganda was a central place, so we had to be very careful what we put on the air. Whenever there was a problem, soldiers would come to us. They would harass you, and you would have to control your movements so you wouldn't annoy them.'

The political and military turmoil of the period created a climate conducive to individual acts of violence against women and girls. This phenomenon has been noted more generally in Africa and Asia: militarization results in 'the mushrooming of a culture of violence against women in which "macho-ness" and brutality are dominant'.[12] As Byanyima commented about the Ugandan situation, 'Women peasants and workers were terrorized in the same ways as men but also had to endure rape. In fact, rape by soldiers became so common that a raped woman was often told she had only herself to blame for getting caught – soldiers were rapists and women were expected to know how to avoid them.'

Gender-based violence was mentioned by many of the women in our sample. A woman living in a village outside Hoima said, 'Amin's government was bad, and Obote II was the worst. Women were badly harassed: most of them were raped, and even young girls were defiled by old men.'[13] A woman who was helping in her husband's shop in a trading center in Lira District remembered that 'Tito Okello's regime though short-lived was full of terror, with killings and raping of women'. The risks were high for girls, especially those going to and from school. A midwife in Fort Portal recalled, 'Girls were raped by soldiers, and most men would "marry" girls forcefully when they were coming home from school in the evenings.'[14] A woman who was a schoolgirl in Kasese District during these years said, 'That was my most difficult period, because as a student I had to travel from the rural area to my school, and that was very insecure. Some of the girls were pulled off the bus by armed soldiers and never seen again, so there was a lot of fear.' Another woman was raped by a soldier while at her teacher training college.

Instability made it hard to operate a business. Under Amin, soldiers commonly extorted money from shopkeepers or arrested them and appropriated their goods. A woman who had just started a grain milling venture in Kampala with her husband and brother noted: 'We could not progress well in our business because of fear. If you started something new, people would say, "This one has a lot of money," and someone would start looking for you.'[15] Women were especially vulnerable. A woman who had recently opened her own tailoring shop in Kampala noted, 'My machines were looted and I lost supplies, so my business was set back a great deal.'[16] Another, who was trying to keep her husband's shop in Lira running, said, 'Women in business were fearful, because we were suspected to have been sending money to our husbands who were in the bush or in exile.' An Arua woman said that under Obote II, many women gave up their businesses entirely and resorted to digging (growing subsistence crops).[17]

Though militarization was damaging to many women, a few found more active and positive roles in the NRM's army in the bush. From the beginning the NRM was attractive to women. Some backed the movement because they shared their male counterparts' idealistic goals: overthrowing a repressive government, restoring democracy, peace, and human rights, and building economic security.[18] They were also attracted by the NRM's advocacy of women's issues. These included both shorter-term, practical gender interests (such as family survival needs, child care, and health services) and long-term, strategic gender goals (such as ending discrimination in employment, education, and politics and securing women's rights to life and dignity). As brutality by government soldiers against women and children mounted, some women turned to the NRM as a refuge. Furthermore, women responded positively to the NRM's mass-based mobilizing strategy, with its attempt to include major segments of society and cut across ethnic groups, religions, and classes, as well as gender. In the local organizations set up by the NRM, women participated fully in choosing leaders and making decisions. Other women joined for personal reasons: to escape from a difficult family situation, follow a boyfriend into the bush, or look for a husband. They did not, however, share a common set of attitudes about feminism or male domination. Apart from the sisterhood that developed among them and the idea that they were freedom fighters alongside their male colleagues, women guerrillas were not exposed to any explicit consciousness-raising activities.

Within the NRA, women played both combat and support roles. Most of them were uneducated rural women, though a few urban women were active too. During the first year women were not allowed to join the camps in the bush, but that position changed. In part because many men had been killed during Amin's reign and the early years of fighting, women came to play essential roles in commanding platoons, guarding prisons, and tracking down traitors who were sending information to government forces. Women of all ages and levels of education in villages and towns provided food, nursed the sick, and comforted those detained in government prisons. Perhaps most importantly, they provided an intelligence network essential for strategic planning.

Participation in the armed struggle had a great impact upon the women involved. Winnie Byanyima, one of the freedom fighters and later an important women's activist and Member of Parliament, argues that 'By joining the National Resistance Movement women were able to address and resolve some of the problems associated with their oppression by men in the larger context of a nationalist, anti-imperialist struggle. For Ugandan women in the early 1980s, there was no alternative for emancipation but to unite with men in an armed resistance. In the process, they acquired a sense of competence, self-confidence, and opportunity for self-determination.'[19] A Western political scientist suggests, 'The years of internal warfare in Uganda had profound effects on women's self-perceptions and men's perceptions of women . . . . It unwittingly thrust women into new roles and situations which fundamentally transformed their consciousness.'[20] Women who joined the NRM 'fought side by side with men. The sight of women carrying both guns and babies on their backs left an indelible impression on many. Women were involved in spying and in smuggling guns into the bush. In the cities, husbands taught their wives to drive and run their businesses in the event that they might have to disappear into the bush . . . . [The fighting] affected women's overall perception of their capabilities.' Such positive assessments of women's place in the army were, however, challenged in 2002 by a former soldier, China Keitetse, in a book – and later film – that alleged sexual abuse and other atrocities against young female soldiers during the bush war.[21]

Economic collapse

The other set of primary changes that affected women were economic. Beginning in 1971 with Amin's coup and creation of a military regime, the country suffered from a combination of global developments and the unwise policies pursued by its own government.[22] The most important international factor was the declining prices for cash crops. Between 1971 and 1978, a sharp drop in the world market price for coffee, Uganda's major export, damaged the incomes of government and producers alike.[23] By 1985, exports of cotton, tea, tobacco and groundnuts had also plunged. Because prices for cash crops were not adjusted upwards by the government-run Marketing Boards, local farmers began shifting back to subsistence agriculture: insofar as they continued to grow cash crops at all, they either stockpiled them or smuggled them across the border for illicit sale. The collapse of the formal economy, leading to a *magendo* (black market) economy, brought hard times for wage-earners, who lost their viability as a group.

Furthermore, the Ugandan government moved away from the outward-oriented policies pursued during the previous decade. 'Local industries were granted significant protection, the size and involvement of the public sector in economic activity expanded considerably, and members of the Asian community, which had dominated the industrial and commercial sectors, were expelled and their properties expropriated. Efficiency and financial discipline suffered, leading to a significant decline in output of about 20 percent during the 1970s.'[24] As the government's revenues dwindled, it relied increasingly on financing from domestic banks, which intensified inflationary pressures. Industrial production also declined. Whereas GDP growth in 1968–9 had been an impressive 11 percent, it declined alarmingly across the following years, dropping 12 percent in 1980 alone.[25] Due to uncontrolled inflation, the purchasing power of wages in 1984 was only one-tenth of its value in 1972. In 1981 Obote initiated a limited program of economic stabilization and adjustment, at the urging of the International Monetary Fund and World Bank. This predecessor to the later Structural Adjustment Programs led to a curbing of the *magendo* economy and inflation and three years of modest economic recovery.[26] But by late 1984 increasing political and military instability led to the abandonment of the program and renewed decline. The overthrow of Obote's second government was followed by economic chaos, including the closure of most of the remaining industries.

Economic insecurity had a negative impact upon women. Women living with husbands might need to supplement the family's income, while those who had been left either temporarily or permanently as heads of their families had to find ways of coping with their situation. As agricultural production shifted back to food crops, some women whose households had previously gained income from cash crops now planted more foodstuffs and sold some to compensate for the lost income. Other women moved into urban or peri-urban areas in the hopes of finding opportunities in trade or paid employment. These shifts commonly redefined gender roles. The position of working wives was strengthened in relation to their husbands: they earned and spent money, became decision-makers, and developed confidence. Even the wives of rich men, realizing that one day they might not have a husband to depend on, went out to earn money. Widows and other household heads who struggled to support their families alone gained experience in working outside the family environment. The economic basis for male dominance was thus weakened.

The women interviewed for this project stressed that economic change forced many women to find a way of bringing in their own income in order to keep their families alive. As NAWOU's Peace Kyamureku explained,

> During Amin's time and during the 1980s, more women started fending for themselves. In the rural areas life was getting worse for the women. There was scarcity, and they became more dependent on agriculture, tilling the land, getting food for survival. But even there, women started also producing some bit of excess for sale. They were in beans or milk, they were participating in that kind of trade, because they had to have a little money. In urban areas, things changed more. Life was hard, everything was very expensive, there were lines, and women had to come out and do some business. Some sold at home, in the sitting room, in the bedroom. Others came into the streets, selling in petty, informal trade or in small markets. So women got economic skills and started trading for themselves.[27]

A similar scenario was painted by UWFT's Lydia Rugasira:

> The rate of inflation was such that the man's salary was no longer sufficient, the woman had to chip in. The terms of trade for the Third World declined in the '70s, prices for cash crops went down, so supplementary incomes were needed, anything to bring in extra income. A lot of people left the villages, because what they were doing there – growing coffee, cotton, selling it – was no longer profitable. So they moved into town. And of course the women also moved into town and started providing services. They sold samosas, rice, simsim balls, but then some of them moved to restaurants and with time opened hairdressing salons.[28]

Two aspects of these economic shifts had particular importance for women: Amin's expulsion of the South Asians, and the problems of inflation, scarcity, and the *magendo* economy. On 2 September 1972, Amin ordered all non-citizen Asians living in Uganda to leave the country within three months.[29] An official account of Amin's 'Economic War' published in 1975 explained that he was told in a dream to expel the Asians; in a speech describing the plan the following day, he 'uttered that historic phrase, "The Asians, they milked the cow, but never fed it"'. Since the procedures Amin put in place did not distinguish between nationals and non-nationals, nearly all the 90,000 South Asians in Uganda departed, leaving behind the wealth they had accumulated, in some cases over several generations. The expulsion of the Asians was followed by harassment of Europeans living in Uganda, leading to more departures.

Although the government argued that Uganda's recent economic problems had stemmed from Indian traders' and industrialists' control of the commercial sector, including cash crop agriculture, the expulsion of the Indians wreaked at least short-term havoc, because there were so few Africans with business or entrepreneurial expertise.[30] The property appropriated from Asians, from local shops to large industrial conglomerates, was given out to Ugandans, mainly those with ties to Amin, creating a new class of inexperienced business operators that included many army men (or their girlfriends). The new Ugandan owners had considerable trouble keeping their ventures going after the initial stock of goods ran out, and many of the businesses failed. The more successful owners engaged in ostentatious display of their wealth, often linked to corruption.

In the longer run, expulsion of the South Asians, while legally and morally indefensible, nevertheless opened up an opportunity for more Ugandans to enter trade. As a cultural historian in Kabale commented, 'We got to know then that a Mukiga could own a shop.'[31] A factor in the decision of Fatuma Kasirye's husband (Profile 2.2) to move his photography shop from Ankole to Jinja in the later 1970s was the business opportunities created by the departure of the Asians, who had been concentrated in that town. Fatuma felt that although there was a shortage of goods, the first steps by Africans into business 'built up a lot of confidence in our people. Now you are seeing second-generation Ugandan traders.' A woman who was a medical student in Kampala during the early years of Amin's regime noted:

> Before Amin, Ugandans were generally not into trade. It was the Asians. If a Ugandan man or woman got a small corner shop, they would be driven out by the Indian in the next shop who would lower his prices below what they charged. Furthermore, Asians had access to credit, whereas Ugandans could not get loans. It was Amin's Economic War that allowed Ugandans to enter shops and sell. But because there was no history of selling among Ugandans, for men or women, they did not know how to run a big business. There was no training, no mentoring. So a big textile shop might drop to just selling bananas.[32]

Grace Ssembatia (Profile 5.1) agreed that, after the Asians left, the Ugandans stocked the shops they had acquired with little other than *chapattis* (an Indian-style fried pancake) and bananas.

At the bottom of the marketing system, a vacuum had been created that allowed some African women to start moving into trade. Eunice Kyamanya (Profile 6.1) said, 'When the Asians left, that was the time that more women came into business. Everybody tried to help themselves, there was no organization. People would get hold of anything and try. But for women it used to be humble business, not as competitive as what men would take. In one small shop, a small room, you'd find 20 women selling. Each one had about the width of one foot, putting there on the ground all her things and selling.' Sarah Kitakule of UWEAL explained, 'Expulsion of the Asians gave the indigenous Ugandans opportunities to venture out into commerce, which was not there before. That also paved the way for some women to get involved in business. A trickle of women began getting involved in shops.'[33] A rhetorically slanted example of this process was provided by *Voice of Uganda*, the government-controlled newspaper. Whereas women's activities outside the home were normally ignored during these years, one article in 1975 described a 50-year-old woman in Kampala who had worked for 18 years as a bride dresser but was then able to take over a tea room in the center of the city after 'the blood-suckers' left.[34] Thanking the President for handing over the economy to Ugandans, she attributed the success of her new venture to his Economic War.

The other major economic change for women stemmed from the combination of inflation, scarcity of goods, and the growth of the *magendo* economy. Inflation was acute, as measured by the cost of a bar of soap for washing clothes. In 1972 it cost about Ush 3; by 1979 it was officially Ush 17 but, almost entirely unavailable in shops, cost Ush50 on the black market; in December, 1985 its price was a minimum of Ush 2,000 in the towns but at least 50 percent more in rural areas.[35] Inflation was particularly hard on government and other waged employees, whose salaries were raised little if any and sometimes not paid at all for substantial periods of time. A woman whose husband was an officer at a virus research station in Arua recalled, 'During Amin's time, money lost its value. The salary we got was not enough to buy necessities: we had to resort to digging for survival. During Obote II, things were no better, as the currency continued to lose value.'[36] The wife of a soldier in Moroto said that, although his salary was still being paid, the money had become valueless. Her family survived on army food rations and the little money she picked up by selling groundnuts on the streets. Many female teachers and nurses in government-run institutions could not get by on their pay, and some of them changed jobs.

As industries and wholesaling activity formerly run by Asians gradually shut down, local shopkeepers were unable to maintain a supply of even basic goods. Kitakule described, 'It was very bad for women. The basics were just *gone* from the table. I remember before Amin, even in my little village there, you'd get jam at the shop, you'd get butter, you'd get bread, you'd get everything. Then suddenly those things just … zuup, those things just disappeared. Even salt was a luxury, soap was a luxury. I remember there used to be lines for supplies when things came in, you'd go queue (stand in line) at different shops. My mum would line up at one place, she'd send us to another shop, so that we could collect enough.'[37] If a family was able to obtain a reasonable supply, keeping it was dangerous in light of the government's prohibition of hoarding. 'When you did get things, you had to be careful, you couldn't keep them in the house. My mum used to put them in tins and then go dig a hole in the ground somewhere in the compound, and bury them there. Because the minute the soldiers or a government agent found a lot of anything in your house, it was called "hoarding" and you would be prosecuted.' When commercially produced goods were unavailable, women experimented with ways of making substitutes from locally available plants. 'I remember at that time we learned of a tree which would work as a soap, the leaves and the fruits. The women would go to this tree and would harvest those things, and that is what they used to make soap. They were just trying to find ways of surviving.'

A shortage of necessary daily commodities loomed large in the memories of the women in our district sample. A teacher in Apac District said, 'During Amin's time, items like soap, salt, and sugar were scarce. People who had them were looted, and the community were made to queue.'[38] When those items appeared, an Arua teacher remembered, 'you had to get in line as soon as they surfaced, or else wait and buy them at high price from smugglers'. Because women were aware that lack of soap and salt led to a decline in hygiene, health, and nutrition, they turned to local substitutes. Fulgencia Apio (Profile 2.3) described how they dried and burned one plant for salt and made soap from the roots of others. A Kabale woman who was selling second hand clothes that had been smuggled from Rwanda said she usually made her own soap from papaya leaves, but she still had scars from injuries she got while fighting for commercially produced soap.[39] An elderly Lira woman offered a fuller description of people's reactions to scarcity during those years:

> When we could not buy necessary items, men and women became ingenious and innovative. The blacksmiths made local hoes, cutlasses, and knives, and women produced local salt and made sugar from sugar cane. In my village, some women used papaya leaves or roots of the local plant called *elila* for soap, but I did not like these because the solution caused cotton clothes to get torn very quickly. I would start filtering fat or any kind of oil, boiling it until a black sediment was left at the bottom of the pot. I would carefully scrape that sediment and compact it in a

container to get shape while it cooled. I then used the tablet for washing clothes and bathing.[40]

Problems intensified during the early 1980s, due to import restrictions and scarcity of certain foods.

The combination of inflation and scarcity promoted a *magendo* economy. Because the majority of the population could not meet their basic needs in normal ways, they resorted to a variety of technically illegal activities.[41] For women, the most important components were black market trade and smuggling. Many women in our sample bought goods that had been brought into the country through *magendo* trade, while a few were themselves crossing the borders, traveling into adjacent regions of Kenya, Rwanda, or Zaire to obtain items for their own family's use. A woman living in the West Nile region said, 'One had to walk to Congo at least once each month, carrying food to sell for essential items like soap, salt, and clothes. This was a very risky business, because if the army men found you, they would take away all your money and leave you empty-handed.'[42] Other women prepared coffee that would be smuggled across the border, for which they were paid not in cash but in bartered goods.

Carrying cash crops or other goods out of the country on a regular basis was so dangerous that at first such trade was largely in the hands of men. But gradually women moved into this niche as well. An adolescent girl living in Kayunga District east of Kampala observed: 'During Amin's years I was old enough to understand. Women experienced suffering. They were carrying coffee on their backs through the valleys to Kenya. I believe that's when women's economic struggles started.'[43] Rugasira's aunt supported her family by going at night across the border to Kenya, buying a few things, and bringing them back for sale. By 1985, women in some parts of southwestern Uganda had replaced men as the main 'exporters' of food-stuffs and fish to Zaire and the main 'importers' of ladies' wear.

A teacher living outside Lira, whose husband was polygamous, described how she augmented her salary:

> Ugandan women are great people. From 1971 they became breadwinners automatically, whether the husband was there or in hiding. Wives were the providers of money and materials. They became *magendo* women. It was a time of turmoil but an eye opener for what women could do. They had to keep the children, pay for their school fees, and care for the husband in the bush as well as their co-wives. I supplemented my income by doing *magendo* business, selling hides and skins. I would load my vehicle in Lira and drive at night. At 5:00 a.m. I would go across to Malaba, Kenya. By doing that I was able to keep my children in boarding schools, pay wages to our workers, and care for my co-wives and buy them clothes, since the husband was hiding. Suffering during Amin forced women to participate in business.[44]

Both the Amin and the Obote governments tried in vain to control inflation, scarcity, and *magendo* activity. Amin fined those who sold at more than the desig-nated prices but employed more draconian measures, including public flogging and death by firing squad, against those who hoarded goods or committed other 'economic crimes'.[45] In January, 1981 the new Obote government ordered market traders and shopkeepers in Kampala to sell food and other essential items at a fraction of their previous free market prices.[46] This attempt to control black marketeering and corruption led the prices of many foodstuffs to drop by as much as 80 percent, which only intensified the crippling scarcities: vendors said they could not afford to sell at the new prices. By the following day *The [London] Times* reported that workers in Kampala found it impossible to buy any food. Nor did police round-ups of hundreds of street traders and confiscation of their goods increase the capital's food supply.[47] But female sellers did not experience the kind of gender-based attacks for causing high prices and shortages that occurred in Ghana during the 1970s.

The *magendo* economy had complex results in social terms, for it pulled both women and men into behaviors that conflicted with accepted norms and values.[48] The availability of cash in the hands of rich *magendo* men raised expectations for the level of bridewealth. For some single women, the chance to earn money through illegal trade loosened the pressure to enter into a traditional marriage; for others, concubinage with a wealthy man offered a way to gain the capital necessary to enter business. For some rural women who were already married but whose husbands opposed their involvement in smuggling or other kinds of illegal trade, *magendo* led them to disengage from marriage in order to set up their own businesses. A Lango song composed around 1980 speaks of a widow forced into *magendo* trade after her deceased husband's male relatives inherited his property; she then faced ill-will from other women who feared that her independent income would lead her to poach on their husbands.[49]

Geographic Mobility and Education for Women

Altered patterns of migration and education helped to shape the experiences of women during these troubled years. Instability led to mass movement of people. It has been estimated that more than 200,000 people left Uganda, in addition to the millions displaced from their homes within the country.[50] The exiles included some of Uganda's leading women. Sarah (Nyendwoha) Ntiro, married to a Tanzanian artist and diplomat, had worked in the Ministry of Education during the early Independence period and in the Vice Chancellor's office at Makerere University during the first part of the Amin period.[51] In 1978, however, she went to Nairobi, where she cooperated with the UN High Commissioner for Refugees in founding the Education Consultancy for Higher Education for African Refugees. Grace Ssembatia (Profile 5.1), then teaching at King's College, Budo and married to a rising lawyer, went to Kenya with her family due to Amin's threats against them. During Amin's rule, Eunice Kyamanya's husband (Profile 6.1) was imprisoned for a year because of his involvement with Obote's first government: she was pregnant at the time and did not know if she would ever see him again. When he was released in 1980, they went into exile in Tanzania. In other cases, only the husband fled the country, leaving his wife in charge of the household. A nurse in Soroti said, 'My husband was being sought, because he was a businessman. The rich, the highly educated were searched for and killed. He took refuge in Kenya.'[52] Women of lower status left too. A Muslim woman from West Nile, a region that suffered great violence under Obote II, explained that when her family went over the border into what was then Zaire, 'We lost everything. Because there was no way of getting money, you would even go three days without food. We lost our children to hunger.'[53]

**Profile 7.1. Working as a driver during the Amin/Obote II years:
'Joyce Munduru'**

Joyce Munduru supported herself and her family while in exile – as well as before and after – by driving vehicles.[54] Although this was an uncommon job for a woman, she used her skill as a trained driver in a variety of settings. Aged 45 years and living in Arua when interviewed, she was divorced and the head of a household that included three of her own six children, the children of her two sisters, and her brother's widow; she provided financial support for the children of two other deceased relatives who were living elsewhere. She lived in a house built during the colonial period as housing for junior (African) members of the civil service. Her dress was made from a colorful 'Kitenge' fabric, and she seemed self-confident and relaxed during the conversation.

Joyce, a Protestant Lugbara woman, was born in 1958 in a trading center in Arua District, where her father was a fishmonger and butcher. Her mother and other female relatives did not do any work that brought them a regular income, but they sold excess food when they needed cash. She went to a local, government-aided primary school, with the encouragement of both her parents. 'My father's attitude toward my education was very good. He wanted all his girls to go on with their education. My mother was very positive also about educating girls. She was the one who paid our school fees, by digging (growing vegetables and selling them). But I was not able to keep on with my education after P 7 (the seventh and final year of primary school) because I got pregnant. Those days pregnant girls were not allowed to continue with their education, so I dropped out.'

After the baby was born, she moved to Kampala, leaving the child at home with her mother. At age 18, she made a decision that was unusual for women of her generation: she joined the police. She went through general training at Masindi, after which 'I was forced by the police authorities to go to driving school'. After completing the training course for drivers, she became a police constable driver in Kampala. She worked 8 hours a day, for pay of 150 shillings per month. She sent some of her earnings home to her mother, keeping the rest for feeding and clothing herself. Although her mother appreciated that she was helping the family, most people in the community disapproved of her work, thinking it appropriate only for men.

Two years later, in 1978, several significant events occurred. Joyce married a businessman with whom she eventually had five children, and she was one of the drivers requisitioned by Idi Amin, then the head of state, for his own use. As she noted, when Amin demanded that the police give him drivers from West Nile, it happened! (Amin was from that area himself and probably felt safer with his own people.) Joyce continued to send much of her income home to her mother, to take care of the child who was living with her.

With Amin's fall from power, Joyce's situation changed dramatically. Because of her close association with him and the reprisals that began under Obote's second government, she was forced to flee the country. In 1981, at age 23, she went across the border from West Nile into Zaire, taking her children with her. Separated from her husband due to the fighting, she was the sole source of support for her household, which included members of her extended family who had also fled to Zaire. In need of income, she approached the French medical NGO, Médicins sans Frontières, to see if they needed a driver.

As she said, 'In exile, one had to survive. Things were very difficult, and I had to earn some money somehow.' MSF was pleased to hire her, and with her earnings she was able to buy food for her family. She noted that many female refugees were forced to start working and that, even within Uganda, after Amin's overthrow 'women started to learn to do things for themselves'. Before that time, 'there were hardships but women did not fend for themselves very much'. For her the transition was relatively easy: 'Since I was in the police, I already knew what it meant to be on your own.'

Joyce's life during the NRM period: When the situation in Uganda stabilized after the NRM came to power, Joyce returned home and was reunited with her husband. They had more children, who were aged 12–25 years at the time of the interview. Over the following 15 years, Joyce kept on driving, working for a series of NGOs in the West Nile area. Because she had 'many willing relatives', care of the children was not a problem. Increasingly, however, tension developed between Joyce and her husband. He was unhappy that she was so independent in financial terms, and 'he refused (prohibited) all my business plans: otherwise I would have made more money than what I have now.' He also reduced his own contributions to the household because she had an income, spending the money on drinking instead. She eventually obtained a divorce. In 2003, Joyce was still working as a driver, now for an NGO that dealt with refugees. She was solely responsible for all the people living in her family. In the future, Joyce expected to continue driving so that she would have a regular salary, but she wanted also to start supplying institutions like secondary schools with food, for a profit and she was building a house to rent out.

Some of the exiles stayed away for many years. A young woman doctor married to an architect left for Nairobi in the mid-1970s.[55] There she did a postgraduate course in public health while her husband worked for the UN Development Program. Later they moved to London, where she did further advanced training and charitable work. They returned to Uganda only in the mid-1990s.

Instability and economic disintegration led to considerable movement of women into Kampala, its peri-urban region, and the smaller towns.[56] Contemporaries were troubled by what they perceived as a flood of female migrants arriving in urban areas, on their own or perhaps with children, but without a husband. Yet Obbo's analysis of women migrants in a poor, peri-urban neighborhood of Kampala in 1971–4 found that by no means all of the women in her sample had come to the city alone: 49 percent either accompanied or followed their husbands to Kampala.[57] Of those who moved independently, many sought greater economic opportunity than was available in the villages, but others were trying to escape from unsuccessful marriages, the negative consequences of polygamy, or the restraints of widowhood.

The increased mobility of women into urban areas undermined customary family patterns. As a historian of Baganda culture commented, women suddenly began to move freely during the 1970s and early '80s.[58] Those living on their own in urban settings were outside male control, leading to lax morality and relationships other than marriage. Parents could no longer control their daughters or play their normal part in marriage negotiations. On the contrary, the girl might be bringing money home to them, a reversal of roles that destabilized relations

between the generations. Geographic mobility worked together with civil distur-
bances and inflation to disrupt familiar practices and weaken family ties.[59]

Education suffered during these years. Under Amin foreign support for
education declined at the same time as Uganda's economic problems decreased the
resources available from the country's own government.[60] Government expenditure on education as a percentage of the Gross National Income dropped from 4.1
percent in 1970 to 1.2 percent in 1980; by the later 1980s it was only 21 percent of
its level in 1970–71.[61] Violence led to the destruction of educational materials and
sometimes school buildings all over the country. Some private schools were
founded in an attempt to fill the gap, but inflation made it difficult for many
families to pay school fees. The expulsion of the Asians removed some of the
qualified teachers in Kampala and other towns, and although Makerere University
and Kyambogo Teacher Training College increased their intakes, nearly half of
the qualified teachers who graduated each year left the country to work elsewhere,
especially in Kenya. Mary Katushabe (Profile 2.4) noted that the importance of
education was questioned during these years, especially when contrasted with the
great wealth of some of the army men and others close to the government.

The problems were compounded for girls. Not only did the threat of violence
make traveling to school dangerous; instability had secondary effects as well.
Margaret Birungi (Profile 9.1), who had hoped to continue her education after her
A-level exams, was unable to do so because her family's life was disrupted by an
escalation in fighting between the NRA and government forces near Hoima.
Although the proportion of girls who received some primary education rose slightly
between 1970 and 1980, the increase would presumably have been much greater
under stable conditions. Furthermore, a study of job expectations among children
aged 12–13 carried out in the early 1980s suggests that the aspirations of girls were
lower than in the early Independence years.[62]

At the university level, though rather more Ugandan women were receiving
professional degrees during these years, their involvement remained fairly constant
in percentage terms. At Makerere University's graduation in October, 1971, 30
Ugandan or other East African women received undergraduate degrees in
education, social work, law, medicine, or agriculture, while another 11 received
postgraduate diplomas.[63] They constituted 20 percent of the bachelor's degrees and
15 percent of the diplomas. In 1978, the 94 Ugandan women who earned undergraduate degrees in a now wider array of professional fields formed 17 percent of
all graduates.[64] Among the Ugandan women engaged in post-secondary education
in 1980, 31 percent were studying law or business, and 25 percent were studying
science/medicine, engineering, or agriculture.

Some women who wanted to train for a profession in this period faced
considerable resistance from their families and others. Miria Matembe, later an
important women's activist, Member of Parliament, and Minister in Museveni's
government, decided while in secondary school that she wanted to study law.[65]
Her father, a small farmer in Ankole, opposed the idea. 'One day when I was
discussing these plans, he attempted to block my way. "No, not my daughter," he
said. "You can't do this, not a girl in my house. You just study nursing or
teaching. You go and study to be a nurse at Mulago [Hospital in Kampala].
Otherwise you will no longer be my daughter".' Matembe decided, however, that
since the government was paying her fees at secondary school and would continue

to do so if she entered the university, 'I didn't really need my father's money or his consent. So, I thought angrily, for me, I will study my law. I can't help it if he doesn't agree.' When she was accepted at Makerere, her father refused to sell a cow to enable her to buy clothing, shoes, and a watch, but she was assisted by an older friend of the family.

The women in our interview sample who were children during these years attained a higher level of education than was the case for the country as a whole, with all of them receiving at least some primary schooling. Nearly half ended their studies with primary or secondary school, while more than a third went on to obtain some kind of certificate or advanced diploma. Fourteen percent graduated from university, and a few continued for postgraduate training. Most of that higher education occurred after 1986, however, when conditions had stabilized again.

Probably because of the economic disruption of the period, seven of these women worked while they were in school to help pay their fees (27 percent), the highest fraction in any period.[66] A Bagisu woman from Eastern Uganda said that when she was 15, in 1974, 'I began working to buy books and shoes for school. Rising at 5 a.m., I would go to school and then run back to my jobs in the afternoon, either picking coffee or growing cotton.'[67] Children were not normally hired for such tasks, but her parents appreciated the money she earned, and other people in the community respected her willingness to work. A Madi woman in Arua, who later became a nursing administrator and businesswoman, displayed her entrepreneurial approach while she was in school.[68] To help pay for her education, she began to design and make tablecloths, which she then took to the market to sell. 'I wanted to raise money for scholastic materials, and this was the only way I could, since I had sewing skills.'

The parents of these girls were less supportive of their education than had been true during the early Independence years, perhaps in part because circumstances were so disrupted that the future rewards of schooling were unclear.[69] Although two-thirds of the fathers backed their education, the remainder were opposed or indifferent during at least part of their schooling. 'My father's attitude was negative. He referred to girls as useless, and he stopped me from going to school.'[70] Several Muslim girls said that their father's position had shifted as they grew older. In one case it improved. 'My father had a Muslim background, and in those days Muslims did not take their children to school. So his attitude was very poor during my early years at school. But when I reached secondary school, he could see the advantages and his interest picked up.'[71] The change could also go the other way. 'My father liked my education and wanted me to be a nurse, so he got me started in training. But because he was a Muslim, he then got me a man, and I was married off, so I had to leave the course.'

The mothers of these girls were more positive, perhaps because a higher fraction than before were themselves engaged in some kind of income-generating activities.[72] Three-quarters of the mothers supported their daughters' education, often helping to pay their fees, while another 15 percent wanted them to be in school but could not provide financial support. A woman whose parents both ran little shops in a trading center outside Hoima said, 'My mother wanted me to study very much and become an important person in the future.'[73] (The daughter now runs a large hardware store and transport business with her husband.) Only 8 percent were negative or indifferent. A Muslim woman who grew up in Mbarara town, where her father was a butcher, said that one of her father's other wives did not like her going to school and influenced him against it.[74]

Repression of Women by the Government and the Press

In addition to the problems caused by political and economic instability, Ugandan women suffered from a campaign of deliberate, gender-based repression. It was enacted through direct government orders and reinforced by the ways women were portrayed or excluded from representation in the press. Perhaps because the Christian churches were themselves being attacked by the government, they did not stand up in defense of women.

In a striking turnaround from the official position adopted during the early Independence years, which had promoted at least qualified public participation for women, the governments of Amin and – to a lesser extent – Obote II assumed a highly negative stance. Except for those occasions when the government wished to present itself to outside observers as supporting the advancement of women, the official rhetoric valued only married women who remained at home, attending to their husbands and children. Female submission and deference were stressed, and husbands were encouraged to discipline their wives. The work of the many women who had of necessity moved into the cash-based economy was either ignored entirely or condemned on the grounds that it constituted inappropriate competition to men and led women to abandon their proper roles within the family. They were not welcomed in government, nearly all their organizations were shut down, and the activities of the few groups that remained were often trivialized. Women visible in public settings were commonly portrayed as sexual objects, leading to repressive measures that regulated their appearance and behavior. It has been suggested more generally that the flip-side of violence against women in destabilized settings is 'contempt for women expressed through reactionary notions of women's proper place in society'.[75] Yet efforts to drive women back into their 'proper' roles in the home are often 'sharply at odds with the reality that many women *have* to seek employment in order to feed their children and themselves'. That was certainly the case in Uganda during the Amin/Obote II period.

The public stance assumed during these years may be explored through the government's policies and actions and through what was published in the newspapers. Because the media were tightly controlled by the government during this period, the papers reveal those positions officials wished to publicize, rather than offering even a semi-independent voice. In 1975, chosen as a sample year, only a single newspaper (*Voice of Uganda*) was published. The articles, editorials, photographs, and letters that its editors decided to print are a reflection of the opinions of the Amin regime.[76] *Voice of Uganda* disappeared in 1979 with the change of government and was replaced by *Uganda Times*, printed until 1984. In 1985 no papers were being published on a regular basis.

Voice of Uganda in 1975 offers a startling contrast to the papers printed between 1955 and 1970. It contained no articles or sections written primarily for women; it displayed no concern with women's issues and no sense that women formed part of the paper's readership. One would barely know from the paper that women were working at all: there was no regular coverage of their activities and no discussion of the problems they faced. The paper printed almost nothing about women completing their education or training or about women's clubs. There were no letters to the editor by women. When women appeared at all, it was usually to be scolded for misbehavior. The few photos of women reinforced conventional and narrow stereotypes of good or bad behavior, both in ultimately sexual terms: they were either loose women wearing short skirts in morally doubtful settings, or beautiful women dressed in 'traditional' clothing who remained in acceptable roles.

The government defined appropriate female dress and appearance, often through presidential decrees that carried the force of law. The penal code of June 1972 prohibited mini-skirts, skirts with a slit that extended above the knee, and trousers, especially hot pants.[77] Urban women were coerced into obeying the decree 'by mobs of men or by soldiers who were empowered to arrest and even enjoy sexual licence over such women'. Although Amin always encouraged women to wear long Ugandan dresses, in 1975 he became aware that loose trousers were part of Islamic women's clothing in other parts of the world, so he revised the earlier decree. Now Ugandan women were permitted to wear pants if they were not tight-fitting. That same year a major in the army who had been named as Governor of Central Province threw a woman out of a dance hall because he 'could hardly tolerate the sight' of her: the photograph shows her from the back wearing long trousers but a skimpy top. The Governor said that he respected 'all women in the province because they the mothers of our nation [sic]. But as mothers they must wear decently.'[78] In 1975 Amin banned the use of make-up and creams, especially skin lighteners. Noting that such preparations made women look like half-castes, monkeys, gorillas, or lepers, he said it was no wonder if men drove their wives away from home when they used these products.

The government also attempted to regulate many aspects of female behavior. As part of the 1972 campaign to enforce morality, Amin ordered the streets of Kampala to be cleared of unmarried women, all of whom were alleged to be prostitutes.[79] Even married women might be picked up by the police if they were not in the company of their husbands. Because a woman could never be certain that she would not be arrested, the streets were sometimes deserted except for policemen. Abortions were banned. Amin was uncomfortable about having Ugandan women study outside the country. In 1975 he prohibited girls from going abroad for training under the sponsorship of foreign embassies, on the grounds that when they returned, they would take jobs in Ugandan government ministries or other organizations and spy for the countries that had arranged for their study.[80]

Articles and letters in *Voice of Uganda* in 1975 echoed the government's repressive stance, drawing implicitly upon the negative corollary of the Domestic Virtue model concerning women who flouted conservative expectations. An article opposing women who wore wigs, had long red fingernails, or painted on a vermilion mouth noted that 'H. E. General Idi Amin has always supported the pure traditionalists'.[81] Challenging Western ideas of slender beauty, it commented, 'In African eyes, it is difficult to separate beauty from usefulness. A useful girl will usually be a beefy one, good at digging as well as at child-bearing.' It quoted a 70-year-old farmer's objection to beauty contests. 'Before the White man came, we told a good girl from a bad one by the way she worked in the fields, by her rate of giving birth, her cooking and her care for husband and children. In the beauty parade, I'm told the judges look at the shape of the girls' legs. Do her legs produce any children?' Enforced marriage was proposed as the answer to immorality. One letter attacked unmarried 'town/city women dwellers, who think that to be free from marriage is to maintain more enjoyable life and comfort'.[82] Because such women 'spoil good married and working-class ladies', cause divorce, and carry venereal diseases, the author called upon 'our beloved President . . . to enact a decree [requiring] women to get married at a certain age'.

The paper also made clear that women were to be disciplined by their husbands, sometimes using Amin's treatment of his wives as an example. An article that focused on women's appearance commented approvingly, 'Husbands and wives are usually affectionate partners – though a good beating for a lazy wife is still considered quite in order.'[83] An editorial criticizing Jomo Kenyatta for not rebutting allegations that his wife was trading illegally said that he had committed a blunder 'by leaving the shrew untamed'. He would not have had this problem 'if only he had followed Marshal Amin's experience in disciplining wives'.[84] An article and photo described Amin's visit to a former wife who was in the hospital after a car accident. Bringing her children with him to listen to the lecture, Amin told her that her wildness and drinking stemmed from the fact that she had converted to Islam but then returned to Christianity. We have no quantitative information about domestic violence in these years, but one suspects it was high.

Politically too, women were sidelined. Parliament (which had contained only two women during the period 1962–71) was suspended under Amin. The few women who were named to government positions had gained his personal approval, which at least implicitly rested upon their personal appearance or social behavior. In 1975, *Voice of Uganda* reported on four women who had been appointed to various government offices, but there was no mention of these women's educational qualifications or work experience.[85] Two of the three unmarried women were shown in photographs: the district commissioner of Busoga Province, and the Ugandan ambassador to West Germany, later named also as ambassador to the Holy See. They were young (one was said to be 27 years old), beautiful, and dressed in 'traditional' clothing. The fourth appointee, a woman named as permanent secretary in the Ministry of Provincial Administration, was described by Amin as having 'good reports and a clean record'. Noting that some women might even prove to be better officers than men because they did not drink, he encouraged her to maintain her dedication to duty. When parliamentary elections were held in 1980 under Obote, only a single woman was chosen out of 145 members.[86] She was named as the sole female deputy minister in a Cabinet of over twenty ministries; one woman served as a permanent secretary and three as under secretaries.

Fear of female sexuality is suggested by the treatment of Elizabeth Bagaya (a princess of Toro before the abolition of the kingdoms) by the government and press in 1974–5. Miss Bagaya, a British trained barrister and former fashion model, was named as Foreign Minister early in Amin's regime. In November, 1974, however, she was dismissed from office when Amin accused her of having sex with an unknown European in a toilet at an airport in France.[87] Miss Bagaya was placed under house arrest for some months in Kampala before slipping across the border into Kenya. In January 1975 *Voice of Uganda* published a supposedly nude photo of

Miss Bagaya taken while she was living abroad and working as a top model for *Vogue* magazine. The accompanying article said, 'It appears that Miss Bagaya was prevented [from pursuing her law practice] by the imperialists who kept harping on her attractive charms until they plunged her into an abyss of immorality. ... This behavior now confirms what President Amin said of Miss Bagaya [about the French airport incident].' Some people said that it was her refusal to submit to Amin's sexual demands that had led to this brutal treatment. That the government was sensitive about its treatment of Miss Bagaya is suggested by a vitriolic article published by *Voice of Uganda* three weeks later. It attacked a journalist who had written in a British paper about why she was removed from office.[88] In remarkably derogatory rhetoric, the responding article accused the British journalist of a long list of offences, concluding that he was 'an international madman now destined for a mad house'.

Women's participation in their own organizations was restricted during the Amin/Obote II period. This was again in marked contrast to the early Independence period. When Amin came to power, he declared that all women's organizations apart from those with a religious function would be abolished.[89] In their place he proposed a national women's organization whose department of religious affairs would take over the functions of the Mothers' Union and the Catholic Women's Guild. *Voice of Uganda* was practically silent concerning women's organizations. When they were mentioned at all, it was usually in demeaning terms. In 1975, for example, a photo shows a meeting of the Uganda Muslim Women's Association for the Central Province.[90] Although the caption says that the women were discussing the activities to be carried out in connection with International Women's Year, it trivializes this issue by stressing that the members spent much of their time marching and drilling, knitting, and making handicrafts. The photograph shows two teams of women – attractively dressed in 'traditional' clothing – having a tug-of-war with a long rope.

In 1978 Amin passed a decree establishing the National Council of Women (NCW) and banning all other groups like the YWCA.[91] Some organizations became dormant, while others operated quietly underground. The change can be seen in the records of the Mothers' Union. Whereas the MU had been organizing seminars in 1971 on such topics as 'The Church and Politics,' promoting the civil and political education of women and discussing how church women should participate in government and the economic life of the nation, by 1977–8 it was reporting a declining membership, shrinking income from fees, and a return to a teaching program that focused narrowly on household skills.[92] Furthermore, whereas Ugandan women had taken part in international organizations during the early Independence period, the Amin/Obote II era interrupted this pattern. It was dangerous for women to participate in outside activities without the government's approval (which was rarely granted), and the economic collapse made it difficult to finance foreign travel. Yet at least a few organizations, like the MU, quietly maintained some international contacts.[93]

Although Obote allowed some women's organizations to resume operations, his UPC attempted to turn the NCW into a party organ and force other groups to support it. These efforts were not entirely successful. In 1983, for instance, the bishop of Kigezi Diocese sent an angry letter to the UPC's district head in Kabale.[94] In it he protested against an order sent to the local Mothers' Union, instructing it to go to Tororo, on the other side of the country, to take part in a political rally organized by the UPC. While, he said, individual members of the Mothers' Union were free to take part in politics, the organization as a whole did not align itself with the UPC or any other party. Furthermore, although 'the Mothers' Union is a gifted Christian women's group in singing Christian songs and rejoicing and dancing, it is not a "singing or dancing club". I would not be happy therefore to see the Mothers' Union criss-crossing Uganda, singing and dancing at Government functions.' After Tito Okello seized power, the NCW organized a march of more than 2,000 women in the streets of Kampala in September, 1985, rallying for peace and protesting against the mistreatment of women by the military.[95] This, the only peace march in the period, made clear the NCW's determination to become an autonomous organization.

The International Women's Year (IWY) proclaimed by the United Nations for 1975, and the international women's congress held in Mexico in connection with it, placed the government of Uganda in an awkward dilemma. While Amin wanted to appear in the eyes of the world a modern, progressive ruler – sometimes a ruler who accepted socialist principles – in fact he had no sympathy with the goals identified by the UN for the women's year.[96] After some initial grumbling, the government decided to cooperate with the IWY at least on the surface. In a speech on 1 May, Amin linked issues of labor with the IWY, praising Uganda as a country where men and women were equal in their work.[97] (He also denounced women who were guerrillas, spies, hid weapons under their wigs, or revealed the secrets of their husbands or lovers to 'imperialists or Zionists'.) The speech made by his then favorite wife, Mrs. Madina Amin, noted women's achievements in Uganda but stressed that 'the greatest responsibility we have towards our society is that we are mothers. We are either actual mothers or potential ones but the fact remains that we are mothers. We must at all times play the role of mothers to our men.'[98] The government agreed to let a small delegation go to Mexico in June, but it did not pay for the trip: all finances had to be raised privately, in part through a dinner dance held in April.[99] The only article in favor of women's rights was published in *Voice of Uganda* several months after the Mexican meeting on a page that talked mainly about entertainment, and the meeting had no official impact in Uganda.

A better reflection of the government's attitude towards the IWY came in the letters, poems, and cartoons that *Voice of Uganda* chose to print in 1975. Some letters argued that the IWY's goal of equality for women reversed the law of nature or was impossible because 'women are physically, psychologically, and categorically weak. Therefore the equal rights they are fighting for will not be equal to their strength.'[100] Men were worried that the Ugandan women who went to the meeting in Mexico would come back with undesirable ideas. A poem in the *Voice*'s Literary Corner simultaneously ridiculed and lamented 'women's war for equality'.

Who will sew a button on dad's shirt? For you
will be equal; Who will do it at all? Never mind woman;
Who will mend the ageing trouser? For you will
Be like dad; You will insult him much; But don't lose hope;
I cry for the 'good old days,' when you were quiet
And never warring: You will remain so but better recognized.[101]

Illustration 7.1 Cartoon about International Women's Year,
Voice of Uganda, 29 April 1975

A cartoon (Illustration 7.1) suggested male fear that if poor women learned about the IWY, they would demand outrageous privileges, like eating chicken (reserved for men in some Ugandan cultures).

Despite official and informal opposition, the IWY did have an impact on some women, encouraging them to speak out for their rights. A moving speech was given in 1975 at an exhibition of craftwork in Ruwenzori Diocese by Betty Kanyamunyo, the women's worker and MU coordinator for the province.[102] Kanyamunyo offered a powerful restatement of the image of women common during the early Independence period: women could be engaged in public activities, contributing to their country, while still carrying out their duties at home. Calling on more women to get involved in the MU, she commented: 'The Church and society needs our service. We can organize our houses well and combine our place at home as mothers and wives with the service to the society or church and the nation. We have to come to an agreement with our husbands about it and inform them on the work we are doing and get them to be interested in it.' Although she emphasized that 'our families should always come first,' she continued:

> For centuries, the women have been kept in the rear in the life of the society. If we consider our own tribe we come from, what places were given to our mothers, grandmothers? Digging in the field, bringing up children and looking after the ordinary affairs of the home made up the life of most of the women in Uganda. We may perhaps have unpleasant memories of how our own relatives, Aunties, Mothers, Grandmothers, objected to our going to school. Even if education was

good for us, surely primary education was more than we needed, high education was for our brothers not for us.

Women must realize, Kanyamunyo continued, 'that persons without self-respect are unable to accomplish great things, because their feelings of inadequacy pull them down from the mountain that they hope to climb. This is very often the point where we as women fail.... We have to learn that self deprecation is not a virtue, but it is a sin because it allows us to escape responsibility by claiming ignorance and inadequacy.' She concluded her talk by referring to the IWY and its demand for women's rights. 'What are these rights we are looking for now? It is up to women, every one of us, to work hard to be recognized as equals to men in a developing society. We need to be aware of our potentials and abilities to apply them in a meaningful way, and at the same time men should recognize women as their equals and so build together on a new society.'

We gain a personal sense of how women's awareness of their rights and their ability to organize increased during the later part of the Obote II period from Eunice Kyamanya's account (Profile 6.1) of her own participation in women's activities. Between 1981 and 1985 she was working for Radio Uganda, after she and her husband returned from exile. In 1982, she said, the wife of one of the government ministers returned from a visit to Nairobi full of enthusiasm about an association started there for media women. 'She mobilized us, saying, "We have problems that are peculiar to us as women working in the media." When we set up the Uganda Media Women's Association, one of our objectives was to share skills and network, but we were not very experienced. Little by little, we learned. We read about the UN's Convention on Eliminating Discrimination against Women [CEDAW], we agreed that we would not promote songs that misrepresented women, we monitored newspapers and radio programs to see where women and their concerns were not properly addressed.'[103]

The Uganda Media Women's Association became more active in 1984, in conjunction with Uganda's first celebration of International Women's Day. 'Somebody at Radio Uganda received a transcription of a program from New York, describing an International Women's Day. We began talking about it, saying, "We have never heard about it, but we must join in celebration of this day." We rang the Women's Desk at the UPC Secretariat to tell them, and they contacted the first lady, Mrs Obote. She said, "Yes, we must". So we moved very fast, we organized, we prepared a statement of women's complaints. At the first Uganda Women's Day, held at the State House in Entebbe, the President came and addressed us. He challenged us, saying, "You women, you are the ones who do most of the digging. Uganda is an agricultural country. You complain of poverty, so why don't you sell produce to improve your own lot?"'

The biggest impact came from the International Women's Conference held in Nairobi in July 1985. On the job Eunice was involved in spreading official information about the meeting, since the government used Radio Uganda as its publicity office. As the conference approached, the NGOs and women's organizations of each nation were charged with preparing a 'country paper' that documented their particular situation. Eunice represented the Uganda Media Women's Association on the committee that wrote Uganda's paper. She was then asked to attend the official conference as a member of the government delegation as well as representing the Uganda Media Women's Association at the parallel conference organized by NGOs and women's organizations.

Obote's government was concerned about the possible repercussions of the conference. It attempted to control who went to the NGO wing of the conference, denying visas to some of the more militant women who had hoped to participate. Obote did not trust even the official delegates.

> Before we left, the President spoke to us. For him, he was not converted to believing in this meeting. I think that he feared that when we went out, we would come back with bad ideas, we would be over-vocal about the liberalization of women. He said, 'You are going to meet people who are coming from better developed countries. Don't put your heads too high in the sky. Remember that the Convention [on Eliminating Discrimination against Women] has not been passed by all countries.' But because I had been involved in these other activities, I was determined to go. I had a 5-month-old baby, but I told my husband, 'You take care of the baby, I have to go to this Conference.'

Obote's reference to CEDAW was certainly intended as a threat: Uganda ratified the Convention only on 22 July of that year, a week after the opening of the Nairobi Conference. But, as Eunice pointed out, 'Obote left before he could see the results of the Conference. I had just come back from Nairobi, I had not even unpacked my suitcase, when we heard on the radio about Tito Okello's coup.'

The Ugandan women who went to Nairobi were indeed transformed, as Eunice explained. 'Our experience there was that some people had gone ahead of us. For example, we learned from workshops that in Kenya they had started addressing issues like men who spent too much of the family income on pleasing themselves outside the home, eating meat, when there were poor meals in the family. One lady came to a workshop who had been driven out of her home by her own husband, who had found a younger girl. But they told us we had legal rights, we could organize, we could do something about it.' The excitement and optimism of that period came to life as Eunice told of what followed.

> When we came back here, everything mushroomed. Women's groups came back, we rose up, and the impact was so great. Women were really mobilized. ACFODE was the most important, but many organizations were formed. The Uganda Media Women's Association covered all this activity, even though we had no office, no money. But we worked together to publicize what women were doing, in all the different parts of the country. Information went out about women, for the very first time.

Women's Work and Domestic Virtue

Women's work

The political and military disruption and economic uncertainty of the Amin/ Obote II period forced hundreds of thousands of women to find ways of generating some income, despite the opposition of the government and media. For many rural women coping with the impact of violence and economic collapse, especially those who found themselves at least temporarily as household heads, it seemed safest to remain in the village. Kitakule described this as a matter of simple survival: if women came to town, they could not be sure of finding food for their children or a place to live.[104] 'In the village you know that you have a garden, you can plant greens, if you are lucky to have salt, you can put some salt in the greens, and cassava. At least you are able to feed the children. They might have to drop out of school if you are not able to meet their school fees, but they are alive.' Furthermore, as production of cash crops diminished and then almost ceased entirely, rural women had more time and labor to devote to growing food on a subsistence basis.[105] In towns too, women took up backyard farming to feed their family in the face of inflationary prices.

Yet even those households that grew virtually all their own food needed at least a little cash. Many women therefore tried to earn money by selling surplus crops or through other activities. Of the mothers of women in our district sample who were living in villages or peri-urban areas during this period, only 19 percent had no income-producing activities at all. As Kitakule said, 'My parents would go to the garden, and if there was a bunch of sweet bananas, instead of our eating it, they would put in on a stool by the roadside. If you're able to sell it, you can use that money for what you need to buy.'[106] The problem for rural women was that they had no information and no capital for growing anything other than the familiar food crops, which all their neighbors were doing as well. While demand was therefore limited to Kampala and other large towns, the disappearance of Indian-run distribution systems meant it was hard to get food to urban markets.

Though many rural women were thus responsible for feeding their families and often generating a cash income as well, their contributions were not recognized. Tadria pointed out in the mid-1980s that gender-based valuation of labor remained strong: 'A man is highly regarded because he is essentially a cash earner (even if he is not earning cash), whereas a woman is underrated because she is regarded essentially as a dependant (even if she is earning cash).'[107] 'The important roles played by women in household and village economies are not suitably remunerated either in kind or material.' The undervaluation of women's work is reflected in the few mentions of women in agriculture in *Voice of Uganda* in 1975. One photograph showed a well-dressed, smiling woman throwing food for her sparkling clean pigs, over a caption that said that animal farming might be well suited to women, who care for them as they do their own babies.[108] An article in the 'Farming Voice' column commented that women often shared farm work with their husbands. Other evidence indicates that women provided the majority of agricultural labor, in many cases being over-burdened by physical demands even if an adult male was present in the household.[109] These observations complicate the debate over the 'feminization' of food production in twentieth-century Africa.

Other women decided to leave their villages in search of better opportunities. The problem was that few of the women who flocked into the towns had any employable skills, any capital, or any experience in earning money. The first step for many was therefore making and/or selling drink or food on a very small scale, carrying skills learned at home into the cash-based economy. Obbo's study of poor migrant women in Kampala in the early 1970s found that, of those who had some kind of income, 39 percent were brewing and selling beer or distilled drinks or working in bars; another 11 percent cooked and sold food.[110]

Profile 7.2 Making ends meet by selling food and drink: 'Jane Kamusiime'

Jane Kamusiime, interviewed when she was in her mid-fifties, supported herself by selling maize flour in the main market in Kabale town.[111] Probably born around 1947 (she did not know the year but estimated her age by having gone through the menopause), she had never married. She had cohabited with at least one man and had two children, though 'one has not been heard from in a very long time and the other died'. In 2003 she was supporting the grandchildren who lived with her. At the time of her interview, Jane was seated on a low stool at her stall in the section of Kabale market devoted to the sale of flour. Her stall, roughly 6 x 8 ft. in size, faced onto one of the walkways in the market; it had a metal roof over it and other stalls on each side. She had a large bag of flour open beside her, using a metal cup to scoop it out for customers. Between sales, and while chatting with people who came by, she wove baskets.[112]

Jane was born in a village outside Kabale, where her father and mother 'were just cultivating crops to feed the family'. A Protestant Mukiga, she never attended school and was therefore illiterate and innumerate throughout her life. Her parents were pleased when she began to work at a young age.

During Amin's regime, her life became difficult. Because 'the economy was in a shambles, money became hard to get'. When she tried to find ways to bring in some income, she discovered that 'working conditions were harsh'. She therefore migrated to the town of Kasese, where she and her two young children moved in with a man, sharing the single room he rented. As he was not able to support them fully, she began to brew and sell beer and other alcoholic beverages. The man ('my husband at that time') gave her the money with which to start brewing. Sale of alcohol was illegal during Amin's rule, so Jane 'sold from under her bed,' keeping her brew hidden from official notice. She worked every evening and night, from 6:30 p.m. to 1:00 a.m., earning what she described as the equivalent in contemporary terms of Ush 1,000 (US$0.50) per night.

Like other women engaged in this trade, she was vulnerable. She was frequently harassed, by soldiers and others, some of whom demanded money in return for not reporting her, and she was robbed many times. Yet, because her brewing as well as any sex work she may have done were illegal and looked down upon by others in the community, she could not complain to the police about these problems. When asked in our interview why she had done this risky type of work, she said simply, 'I needed to survive'. She continued to brew and sell for several years, buying food and necessary household things for herself and the children with her income.

After that 'husband' died, while her children were still under the age of ten, Jane moved back to Kabale and began to sell bananas at an informal market on the edge of the town. This was during the Obote II period, when, she explained, trade with nearby Rwanda – much of it illegal – blossomed. Because people now had cash, her new work was more profitable than beer selling. In addition to covering her family's expenses, she even managed to build her own house.

Jane's life during the NRM period: The NRM period was generally favorable for her, though the Rwandan war in the 1990s temporarily hampered cross-border trading. As of 2003 Jane's life was relatively stable. She enjoyed being back in her home area, and she felt a little more secure economically. She earned 'maybe 2,000' Ush a day (US$1), but since she lived in her own house with the grandchildren, she could use her income for other domestic expenses and school fees instead of having to pay rent. As she looked ahead, however, she was concerned that, because she was growing weak, she might not be able to continue working. She had no children to look after her, and she could not afford to pay for medical care.

It should be emphasized that most of the women who moved into trade during these years did so to keep themselves and their families alive, not to gain personal or economic empowerment. Kitakule commented, 'I don't think the war and other changes really promoted women, making them say, "Yes, now I can go out and sell". It was just a subsistence way of surviving.'[113] Most women who entered trade operated on a very small scale, for they had little capital and no access to credit. Moreover, it was dangerous for a woman to be visibly successful in any kind of work, for her home or business might be raided by soldiers or informal bands of armed men and she might be charged with prostitution. Women would later move into more important roles in the sale of food and drink, including in markets and shops, but that came slowly. Tripp claimed that retail trade 'was largely taken over by female entrepreneurs after the expulsion of Asians from Uganda', but our evidence indicates that the transition happened in two stages.[114] Asian shopkeepers were generally replaced initially by Ugandan men and only later by women.

A few women, usually those with capital provided by a relative, did go into business at a somewhat higher level during the Amin/Obote II period. A successful businesswoman interviewed in 2003 recalled: 'Women started getting into trade for the first time. For the first time you could hear women talking about a million Ugandan shillings. It was unbelievable. Most of these women were unmarried, sometimes girlfriends of army men. Very few married or professional women went into business during the 1970s. But it was a start.'[115] Theresa Mbire, trained as a teacher, noticed, after the Asians were expelled, that there were no florists in Kampala.[116] With the backing of her husband, she began selling fresh flowers in a shop on Kampala Road. Whereas the Asians had imported their flowers from Kenya, she decided to buy seedlings, raise them in Kabale, and then transport the flowers to her shop. In 1975 she expanded into a tailoring business and by 1979 had a workshop in Ntinda with hundreds of sewing machines. During the 1979 war, her workshop was looted, so she secured a small industry loan and set up Home Pride bakery. Later she moved into household furnishings.

The businesswomen who made the strongest impression on popular thought were labeled 'the Dubai women'. Taking advantage of the demand created by the shortage of consumer goods, these traders traveled to Gulf countries or, if they had more capital, to London or East Asia to buy clothes and other small items that they brought back to Uganda for sale. These early female importers were described in positive terms by women interviewed around 2000. Kitakule commended the women who went to Dubai with two empty suitcases, bought shirts, and sold them for a thousand dollars on their return.[117] They were sometimes afraid at first of traveling outside of the country, but 'after they got their confidence, these women were able to say, "Ahhh, I know what I want, let me venture out." These Dubai women were genuine businessmen.' Rugasira said, 'I have a cousin whose husband was not making any money. Her friends said, "We'll lend you some money to go to Dubai, buy these things, bring them here, sell them, and make a little bit of difference, support the family." The husband said, "No," but she's stubborn, she went once, she went twice, she went again. So they survived.'[118]

Later commentators pointed out that some of these women were able to make progress in business. Going to Dubai 'was a venue for women to enter business. When they returned, they invested in shops to sell their goods, and many of them built houses, established other ventures, and paid school fees.'[119] Grace Mukasa of

ACFODE noted that some of the women who began by going to Dubai were later able to buy large shipping containers of shoes or clothing, and eventually they moved into international trade at a higher level or became owners of rental property in wealthy neighborhoods of Kampala. These women were thus predecessors of the successful, entrepreneurial businesswomen who rose to prominence at the end of the century.

But they were not treated with respect at the time. Because it was expensive to travel abroad and pay for goods, many people asked where 'the Dubai women' obtained their cash resources. Not surprisingly in light of the dominant representation of women during these years, the answer commonly given was prostitution. Kitakule explained, 'There were people who thought that there was something wrong with any woman who was in business, and that everybody who goes to Dubai is going to sell their body.'[120] Rugasira recalled that when people saw women going abroad to bring things back, they said '"Prostitution, prostitution, prostitution." They said these women were sleeping with Indians, with Arabs, with anyone. Perhaps there was a little bit of that, it being a strange land, but on the whole they were doing honest business. But people stigmatized the whole thing. A friend of mine who went out to buy things was very bold. She said, "If I wanted to do prostitution, I would do it here. I wouldn't have to fly to Dubai".'[121] Kyamureku commented that 'if a married woman tried to go out of Uganda to do business, to go to Dubai to bring things back, then people would start talking: "A married woman! She's doing this or that! When she gets there she gets money because she sells herself." So some women used to go with their husbands, which was an added expense – two air tickets, the extra accommodation – just to stop the talking.'

Because it was difficult for women with no capital to earn an income through 'legitimate' economic activity, some women in Kampala and other towns did seek support through sex work. Prostitutes in Kampala in the mid-1970s ranged from poor women who worked out of their rooms in slum areas or frequented bars to beautifully dressed women who held good jobs or were students but supplemented their earnings through sexual activity.[122] The latter were patronized by foreign diplomats, wealthy army officers, or *magenda* business tycoons. All these women were subject to arrest, extortion, or other kinds of harassment by the police or soldiers. Other women set up informal 'marriages'. In such arrangements, a man provided some or all of the money needed for housing, food, and clothing in return for the women's exclusive sexual services and companionship. The boundaries of such relationships were often blurred. Paid sexual activity with a variety of men might lead over time to a more monogamous relation with a single man; many women who gained money or other kinds of assistance from sex work engaged in different kinds of income-generating activities at the same time. In Obbo's study of poor female migrants in Kampala, for example, only 5 percent of the women described their primary occupation as prostitution.[123] Yet many who had other economic activities earned money at least on occasions from sex, and some of the women who said they were unemployed (constituting a third of her sample) were being 'kept' by men. Some women preferred the freedom of these 'outside marriages'. Furthermore, the collapse of social services and the mushrooming of corruption forced some women to use their bodies to survive.[124] If, for example, a woman needed health care but could not raise enough money to bribe the medical providers, she might be forced to pay with sex.

The political and economic dislocations of these years affected employment patterns among educated women as well. A slowly rising proportion of teachers were women. Of about 29,000 primary school teachers reported in 1975, 29 percent were women.[125] By 1986, handwritten figures generated by the Ministry of Education indicate that 32 percent were women. Most, however, were untrained or worked in the lower two professional grades. Thereza Kamugasa (Profile 8.1) began work as an unlicensed teacher in a primary school near Hoima around 1975. She was invited to take the position even though she had only S 4 ('O level') qualifications and no formal teacher training. Nevertheless, she was well respected in the community and earned enough money to help her mother, with whom she was living. At the secondary level, 19 percent of 4,400 teachers in 1981 were women.[126]

Teachers faced serious financial problems during these years. Because most of them were employed by the government (as were nurses, community development workers, and some office staff), they were hit hard by the growing disparity between inflation and government wages. Rugasira, who grew up in Kampala, remembered that, when she was a child in the 1960s and early 1970s, her mother, a teacher, lived comfortably on her pay: she could even afford a car.[127] Later, however, as economic circumstances became more difficult, her mother bought a little business, which she supervised after school. During the early 1980s, she left her teaching job entirely to concentrate on several businesses. Mary Katushabe (Profile 2.4), whose husband was the headmaster of a secondary school in Kabale, said that their family suffered during Amin's regime because the government defaulted on paying school salaries.

Fewer women were entering nurses' training than had been the case during the early Independence period. At Mengo School of Nursing, for example, 55 students had embarked on the basic course for enrolled nurses in 1960, but in 1972, only 32 new students began training.[128] At Mulago, about 220 student nurses had entered in 1968, but by 1979–82, the annual number had dropped to half that level. In 1980, just 108 new enrolled nurses were registered by the Uganda Nurses and Midwives Council (UNMC), even though Nsambya School of Nursing was now turning out nurses as well.[129] A less pronounced decline is seen in the register books kept by the UNMC for Registered Nurses and those with more specialized qualifications. This was probably because some Ugandan women continued to receive advanced training in Europe at least through the mid-1970s, and some foreign Registered Nurses continued to work in Uganda.

Nurses were adversely affected by the progressive weakening of the government-supported medical system. As primary health care declined, mortality increased.[130] Infant mortality rates rose between 1970 and 1985, and a severe outbreak of sleeping sickness in 1980 was attributed to the instability and poor medical services as well as to the dry weather. A British nurse who visited Mulago Hospital in 1985 (which had been a showpiece when it opened in 1962) noted that the country's political/military problems had led to a serious breakdown in services.[131] The hospital had no proper water supply, and drains and latrines were blocked. Some buildings had become entirely unusable, while in the functioning areas windows were broken and there was no disinfectant, soap, or bed linen. Doctors were often absent from the hospital, attempting to earn money elsewhere. Yet even within this disrupted system, the British visitor was impressed by the dedication of the nurses at Mulago.

Women were apparently moving into secretarial or clerical work at a rapid pace, though we lack quantified information. Because the majority of office workers had previously been Indian men, the expulsion of the Asians left a vacuum filled by some Ugandan women as well as many men. Rather surprisingly in light of Amin's opposition to both labor organizations and women, female workers in clerical, commercial, and other technical positions set up their own wing of NUCCPTE in 1976.[132] Thereafter more women joined the union, and the leadership was compelled to integrate them more fully into the organization, including letting them become shop stewards. They rarely moved up into higher administrative positions, however. A report written in the early 1980s noted that women were minimally represented in government-affiliated parastatals: one branch manager in Uganda National Bank plus four managers and one acting general manager of Uganda Hotels.[133]

The very few women who held industrial positions commonly reported conflict between their jobs, which they undertook from a simple need for money, and their domestic duties. A small sample of women doing industrial work in Jinja in 1978–9, most of whom were young and had children, said that although their husbands generally approved of their work for economic reasons, they themselves felt that their children were receiving insufficient attention.[134] Tension was reported also in a study of absenteeism among women working in 1981–2 for the United Garment Industry Ltd in Kampala: responsibilities at home frequently caused them to miss work.

Other kinds of work are hard to study, in part because the few mentions of them in the press were shaped by political considerations. In 1975, for example, *Voice of Uganda* showed a wedding photograph of a prosperous Ugandan couple. The husband was said to be working in the head office of the Jinja-based Madhvani conglomerate, which had been taken from its South Asian owners and put into African hands; his wife was employed at the similarly appropriated Dunlop Tyre Factory in Jinja.[135] Other photographs showed the female pilot who flew Amin to the celebration of Labour Day on 1 May and a group of women being trained as pilots, standing with Amin. Some of the latter, it was explained, would go into the Ugandan Air Force, while others joined Uganda Airline. The day after that photograph appeared, a fulsome editorial entitled 'Female Society Takes Giant Leap to Glory' commended the new opportunities Amin was offering women by giving them the 'chance to defend the motherland'.[136] Praising Ugandan women for not being provocative or challenging even if they were employed as teachers, nurses, or secretaries, the editorial called on women 'to show how much they can do in such stages to prove their work for more confidence in the future'. A few women worked as housegirls or hairdressers.[137]

Additional information is provided by our district sample. Of those who were children during this period, only 23 percent of their mothers had no regular income-producing activities, the lowest fraction of any of the periods. Even some of these, women involved in subsistence agriculture, merely sold surplus food when they had it. Although an eighth of the mothers were teachers, nurses, or secretaries, the majority were engaged in petty trade. A quarter grew foodstuffs or poultry expressly for market sale, a sixth sold local alcohol, tea, or pancakes, and a quarter worked as assistants in a market or shop.

Fifty women in our sample entered paid work for the first time during the Amin/Obote II period. The proportion in trade rose to nearly a third, the majority making and/or selling food or drink. In contrast to the older groups, five of these women were selling in markets, retailing staples they had not produced themselves, and three were raising food or poultry commercially. The proportion who became teachers or nurses dropped, but there were now eleven secretaries and office workers, an occupation not seen in the previous samples. A slightly lower fraction went into other professions or high-status work, while unskilled or semi-skilled labor took on a more important role, rising from 8 percent in the early Independence period to 22 percent now. Four were sales girls in shops or waitresses in eating or drinking places, while three did manual labor.

These women were on average a little older when they started work than their early Independence predecessors. A smaller proportion were aged 20-24 years and more were aged 25–29. They were also more likely to be separated/divorced or widowed than had been the case before, and many more of them already had children at the time (54 percent, as compared with 25–27 percent in both earlier periods). These patterns stem from the fact that many women who had not worked in the early years of their marriages were pushed into the public economy by the atypical conditions of this period. Furthermore, the location of their employment had shifted as compared with the older women. Fewer were living in Kampala or the villages than had been the case before and about the same proportion in peri-urban areas, but there was a significant increase in those working in district headquarters (from 13 to 36 percent). This suggests that when rural women were forced to seek cash, many moved to urban areas, but in many cases to smaller towns rather than the city.

When asked why they took on the particular type of work they did, the responses of these women were far more functional than those of earlier women. Only a quarter said they chose that employment because they liked or admired it. Half now implied that the *type* of work was secondary: they had to find something that generated income for their home. A woman living outside Hoima began growing extra food to sell on the streets or at the market. She explained, 'My husband had died, leaving me with five young children, so I needed to earn money to keep my family alive.'[138] A young Kampala woman took a job selling spare parts for cars: 'My husband was a civil servant and we became very poor, so I was forced to work to supplement the home income.' Ten percent said that they were called or forced to do this work by the authorities or their relatives, and 12 percent said it was the only work they could get. Lacking any skills and divorced from her husband while in her thirties, Fulgencia Apio (Profile 2.3) moved from Lira District to Kampala, where she took a position as a housegirl.

About a third of the women said that it was unusual for women to do the kind of work they had started. The biggest cluster consisted of secretaries and office workers: such employment was indeed a new opportunity for women. An animal husbandry officer with the government in Hoima said, 'I did field work, treating animals, advising farmers on how to feed and treat them. I was the first lady in the district to work in that way.'[139] A saleswoman in an army shop in Moroto was 'the only woman in the whole barracks who was doing that kind of work. This was a surprise to many people.'

Although working was necessary for many of these women, it was not always greeted positively by others. Older gender conventions conflicted with economic reality. While most said their husbands or other close relatives approved of their work, a quarter faced opposition or at best a qualified reaction within the family. The Hoima woman who began selling excess food said, 'The in-laws, especially the brothers of my late husband, did not want me to do it. They opposed my working and said I should stay at home.'[140] The Kampala woman who sold car spare parts explained, 'My husband did not like my work at first. He was worried because I was a young lady. But we needed the money, so he did not do anything about it.'

Three-quarters of the women in our sample thought that people in the community regarded their work in a favorable light, even if they were unusual in pursuing that occupation. Several secretaries noted, for example, that they were admired, with other girls deciding to follow their example.[141] Other people might even help women to circumvent their husband's objections. A woman who was selling second-hand clothes in village markets outside Kabale explained, 'My husband did not like my work because he said I was going to become a loose woman. But other people did not mind. They even used to help me by carrying my pack of clothes to the taxi (minibus), so I could leave home pretending I was just going to town.'[142]

Among the women in our sample, 15 changed from their initial type of work to another during the Amin/Obote II years. (Here we are looking at those who moved to a different kind of economic activity, not just changing employers.) This was to a large extent a 'brain drain' of educated and experienced women who could no longer afford to remain in professional work: ten of the women had worked as teachers, in medical fields, or as an animal husbandry officer before shifting to more lucrative occupations. The fact that government wages were not paid regularly and did not keep up with inflation was an important consideration. The five teachers, who had worked in their original jobs for 12–33 years, set up a private nursery school, went to work for the Bank of Uganda, tried commercial agriculture, became a resident matron at a boarding school, or took a paid position with the Mothers' Union (Mary Katushabe, Profile 2.4). Of the three nurses, all of whom had worked in hospitals for many years, one began brewing beer and selling produce, another became a note examiner for the Bank of Uganda, and the last took a position as a nurse with a textile company. A medical doctor went into real estate while in exile, and an animal husbandry expert began to raise heifers on her own.

The Domestic Virtue model and its 'Petty Urban Trade' variation

The repressive policies of the government and the press's attitude towards women, especially under Amin, were based upon a negative and exaggerated version of the original Domestic Virtue model. Relying on the model's corollary about 'bad' women, the official position stressed women's harmful potential, especially their sexuality, when outside the home, while at the same time ignoring the contributions they were making within the public domain. Only when the government and the press wished to present Uganda to outside observers as a socialist or Westernized society did it talk about women's actual roles in the economy and community.

Official backing for an older conception of Domestic Virtue bore no relation to the changing realities of life for many women. Many rural women were growing extra food for sale or were undertaking small income-generating activities on the side, a pattern that accorded with the basic Domestic Virtue model so long as they continued to meet its other requirements. A growing number of educated women were moving into the wider range of positions now accepted by most Ugandans as appropriate for them, including teaching, nursing, government positions, and clerical or office work. The Service Career variation of the Domestic Virtue model was thus expanding in scope and membership, even though the government and the press no longer provided recognition or praise for those who followed it.

A new challenge to the original model came from the many poor women who were entering the cash-based economy in urban settings as petty traders or other kinds of low-status workers. Although this pattern had started to appear in the early Independence years, it expanded enormously during the unsettled Amin/Obote II period. These women came into Kampala or the towns because they were looking for ways of earning money, due to some mixture of economic and demographic problems. Either they were married but their husband could not provide the cash required to support the family; or they were household heads, at least for the time being, with children to raise. Even if they had a husband, these petty traders normally worked on their own. To gain money they made and sold food or drink or did service work associated with women's domestic roles. Many of them struggled just to stay alive, juggling multiple ways of bringing in money, some of them illegal. As was to be the case in the NRM period, very few who started at the bottom of the economic system were able to rise above subsistence level. Furthermore, these women bore a substantial physical burden, since they could not afford to hire domestic help. They therefore had to do all their normal work at home, in person, as well as carrying out their income-generating activities.

Because most of the women had little if any education, and the kinds of work they did were not of high status, they did not qualify for inclusion in the Service Career version of the Domestic Virtue model. The government disapproved of their activities and did not acknowledge their contributions within the informal economy. Yet other people in their communities recognized that these women were working of necessity, usually to provide for their children, and they were respected for doing so. Hence they could not be regarded as 'bad' women under the Domestic Virtue's corollary, though they might be living without a husband. Their work posed little direct challenge to male roles, since few men wanted to engage in trade at such a low level or to earn money through jobs linked to a domestic setting. At the same time, however, the fact that female household heads were earning their own money and deciding how to spend it undercut earlier assumptions about male dominance within the family.

This situation forced the development of a second variation of the original model, one we term the Petty Urban Trade version. It allowed small sellers and low-status workers in the towns to be respected as good women and to maintain a positive identity if they were seeking money to sustain their households, particularly to care for and educate their children. Most of their economic activities were now defined as legitimate, even if they involved alcohol, though sex work was still not generally accepted. Widows and single women were included in the definition if they had children. Motherhood had thus trumped marriage as a requirement for good womanhood. Those who headed their own households were allowed to make decisions.

If we return to the original model, we see that its expectations had been adjusted as follows:

- All women should marry. *This requirement had now been downplayed, with a niche created for widows and unmarried women.*
- Women are mothers. *This assumption remained the strongest single feature, applying even to unmarried women.*
- Women have practical duties within the household. *This expectation also retained its force, justifying women's need to work outside the home to earn money to support their families.*
- Women's work is done within the homestead except when going out for wood and water. *This component was abandoned, though women were still expected to be at home when not working.*
- Women are subject to male authority. They are submissive and deferential to men, including their husband, his male relatives, and other men in the community. *This notion was powerful in social terms, but women were allowed to interact on a more even basis with men in a working environment.*
- Women are not decision-makers. *This idea was undermined by women's role as household heads and their economic independence.*
- Women may use resources, such as land and domestic property, but they do not control them. *This concept became largely irrelevant when a woman moved to an urban area and undertook her own work.*

As a corollary, poor women who were living without a husband but working to support their children could no longer be regarded automatically as sex objects or prostitutes. The actual necessities of women's lives had thus led to a new version of the Domestic Virtue model, one that was to remain important during the NRM period as well. Society's willingness to validate these women's work in the face of government opposition demonstrates that practical pressures can outweigh official policies.

The Amin/Obote II years affected many aspects of women's lives, generally in negative ways. The combination of violence and instability plus economic collapse forced both female household heads and currently married women into the cash-based economy. Their entry into the market world was facilitated by the expulsion of the South Asians, the rise of a *magendo* economy, and the migration of women into urban areas. At the same time, however, girls and women were endangered by gender-based violence and suffered from the disruption of education and health care. Though many more women were working, they did so in the face of governmental and media disapproval. The repression of women and their organizations that was such a pronounced feature of this period rested upon an exaggerated version of the older Domestic Virtue model, but that definition again demonstrated its adaptability by developing a Petty Urban Trade variation to legitimate the work done by poor women to support their families. In the next chapter we follow these patterns into the NRM period.

Notes

1 CultHist3 (see Appendix B) emphasizes that if the changes occurring by 1970 had been allowed to continue on a gradual basis, Uganda would have integrated more smoothly into the global economy. But the abrupt disruption of older patterns removed the foundation that had been being created, forcing women into unfamiliar economic and

social roles.
2 For fuller accounts, see Tumusiime, *Uganda 30 Years*, Jørgensen, *Uganda*, Museveni, *Sowing the Mustard Seed*, Decalo, 'Military Coups', and Tripp, *Women and Politics*.
3 See, for example, her *African Women*.
4 For information about these women's ethnic and religious affiliations, current type of work, and current marital status, see Appendices C8-9.
5 Tamale, *When Hens Begin to Crow*, p. 16.
6 Watson, 'Uganda's Women.' Life expectancy at birth for both males and females dropped by about 1.5 years between 1970 and 1985 (World Bank, *Africa DataBase, 2003*). For below, see Byanyima, 'Women in Political Struggle,' p. 133.
7 The total population in 1969 was about 9.5 million and rising (U. President's Office, *Report on the 1969 Population Census*, Vol. IV, p. 40).
8 Nalwanga-Sebina, 'Report on a Five-Day Survey.' For below, see Lira7.
9 Hoima14.
10 Kabale15. For below, see Hoima8.
11 Hoima20.
12 Sen and Grown, *Development, Crises*, p. 67. For below, see Byanyima, 'Women in Political Struggle,' p. 133.
13 Hoima5. For below, see Lira4.
14 Hoima3. For below, see Kampala23.
15 Kampala16.
16 Kampala20. For below, see Lira4.
17 Arua14.
18 Byanyima, 'Women in Political Struggle,' and Wakoko and Lobao, 'Reconceptualizing Gender' for this paragraph and the next. Cf. Urdang, 'Women in National Liberation Movements,' and Coquery-Vidrovitch, *African Women*, pp. 195–9.
19 'Women in Political Struggle,' p. 129.
20 Tripp, 'Gender, Political Participation,' p. 115, for this and below.
21 *My Life as a Child Soldier in Uganda*, discussed in *Monitor*, 17 February 2002.
22 O'Connor, 'Uganda: The Spatial Dimension,' Edmonds, 'Crisis Management,' and Hansen and Twaddle, 'Introduction' to *Changing Uganda*.
23 Ellyne, 'Economic History.' For below, see World Bank, *Africa Database, 2003*.
24 Busingye, 'Impact of Structural Adjustment Programs,' p. 11, Ellyne, 'Economic History,' *New Vision*, 29 July 2003, M. Snyder, *Women in African Economies*, pp. 18–19, and Basirika, 'Structural Adjustment.'
25 Jamal, 'Ugandan Economic Crisis,' p. 122.
26 Belshaw, 'Agriculture-Led Recovery,' and Edmonds, 'Crisis Management.'
27 TB2.
28 TB8.
29 *Uganda 30 years*, pp. 46–7, and U. Min. of Information and Broadcasting, *Uganda's Economic War*.
30 Wakoko and Lobao, 'Reconceptualizing Gender'.
31 CultHist1 (see Appendix B).
32 Kampala17.
33 TB7.
34 7 July 1975.
35 See Harmsworth, 'The Ugandan Family in Transition,' for this and below.
36 Arua3. For below, see Arua11.
37 TB7 for this paragraph.
38 Lira11. For below, see Arua3.
39 Kabale10.
40 Lira11. She demonstrated this method of making soap to the interviewer.
41 Banugire, 'Towards an Appropriate Policy Framework,' and Prunier, 'Le "Magendo" en Ouganda.'
42 Arua13.
43 Jinja10. For below, see TB8 and Syahuka-Muhindo, *Understanding Women's Participation*, p. 37. For women in Lusaka, Zambia, 1971-85, see Hansen, 'The Black Market.'
44 Lira2.
45 E.g., *Voice of Uganda*, 26 June 1975; *The [London] Times*, 25 January 1975, p. 3, and 26

March 1975, p. 7.

46 *The [London] Times*, 26 January 1981, p. 6.
47 Ibid., 27 January, p. 6. For below, see Clark, 'Gender and Profiteering,' Robertson, 'The Death of Makola,' and her *Sharing the Same Bowl*.
48 Harmsworth, 'The Ugandan Family in Transition,' p. 94. For below, see Syahuka-Muhindo, *Understanding Women's Participation*, pp. 33–8.
49 Ebila, 'Portrayal of Gender Relations.'
50 Snyder, *Women in African Economies*, p. 18.
51 Tripp and Kwesiga, *The Women's Movement*, p. 206.
52 Lira6.
53 Arua8.
54 She was interviewed on 14 February 2003 by Judith Ruko, mainly in Lugbara, with a little English (tape: Arua10). By the standards of that community, the interviewer judged that she was of middle economic level: not wealthy, but living quite comfortably.
55 Kampala17.
56 By 1985, the urban population constituted 9.9 percent of the national total, as compared to 8.0 percent in 1970 (World Bank, *Africa DataBase, 2003*.
57 *African Women*, esp. ch. 5. Because Obbo recorded the situation before the worst of the violence and economic hardship, her account probably documents an intermediate position, one lying between that of the early Independence period and what would have pertained 5-10 years later. For female migrants in Transkei, South Africa, see Redding, 'South African Women.'
58 CultHist2 (see Appendix B).
59 Harmsworth, 'The Ugandan Family.'
60 For this and below, see Ssekamwa, *History and Development of Education*, pp. 184–7, Kwesiga, *Women's Access to Higher Education*, p. 210, and Bigsten and Kayizzi-Mugerwa, *Crisis, Adjustment*, p. 119.
61 World Bank, *Africa DataBase, 2003*.
62 The proportion of girls among primary school students rose from 39 percent in 1970 to 43 percent in 1980 (UN, *WISTAT, 1999*). For below, see Opolot, 'Occupational Aspirations of Primary School Leavers.'
63 Makerere University, 'Installation and Graduation Ceremony, Makerere University, 9 October 1971.'
64 Makerere University, 'Graduation Ceremony, 7 October 1978.' For below, see UN, *WISTAT, 1999*.
65 Matembe, *Gender, Politics, and Constitution Making*, pp. 6–12 and 18–19 for this paragraph.
66 Two were employed as untrained teachers at a lower level, two brewed and sold alcohol, two made and/or sold clothing or domestic goods, and one counted money in a bank.
67 Jinja10.
68 Arua7.
69 Many parents in Buddo County in 1976 said that they were only sending their daughters to school because it would lead to paid employment. They had grave reservations about the negative behavior displayed by educated girls, including an unwillingness to show proper respect to their parents and later to their husbands (Kirunda, 'Women's Education in Buddo,' as cited by Kwesiga, *Women's Access to Higher Education*, p. 166).
70 Arua4.
71 Arua1. For below, see Kampala4.
72 See later section in this chapter.
73 Hoima1.
74 Kampala4.
75 Sen and Grown, *Development, Crises*, p. 67 and, for below, p. 75. For South Africa, see Unterhalter, 'Constructing Race'; for Mozambique, see Sheldon, *Pounders of Grain*, ch. 5, esp. p. 154.
76 We would normally have used 1985 as another sample year, but only scattered issues of two papers survive. *The Star*, which appears to have been run off on a copy machine, came out only in January and February. Expressing strong opposition to the Democratic Party and Ssemogerere, it presented a somewhat more positive picture of women and their activities. *The Weekly Times*, which had been banned in 1981, was allowed to resume publication in August 1985, at the time of Tito Okello's coup, when it was clearly

controlled by his government. See also Appendix A.
77 *Voice of Uganda*, 14 February 1975. For below, see Obbo, 'Sexuality and Economic Domination,' p. 81.
78 *Voice of Uganda*, 13 May. For below, see ibid., 6 May.
79 Tripp, *Women and Politics*, p. 49. For below, see Byanyima, 'Women in Political Struggle,' p. 133.
80 *Voice of Uganda*, 8 May.
81 7 January 1975.
82 17 March 1975.
83 7 January 1975.
84 4 November For below, see 19 March.
85 23 April, 29 January, 17 January, 21 January, and 15 May.
86 Tamale, *When Hens Begin to Crow*, pp. 15–18. For below, see Ayuru, 'Sensitised Women.'
87 *Voice of Uganda*, 24 January 1975, and *The [London] Times*, 25 January 1975; cf. Bagaya's *Elizabeth of Toro*.
88 14 February 1975.
89 Tripp, *Women and Politics*, pp. 49–51 for this and the next paragraph unless otherwise noted.
90 18 March 1975.
91 The NCW was an early example of what has been described as 'state feminism' (Okeke-Ihejirika, *Negotiating Power and Privilege*, pp. 21–2).
92 UCU Mukono IMU 110/6 vs. IMU 17/6.
93 UCU Mukono IMU/114/6 and 113/6.
94 UCU Mukono 1MU 38/3.
95 Tripp, *Women and Politics*, p. 51.
96 The only positive report concerning female equality associated with IWY in *Voice of Uganda* concerned the success of the Soviets in educating girls and providing equal work opportunities for women (26 March).
97 *Voice of Uganda*, 1 May 1975.
98 2 May 1975.
99 7 April. For below, see 22 September 1975.
100 E.g., 9 March and 5 May. For below, see 31 March and 10 April.
101 21 August 1975. For below, see 29 April.
102 See UCU Mukono 1MU 40/3, for a typed copy of her address.
103 UN, Dept. of Public Information, Convention on the Elimination of All Forms of Discrimination against Women, April, 1984. The Convention was passed by the General Assembly in December 1979.
104 TB7.
105 Jamal, 'The African Crisis'.
106 TB7.
107 Tadria, 'Changes and Continuities,' pp. 82 and 89; for below, see her 'Changing Economic and Gender Patterns,' chs. 4 and 5, esp. p. 90.
108 14 February 1975. For below, see 28 November.
109 Andama-Harmsworth, 'The Economic Status of Rural Women,' as summarized in Musoke, *Research on Women*, pp. 20–21, and Kwesiga, *Women's Access to Higher Education*, Table 6.3. For below, see, e.g., Whitehead, 'Rural Women and Food Production,' and cf. Kisekka, 'El papel de la mujer.'
110 Obbo, *African Women*, pp. 124–5.
111 She was interviewed on 5 February 2003 by Jean Kemitare in Rukiga (tape: Kabale7). Marjorie McIntosh met her the day before this interview, at her stall. The interviewer felt that by the standards of that community, Jane's economic level was low but adequate.
112 The fiber was prepared by local women from reeds growing in wet areas, which were cut, soaked, and pounded until they gained the necessary texture and flexibility. Jane had a pile of these prepared fibers beside her, using the full reed for the structural units of the basket and a thin strand pulled off lengthwise as the thread that bound the rows together. To add color to her baskets, she made creative use of an old bag made of sturdy colored plastic, originally intended for carrying charcoal, potatoes, or other heavy objects. She ripped thin strands from the edge of the bag and wove them in with the reed

material, producing attractive patterns of blue and white against the tan background.
113 TB7.
114 'Gender, Political Participation,' esp. p. 112.
115 Kampala17.
116 *New Vision*, 25 October 1989.
117 TB7.
118 TB8.
119 Joy Kwesiga, interviewed in 1998: Snyder, *Women in African Economies*, pp. 19–20. For below, see TB1.
120 TB7.
121 TB8. For below, see TB2.
122 Bakwesegha, *Profiles of Urban Prostitution*, ch. 3.
123 *African Women*, pp. 124–5.
124 Byanyima, 'Women in Political Struggle', p. 133.
125 World Bank, *Africa DataBase, 2003*. For below, see U. Min. of Education, typescript, 'Education Statistics Abstract, 1986,' kindly located and made available to Marjorie McIntosh by Mr. Lule at the Ministry of Education.
126 UN, *WISTAT, 1999*.
127 TB8.
128 Mengo School of Nursing and Midwifery, Kampala, *Register of Nurses*, Book A. For below, see Mulago School of Nursing and Midwifery, Kampala, *Register Book of Nurses and Midwives*.
129 *Register Book of Enrolled Nurses*, Book II, UNMC. For below, see *Register Books of Registered Nurses*, 1–2, and *Register Books of Sick Children's Nurses and Mental Nurses*.
130 Bigsten and Kayizzi-Mugerwa, *Crisis, Adjustment*, p. 122. For below, see World Bank, *Africa DataBase 2003* and *The [London] Times*, 26 January 1980, p. 5.
131 Holden, 'Colonial Sisters'.
132 Asowa-Okwe, *The Dynamics of Women Participation*, pp. 24–6.
133 Ayuru, 'Sensitised Women'.
134 Nabunya, 'A Survey into the Socio-Economic Conditions'. For below, see Senyondo, 'Female Absenteeism in Industry,' as summarized in Musoke, *Research on Women*, p. 46.
135 7 January 1975. For below, see 2 May and 12 August.
136 13 August 1975.
137 For women working in the households of more prosperous relatives and as hairdressers, see Obbo, 'Stratification'.
138 Hoima8. For below, see Kampala10.
139 Hoima15. For below, see Arua16.
140 Hoima8. For below, Kampala10.
141 Lira1 and Lira3.
142 Kabale10.

Eight

Broader Developments for Women during the NRM Period
1986–2003

With the establishment of a government in 1986 by Museveni and the National Resistance Movement, based upon a one-party system, Uganda began its transition to a normal life. Military and political stability were restored in much of the country, and the kingdoms were permitted to return as 'cultural,' not political, institutions.[1] With government encouragement, a free market economy flourished, though the much touted economic development visible at the national level by the mid-1990s was uneven in regional and social terms. Property appropriated from South Asians during Amin's regime was returned by the government to its rightful owners. Poverty intensified at least temporarily, due to two factors: the reforms introduced by the government, part of the Structural Adjustment Programs (SAPs) demanded by the international financial institutions; and Uganda's disadvantaged position as a producer of simple agricultural goods within a global economy. Women were disproportionately present among the needy, despite attempts to mitigate poverty. The NRM introduced several affirmative action measures that gave women an advantage in government at all levels and in education. Women's organizations, NGOs and CBOs working with women flourished through the 1990s, devoting much of their attention to legal rights and poverty. Women faced serious challenges in the area of reproductive health, and despite the government's prompt and energetic action, HIV/AIDS was a major national tragedy, with particular consequences for women.

During the NRM period women were working outside the home in higher numbers and proportions than ever before. Many poor women were obliged to work to support their families, whether as household heads or to supplement the income of their husbands; most of them remained in small-scale production and/or retailing of food, drink, cloth, or clothing. But entrepreneurial business activity, professional work, and other types of employment increased among women of middle and higher status, thanks in part to the improved educational opportunities available at the secondary and university level. At least during the first decade of the NRM years, women and their issues, including ones specific to working women, were actively discussed in the press and women were portrayed in favorable terms. Positive media coverage was due in large part to the government's advocacy of women as full members of the public world, including in decision-making roles. Gender tension, though seldom mentioned in the press, was nonetheless acute. We also encounter continuing debate over the three clusters of issues concerning women that surfaced in the early colonial period: marriage and domestic relations; inheritance rights and landholding; and women's role as decision-makers in the public sphere.

By 2003, though most people still accepted some form of Domestic Virtue thinking, a new gender formulation was emerging. It was made necessary by the success of some highly visible and well-respected women who were competing actively in the private sector, the professions, and government or politics. These entrepreneurial women generally played redefined roles within their families as well. An alternative set of gender definitions was beginning to appear that accepted the contributions of these women, so long as they continued to accept responsibility for their households and – if married – display appropriate respect for their husbands and their male relatives in public. A modified set of expectations likewise emerged for their husbands, who were allowed to interact more fully with their wives, children, and households without losing respect as males.

This chapter explores the general developments that expanded women's options during the NRM period. We look first at changes in the areas of politics and the economy and then at the NRM's pro-women policies in government and education and the mood of disillusionment visible by 2003. After examining women's organizations and their activities, we consider demographic and health issues. The following chapter looks at women's work, media portrayals, gender tension, and Domestic Virtue attitudes, including the impact of the successful entrepreneurs. In both chapters we draw upon information from all our interviews, including the full district sample of 113 women.[2]

Political and Economic Stability Restored

The political context of women's lives during the NRM period differed greatly from the preceding years. The new government brought peace and stability to much of the country, though the north and sometimes the western or southern border areas continued to experience military violence into the early twenty-first century.[3] Following the pattern developed by the National Resistance Army during the period of guerrilla struggle, the new government reworked the system of local control. In an attempt to integrate and empower the peasants, the NRM abolished the position of chief, substituting for it a pyramid of resistance councils (meetings of all adults living in a particular area, including women and immigrants) and resistance committees, elected by the councils.[4] Women were also named to high offices within the central government and its bureaucracy.

For working women peace was of inestimable value. Among the women in our district sample, the most commonly cited positive feature of the NRM years (mentioned by 42 percent) was that this government had brought peace, security, and stability. Peace was especially important to women who had been children during the Amin/Obote II period and had that baseline for comparison. Some women gave Museveni personal credit. A woman who ran a hairdressing salon in Mpigi said, 'In earlier days there were murders by soldiers, but now Museveni has controlled the army.'⁵ The proprietress of a shop and little restaurant in a trading center outside Mpigi explained, 'This has been the best time for me. We used to sleep in the bush, but now we live in our houses and we are able to work without any disturbance. For me, Museveni is my man.' For some women, peace means freedom from sexual violence. A woman who was braiding hair while seated under a make-shift roof of papyrus in the industrial section of Arua commented: 'This period is quite good because there is no insecurity. We can sit the whole day beside the road plaiting hair and reach home late in the evening without any problems.'⁶ A Hoima woman who offered private secretarial services echoed this statement: 'In the current regime there is peace. You can walk in the middle of the town at 4 in the night and no one will tamper with you.'

Ongoing fighting in the north between government forces and the Lord's Resistance Army/Kony troops was treated in divergent ways by the women in our sample. Rather surprisingly, the great majority simply ignored the situation, stating or implying that peace had been extended to all Ugandans. Thereza Kamugasa (Profile 8.1) said, 'From the time Museveni entered Uganda as the president, peace has prevailed all over the country.' A woman who works as a housegirl in Arua, not far from some of the worst areas of fighting and home to many of the refugee camps, said 'Since the NRM government took over power, there has been no war'.⁷ Such responses suggest that many Ugandans set up regional boundaries in their own minds, based upon administrative area and ethnicity, that allowed people in stable parts of the country to shut their eyes to what was happening elsewhere. Only a small group mentioned the fighting as a serious problem. Such reactions were concentrated among those living in Lira, close to the disturbed areas, and among more educated or older women. A civil servant working for the Lira Municipal Council reflected, 'The war going on in the north has destabilized the region. Currently cattle rustlers are coming, saying that they want to graze their animals, but later they take our cows and rape our women.'⁸ Angela Akello (Profile 2.1) emphasized the negative impact of the conflict, while Eunice Kyamanya (Profile 6.1), though retired, was interviewed at the end of a workshop to train media women to contribute to peace-building efforts in the north of Uganda.

The economic world likewise changed significantly after 1986. During the NRM period, the formal economy became functional again. The standard of living for some people rose, and the country undertook reforms designed to bring its economic and social policies into line with the concerns of international organizations. Various measures indicate economic growth at the national level, including the rising Gross Domestic Product.⁹ Rapid inflation between 1985 and 2001 was apparently being brought under control in 2002–3. Production of food crops consumed within the country increased, though export crops displayed a more mixed history.¹⁰ Ownership of goods related to communication (radios, television, mobile telephones, and personal computers) and transportation (motor vehicles) improved but remained low by global standards.¹¹ In 2000–2001, for example, 52 percent of Ugandan households had a radio (78 percent in urban areas and 47 percent in rural), but only 6 percent had a television and 3 percent a telephone. Mobile phones were soon to effect a communication revolution, though the number of landline telephones remained very small even in urban areas.

Partly because of broader global concerns, and partly because some nations or organizations were particularly eager to assist Museveni and the NRM, foreign money became available in several forms. In addition to funds provided by the international financial institutions, primarily the World Bank and the International Monetary Fund, assistance was given by the development agencies of the UN and individual nations, especially the Scandinavian countries and the Netherlands. Other kinds of economic help were offered by international NGOs. Foreign donor money as a fraction of the government's total income rose sharply during the NRM period.[12] By 2003, 54–7 percent of the country's total budget came from foreign sources (including individual remittances). While outside money was essential to Uganda's economic revitalization, it often had strings attached. The World Bank and IMF would only grant loans if the government agreed to certain kinds of economic and fiscal policies; development agencies and NGOs commonly had their own goals. The presence of what became known as 'donor-driven agendas', in economic and social terms, had a major impact upon women.

The international monetary organizations demanded a renewal of the SAPs that had been started on a limited basis in 1981 but abandoned three years later. In 1987 the NRM government began a program of economic recovery that included two main types of policies.[13] The first, designed to reduce government expenditure, included austere monetary policies, cutbacks in social services like health and education, privatization of public services, and 'retrenchment' (laying off employees) in the civil service. The second, intended to improve agricultural and industrial productivity, focused upon currency devaluation and market liberalization. Similar programs were being required of all sub-Saharan countries by the World Bank and IMF, but the NRM implemented them with special vigor. Although it was recognized at the time that these changes would cause some degree of suffering in the short term, the financial organizations argued that the benefits would soon start to be felt, resulting in a healthier economy and society longer-term. Some improvement was seen in industrial investment and physical infrastructure, especially roads, and the total Gross Domestic Product increased.

But in Uganda as in much of Africa, the SAPs did not work out as planned. Household poverty worsened, at least for the first 10-12 years after 1986. The most direct measure of the standard of living is real wages (the purchasing power of wages). In 1985 average real wages in Uganda were at a scaled value of 5.4, a figure that dropped to 3.2 in 1990 and to 1.4 in 1995.[14] It may be that the proposed benefits of SAPs were starting to be felt by the turn of the century, however, for in 2001 real wages bounced back to 3.4. Yet Uganda remained one of the poorest countries in the world. In 2002 it ranked 158 out of 174 countries in the UNDP's *Human Development Index*, which includes per capita incomes, the adult literacy rate, and life expectancy at birth.[15] Although the government's much touted figures that overall poverty as measured by *incomes* fell from 56 percent in 1992 to 35 percent in 2000, these gains were distributed unevenly in regional terms. In the war-torn north of the country, 66 percent of the population still lived in poverty in the latter year.[16] The country's economic problems were accentuated by the nature of Uganda's increasing involvement in the global economy, limited primarily to its role as a producer of agricultural exports of limited value.

SAPs had particularly negative consequences for women.[17] By 1993–5 there was public discussion of the programs' failure to improve women's lives, due in part to their heavy involvement with the informal economy.[18] A report written in 1997 on Uganda's economic structures, processes, and policies from a gender-sensitive perspective suggested that the economic reform programs had intensified the following: unpaid labor for women, men, and girls; gender inequalities in access to product markets and to social and physical infrastructure; and gender inequalities in economic power within households.[19] The SAPs imposed handicaps at higher economic levels too. Virtually no women had the resources to bid success- fully for the businesses or services that were being privatized. Sarah Kitakule of UWEAL said:

> Liberalization of the economy opened up opportunities, because before there was a monopoly, the Marketing Boards and so on. When government freed up the economy, women had a chance to participate. But they were at a disadvantage, because liberalization has created tougher competition. Most of our women have very limited capacity to engage in large-scale enterprises, to enjoy economies of scale. So it is tough for them.[20]

Likewise, while global trade may have expanded opportunities for some Ugandans, few women operated the kind of large import-export businesses or factories that benefited.

Regardless of the precise impact of SAPs, poverty was clearly more acute for women than for men, in Uganda as in other parts of the world.[21] In the late 1990s, at least one-third of all women in the country lived in absolute poverty, defined as being unable to meet their basic needs.[22] For those who were married, cultural expectations dictated that, in the face of limited resources, men and boy children should be fed, clothed, and given medical care first. The consequences were even more severe in households headed by women, as were 29 percent of all family units in 1991 and 27.5 percent in 2000–1.[23] Women's ability to satisfy their households' economic needs was curtailed by lack of employment opportunities, low real wages, and the problems that confronted those who operated outside the formal economy. In the late 1990s, the government began a 'participatory poverty assess- ment', in which district meetings were held throughout the country to identify the features of local poverty, with particular attention to gender issues.[24] The resulting set of measures, the Poverty Eradication Action Plan (PEAP), recognized the challenges faced by women and their role in ameliorating poverty. A discussion paper on 'Challenges and Prospects for Poverty Reduction in Northern Uganda,' for example, published in 2002, described how the militarization of the north had affected women: the loss of male household heads and other relatives, vulnerability to sexual abuse and sexually transmitted diseases, and economic weakness.[25]

Women were also hit by retrenchment, through the loss of their own jobs or those of their husbands or fathers.[26] The government's civil service, a structure inherited from previous regimes, was about one-quarter female in 1987. It was described as 'on the brink of collapse and in need of a drastic overhaul. It had become large, inefficient, unproductive, unresponsive to national needs, utterly demoralized and generally incapable of delivering the services or performing the functions that it had been set up to achieve.'[27] Pushed by the IMF and World Bank, the NRM appointed a commission in 1989 to review the structure and functions of the civil service. Over the next few years 3,400 staff members were laid off with small pensions, and it was expected that by 1994 about 63,000 employees would have lost their jobs. Local governments too participated in the retrench- ment. Several of the women in our sample were themselves laid off, forced to find other – and generally less secure – sources of income. A woman who had been sweeping roads for the municipal council of Kabale for 19 years was laid off, after which she began selling porridge and other foodstuffs in the taxi park.[28] One Hoima woman, who had been a clerical officer at a government-run school for nine years, took up trade in groundnuts and beans, while another began to sell secondhand clothes after her program in the local office of the Ministry of Housing, Works, and Communication, where she had been a clerk, was scrapped.

Economic change was mentioned as a key feature of the NRM period by 41 percent of the women in our sample. In positive terms, they commented that goods were readily available, growth was occurring, and women were now active players in the economy. Such features were mentioned especially by women who had grown up in the disastrous economic milieu of the Amin/Obote II era. Development and improved communications were major themes. Grace Ssembatia (Profile 5.1) observed: 'There has been some development in this era. Even people in the village own radios now, and grass thatched houses are rarer.' A successful businesswoman in Hoima said, 'The regime of Museveni has contributed a lot. For example, there are now mobile telephones. I have just sent some money to Kampala and it will reach there immediately.'[29]

Some women attributed the economic improvement to greater security. As a primary school teacher in Arua noted, 'This period has brought in increased stability. One is able to work to get income without worrying about insecurity.'[30] But they stressed that, to thrive in this economic world, planning and hard work were important. The owner of a carpentry shop in Kabale said, 'One can earn in this regime. But it takes proper planning, not just copying other people's businesses because you think that is a good income earner.'[31] The housegirl in Arua agreed: 'Everything is available in the market if you have the money. You have to have brains and to work very hard to get things and survive.'

Women were said to have shared in economic development. A retired teacher in Lira noted: 'Women are now as competitive as men in business undertakings. They can move about and go looking for commodities to stock their shops.'[32] A Kabale woman explained, 'Now there is development. Even women can do some work. For example, I am making coffins. Before it was unheard of for a woman to have such a business. In addition, in the home before, women could not plan for development, you could not even sell a goat. My late husband had a lot of money, but because women were not allowed to discuss it, we could not make plans.' Positive sentiments about the economy and women's place in it were expressed even by a woman seated on the ground in a quarry on a hillside above Kabale, using a wooden mallet to break up stones, in return for wages of Ush 1,000 per day (US $0.50). 'Working conditions are better now, and one is able to earn an income, save, and look after your own home. This is the most favorable period for women, because you can work for your own money, without being given it by a man, and you can use it as you wish.'[33]

Other women linked the economic situation for women to political improvements. As Eunice Kyamanya (Profile 6.1) said:

Museveni has brought about a big change for women. He was younger and better informed. Because of his experience with liberation movements, he involved women right from the beginning. He supports women, and women who work have been empowered to do a lot of things. The environment changed when we had backing from the head of state. He said, 'Once you solve women's problems, half the nation's problems will be solved.' This was very interesting, a big change from what we had heard before. Now we were empowered, now we could move forward together. Those affirmative steps the government has taken have helped the microfinance institutions and the economic environment for all women.

There were, however, dissenting voices. A quarter of the women, especially those who had grown up in the colonial and early Independence periods, pointed to the economic problems of the NRM years. A health service administrator in Jinja commented, 'The NRM period has affected the economic front. It has deprived Uganda. You have to work harder in order to get enough money. One job is not enough for survival.'[34] Several women noted that the gap between rich and poor had increased. A secretary in Mpigi said, 'People who have, have a lot, and those who don't, have nothing at all. Recently many people have been laid off from jobs.'[35] The owner of a small stationery shop in Jinja was discouraged: 'Business is very bad, and now in the 2000s things have turned from bad to worse. That's why some of us are quitting business.'

The NRM's Pro-Women Policies

Certainly by 1988–9 and to some extent right from its inception, the NRM government presented itself as sympathetic to women's concerns and eager to pull them into political participation.[36] A good example is a speech given by Museveni at the International Women's Day (IWD) celebration in March 1989.[37] Noting that women must participate in the political process and play an equal role in guiding development efforts, he stressed their importance in increasing agricultural production and the need to offer financial assistance to rural women. IWD, he said, highlighted the struggle by women for their rights and equality. It reflected the determination of women to play a larger role in the economic, social, political, and cultural life of Uganda; it symbolized women's solidarity in the struggle for world peace and stability; and it demonstrated the ability of women to work for their own emancipation. In an analysis that showed considerable gender awareness, he promised that the government would 'strengthen the position of women in the economy by raising the value and productivity of their labour and giving them access to control over productive resources such as land, capital, seeds, fertilizers, and tools'. Presidential language of this kind continued into the 1990s. In 1995, Museveni's speech at the celebration of International Labor Day called for 'the protection of women's rights so that they can benefit from their own labour and have greater access and control over productive resources'.[38] Noting that poor governance excludes women from the decision-making process, he said the NRM had empowered women to enable them to realize their full potential.

His comments were not merely a rhetorical strategy, for the government introduced pro-women policies in several key areas. It supported affirmative action measures that reserved seats for women in government, promoted new procedures that favored women in university admissions, and recognized the special importance for girl children of instituting free primary education. During the years between 1986 and around 1998, most women in Uganda felt that the country was moving forward and that their own position was improving, thanks in large part to the NRM's active backing.

This favorable stance stemmed from several considerations. When the NRM came to power, Museveni himself and many of those around him were heavily influenced by socialist thought, including the goal of equality among all people regardless of their sex. Museveni later accepted a free market economy, and he believed that women should continue to fill customary roles within the family, but he remained committed to women's participation in government and education. Furthermore, women had been part of the NRA's bush war, serving as soldiers and support workers. The NRM therefore felt that they had demonstrated their loyalty and capacity and deserved to be rewarded by full involvement in the new regime. Museveni may also have been seeking to expand his political legitimacy by enlisting the backing of women. When the NRM took power, the new government had little claim to authority beyond its defeat of the opposing forces in battle. One of the tasks facing Museveni was to persuade Ugandans and foreigners alike that his regime was able to win popular support. By advocating a series of policies that improved the status of women, he was building a powerful group of backers. Although the first four women appointed to ministries in his government were all members of the educated elite – indeed, all graduates of Gayaza High School – Museveni showed far greater concern than any previous leader with the plight of rural women. This widened his appeal still further and reinforced the government's attempt to create a populist and pan-Ugandan image.[39] Modernizing governments in other developing countries have similarly used women as allies in their struggle against more conservative factions. But 'a top-down attempt by the state to improve women's civil status as a wedge against "traditional" power blocs in society often creates simmering tensions'.[40] Such tensions were to be clearly visible in Uganda.

Active interventions in government and education

The NRM vigorously promoted women's participation in government. From the early years of the Movement, when the country was run through resistance councils and committees, women were involved. At the local level, certain seats were set aside for women, a policy reflected in the Constitution of 1995 and the Local Governments Act of 1997. According to the latter, councils at all levels, including districts, sub-counties, municipalities, and towns, were required to include at least two women among their six members.[41] The Act argued that affirmative action was necessary 'to ensure democratic participation in, and control of, decision making by the people concerned; and to establish a democratic, political and gender sensitive administrative set-up in Local Governments'. Women were guaranteed places in higher levels of the NRM government as well. In the 1989 elections for the National Resistance Council, 34 seats out of 241 were set aside for women, as were 39 out of 274 in the Parliamentary elections of 1996.[42] Other women were chosen through competition for open seats. Whereas in 1980 only 1 out of 126 seats in Parliament had been held by a woman, in 1989 women held 41 seats (17 percent), a figure that rose in 1996 to 52 seats (19 percent).

Partly in response to pressure from ACFODE and national and international NGOs, the government created a Ministry of Women in Development in 1988.[43] In 1991 it became the Ministry of Gender, Youth, and Culture and was later reconstituted as the Ministry of Gender, Labour, and Social Development. The ministry's charge was to take the lead in educating women, advocating women's issues, and liaising with other governmental bodies to achieve gender-responsive strategies in all areas. To increase its contact with women throughout the country, the ministry opened district offices in 1995.[44]

Women were active players in the process that led to the 1995 Constitution. The production of Uganda's constitution was a remarkable effort in democratic education and mass participation. It was spread over several years so as to involve people in every village throughout the country in a first round of meetings about what a constitution was; a second round discussed what provisions Uganda's constitution should have. One of the four topics considered in these seminars was the place of women and their concerns within the constitution. The number of women involved in the coordinating bodies was not large. Only two women, one of them Miria Matembe, sat on the initial Constitutional Commission of 21 people, named in 1989, which ultimately produced a draft constitution.[45] When the Constituent Assembly, charged with debating the draft constitution and preparing a final version, was elected in 1994, 51 women were among the 284 delegates (18 percent), most of them chosen for reserved seats. The women Constituent Assembly Delegates (CADs) worked hard to embed women's rights in the final draft, prepared in 1995, and the Women's Caucus they set up cooperated closely with other women's organizations.[46] After the constitution's approval by the electorate later in 1995, the former secretary of the Constitutional Commission was quoted as saying proudly that the document guaranteed women more preferences than any other national constitution worldwide.

By the early twenty-first century, women were active throughout the government. Some had been named to highly visible positions, including Dr Speciosa Wandira Kazibwe as Vice President and Miria Matembe as Minister of State for Ethics and Integrity. In addition to elected politicians, other women held positions within the bureaucracy, the military, and parastatals. Government officials were more aware of women and their concerns than in the past and were supposed to include gender as a factor in planning.[47] At the local level, some women MPs were active within their constituencies, talking about economic development, family planning, and other issues.[48] Women councilors in local bodies were thought to be effective in disseminating information to their constituents and were commonly named to financial positions because they were seen as detached from the old centers of local power and less corrupt.[49] In Mbarara, more women than men were elected in 2002 to the District Council, and a woman was chosen as its speaker. Women also stood for some of the seats reserved for youth and people with disabilities.

Public perceptions of women who were involved in government included some positive features. Women were respected for their competence, including Rebecca Kadaga, Deputy Speaker of the Ugandan Parliament and formerly head of FIDA, G. N. Bitamazire, Minister of State for Primary Education and first president of NAWOU, and Justice Julia Sebutinde, the head of a series of Commissions of Inquiry into corruption or misappropriation in government-related bodies.[50] The queen of Buganda, herself a career person, was reported in glowing terms as she promoted women in development and participated in community affairs.[51] At a meeting in March, 2003, Ugandan women leaders listed 'improved visibility for women/gaining a voice', 'political/legal gains', and 'decision-making/leadership' among the top improvements for women since 1986.[52]

The other area in which the NRM government actively promoted girls and women was education. During the late 1980s, the government, prodded by NGOs, became concerned about the relatively low proportion of women enrolled in universities.[53] At a workshop on 'Women, Law and Development' in 1989, the first deputy prime minister expressed his alarm that of 1,640 students admitted to Makerere University that year, only 373 (23 percent) were female. He commented that 'women's education was lagging behind men's because society grooms a woman for marriage and hence early school drop out'. The following year, the government introduced an affirmative action measure designed to increase the number of women entering Makerere and the few other public universities.[54] Female applicants were henceforth awarded an extra 1.5 points on top of their earned secondary school examination scores, a policy justified on the grounds that girls' schools frequently provided less rigorous education than did boys' schools and that girls had extra responsibilities at home that kept them from schoolwork. This policy proved at least partially effective. The enrollment of women at Makerere rose to 35 percent in 1999 and 41 percent in 2002; the proportion of female graduates increased from 28 percent in 1995 to 38 percent in January 2003.[55]

More important in terms of the number of people affected was the government's policy of Universal Primary Education (UPE), which offered free schooling at the primary level. Prior to 1997, parents had been required to pay fees even in government-supported schools. Many poor families could not afford the cost, and if they had to choose which children to send to school, they generally preferred boys. Though the fraction of all school-aged children who were enrolled in primary education had been rising gradually over time, as late as 1992 only 46 percent of all girls and 56 percent of all boys were attending school.[56] Literacy was also low, especially among women: in 1990, 55 percent of women aged 15 and over were illiterate, as compared with just 32 percent of men.

The government's thinking about mass primary education was influenced by studies that demonstrated the special long-term significance of educating girl children. Girls who had completed primary school were likely to marry at a later age, produce fewer children, and invest in the health and education of those children. In the first stage of the UPE project, started in 1997, each family was allowed to send four children (of whom at least two had to be girls) to government-supported primary schools without paying fees, though they still had to provide a uniform and some supplies. The program was extended several years later to cover all children. UPE resulted in a huge increase in primary school enrolments, from 3.4 million in 1996 to 6.9 million in 2001.[57] Despite a large rise in government expenditure and attempts to train more teachers, class sizes in the early years of UPE were very large, and school buildings, libraries, and books were inadequate. In 2002, only 60 percent of schools were able to meet the target ratios of one teacher per 55 pupils and one desk per three pupils.[58]

As intended, the impact of UPE was particularly marked for several categories of children. In 1992, only 51 percent of poor children of primary school age had been enrolled, as compared with 82 percent of rich children.[59] By 1999, however, 84 percent of poor children were in school, as were 85 percent of rich children. Female enrollments rose more sharply than did male. By 2000, 88.8 percent of all girls of primary age were in school, as were 89.3 percent of all boys. Girls' enrollment had thus increased by 95 percent since 1992, whereas boys' had risen by only 59 percent. In 2001, girls constituted 49 percent of all primary school children, and UPE was bearing fruit in terms of literacy.[60] Further, more girls were continuing their education: 44 percent of secondary school students were female in 2001. By 2002 a few schools were beginning to allow adult women to return to education.[61]

Other improvements in female education extended these government initiatives. Women's organizations displayed strong interest in the training of girls and women. They were concerned about the ways in which gender affected students' performance, and they worked hard to persuade more girls to do science subjects in school and to pursue such fields as mathematics and engineering at university level.[62] Women leaders expressed concern about the ongoing importance of the elite boarding schools, which many of them had attended but which they felt had an excessively narrow clientele. ACFODE was instrumental in the creation of the Department of Women's Studies at Makerere University, the first such program in sub-Saharan Africa. Beginning operations in 1991 after five years of lobbying and planning, the new department served as a designated research center for women. It also offered undergraduate courses in gender and development and an MA degree.[63] When the department started, it was housed in a small basement room with one table, three chairs, one borrowed typewriter, and several cardboard boxes of books. By October 2001, the department (renamed Women and Gender Studies) had graduated 97 MA students and added a large undergraduate program in Gender and Development. In July 2002, the department moved into a spacious new building of its own, just in time to host Women's Worlds 2002, an international women's congress attended by 2000 delegates from 90 countries and covered extensively by Uganda's newspapers.[64]

Practical education was expanding too. Some women gained access to training in business and computer skills through short courses for adults. The Mothers' Union, for example, set up a training center in Mukono in 1989 which included business management among its classes, and in 1995 it opened a vocational training center in Kampala that focused on computer science as well as other practical subjects.[65] Within our district sample, 30 percent of the women had received some form of training in business management, and 16 percent had acquired some computer skills. If the third of our sample who received practical training as adults proves representative of all working women, this type of instruction will certainly make a difference over the longer run.

An area heralded as offering great potential for women was training in Information and Communication Technology (ICT), the cluster of new forms of communication that were transforming how information was transmitted and business done in the early twenty-first century. Idealists spoke of how the ICT revolution would help developing countries – including their women – to 'bridge the digital divide,' thereby moving into the twenty-first century on a more equal basis with the developed world.[66] By 2003 several Ugandan institutions were offering short courses and longer certificate programs in ICT, with preference sometimes given to women.

Working women benefited from the government's advocacy of women. Many people concerned with women's issues and their economic roles argued that, when people saw that women held positions of power in government and functioned effectively in decision-making roles, they were more receptive to women's participation in middle and higher strata of the business world and professions as well. Improved access to schooling and training likewise helped to create a climate conducive to women's work. As a woman in our district sample who runs a small shop and restaurant in Mpigi commented, 'Our mothers suffered a lot, but for us, we are now okay. In the past, if you hadn't gone to school, you were just too stupid. You sat behind in the kitchen. Women used to be in the background, but now we are considered as human beings. Now, we are enlightened. Even if you are illiterate, you are taught skills.'[67]

The NRM's perceived advocacy of women created widespread popular backing for the Movement among women, especially in rural areas. In our district sample, more than a quarter of those interviewed voluntarily praised the NRM for the improvements it had brought for women. A retired nurse in Lira, who supplemented her pension by operating a drug shop, said 'Thanks to the NRM, more women are now working, they have got good educations, and many of them are in high positions, especially in politics and other professions, which was not there in the past. Women are now doing well.'[68] Another Lira woman, who ran a shop that sold clothes for women and children, commented:

> NRM has brought a good change. Women's economic and political status has improved. In the old days, women's voices would not be heard. But from 1986 to date there is an immense change in women's economic, political, and social participation. Before, women never owned land, unlike today when women have money of their own to buy assets like land, houses, and other things. Women know their rights, and some men today respect them.

The improved status of women was linked in some of our interviews with broader issues of political involvement and freedom of speech. A secretary in Lira, who raised poultry on the side, explained: 'Politically women have come up. In the past politics was mainly done by men, but currently tough women are in politics, especially now there is affirmative action. There is freedom of speech, and women's rights have made them do away with their inferiority complex. The majority of women are now vigilant and active in politics.'[69] A secretary at a primary school in Hoima said, 'NRM has listened to the voices of the underprivileged, especially women, children, and the disabled'; a personnel officer in Jinja emphasized that 'in this period there is freedom of expression'.

Among our sample, the few negative comments about Museveni and the NRM were limited to statements like 'stealing has become normal and the level of trust-worthiness of public officials has gone so low' or 'corruption is spoiling Museveni's good name'.[70] The extent of support for the government among these women, most of whom lived in smaller communities, contrasts with the disaffection observed among a rising number of urban women. In addition, women who had criticisms of the government and President may not have felt comfortable expressing them to unknown interviewers.

Disillusionment and backlash, 1998–2003

Despite the great advances for women made possible by the NRM's affirmative action policies, activists were increasingly downhearted in the years after 1998. Their disillusionment stemmed in part from the realization that enacting pro-women measures was not enough: implementing them effectively in the face of deeply rooted habits of male authority and female submissiveness was a major challenge. The government's commitment to women seemed to be decreasing, while problems such as corruption and ongoing fighting in the north loomed large. Furthermore, a strong backlash was developing against what were perceived as the unfair advantages given to women. By 2003 many people who worked on women's issues were gravely concerned. Rather than fighting for additional rights for women, they were now worried that they would not be able to hold on to the gains previously made.

Some of the discouragement among women leaders was due to their growing awareness that affirmative action had not achieved as much as they had hoped. In 1998, women held only 13 percent of 92 posts at the ministerial and sub-ministerial level, and in 2002 a discouragingly small proportion of women held decision-making positions elsewhere in the public sector: 20 percent women among permanent secretaries and 19 percent among under secretaries, 15 percent among judges, 23 percent among chief magistrates, 10 percent among resident district commissioners, and 8 percent among ambassadors.[71]

The government bureaucracy's ostensible sensitivity to women's issues was shown to be limited, though some statistics were now broken down by gender, as women activists had demanded. CEEWA-Uganda conducted a study in 1998 that examined the attitudes of 60 important people in seven branches of the central government concerning the role of gender factors in planning. Although 86 percent of the officials claimed they had some knowledge about gender issues, only 53 percent said they took these issues into account when making decisions.[72] The great majority (92 percent) said they did not have any idea how gender-disaggregated data could be generated. Many parastatals and government-sponsored initiatives, including important economic ones, paid little attention to women's concerns.[73] At the turn of the century activists were still pushing the NRM to put more women into positions of power at all levels and to enforce gender concerns within the bureaucracy.[74]

Even though women were guaranteed seats in local government bodies and Parliament, they found it difficult to compete with men because of gender-based obstacles.[75] Women faced disadvantages when campaigning. They were expected to fill conventional female roles: unmarried candidates were seldom taken seriously, and even married women needed to dress conservatively, behave modestly around other men, and make clear that they had their husband's backing. People worried that if a woman were elected to a local council, she might abandon her husband in favor of men she met there.[76] A lecturer at Makerere University had to kneel at public meetings when requesting men's support for her candidacy; several newspaper photos showed other female candidates kneeling while soliciting votes.[77] Women were often unable to compete with men financially while seeking election, because they controlled fewer resources of their own. In one literary representation, a school teacher standing for office was first criticized because she was a single mother and then faced a crisis when she could not afford to pay what the male candidates provided while campaigning.[78] More women than men were excluded from government because they did not meet the constitutionally imposed requirements for formal education. In Mbarara, the woman nominated by President Museveni in 2002 to be the resident district commissioner was disqualified because of insufficient education.[79]

Once elected, women were not always effective advocates for gender equity. Many women's representatives in national and local government bodies did not perceive themselves as responsible for presenting women's issues, and they often stayed silent in debate. Seldom did they assume leadership roles, apart from being named as vice-heads of committees or other bodies, positions that normally conveyed little actual power. Those politicians who stepped outside accepted female roles faced severe criticism and sometimes ridicule. Even women who had previously been applauded as effective fighters for women, like Maria Matembe and Winnie Byanyima, were by 2002–3 commonly regarded as excessively aggressive and out of line. Vice-President Kazibwe had initially been represented by the press in dismissively female but generally positive terms: as 'mother of four,' 'baby faced,' or 'a good Catholic DP girl'.[80] Later she became controversial because of her outspoken comments about men. When she announced in 2002 that she was seeking a divorce on grounds of domestic violence, she triggered a firestorm in the media for talking publicly about matters that should be kept within the home.[81] Even some women activists felt that she had harmed the cause by providing fuel to those who argued that women who were powerful in public venues could not be restrained within marriage. Although Kazibwe was not formally removed from office, within a year she had resigned, going to Harvard University in the US for advanced medical study.

Burnout and political disfavor reduced the number of effective women leaders. Some of the older women had lost their willingness to fight, after repeated disappointments. In 2002, when Matembe was asked about the attempt by women's organizations and a few women MPs to get a clause on co-ownership of land by women added to the Land Amendment Act, she said: 'I have lost hope about that provision. The clause will never get [to Parliament]. I don't think anybody will struggle harder than I did. I wish them all the best, they can try. I have fought enough on causes of women, let the young people fight. You never know, God may come to their rescue. My energy died a long time ago.'[82] Byanyima, a long-time fighter for women's rights, lived under threat of imprisonment because of her husband's challenge for the presidency in 2001 and her own criticism of the government.[83]

In schooling as well, it was becoming increasingly clear that simply offering girls equal opportunities for education did not solve the underlying problems. The school drop-out rate for girls was rising again early in the new century, after several decades of improvement. Among the factors that contributed to this troubling development were the need for their labor at home and the fact that girls who became pregnant, in some cases through rape, might not be allowed to remain in school.[84] Muslim girls were particularly unlikely to continue into and through secondary school. An article in *The East African* written several weeks after Women's Worlds 2002 pointed out that the conference had had little practical impact upon the problems faced by women in Uganda. 'Education is critical to the advancement of all women, yet nothing is done when greedy fathers marry off their teenage daughters to rich old men. As long as the world fails to back the women's emancipation rhetoric with concrete financial and legal empowerment, conferences such as the one that took place at Makerere will come to naught.'[85] This ambivalence was echoed at the women leaders' meeting in March 2003: improved education was cited as one of the top five gains for women since 1986, but 'limited education' was on the list of current problems for women.[86]

Nor did ICT offer the benefits to women that early enthusiasts had hoped. In

Uganda as in many other countries, women were at a severe disadvantage in profiting from the new technologies. Few families had a landline telephone at home, so women could not access ICT there, and they were less likely than men to work in settings that had an ICT connection. The government displayed little concern with women's issues in planning for ICT.[87] Even when ICT facilities and training were available, women were generally reluctant to pursue them. In 2000 CEEWA-Uganda undertook a test project for small businesswomen, hoping to empower them economically through the use of ICT.[88] The impact of the experiment was disappointing. The intended beneficiaries made less use of the facilities than had been expected, and they generally ignored computer-based forms of ICT. In rural Telecentres, mobile telephones were the most heavily used facilities, with photocopiers and FAX machines next, if they were working. These outcomes resulted from gender-based factors. Women were busy, it was difficult for them to travel to the Telecentres, and the opening hours and training sessions were scheduled at times that proved inconvenient for them. Some husbands forbade their wives to go to the centers, and many women lacked the skills and confidence to utilize the services due to illiteracy, innumeracy, language, and content.

The sense of discouragement that resulted from a realization that gender problems could not be solved simply by pro-active measures was compounded by a feeling that the government no longer cared about women's issues. In 1998 the NRM did not support proposed changes to the Land Act that would have given women greater rights over family land, nor did it back the introduction of a Domestic Relations Bill.[89] By 2003, the heady optimism about women's progress visible during the earlier 1990s was gone. Miria Matembe and several other important women were removed from office by Museveni that spring, and replaced by men. Another effort to reform the land laws failed, and a moderate Domestic Relations Bill was abandoned before it was submitted to Parliament.

Wider political problems contributed to a sense of discomfort. In the north of the country, fighting between government forces and the LRA/Kony rebels continued through 2003. As had been the case during the Amin/Obote II period, women were harmed disproportionately. They faced destruction of houses and fields by soldiers and guerrillas, murder of family members, rape, abduction of children, and the many hardships of living in refugee camps, including sexual abuse.[90] Corruption in government brought practical problems for women trying to earn money and contributed to worry about the feasibility of democracy within the country. A historian of Bakiga culture commented in 2003 that democracy and development had intensified corruption.[91] This view was echoed by an expert on Baganda traditions, who suggested that Uganda had not moved through the stages needed to implement a representative form of government successfully. Some educated urban women felt that corruption, the government's attempts to curtail freedom of speech and the press, and greater use of state violence were all associated with the government's decreasing commitment to women.[92]

Women at many levels of society realized that the forthcoming Presidential and Parliamentary elections, to be held in January 2006, might have an impact upon the standing of women. Our district interviews took place during the first four months of 2003, a time when permitting multiple political parties was under discussion but the question of whether the Constitution should be changed to lift the presidential term limit for Museveni had not yet become a hot issue. The guidelines we provided to our interviewers included the following statement, which would have been translated into local languages in various ways: 'No one knows right now what will happen politically in 2006. Do you think that women who work will be secure, regardless of political events, or do you think their position may be affected by what happens in the government?'

Of those who had an opinion, nearly half thought that working women would not be affected by the political situation: women were sufficiently grounded within the economic system to maintain their position regardless of who ran the country. Most attributed that security to wider changes affecting women, primarily education and their current participation in government. Women who had some money of their own, it was suggested, would be especially safe. Such responses suggest that governmental support for women was seen as a facilitating but not a necessary criterion for women's ability to earn an income. Another 13 percent felt that working women were at risk, that they would be affected adversely in economic or political terms by a change of government. Several feared that if the NRM left power, a new government would not favor women. Two-fifths of the sample gave a qualified answer, pointing mainly to the generic dangers of political instability at the time of the next elections and thereafter.

By 2003, a strong backlash against the special privileges given to women by the government's affirmative action policies had emerged. Even during the period of constitution building in the mid-1990s, some men had expressed reservations about women's great effectiveness in securing their rights within the new document. In 1995, *New Vision*, generally sympathetic to the NRM's agenda, published an article entitled 'Equal before the law'.[93] Though it ostensibly challenged the fear that the

Equal before the law

By A Special Correspondent

Not long ago, in the affairs of men and nations women, like children, were sup-

SOME men have expressed fears that the new constitution has placed women above men. It has done no such a thing. All it has done is uplift women's rights and protect their interests which have been denied them through customs, traditions and beliefs.

the past, the new constitution of Uganda is welcomed as a breath of fresh air in a world that has been largely unfair and unjust. From now henceforth in Uganda, women are to be accorded quality with men not just in

Illustration 8.1 Cartoon about Constitutional Rights for Women, New Vision, 29 November 1995

new Constitution had placed women above men, it was accompanied by the cartoon shown in Illustration 8.1. In 2003, many men and some women – from the level of Parliament down to the villages – felt that women had received unfair advantages and that change was needed. The commission that was reviewing the 1995 Constitution was under pressure to reduce the number of seats reserved for women, and Makerere University was being pushed to revisit its policy of granting additional points to female applicants. In March 2003, women leaders summarized these problems on their list of the major challenges women currently faced: 'problems in sustainability/lack of a shared vision/limited awareness and use of gender tools', 'insufficient or ineffective government support for women's issues', and 'backlash against the gains made by women, on the part of men and some other women'.[94]

Women's Organizations

One of the most conspicuous features of the NRM period, at least between 1986 and around 1998, was the vitality of the Ugandan women's movement.[95] Those were exciting, optimistic years for activists. Women's organizations and NGOs or CBOs dedicated to women's wellbeing were numerous, active, and generally effective. Some were rooted in the past (including church-based organizations), but many were created after the Nairobi Conference and the establishment of the NRM government. Undertaking public advocacy, education, and/or specific improvement projects, some also attempted – generally without much success – to bridge the gap between educated, urban women and rural women.[96] Although many of the NGOs were international, they had primarily Ugandan staffs, as did all the local organizations: both types developed the capacity of the women who worked for them as well as those whom they assisted. In some situations these groups worked in tandem with the government, but they also pushed public officials for new policies and monitored government enforcement of measures that affected women.[97] They focused on two main areas: legal rights and social justice; and female poverty and access to credit.

Improving women's legal rights – especially their ability to inherit and hold land – was a major goal. In 1991, women were estimated to own 7–26 percent of all land in Uganda, and their holdings were generally smaller than those of men.[98] In many of the country's ethnic groups, women did not have an equal claim to family land, they found it hard to purchase land on their own, and widows had no right to the land on which they had lived and which they had farmed while their husband was alive.[99] Women's organizations undertook two strategies in approaching these issues. On the one hand, they promoted changes in legislation. They pushed for the Land Act of 1998, which would have given women greater tenurial security, and when it failed to win Parliamentary approval, they continued to call for changes in the laws that would enable married women to co-own property.[100] They also wanted repressive family laws that discriminated against women in the areas of divorce and child custody to be scrapped, and they worked (unsuccessfully) for the passage of new laws on sexual harassment and domestic relations, such as making physical abuse a crime and outlawing marital rape.

At the same time, women's groups were educating and assisting women about their rights. In 1988 the 60 members of the Uganda branch of FIDA, the

International Federation of Women Lawyers, opened a legal clinic for needy women in Kampala.[101] The president of FIDA, Rebecca Kadaga, said that the clinic would offer advice on the succession of land and estates, family law, maintenance and custody of children, and divorce settlements. FIDA also intended to prepare a pamphlet describing laws relevant to women in simple terms and to travel throughout the country to conduct legal education sessions with women. Legal aid clinics were later set up by other NGOs in district towns. Some of the problems faced by uneducated women who came for help to these clinics are painfully documented in *Tears of Hope*, a collection of narratives recorded by members of FEMRITE, the Uganda women writers' organization.[102] Such activity did heighten the legal awareness of some women. In 2002 a hawker sued the Kampala City Council, charging that the police had beaten her while trying to remove her from the streets; in Mbarara a woman sued the local newspaper for defaming her by saying that she maltreated customers and solicited men sexually at the shop where she worked.[103] The press reported that sex workers had petitioned Parliament, asking that their profession be legalized and that better working conditions be established.

The picture nevertheless remained fairly bleak as of 2003. Legal constraints (including women's ignorance of the law and of how the judicial system worked) stood in the way of their advancement.[104] Bridewealth was still demanded in some areas, promoting a sense that a man had paid for the services provided by his wife and making it difficult for a woman to leave an abusive husband (since her parents would need to return the bridewealth to the man). Despite reforms in the Constitution concerning women's right to inherit land, the ability of rural widows to keep possession of marital property was often limited in practice by the claims of the man's family.[105] Inheritance rights of daughters or co-wives were even less secure. Because women were not perceived as rightful landowners, even when they did nominally have title, use of land was often controlled in practice by their husband or another male relative. Also ill-defined were whether a woman could inherit a business she had operated jointly with her husband and whether she could leave her business to her own heirs.

Violence against women was a major problem, though – except for the commotion following Vice-President Kazibwe's divorce announcement – it was rarely discussed in public. Wife beating was evidently widespread.[106] Physical chastisement was not illegal, so long as the wife was not severely injured, and it was seen as legitimate by many men and women alike if a woman displeased her husband. In one short story, a woman angers her husband by complaining that he is spending their family's money on other women.[107] When he beats her, male neighbors refuse to interfere: 'That is the culture. The man is disciplining his wife and that is their business.' Uganda's churches and mosques acquiesced in this pattern. They commonly advised abused women to accept domestic violence with a forgiving spirit and to remain with the man unless their own lives or those of their children were in danger.

Women of all ages – but most worryingly girls – were commonly seen as objects for the sexual gratification of men.[108] In 2002 educators and the media were concerned about the soaring problem of defilement (forced sexual activity) of girls. Workshops held in connection with the 'Day of the African Child', a UN-sponsored project, included discussion of the problem that older men were increasingly enticing young girls into sex, believing them to be free from HIV/AIDS; a popular local drama group presented a play dealing with defilement, including music and video clips, in communities across the country.[109] In Mbarara, the police reported that 50 girls were raped every month but the culprits were rarely punished. Fourteen girls were said to have dropped out of one primary school in Busia District the previous year 'after they were impregnated by their teachers and fellow pupils'.[110] When efforts in 2003 to persuade Parliament to consider a Domestic Relations Bill and to enact stronger measures against sexual violence proved unsuccessful, the Uganda Women's Network commissioned a report exploring the relationship between the proposed bill and the country's Poverty Eradication Action Plan.[111] The goal of the study was to demonstrate the consequences of marital insecurity and domestic violence for women's economic situation. The women leaders who met in March, 2003 noted that certain legal gains had been made but felt that 'inadequate laws on some matters of vital concern to women,' including landholding and domestic violence, remained a major problem.[112]

Poverty was the second main focus of women's groups during the NRM period.[113] Often working together with government initiatives, women's groups ran workshops in various regions of the country on how to combat poverty and set up small-scale enterprises.[114] Within local communities, a few women founded co-operatives, advocated during the later 1980s and early 1990s as a means of helping rural women to pool their resources and labor and thereby participate in economic development. Women's cooperatives grew wheat and passion fruit, prepared chicken feed, and set up a tailoring project.[115] But the cooperatives faced serious problems – including the lack of literacy and other skills of most of their members, poor management techniques, and weak profits within an inflationary economy – and most of them failed fairly quickly. A limited number of women took part in unions or other workers' organizations, groups permitted though not encouraged by the NRM government.[116]

Women selling in several of Kampala's markets organized themselves as well. In Kiyembe market, a protracted struggle in 1986–94 pitted members of a cooperative of women vendors against the local council and town clerk, who evicted them from their market stalls. The dispute, barely mentioned in the newspapers, was used as a case study in a research project interested in 'why women in Uganda often find that they have to organize along gender lines to protect their interests'.[117] The author concluded that the conflict 'reveals the depths of male bias against women in society and how quickly this bias becomes politicized when women attempt to make even small claims on resources'. The women who sold in Owino market, Kampala's largest and at times roughest venue, organized during the mid-1990s. In 1995, when the Owino Women's Group was said to include 75 percent of all the vendors at Owino, it was addressed and encouraged by the Vice President, Dr. Kazibwe.[118] The group later agitated for improved sites for their stalls and organized a benefit to raise money for their own building.

Another approach to poverty involved granting small loans to women, in the hope that they would use the money to improve the ongoing economic situation of their household. In 1995, there was great interest in the government-backed *Entandikwa* project.[119] This loan fund reserved 30 percent of its money for women, and women's organizations joined the government in encouraging individual women and groups to apply. What proved a somewhat more successful approach was developed by the microfinance institutions (MFIs). These loaned money to poor women who lacked the collateral to qualify individually for commercial bank loans so that they could develop or expand income-generating activities.[120] In this approach, women generally joined together into groups that collectively assumed responsibility for small loans to their members. The money came from governmental bodies or NGOs, the latter usually funded by foreign organizations. Often involving regular weekly meetings at which women paid in small sums to repay their loans and sometimes put a little into savings, some MFIs also trained their members in simple financial skills. In return, the women had to pay a high rate of interest (usually around 30–35 percent per annum) for short-term loans, seldom longer than 3 months. Agricultural projects rarely qualified for support.

MFI programs for women became common during the early 1990s, and by 1995 the Uganda Women's Finance and Credit Trust, the first large organization, had 8,000 clients.[121] During the later 1990s, MFIs blossomed, with 65 programs active in 2000. These organizations proved to be helpful to women with existing small businesses who could use a short loan to expand their scale of operations. The loans were less successful, however, among very poor women who did not know how to use their cash to generate profits or who spent it on essential household purchases, school fees, or health care. If that happened, they might be able to handle the weekly payments, but they could not repay the capital at the end of the loan. When the government proposed a national strategic plan for microfinance in 2002, an analysis of the proposal commissioned by ACFODE argued that it would have unintended but strongly negative consequences for the neediest women.[122]

Furthermore, very few borrowers succeeded in using their loans to move out of poverty. This was due largely to the high interest rates charged, the short duration of the loans, and the small sums granted.[123] Most women found it difficult to expand their business income sufficiently within a few months to be able to return the principal at the end as well as paying the weekly interest. Because there was great pressure from other members of the group to repay the loan, some women were forced to sell their business stock or household goods to avoid defaulting. Others took out a second loan from a different MFI to cover the first, thereby becoming trapped in escalating indebtedness. Pathetic situations were described in which even basic necessities like cooking utensils and bedding were confiscated by the MFIs. By 2003 there was a growing concern among those who worked with the poor that access to MFI credit was in some cases worsening the poverty of vulnerable women.

As an alternative to an MFI loan, some poor women combined voluntarily into informal social support networks (*munno mukabi*) or rotating saving and credit associations (ROSCAs).[124] In the latter, each woman paid a small amount to the group regularly and received the full kitty on a rotational basis to use for larger expenditures. Many ROSCAs also kept a small loan fund in case members encountered special emergencies. In such groups, no interest was charged, but members might have trouble enforcing payment from their fellows. ROSCAs became increasingly popular with very poor women during the late 1990s, as concern mounted about being unable to handle an MFI loan and its interest.

Furthermore, needy women sometimes found the social climate of a ROSCA more welcoming. A study carried out in the Masaka region in the mid-1990s found that very poor women hesitated to join formal credit groups because they could not afford proper clothing to wear to meetings, they feared the embarrassment of being asked to read or write if they were illiterate, and they felt they could not contribute to running the group since they had no experience in local political, religious, or social welfare organizations.[125]

The impact of improved access to credit is seen in our district sample, half of whom said their lives and work had been assisted in this way. Seventeen percent had received loans from MFIs and 7 percent from commercial banks. More than a quarter had obtained credit of other kinds: from government-supported poverty alleviation projects, HIV/AIDS organizations, business groups, religious bodies, or local credit and savings groups. Three highly successful businesswomen in Kampala had obtained loans together with their husbands, two from commercial banks and one (who is in real estate) from an international lending institution in Nairobi. At the other end of the spectrum, ROSCAs were mentioned by several of the very poor women as providing valued assistance at times of a cash crisis. Jane Kamusiime (Profile 7.2), a small market seller in Kabale, belonged to such a group, and Angela Akello (Profile 2.1), a Community Development officer in Lira, praised ROSCAs for helping destitute women to buy at least basic household items, like bedding and cooking pots.

Despite their energy and fine goals, women's organizations in Uganda were not always effective. Even in their heyday prior to 1998, they faced severe challenges. Outside funding could cause problems. An NGO that received money from foreign sources to address women's issues, even if it was staffed entirely by Ugandans, was open to the charge of promoting Western feminism or other values that were not well suited to the Ugandan context. Conversely, NGOs were subject to criticism by Western feminists that they were not pushing for sufficiently radical change and/or were not achieving even their modest goals.[126] Tension was visible within organizations as well. As Tripp observed, 'The availability of donor funding to NGOs and local organizations has created new struggles over accountability and donor dependence, not just among groups competing for these scarce resources, but more importantly within the organizations themselves. It also takes on class dimensions, since those most likely to apply for these resources are the better educated, better connected and better informed parts of society.'[127]

Women's groups found it difficult to work effectively together. The theme of lack of cooperation within and among women's associations emerged early in the NRM period. An article by an unnamed ACFODE reporter about International Women's Day in 1989 concluded:

> Ugandan women have a long way to go. Despite special consideration by the NRM government, the women are still passive and have not shown positive awareness in struggling for the women's rights and the nation's political survival. Today, women are split between warring factions. Women's organizations are on each other's necks while individual women haunt each other, fighting for funds, men, success and undermining each other. The groups are characterized by gossip, passivity, malicious propaganda, frustrations and inferiority complex. As long as the Ugandan women are still divided and unrealistic about their common goal, they will always be ruled and be bullied.[128]

During the constitution-building process, some women Constituent Assembly Delegates and CBOs were unwilling to participate in the effort to develop a shared women's agenda. Matembe blamed urban women in particular for their failure to contribute.[129] In 2002 a report by ActionAid Uganda criticized the leading women's associations for their ongoing elitism and failure to campaign energetically on behalf of the issues that affected the lives of rural women.[130] ACFODE acknowledged 'glaring challenges' and revised its strategies, including reaching out to younger women and developing linkages with grassroots women.

Participation in women's organizations was declining by 2003. Many groups reported smaller memberships, scant involvement by younger women, and unwillingness to invest time in the group's activities. Some capable and energetic women, the kind who might formerly have helped to run organizations, had decided that they needed to acquire financial security for themselves and their families. This tendency was heightened by uncertainty about what would happen in the 2006 elections, leading people to feel that they must have a solid economic base of their own to weather possible political trouble. In our district sample, few of the working women – except those in Kabale – were involved in women's organizations or other community groups. Income-generating activities and civic participation competed for their limited time. Since participation in organizations or community projects was generally not remunerated, few women were likely to prioritize it over work that offered a profit.

Women activists in 2003 were troubled by women's decreased willingness to work together for the common good. Several of our torchbearers reported severe infighting among women themselves, which they described only partially in jest as the Ph.D. ('Pull Her Down') syndrome. Women, they feared, were becoming their own enemies, in business, politics, and higher education, undermining the gains previously attained. Women leaders likewise identified 'poor communication among women/lack of mutual support/isolation' as a major challenge, one they thought was reinforced by 'insufficient support for each other' and by 'poor information flow among women, extending from the top all the way into the household and rural communities'.[131]

Since many women's NGOs were funded by foreign money, a grave emerging problem in 2003 was that donors' interests were shifting. Partly because the money granted to women's projects had produced fewer positive results than was hoped, some of the leading foreign backers were giving notice that when current grants or contracts were finished, they would not be renewed. In many cases the money would go instead to supporting 'transparency' in government (efforts to lessen corruption). Fear of 'donor fatigue' was leading some of the largest organizations to cut back on expenses and plan for a more limited future.

A sense of nostalgia for better days in the past may have contributed to a desire to document the history of the women's movement. The 'Women & Men' section in the *Monitor* in March, 2002 included an article about recent books by Sylvia Tamale and Aili Mari Tripp on Ugandan women's participation in politics.[132] Publicity likewise accompanied the appearance in 2002 of *The Women's Movement in Uganda: History, Challenges and Prospects* (edited by Tripp and Joy Kwesiga), Miria Matembe's account of her own experiences (*Gender, Politics, and Constitution Making*), and the celebration of the YWCA's Golden Jubilee.[133] The Forum for Women in Democracy (FOWODE) compiled and exhibited a collection of photographs of women active in public life from 1940 onward.[134] A Ugandan woman member of the East African Legislative Assembly who viewed the photographs commented, 'This is very innovative. We have always been told that the women's struggle started with Museveni, but this exhibition shows it started long before 1986.' The exhibit drew attention to some of the problems facing current women's activists. One photograph showed Winnie Byanyima behind bars in a police cell. FOWODE also published a book of autobiographical statements by women politicians plus booklets of photos and cartoons.[135]

Reproductive Health and HIV/AIDS

Demographic and health factors had a powerful but largely negative effect on working women during the NRM period. A key influence promoting their participation in the market economy was the marked increase in the size of Kampala and the towns during the later part of the century, due mainly to immigration. The urban population expressed as a fraction of the total population (which was also rising) grew from 10 percent in 1985 to 14.5 percent in 2001.[136] Women who lived in urban areas were more likely to need a cash income but also had more opportunities for obtaining it, despite their common lack of employable skills. The rapid and unplanned nature of urban expansion led to a housing crisis, a problem especially acute for women.[137] Continued migration disrupted village families as young people moved away in search of better opportunities, sometimes leaving behind old or sick people with no one to look after them. While some Ugandans were shocked by the impersonal 'old people's homes' they had heard about in North America and Europe, one of the women in our sample − a former nurse who had become a successful businesswoman − hoped to set up a residential nursing home for the elderly.[138]

Culturally defined gender expectations promoted large families but limited women's access to good quality reproductive health care.[139] The total fertility rate (number of births per woman) was very high but declining slightly by the end of the century. Between 1965 and 1985, according to the World Bank's figures, it had varied between 7.04 and 7.22 births per Ugandan woman, but in 1990 it went down to 6.98 and in 2000–1, the latest value, to 6.9.[140] Rural women had many more babies than urban women, while poor women had many more babies than wealthier ones. The average age at first marriage during the 1990s was 19 years for women as compared with 24 for men; among women aged 15–19, 50 percent had already married, as compared with 11 percent of men. It was hoped that improved female education would help to curb population growth and early marriages. In 2000–1, women with no education had an average of 7.8 children and those with a primary education had 7.3, but women with a secondary education had a mere 3.9.[141]

The availability and quality of reproductive health counseling and care were generally low. Both maternal and infant mortality showed a slight but disconcerting *rise* in the early twenty-first century, after years of slow decline.[142] Family planning was limited: only 15 percent of currently married women used any kind of contraception in 1991–8. Prenatal care appeared to be moving in a more positive direction: 87 percent of pregnant women in 1996 received medical attention.[143]

But in 2002 UNICEF reported that the rate of deaths from pregnancy-related causes had risen to new heights, due largely to inadequate prenatal care.[144] An indirect indicator of infant and maternal health is who assists the mother at the time of delivery. Here there were wide discrepancies between rural and urban patterns in the early 1990s. In the villages, only 32 percent of mothers were assisted by a doctor, trained nurse, or trained midwife; 55 percent were assisted by a traditional birth attendant, relative, or friend; and 13 percent gave birth with no one else there at all. In towns, a much higher fraction of women were helped by a trained professional.

Women's ability to succeed in their income-generating activities was affected by reproductive health practices. A woman who had six or seven children was pregnant or breastfeeding throughout most of her fertile years. Poor care increased the chances that she would become ill or die as a result of pregnancy or childbirth. These problems constrained women's ability to contribute economically to their own households and to national growth, while at the same time weakening their chances for personal development. The women in our district sample had smaller families than average (probably because our sample was skewed in favor of educated women working in non-agricultural areas). If we look only at women aged 50 years or more whose childbearing years were presumably over, the average was just 4.8 children per woman. It is not clear to what extent these women had deliberately limited their family size while married as opposed to being widowed, separated, or divorced. Multiple causalities related work and family size. A woman on her own with a young family may have had to work, as may older married women with many children whose husbands' earnings were insufficient. Women of any marital status with only a few children had more time and energy to devote to income-generating activities than did mothers of large families. Conversely, women who lived in or near a town and had their own earnings were more likely to learn about and be able to afford family planning options.

By far the greatest health problem to confront Uganda during the NRM period has been HIV/AIDS, which by the later 1980s was becoming a serious issue in much of sub-Saharan Africa. Although many countries refused to admit that the disease was present in their own populations, the NRM government took the lead in discussing HIV/AIDS publicly and working with international bodies to mount educational campaigns that tried to limit transmission of the virus and de-stigmatize the illness. In 2003, an estimated 820,000 Ugandans were said to be infected with HIV, constituting 8 percent of the population. If these figures are correct, they constitute a real achievement, for this was only half the rate in 1992. But many people had already died, and an estimated 1.7 million children had been orphaned by HIV/AIDS, losing either their mother or both parents. As was the case during the Amin/Obote II period, high mortality forced those women who were left in charge of households to find some way of supporting themselves and their children.

In Africa – unlike the initial North American and European pattern – it quickly became clear that HIV/AIDS was infecting women too, not just men. It was estimated at the end of 1997 that 49 percent of the Ugandans who were HIV-positive or had AIDS were women. Women were susceptible to the involuntary contraction of HIV/AIDS through rape, especially common during the unsettled period prior to 1986 when HIV/AIDS was spreading among soldiers. The ability of women to demand that their sexual partners use a condom varied with marital status. Among some single women, efforts to promote condom use were proving successful by the turn of the century. A report by UNAIDS/WHO in 2002 stated that the number of unmarried women between the ages of 15 and 24 who insisted on condom use had doubled between 1995 and 2001; the proportion was expected to reach 28 percent by the end of 2004.[145] Increasing awareness among younger women stemmed in part from the activities of NGOs and such targeted newspapers as *Straight Talk*. For wives, the problem was more difficult. As early as 1989 an article about women's knowledge of AIDS commented that, because married women were generally monogamous themselves, they believed they were safe from HIV infection.[146] Yet cultural patterns allowed husbands to have multiple partners, while wives could not deny sex to their husbands or insist that they use condoms.[147] Men therefore brought the infection home.

The multiple effects of HIV/AIDS were revealed clearly in our district sample. Some women described the epidemic as a national issue. Mary Katushabe (Profile 2.4) identified HIV/AIDS (together with poverty) as the great unresolved challenges of the NRM period. But several women gave credit to Museveni and his government for their efforts to combat the spread of the disease. A woman who ran a clothing shop in Lira commented, 'The AIDS scourge started and spread like bush fire. It started as a disease of urban areas but has now spread to rural ones. The NRM came out openly to sensitize people about the dangers of HIV/AIDS and how to protect themselves from contracting it.'[148] In more personal terms, many of the women mentioned the death of parents, aunts or uncles, husbands, siblings, children, or grandchildren. Two small businesswomen in Mpigi said, 'I have lost many relatives and some more are currently down' and 'almost all my clanspeople have died of AIDS'.[149]

The death of a husband, partner, or other male relative often meant a drop in household income and loss of personal support. A woman who owned a bar in Arua commented, 'I lost the father of my child to HIV/AIDS. Although we were not married, he was helping with the child's upkeep. I have also lost many other friends and relatives who used to help me in my work.'[150] The proprietress of a shop in Mpigi said that if her daughter's father had not died of AIDS, he would have supported the child. A saleswoman in a stationery shop in Jinja said, 'AIDS has given a great blow to many of us. I lost three brothers who were strong pillars in the family, so things are very difficult.'[151]

Children left as orphans through the death of their father or both parents were frequently absorbed into the households of female relatives. Because working women were perceived to have extra cash resources, this responsibility was likely to fall upon them. A primary school teacher in Jinja was raising the children of an uncle who had previously assisted her and to whom she was close.[152] Angela Akello (Profile 2.1) lost several siblings but received help in providing for her orphaned nieces and nephews from a community HIV/AIDS initiative. Seven elderly women were looking after orphaned grandchildren. The burden of caring for orphaned children did not necessarily fall upon the women with the highest earnings. Of the 42 women who said they had 5–18 or 'many' dependants and who reported their earnings, 29 percent had a monthly income of less than Ush 100,000 (US$50), 48 percent earned Ush 100,000–499,999 (US$50-249), and 24 percent earned Ush 500,000+ (US$250+).

Profile 8.1. Coping with HIV/AIDS: 'Thereza Kamugasa'

Thereza Kamugasa was a 50-year-old widow whose husband had died of AIDS and was herself HIV-positive.[153] Although she had begun her working life as a teacher, she was in 2003 supporting herself and her family by growing and selling vegetables: she was too ill to hold a regular job. She lived in a modest house in a village some distance from Hoima, surrounded by plots of sweet potatoes, cassava, and beans. When interviewed, she had just come in from working in her garden and was dressed in muddy clothing. After welcoming the interviewer and sitting down with her on the floor to talk, she answered in an open manner the questions put to her. Although she cried during the conversation, she commented at the end that talking about her problems had given her some sense of relief.

A Protestant Munyoro, Thereza was born in 1953 in the Mulago area of Kampala, where her father was an administrator in the hospital. While she was still young, her father divorced her mother and thereafter did not pay anything to help raise the children. Her mother took them back to Hoima town, where she worked as a nurse to support the family. She must have earned a fairly good income, for Thereza attended a prominent girls' primary school in Hoima, which she said was such a good school they even had two uniforms! She went on to secondary school, where her teachers affected her life by encouraging her and the other girls to work hard. The pupils had to dig in the school's garden, so she also learned how to grow food – a skill that subsequently stood her in good stead.

When Thereza finished S 4 in 1976, the education sector was lacking personnel and she was invited to take a position as an unlicensed teacher in a primary school. She was in her early twenties – still unmarried, without children, and living with her mother – when she began work. She did not receive any teachers' training but drew upon what she had herself learned at school. Her relatives were happy that she had this job, and other people in the community respected teachers very much. She worked from 8:00 a.m. until 5:00 p.m. and earned Ush 30,000 per month. In control of her own earnings, she gave some to her mother for household maintenance and used the rest to buy clothes and other items for herself.

In 1976, when she was 23, Thereza married, as her husband's first and only wife. He did not like her to work outside the home and after two years insisted that she give up her teaching job. He told her to take up tailoring, but he did not give her any money for training and refused to buy the sewing machine he had promised her. She therefore stayed at their home in a village outside Hoima, bearing and taking care of their four children, while her husband worked for a salary. During the Obote II period, they suffered harassment on political grounds, and her husband was taken away from home for two months, during which time she had trouble providing for the children. She was grateful to the NRM for restoring order: 'From the time Museveni entered Uganda as the president, peace has prevailed all over the country. There is development everywhere, and people have prospered.' Her husband was evidently among those who prospered, for during the latter part of his life he had a good job in Kampala, employed by the Uganda Revenue Authority. Little of his income made its way back to Thereza, but his HIV virus did.

After her husband's death from AIDS in 1994, when she was 41, Thereza

---

needed to generate an income of her own. She was eager to continue educating her children, and that meant money for school fees. She was therefore pleased when she was approached by the AIDS Control Programme (ACP) of the United Nations Development Program. She had been recommended to them as a well liked and educated person, though she lived in a village. From the position they offered her as an outreach worker, plus a variety of other little income-generating activities, she brought in enough money to send her children to boarding schools in Kampala: 'I wanted them to obtain a quality education.' She was able to support her older two daughters through the university, while the younger two children completed all or most of secondary school.

But she reaped little reward from her struggle to educate them. Of the older daughters, both Makerere graduates and married but not working, the first was completely estranged from her mother in 2003: Thereza had never met her son-in-law and did not know where they were living. The second daughter rarely came to see her mother and provided no financial assistance. Thereza's son had completed S 6 and qualified for the university, but because she could not pay, he did not continue. In 2003 he was working voluntarily for an NGO, drawing no salary but hoping for paid work later on. The youngest girl left school after S 4 due to lack of funds. She became an unlicensed teacher, leaving her child with Thereza. Thereza's neighbors taunted her, saying, 'You educated your children, but you are no better off than us. You still have to go to the garden to dig the way we do.'

Over the past few years Thereza's life had become much more difficult, due to a combination of poverty and her illness. After leaving the ACP several years before, because she was no longer well enough to work on a regular basis, she took a position as a part-time cook for World Vision, an NGO that had just opened a branch in Hoima. But she soon found she could not handle that job either: she had many illnesses that kept her at home, due to her damaged immune system, but she could not afford medical treatment. With no other source of income, she decided to go to the government pension office in Kampala to claim her husband's pension. There she found that her oldest daughter had preceded her. Claiming that Thereza was dead, the daughter and her husband had appropriated the entire Ush 3 million (US$1,500) in the account.

Being HIV-positive brought social problems as well. Thanks to the government's energetic promotion of HIV/AIDS awareness and prevention, the secrecy and shame associated with the disease had largely dissipated in many parts of the country, especially in the towns. But in Thereza's isolated village, older attitudes continued. After her husband's death, when she was tested for HIV/AIDS and found to be positive, she decided to make her condition known publicly. 'Unlike most of my village mates and friends, I no longer believe it is a stigma to be an HIV carrier.' Having recently converted to a 'born again' Christian denomination, she stood up in church, telling the congregation that she was HIV-positive and asking for their support and prayers. She has refused to think about becoming close to another man, 'because as a Christian I believe that infecting other people with this deadly disease is committing the sin of murder'. But her openness is not respected by everyone in her community. Some people insult or shun her, and as she walks along the roads going to church or to visit a friend, she hears people saying to each other, 'There is that AIDS carrier passing by.'

In 2003 Thereza was supporting her household (consisting of herself, her mother, her grandchild, and sometimes her younger two children) by growing their food and producing some vegetables for sale. Because she could not afford to hire any workers, she did all the manual labor in the garden herself, though she could no longer dig for long periods at a time. If she had extra money, she bought additional produce from other neighbors and sold it, to increase the profit from her own vegetables. But that profit was very low. In a good month, with many customers, she might earn Ush 40,000 (US$20). She also picked up some money by working occasionally as a secretary for a local government official. Because she had her own house, she used most of her income to buy food and clothing, with milk and meat as extras at the weekend. Despite the problems she had confronted, Thereza ended the conversation by saying, 'I thank God who has enabled me to live despite these challenges.'

Women were defined culturally as carers, a role that often conflicted with their income-generating activities.[154] Fourteen percent of our sample said that HIV/AIDS had harmed their work because they were expected to look after relatives even when it interfered with their own economic activities. A 20-year-old woman in Mpigi who was an apprentice tailor in a shop run by an older woman noted, 'When relatives are sick, they call you to go and nurse them because you are young. Other people who earn more money can then go on working. They believe that you are always available and your income does not matter. They do not realize that you need your earnings for your own upkeep.'[155] A teacher in Jinja said she had often had to miss work, sometimes for long periods, to tend relatives when they were ill. When Joyce Munduru's brother (Profile 7.1) was ill with HIV/AIDS, she depleted her savings and stopped work on the house she was building in order to look after him, as she was the only person in her family who could afford to do so. A dressmaker in Arua who lost two children to HIV/AIDS noted that when they were ill she not only spent money buying medicines for them, she lost customers because of the time she spent at the hospital taking care of the children: 'My clients would wait for their dresses in vain and lose trust in me.'[156]

HIV/AIDS impaired women's work in other ways as well. A shopkeeper in Mpigi said that some of her customers had died before paying the money they owed her; one of her neighbors, who raised food to sell, complained about the amount of time she had to spend away from her business going to burials.[157] A personnel officer in Jinja's local government explained, 'Here at my place of work absenteeism is high, people are bedridden for months, and you continue to pay them. And even for staff who are not sick, they have to go and look after a sick sister, a relative.' A district medical officer in Jinja likewise noted that HIV/AIDS had increased the workload and was psychologically stressing for all the staff.

Some women became involved in HIV/AIDS prevention or nursing. Margaret Birungi (Profile 9.1) talked openly with her employees about the disease and its relation to sexual practices and bought condoms for the men. Another woman, who started work as a women's project officer for the Catholic Diocese in Kabale, developed a successful international career with a progression of NGOs focusing on HIV/AIDS. She commented in her interview: 'The advent of HIV/AIDS and the President's openness about it thrust me into such work. I was first employed in an AIDS information center and then gradually grew in the NGO world as a result.'[158] Several nurses in Arua commented on the emotional pain and physical risk of working with AIDS patients. 'In my work it is pathetic and demoralizing to see HIV+ people whom you know you cannot help much because screening facilities are not there in the health units. I also lack counseling skills for dealing with such people.'[159] 'At the work place government does not provide protective clothing and disinfectants. The fear of contracting AIDS while at work is great, because we handle body fluids like vomit and sputum.'

Yet Peace Kyamureku of NAWOU pointed out that the HIV/AIDS epidemic, despite its grievous consequences, had encouraged women to fend for themselves.

> I think we've really learned a lot from AIDS. One time at a workshop someone said, 'What are the advantages of HIV/AIDS in Uganda?' I was really shocked. How can someone say that when people are dying? But as we discussed it, as we looked at it, we realized it has brought certain benefits. Women, and even children now, they know that someone might die, anyone could go. Before, it was the men who always worked, who brought money, who did things. But now, because of AIDS, women have started getting skills. Even men are telling their wives, 'Well, why don't you start working? What if I'm not there?' The same thing with the children, 'Learn a skill, learn how to do something when I'm not around.' So I think because of that, out of necessity, women have tried to do many more things.[160]

The NRM period thus offered both gains and challenges for women. The restoration of peace to much of the country and the growth of a functional economy provided a solid base for the pro-active policies the government introduced for women in the area of political participation and education. By around 2000, however, there was a mounting sense of discouragement among women leaders. Women's organizations tackled the key issues of legal rights and poverty, but with limited success. Reproductive health problems and HIV/AIDS affected all women, with particular consequences for those who were working. It is to women's economic roles, together with representations, gender tension, and Domestic Virtue thinking, that we now turn.

Notes

1 People in Ankole chose not to re-establish their monarchy, but the kingdoms of Buganda, Bugisu, Bunyoro, and Toro were restored.
2 See Appendix C for quantitative information. Because only 6 women in the sample were children during the NRM period, their family background and education will not be described.
3 For a description of events, see, for example, Tumusiime, *Uganda 30 Years*, and Museveni, *Sowing the Mustard Seed*, chs. 13–14.
4 Mamdani, *Citizen and Subject*, pp. 200–3 and 207–10.
5 Mpigi13. For below, see Mpigi6.
6 Arua8. For below, see Hoima4.
7 Arua14.
8 Lira7. See also Natukunda and Birungi, 'Women at War.'
9 World Bank, *Uganda's Recovery*, and Tumusiime, *Uganda 30 Years*, pp. 95–102. In 1980 the indexed GDP was 1.2 but grew to a peak of 5.86 in 1995 (measured against current US dollars) before settling slightly to 5.7 in 2001 (World Bank, *Africa DataBase, 2003*).

10 World Bank, *Africa DataBase, 2003.*

11 The number of radios per 1,000 people was 88 in 1985, 116 in 1990, and 120 in 1995; the number of television sets per 1,000 was 6 in 1985, 11 in 1990, and 26 in 1995; the number of mobile phones per 1,000 was zero through 1995 but 14 in 2001; the number of computers per 1,000 was 0.5 in 1995 (World Bank, *Africa DataBase, 2003,* CD-ROM). In 1990 there were just 1.7 vehicles per 1,000, a figure that had reached 3.7 in 1995. For below, see U. Bureau of Statistics, *Uganda Demographic and Health Survey 2000–2001,* p. 18, and World Bank, *Africa DataBase, 2003,* CD-ROM.

12 Indexed Net Overseas Development Assistance (ODA) as measured in constant US dollars was between 1.1 and 1.95 in 1965–80, but it was 6.9 in 1990 and 8.0 in 2001 (World Bank, *Africa DataBase, 2003,* CD-ROM).

13 See, e.g., Ellyne, 'Economic History', Tukahebwa, 'Privatization', Lateef, 'Structural Adjustment', Ochieng, 'Economic Adjustment Programmes', J. B. Mugyenyi, 'IMF Conditionality', IMF, *Uganda: Adjustment with Growth,* Bigsten and Kayizzi-Mugerwa, *Crisis, Adjustment,* and, for a later perspective, Mkandawire and Soludo, *Our Continent.*

14 World Bank, *Africa DataBase, 2003.* For below, see World Bank, *Uganda: Growing Out of Poverty* and *Uganda: The Challenge of Growth,* and cf. Jamal, 'Changes in Poverty Patterns'.

15 UNDP, *Uganda Human Development Report 2002.*

16 U. Ministry of Finance, Planning and Economic Development, 'Challenges and Prospects for Poverty Reduction in Northern Uganda'.

17 Basirika, 'Structural Adjustment', pp. 86–7, Busingye, 'The Impact of Structural Adjustment Programs', M. R. Mugyenyi, 'The Impact of Structural Adjustment Programmes', Butegwa et al., 'Private Sector Development', and Gladwin, *Structural Adjustment.* For liberalization of trade, see A. Hale, 'What Does Trade Liberalisation Mean?' and her 'Women Workers', IWGGT, 'Gender and Trade', and Kiggundu, 'Women and Trade'. For other African contexts, see Mupedziswa and Gumbo, *Women Informal Traders,* Clark and Manuh, 'Women Traders in Ghana', Kiteme, 'The Socioeconomic Impact', and Sheldon, *Pounders of Grain,* ch. 7.

18 World Bank, *Uganda: Social Sectors,* Uganda National Council of Children, *Equity and Vulnerability,* and *East African,* 6–12 March 1995, *New Vision,* 1 June 1995, and *Monitor,* 20–22 September 1995.

19 Elson and Evers, 'Gender Aware Country Economic Reports'.

20 TB7.

21 E.g., Newman and Canagarajah, *Gender, Poverty,* and World Bank, *Gender, Growth.* For the response to poverty of women's organizations and NGOs, see later section in this chapter.

22 U. Ministry of Finance, *National Program for Good Governance in the Context of PEAP* (2001), as cited by Lucas, 'Locating Women'.

23 UN, *WISTAT, 1999,* and U. Bureau of Statistics, *Uganda Demographic and Health Survey 2000–2001,* p. 11.

24 E.g., U. Ministry of Finance, Planning and Economic Development, *Uganda Participatory Poverty Assessment Process, Kalangala District Report* and *Kampala District Report.* For below, see U. Ministry of Gender, Labour and Social Development et al., 'Engendering Uganda's Poverty Eradication Initiatives'.

25 U. Ministry of Finance, Planning and Economic Development, *Challenges and Prospects* p. 54.

26 See, e.g., *Monitor,* 26–28 July 1995, and Wanyoto, 'Retrenchment'.

27 Nankunda, *Civil Service Reforms,* pp. 2–3 for this and below. The projected cuts constituted around a quarter of the number of people in the Civil Service in 1987 (U. Min. of Planning and Economic Development, *National Manpower Survey, Census of Civil Servants,* 1988, Table 5).

28 Kabale6. For below, see Hoima10 and Hoima5.

29 Hoima14.

30 Arua3.

31 Kabale11. For below, see Arua14.

32 Lira11. For below, see Kabale10.

33 Kabale18.

34 Jinja9.

35 Mpigi11. For below, see Jinja1.

213

36 Tripp suggested that Museveni was not initially committed to women's issues and was pushed into supporting them by women's organizations and NGOs (*Women and Politics*, ch. 4). Cf. Boyd, 'Empowerment of Women'.

37 *New Vision*, 9 March 1989.

38 *New Vision*, 2 May 1995.

39 *Weekly Topic*, 10 August 1988.

40 Sen and Grown, *Development, Crises*, p. 76.

41 *The Local Governments Act, 1997*, pp. 15 and 25–6. For below, see ibid., p. 10. The Act also required membership by people representing young people and those with disabilities.

42 Tripp, *Women and Politics*, pp. 70–71. See also Tamale, *When Hens Begin to Crow*, chs. 3–4, and Matembe, *Gender, Politics, and Constitution Making*, ch. 5.

43 Tripp, *Women and Politics*, ch. 4. See also Kyasimire, 'The Role of Women'.

44 See, e.g., *New Vision*, 15 November 1989 and 3 March 1995.

45 See Matembe, *Gender, Politics, and Constitution Making*, chs. 4–5, Tamale, *When Hens Begin to Crow*, ch. 5, and Tripp, *Women and Politics*, ch. 4, for this and below.

46 *New Vision*, 13 February and 22 July 1995. Key players were Winnie Byanyima and Miria Matembe. For below, see *New Vision*, 17 November.

47 For a good example, see Uganda National Agricultural Research Organisation, *Outreach and Partnership Initiative*.

48 See, for example, *Orumuri*, 12–18 August 2002 (2 articles).

49 See, for example, *Bukedde*, 27 May 2002, and *New Vision*, 8 March 2002. For below, see *Orumuri*, 17–23 June and 20–26 May 2002.

50 *New Vision*, 24 October and 4 December 2002, *Monitor*, 31 October 2002, and Kwesiga, 'Leaders within Limits'.

51 See, for example, *New Vision*, 7 November 2002, *Bukedde*, 1 and 10 March 2002, and CultHist4 (see Appendix B).

52 See Appendix D.

53 Although the number of female students was rising (from 744 in 1970 to 1323 in 1980), the fraction of women remained fairly constant (18–20 percent in 1970/71 and 1980/81): UN, *WISTAT, 1999*. For below, see *New Vision*, 4 October 1989.

54 See Kikampikaho and Kwesiga, 'Contributions of Women's Organisations', for this and below.

55 *Monitor*, 20–23 January 2003, and Makerere University, *Graduation, 17th January 2003*. See also Kwesiga, *Women's Access to Higher Education*, and Mafatle, 'Determinants of Women Enrolment'.

56 World Bank, Human Development Network, Education Notes, April 2002. The fraction of all girls enrolled in primary school had grown from 30 percent in 1970 to 43 percent in 1980, while that of boys rose from 44 percent in 1980 to 56 percent in 1980 (World Bank, *Africa DataBase, 2003*). Of those children enrolled in primary school, 39 percent were female in 1970, 44 percent in 1985, and 45 percent in 1995 (Kwesiga, *Women's Access to Higher Education*, p. 97, and UN, *WISTAT, 1999*). For below, see UN, *WISTAT, 1999*.

57 World Bank, Human Development Network, Education Notes, April 2002, and U. Ministry of Education and Sports, *Education Statistical Abstract, 2001*. Real per capita education expenditure by the government in constant 1995 US dollars rose from 6.5 in 1995 to 13.2 in 2001 (World Bank, *Africa DataBase, 2003*).

58 Kwesiga, *Women's Access to Higher Education*, p. 93.

59 See World Bank, Human Development Network, Education Notes, April 2002, for this and below.

60 Kwesiga, *Women's Access to Higher Education*, pp. 91–7. For below, see U, Bur. of Statistics, *Uganda DHS EdData Survey 2001*, pp. 14–15, and Kwesiga, ibid., p. 97.

61 E.g., *Bukedde*, 18 February 2002, and Mt Masaba High School in Mbale.

62 *New Vision*, 13 May 1989 and 19 April 1995; *New Vision*, 7 March 1989 and 14 January and 3, 5, and 10 October 1995. For below, see *New Vision*, 17 June and 24 Aug. 1995, reporting on Gayaza High School's 90th birthday celebrations, and Kikampikaho and Kwesiga, 'Contributions of Women's Organisations'.

63 *New Vision*, 13 May 1989, and Mukasa and Tanzarn, *Celebrating 10 Years*, pp. 9–13.

64 E.g., *Monitor*, 3 April and 22 July 2002, a special section on 'Women's Worlds Congress'; *New Vision*, 12 March, 2 and 23 July 2002. Grace Bantebya Kyomuhendo was the

convener of the congress.
65 *New Vision*, 27 February 1989 and 26 July 1995, and, more generally, Tinkasiimire, 'Women's Contributions to Religious Institutions'.
66 E.g., Rathgeber and Adera, *Gender and the Information Revolution*, and Norris, *Digital Divide*.
67 Mpigi6.
68 Lira17. For below, see Lira3.
69 Lira15. For below, see Hoima5 and Jinja7.
70 Kampala20 and Kabale14.
71 UN, *WISTAT, 1999*, and UN, *The World's Women 2000*, p. 172; Kwesiga, *Women's Access to Higher Education*, p. 122.
72 CEEWA–U, *Gender Analysis for Economic Decision Making*.
73 *New Vision*, 25 November 2002, referring to a study of the Strategic Exports Initiative.
74 Tamale, *When Hens Begin to Crow*, chs. 2 and 7.
75 Ibid., esp. chs. 3-6 and 8, and Tripp, *Women and Politics*, esp. ch. 11.
76 Kwesiga, 'Leaders within Limits'.
77 Ahikire, 'Of Local Democracy', *New Vision*, 8 March 2002, and *Bukedde*, 18 June 2002.
78 Okurut, 'The Eyes of a Heifer', in her *Milking a Lioness*, p. 57.
79 *Orumuri*, 5-11 August 2002.
80 Kiguli and Kiguli, 'Representations of Women Leaders'. For below, see the summary in *East African*, 5-11 August 2002.
81 See Chapter 9.
82 *Monitor*, 23 July 2002.
83 *New Vision*, 13 May and 29 July 2002, and *Sunday Vision*, 2 June 2002.
84 See, e.g., Keshubi, 'Joanitta's Nightmare', in Okurut and Barungi, *A Woman's Voice*, p. 28.
85 12–18 August 2002.
86 See Appendix D.
87 E.g., U. Ministry of Works, Housing and Communications, 'National ICT Policy', draft, May 2002.
88 CEEWA-U, 'A Baseline Study on … ICTs', and CEEWA-U, 'ICT Project, Evaluation Report'.
89 Matembe, *Gender, Politics, and Constitution Making*, ch. 7.
90 Natukunda and Birungi, 'Women at War'. For powerful examples, see Okurut, 'Letter of a Daughter' and 'Refugee Girl', in her *Milking a Lioness*, pp. 34 and 18, and De Nyeko, 'Chained', in Barungi, ed., *Words from a Granary*, p. 16.
91 CultHist1 (see Appendix B). For below, see CultHist2.
92 For critiques of the NRM's treatment of women, see M. R. Mugyenyi, 'Towards the Empowerment of Women', Tamale, *When Hens Begin to Crow*, esp. chs. 5–7, and Tripp, *Women and Politics*, esp. chs. 3–4.
93 *New Vision*, 29 November 1995.
94 See Appendix D.
95 Tripp, 'Gender, Political Participation', 'Local Women's Associations', and her *Women and Politics*, Kwesiga, 'The Women's Movement', Dicklich, 'Indigenous NGOs', Tripp and Kwesiga, *The Women's Movement*, and Kwesiga, 'The Women's Movement in Uganda Revisited'.
96 ActionAid Uganda, *Footprints in Social Transformation*, and Bitamazire, 'The NGO Perspective'. For below, see Dicklich, 'Indigenous NGOs'.
97 Kharono, 'Imperatives for International Donor Action', Wakoko and Lobao, 'Reconceptualizing Gender', and Nalwanga-Sebina and Natukunda, 'Uganda Women's Needs Assessment Survey'. More generally, see Staudt, 'The Impact of Development Policies'.
98 Elson and Evers, 'Gender Aware Country Economic Reports', p. 20.
99 Sebina-Zziwa, *Gender Perspectives on Land Ownership*, and 'The Paradox of Tradition'.
100 Matembe, *Gender, Politics, and Constitution Making*, ch. 7. For below, see *New Vision*, 13 May and 29 July 2002, and *Sunday Vision*, 2 June 2002.
101 *Financial Times*, 4 March, and *Star*, 7 March 1988.
102 Edited by Ageta Anne Wangusa and Violet Barungi.
103 *Bukedde*, 24 September 2002, and *Orumuri*, 7–13 October 2002. For below, see *Monitor*, 8 March 2002.
104 World Bank, 'Report of Study on Legal Constraints' (1995), FIDA Uganda, *Annual*

215

Report, 1998, and Martin and Hashi, 'Law as an Institutional Barrier'.

105 Asiimwe, 'Making Women's Land Rights a Reality', and 'Women and the Struggle for Land'. See also Kiguli, 'Mad Apio', in Okurut and Barungi, *A Woman's Voice*, p. 16, Okurut, 'The Muscle of the Law', in her *Milking a Lioness*, p. 90, and Munyarugerero, 'Maria Demands Her Share', Batanda, 'For Our Children', and Ntakalimaze, 'Taste of Betrayal', all in Wangusa and Barungi, *Tears of Hope*, pp. 53, 75, and 131.

106 For fuller discussion, see Chapter 9.

107 Okurut, 'The Reward', in her *Milking a Lioness*, p. 2, and cf. her 'Milking a Lioness', p. 7, in ibid.

108 E.g., Tindyebwa, 'Looking for My Mother', and Barenzi, 'Behind Closed Doors', both in Okurut and Barungi, *A Woman's Voice*, pp. 1 and 22, Okurut, 'A Virgin for the King', in her *Milking a Lioness*, p. 16, and Ekochu, 'Not Until I Find My Daughter', in Wangusa and Barungi, *Tears of Hope*, p. 151.

109 *Sunday Vision*, 16 June 2002; *Sunday Monitor*, 12 May 2002. For below, see *Orumuri*, 3–9 June 2002.

110 *Bukedde*, 12 June 2002.

111 Tanzarn, 'The Link between the Domestic Relations Bill and the Poverty Eradication Action Plan'.

112 See Appendix D.

113 Although women leaders cited economic improvement for women as a major gain since 1986, they felt that poverty and continued economic constraints were among the most serious problems that women faced in 2003 (see Appendix D.)

114 *New Vision*, 4 January and 3 October 1995. For below, see *Monitor*, 15–17 May and 15–18 December 1995, and *New Vision*, 3 October and 4 November 1995.

115 *New Vision*, 11 August and 25 October 1989, and Muhumuza, et al. 'Uganda Cooperative Alliance', as described by Musoke, *Research on Women*, pp. 25–6. For below, see Muzaale, 'A Study of Women Involvement', and Mupawaenda, 'Problems Faced with Women Co-operatives'.

116 *New Vision*, 23 and 30 August and 5 December 1989, *Monitor*, 17–20 November 1995, Ahikire, 'Worker Struggles', and Asowa-Okwe, 'The Dynamics of Women Participation'.

117 Tripp, *Women and Politics*, ch. 8, esp. p. 161.

118 *New Vision*, 6 February 1995. For below, see ibid., 18 May and 17 August. See also, for market women in Owino and other Kampala markets, Davis, 'Time Is Money?'

119 *New Vision*, 11 January, 8 February, 7 and 16 March, and 2 May, and *6ᵗʰ of February*, May.

120 Wavamuno, 'Women Credit Situation', as summarized in Musoke, *Research on Women*, pp. 30-31, Musoke and Amajo, 'Women's Participation', and Ssemogerere, 'Mobilisation of Domestic Financial Resources'.

121 *Monitor*, 17-19 July 1995. For assessment of MFIs, see Wright et al., *Vulnerability, Risks*, and Muwanika, 'Empowerment of Women'.

122 U. Ministry of Finance, Planning and Economic Development, 'Strategic Plan for Expanding the Outreach and Capacity of Sustainable Microfinance', and Sekabanja, 'Situational Gender Analysis'.

123 Kasisira, 'Credit to Ugandan Women', Kateregga, 'Women's Experience with Credit', Kiiza et al., 'Accounting for Gender', Snyder, *Women in African Economies*, ch. 3, and Omitta, 'Challenges of Empowering Women'.

124 Snyder, *Women in African Economies*, ch. 3, Birungi, 'Perspectives for the Evolvement of Kinship Credit Systems', Magyezi, 'The Role of Informal Credit Schemes', and U. Ministry of Women in Development, Culture, and Youth, 'Women's Informal Credit Groups'.

125 Pickering et al., 'Women's Groups'.

126 Porter and Judd, *Feminists Doing Development*.

127 Tripp, *Women and Politics*, p. 198.

128 *New Vision*, 7 March 1989. For below, see ibid., 29 March and 4 April 1995.

129 *New Vision*, 28 October 1995

130 ActionAid Uganda, *Sisterhood?* For below, see *New Vision*, 17 May and 19 November 2002; *Monitor*, 17 May 2002.

131 See Appendix D.

132 8 March 2002. In 1995 ACFODE had produced two films documenting Ugandan women's experiences and prepared a record of its own history and achievements (*New Vision*, 4 April and 14 November.)

133 *New Vision*, 23 July 2002, *Bukedde*, 30 July 2002, and *New Vision*, 9 October 2002.

134 *East African*, 17–23 June 2002.

135 Byanyima and Mugisha, *The Rising Tide*, FOWODE, 'Ugandan Women in Public Life', and its 'What A Pity This Child Was Born a Girl!'

136 World Bank, *Africa DataBase, 2003*.

137 See, for example, Kateregga, 'A Gender Assessment', Ntege, 'Women and Urban Housing Crisis', and Manyire, *Gender and Housing Development*.

138 E.g., CultHist2 (see App. B); Kampala 16.

139 See, for example, Bantebya Kyomuhendo, 'Treatment Seeking Behaviour', her and Ogden's 'Six Women', her 'Low Use of Rural Maternity Services', and her 'Decision-Making in Poor Households', Kwagala et al., 'Health and the Economic Empowerment of Women', and Neema, 'Women's Organisations'.

140 World Bank, *Africa DataBase, 2003*, and U. Bureau of Statistics, *Uganda Demographic and Health Survey, 2000–2001*, pp. 41–4, for this and below. Birth rates at this level led to a rapid rise in the total population during the NRM period despite losses from AIDS. From 14.3 million people in 1985, the population grew to around 24 million in 2003 (World Bank, *Africa DataBase, 2003*, and UN, *WISTAT, 1999*). See also UN Children's Fund, *Children and Women in Uganda* and Uganda National Council for Children, *Equity and Vulnerability*.

141 U. Bureau of Statistics, *Uganda Demographic and Health Survey, 2000–2001*, p. 44.

142 Ibid. For below, see UN, *The World's Women 2000*, p. 47.

143 Ibid., p. 80. For below, see *Monitor*, 25 February 2002.

144 UN, *WISTAT, 1999*.

145 *Monitor*, 10 December 2002.

146 *New Vision*, 13 September 1989.

147 In 2000, when asked whether a wife is justified in refusing sex with her husband, 76 percent of women said yes if she knows he has sex with other women, 89 percent if she has recently given birth, and 91 percent if she knows he has a sexually transmitted disease (U. Bureau of Statistics, *Uganda Demographic and Health Survey*, p. 38). For minimally fictionalized representations of the relationship between HIV/AIDS and physical violence, see Okurut, *The Invisible Weevil*, and Isegawa, *Abyssinian Chronicles*.

148 Lira3.

149 Mpigi4 and Mpigi6.

150 Arua1. For below, see Mpigi12.

151 Jinja1.

152 Jinja10.

153 Thereza was interviewed by Beatrice Tumushabe, in Runyoro, on 19 March 2003 (tape: Hoima7). The interviewer judged that by the standards of that community, Thereza's economic level was low but adequate, living above the bare minimum.

154 E.g., Nalwanga-Sebina, 'Women and AIDS', Obbo, 'Gender and Urban Poverty', her 'What Women Can Do', and 'Who Cares for the Carers?', and Wallman, *Kampala Women Getting By*.

155 Mpigi18. For below, see Jinja10.

156 Arua11.

157 Mpigi9 and 3. For below, see Jinja7 and Jinja10.

158 Kampala23.

159 Arua2. For below, see Arua7.

160 TB2.

Nine

Work & Gender Issues in the NRM Years

Having traced the broader developments that affected women during the NRM years, we turn now to more specific issues. This chapter begins with an examination of women's work, followed by discussion of how women and their concerns were portrayed in the newspapers. After an exploration of the high level of gender tension and domestic violence visible in this period, the final section examines Domestic Virtue thinking during the NRM years and the emergence of a new gender formulation that supported the activity of successful entrepreneurs.

Women's Work

The diversity of women's economic roles during the late twentieth century is demonstrated in a variety of research studies and in Ugandan newspapers. They make clear that women were engaged in a far wider range of economic activities than at any previous time, including occupations previously defined as male. In some cases women were now succeeding at middle or even upper levels of business and the professions. This expansion stemmed from economic need or a desire to use one's education and from the NRM's affirmation of women as active participants and decision-makers within the public domain. In the media, women's work had become so common that it was taken for granted, rather than being newsworthy in its own right. In 1995 and 2002, many references to women's businesses or jobs occur not in articles focusing specifically on *female* activity but rather in discussions of that *type of work*.

General features
Government statistics make clear that during the NRM period the great majority of women continued to work within the family or were self-employed. During the 1990s, 54–8 percent of economically active women were unpaid family workers, 36–9 percent were self-employed workers or employers, and 5–7 percent were waged or salaried employees.[1] Yet, as Winnie Byanyima argued forcefully at the time of the Beijing Women's Conference, such figures do not adequately reflect

either the demands on women's labor or their contributions to the economy.[2] While women's work is often undervalued for cultural reasons, there are also objective difficulties in evaluating the economic contribution of women's unpaid work within the household and their role and level of underemployment in the informal economy.[3] Hence even the most recent government statistics tend to under-record women's participation.

The Uganda Demographic and Health Survey for 2000–1, which attempted to get at the realities of women's work, shows that 73 percent of women aged 15–49 were currently 'employed' (i.e., were working in some way, including on their own family's land) and another 6 percent were not employed at the time of the survey but had been at some time during the previous 12 months.[4] Of currently employed women, 77 percent worked in agriculture and the remainder in other occupations: 10 percent in sales and services, 7 percent in unskilled manual labor, and just under 3 percent each in professional/technical/managerial work and skilled manual labor.

Women's earnings were generally lower than those of men. Among non-agricultural workers in 1995–6, women received between 56 and 83 percent of the wages paid to men, depending on the region.[5] Nor did all women control how their income was spent. In 2000–1, 60 percent of currently employed women decided independently how their income would be used, while 25 percent decided jointly with a husband or someone else; for 15 percent of the women, another person decided. Yet their income was important to the family's financial situation. When asked what proportion of household expenditures their earnings covered, 24 percent of the married women said they paid for all expenses and another 38 percent said they paid for half or more.

Of our district sample, 40 women entered paid work for the first time during the NRM years. Thirty percent went into some kind of business, the majority making or selling food or drink. The proportion of teachers, nurses, and secretaries continued to decline as compared with earlier periods, now only 38 percent, while only 8 percent engaged in other kinds of skilled or high-status work. A quarter of the women provided unskilled or semi-skilled labor, with the largest groups in hairdressing and domestic work. Fewer of the women than in the past were in their teens (16 percent) or unmarried (53 percent) when they started work, with higher fractions aged 25–40 and married.

When asked why they decided to take that particular kind of work, only a quarter said they liked the job or had talent or training for it. Most emphasized the need for money for their families or to support themselves. A woman who runs a hairdressing salon plus shop in Arua said, 'I wanted to avoid financial problems when my husband was delayed in Congo.'[6] A young woman who grew up in a village near Masaka explained, 'I took a job as a housegirl in Kampala because rural life was so hard and we were so poor.' Another group said that they entered the only type of work available or that they had no choice because of their lack of education or skills. Several were encouraged by their parents or husbands to join them in their business. The husband of a Muslim woman interviewed in Kampala said that he had set up a shop for his wife 'to increase the family income and to keep her busy so that she avoids joining gossip groups and being influenced into improper behavior'.[7] Fewer of the women worked in villages than had been the case before, with an increase in the fractions in district towns or peri-urban areas.

In a reflection of how necessary and hence how common women's work had become, 87 percent of the sample said it was usual for women to do the kinds of activity they entered, and 84 percent said their work met with approval from their husbands and other relatives. Only 7 percent said their families opposed their work, and 10 percent met a mixed or qualified response, in most cases from a husband who initially opposed the idea but later accepted the wife's activity. Just one woman said that her parents objected to her work (as a copy typist) because they expected her to get married.

Yet in the broader community some resistance remained. Twenty-two per cent said that other people regarded their decision to enter such work negatively, and 14 percent faced a mixed response. In some cases objection stemmed from the nature of the work. A woman in Lira said she was criticized because she sold beer as well as other goods in her shop.[8] A bar keeper in Hoima, who had young girls available to attract customers and sell sex, claimed (somewhat disingenuously): 'Other people do not like my work. My parents wanted me to carry out some other business, but the money I have is too little to start a business.' Several women said that objection to their work among people in the community stemmed from envy, because their income allowed them to live better than others.

Participation in the market economy brought many benefits for women. In the simplest terms, their own economic circumstances and those of their family improved. Of the women in our district sample, 91 percent said that their current work enabled them to provide essential commodities (food, clothing, and some-times housing) for their own or their relatives' households, a feature especially important for those with large numbers of dependants. Half of the women paid school fees for their children, the highest fraction in any period. A rising concern was building a house – for their own residence, for an elderly relative, or to rent out – and an eighth of the women spent part of their earnings on personal effects for themselves.[9]

Working also offered secondary advantages for women. Some of the women in our sample emphasized that, because they had their own incomes, they were freer from their husband's control. As a nurse who runs a clinic in one of Kampala's suburbs noted, 'Life is better today, for we can get our own money, we can afford to make decisions. In earlier days our mums could only depend on the man.'[10] An education officer in Jinja commented, 'When my mum wanted to visit her parents, she would ask my dad, who would tell her to wait for two months. But now, you get your own money and you just inform him: "My dear, I am going to visit my parents and I have my money." If he contributes, okay, but if he does not, you can afford to buy yourself what you will take to your parents.' Other women stressed their independence from other men in the community. A hairdresser in Lira asserted, that because she has her own money, 'nobody can shout at me now'.[11] A labor officer in Arua observed that she had acquired status, respect, and dignity and could not be pushed around by men any more. Work increased women's social exposure, sometimes allowed them to travel (for example, Mary Katushabe, Profile 2.4), and promoted the develop-ment of new patterns of behavior. Thus, Angela Akello (Profile 2.1) rode a motorcycle to reach dispersed village women around Lira in 2003, though she was in her late fifties.

Types of work

Of the many kinds of work in which women engaged during the NRM years, agriculture remained the most common – to raise food for the family and/or to gain a cash income.[12] In 1994, 89 percent of all Ugandans lived in rural areas, gaining their livelihoods from smallholdings. It was estimated in 1997 that 90 percent of rural women and 53 percent of rural men were engaged in agricultural production. Women provided 80 percent of the labor for food grown for consumption within the country. About two-thirds of that food was retained for the family's own use, though the share was declining. As poverty worsened, food production by women living in towns and cities was increasingly important, for domestic consumption and sometimes for sale.[13] In the newspapers we hear especially about farmers' income-generating activities. Individual women profited from such familiar projects as growing maize and producing poultry.[14] Women's agricultural groups were becoming common in most regions of the country, in some cases producing familiar cash crops like cotton or rice, in others moving into new ventures like beekeeping or mulberry trees and silk worms. Even when agricultural items were grown for export, women were the primary workers, whether on family farms or as paid laborers in commercial agriculture.[15] For traditional exports, women provided 60 percent of the labor; for newer types of exports, like fresh flowers, they provided 80 percent. In a related area, women were becoming involved in the processing and marketing of fish after it was brought to shore, though a strong prohibition in many Ugandan cultures against women going out in boats to fish remained largely intact.[16]

Any labor expended on crops raised for sale had to be added to women's production for their own family's consumption. Rural women's time was highlighted as a major development constraint: they already worked 12–18 hours per day, not only in agriculture but in supplying labor for family and community care.[17] Rural women commonly spent about four hours daily gathering wood for fuel and bringing home water. Studies of village women in Uganda and several other African countries found that they moved (without mechanical assistance) an average of 26 metric ton-kilometers per year, especially wood and water. Yet women were less likely than men to make decisions and to control resources and benefits when crops were grown for sale.[18]

Rural women who wanted to earn cash often lacked information about their options and confronted serious infrastructural problems. These included inadequate transportation, the difficulty of obtaining water and fuel, poor access to electricity, and the absence of sources of agricultural power other than female labor (i.e., using animals, mechanized equipment, or other technologies). The demand for paid agricultural labor was limited, and married women who farmed with their husbands might have trouble gaining access to the profits. Nor did the government's Agricultural Extension Services assist women effectively.[19]

For women involved more fully in the market economy, the most common area was business, trade, or manufacturing.[20] One finds great diversity both in the types of activities women pursued and in the scale of those activities. At a lower economic level their participation was often dictated by ongoing poverty, which forced both unmarried and married women to bring in an income to support or help support their families. Businesswomen were therefore concentrated within micro- and small-scale enterprises (MSEs).[21] A study carried out in 1995 shows that the largest group of Uganda's MSEs (46 percent) were owned by women, as compared with 38 percent owned by men and 17 percent multi-owned or ownership not known.[22] Retail trade accounted for 60 percent of all female-owned enterprises; another 16 percent produced beverages; 9 percent made textiles; and 9 percent offered services. Female-owned enterprises were far more likely to have just a single worker, almost always the owner herself, than were male-owned businesses. They were also less heavily capitalized than male businesses. Forty percent of the women's enterprises had no more than Ush 10,000 (US$6.60) in current capital, and only 16 percent of women-owned businesses had capital of Ush 200,000 (US$132) or more.

Clearly women's ability to compete successfully in business was still severely constrained. Various analyses done during the 1990s explored the factors that handicapped their ability to succeed.[23] In 1990, Dr Kazibwe, then the Vice President, highlighted some of the challenges confronting women in business and industry, factors that kept most of them in petty trade.[24] She noted that a woman's time is 'co-ordinated,' in that a variety of activities must be performed within the same block of time, 'as opposed to a man's time, which is 'segregated' – he can concentrate on only one task at a time'. Other problems that hindered women's participation were the following:

- Because of multiple responsibilities, women cannot move away from home to pursue business elsewhere.
- Too much of their time is spent doing work that could be assisted by simple technology.
- Women lack capital, and because they have no property rights, they cannot borrow money to start businesses.
- Their skills are limited by poor education.
- In marketing, women 'are a disaster'. They lack bargaining power because their projects are small and scattered physically; lack of appropriate technology raises prices, so buyers are not willing to pay; lack of specialization results in inferior products that cannot compete; they lack market knowledge and skills concerning packaging and advertisements; and they commonly operate in an environment where purchasing power is low and transport difficult.

In a pattern that limited the ability of women to expand their businesses, all but the wealthiest women generally used their earnings primarily for family purposes. A study carried out in the late 1990s of female participants in Kampala's informal economy, many of them market sellers, showed that the women first used their income for daily needs.[25] If they had profits beyond what was needed for immediate expenses, they employed them in the following sequence: first, to pay for their children's education; second, to buy a plot of land; third, to build a house on that land; and lastly, if circumstances permitted, to expand their business. Because poorer women rarely reinvested their profits, their businesses generally remained at a subsistence level. Even if they had an opportunity to grow economically, they usually did so laterally (for example, opening a second stall) rather than moving into a larger, more capital-intensive activity.[26] In our district sample, only 13 percent of the women reinvested any of their proceeds in their businesses.

Among the various ways in which women participated in business during the NRM period, the most common was still production and sale of food and drink at lower levels. Women now dominated market selling. Some sold food they had grown or processed themselves, but most obtained their supplies from wholesalers. Cooked food had become more important. Newspaper accounts show women of diverse cultural and religious backgrounds offering food in Kampala's city and suburban markets as well as in other parts of the country.[27] Other women continued to brew local alcohol for sale, while a smaller number participated in what was known as 'Busia trade', named after a pair of towns that straddled the Ugandan-Kenyan border. This 'informal' trade between countries attempted to take advantage of price differentials while also avoiding payment of import-export taxes.[28] As Margaret Birungi (Profile 9.1) discovered, cross-border trade could yield high returns, but it was risky both economically and in terms of personal safety.

Many women offered their food and drink outside formal markets or shops, to avoid paying rent. Street traders increased in number.[29] Especially popular were the night markets held between around 6 p.m. and midnight to serve customers who had been at work during the day. Seated on the ground or at a table alongside busy streets, aided by light from a candle or paraffin lamp, these women sold cooked food for immediate consumption as well as food and other items to take home.[30] Market sellers and other small businesswomen who dealt in food were vulnerable to competition from the new, foreign-owned supermarkets that were opening in Kampala and the larger towns.[31] Women with disabilities faced special challenges.

A few women were starting to move into medium- or large-scale businesses involving food or drink. In 1995, a female dealer in grains from Mbarara was robbed of millions of shillings, a Makerere graduate in economics was named as chief executive of the Ugandan Grain Milling Company in Jinja, and a woman became the quality control manager at Coca-Cola bottling.[32] Women were taking senior positions in restaurant and hotel management, and some were experimenting with new types of products.

Work with textiles and clothing was also common. While most women continued to run small local stalls or shops, selling cloth or used clothing and sometimes offering simple tailoring, others again moved to higher levels.[33] In 1995 one woman ran a tailoring school in Kampala, two women (one a graduate of King's College, Budo) went into fashion design, and a woman who had been trained in London concentrated on bridal wear.[34] A book published in 2002 about successful businesswomen in the (British) Commonwealth featured two Ugandans involved in clothing or furnishings.[35] Mary Kisitu, who had received degrees in biochemistry from Makerere and Loughborough University in the UK, said she inherited a talent for tailoring from her mother. Using an old sewing machine, she began designing and selling clothing, a business that gradually evolved into Lakai Uniforms, a company that served a clientele of banks, hotels, government agencies, and hospitals. Alice Karugaba, who had obtained a diploma in secretarial studies in England, began work as a secretary. When, however, she found in 1979 that she could not sustain herself and her four children on her salary, she began baking bread, then moved into groceries, and later used all her capital to set up Nina Interiors. This business, which retailed top quality office and domestic furnishings and specialized in upholstery work and window dressings, had 31 full-time employees by 2000.

Other women participated in new types of business ventures. They worked in floriculture and tourism, directing several of the large travel companies.[36] They served as executives for airlines and for aviation and delivery services. They headed an industrial design and engineering firm and a plastic products company; a group of businesswomen from Jinja opened a mattress factory.[37] Women were found at the top of some of the country's leading economic associations, named as executive director of the Uganda Manufacturers Association and president of the UNCCI.[38] Even the conservative world of banking and finance was starting to open up to women. In 1995 a woman was named as managing director of the Bank of Baroda, and a group of businesswomen planned to launch a bank of their own in 1997.[39]

In the professions, women continued to work primarily as teachers and nurses. Among primary school teachers, the total number rose sharply (from 74,000 in 1986 to 103,000 in 1997 and higher still with the introduction of UPE), but the proportion of women held steady at 30–33 percent.[40] Nearly a third of all primary teachers in 1997 had no formal teaching qualifications, but women were less heavily represented in this group than men. In secondary schools, women constituted 18 percent of the teachers in 1997. Teachers' salaries remained low, and a study of education published in 1997 encouraged teachers to be 'economically progressive', supplementing their school income with other activities, such as market gardening, keeping poultry and swine, and trade.[41] Almost as an afterthought, the author reminded teachers that they 'need to be careful to see that these activities for self improvement do not prevent them from doing effectively and efficiently their teaching duties'. At universities, 20–21 percent of the instructors were women in 1996–8. Among all institutions of tertiary education in 1997, women formed 54 percent of the teaching staff in the field of agriculture, 32–4 percent in veterinary medicine and technical subjects, but no more than 25 percent in all other areas, including education.

Among nurses, the number of people being admitted into training programs at Mengo and Mulago Schools of Nursing was not significantly higher at the end of the century than it had been during the late 1970s and early 1980s, but the sex distribution was changing. Prior to the NRM period, nearly all of the students enrolled in the program for basic nurses at both institutions had been female, as were all in the midwifery courses.[42] But of the student nurses who started at Mulago between November 1999 and January 2002, fewer than three-quarters were women; in several intakes the fraction was only 64 percent. Instructors in the program noted that men were now entering nurse's training in order to become clinic or hospital administrators. The same trend is seen among those registered by the Uganda Nurses and Midwives Council. Whereas most enrolled and registered nurses were women through the 1990s, in the new category of 'Nurses with Comprehensive Qualifications,' a higher form of qualification introduced only in 1995, men constituted an increasing fraction of the Ugandans registered.[43] This transition accords with the wider observation that if a type of work previously done by women within a patriarchal society gains in status or starts to yield a better living, it will be taken over by men.[44]

The government and its affiliated institutions offered a growing range of employment opportunities to women. In addition to the upper-level politicians and ministers discussed above were thousands of civil servants. Some were hired by the central government, while others were employed by local bodies, either in skilled work, such as a district agricultural officer, or in jobs like cutting grass and tending the gardens for a municipality.[45] Women also found employment in parastatals and regulatory bodies, and some moved into the police force, though only a few succeeded in rising to the upper ranks.[46] Women were welcomed into the army, especially during the first NRM decade. At International Women's Day celebrations in 1988, where Museveni inspected a female guard of honor, he described the contributions of women soldiers while the NRA was fighting in the bush.[47] He said he had 'received a lot of resistance from male chauvinists, parents and soldiers against the recruitment of women into the army. They thought women were being taken as prostitutes. But women soldiers have demonstrated their capability and even proved to be better combatants than some male soldiers.' By 2002, however, *Bukedde* presented women in the army in negative terms, calling them 'tough'.[48]

NGOs concerned with women's issues offered other opportunities. Even internationally funded organizations believed in hiring local women as part of their capacity-building goal. Thus, a woman who had been buying foodstuffs in one market and selling them in another took a job as a cook for the Red Cross in Arua. 'The pay there was good, and I needed money for looking after my children since my husband was very irresponsible and always drinking.'[49] Joyce Munduru (Profile 7.1) found employment as a driver with a non-profit organization after her return to Uganda from Zaire, and Thereza Kamugasa (Profile 8.1), herself coping with HIV/AIDS, was hired by an NGO to offer education and support to others, so long as her own strength was sufficient. Women were taken on at higher levels too, as program officers and project coordinators.[50]

The burgeoning world of the media and arts involved many women.[51] A group of school children visiting *New Vision*'s office in 1989 were greeted by the white male editor-in-chief and the female Ugandan administrative officer. In 1995 women served as librarian and deputy marketing manager for *New Vision* and worked as presenters and producers for Capital Radio and Radio Sanyu.[52] Eunice Kyamanya (Profile 6.1) was an important figure in Radio Uganda during the NRM period, covering some of the country's leading events. A gallery exhibit in 1995 featured the work of 11 women artists, and 20 women from various musical groups joined together for a special performance.[53] Women also danced: in cultural performances with the Ndere Troupe, with a band performing at a party hosted by the Chinese construction firm that built the second hydroelectric power station at Owens Falls in Jinja, and with the Afrigo Band as it set off for a European tour.

A wide range of other activities brought women into the public economy. Some of these had roots in earlier periods. Handicrafts were still being promoted in 1995 as a way to earn money. Kitgum women made pots to bring to market, NAWOU taught Muslim women basket weaving, and the Wandegeya Women's Club in Kampala had craft stalls that sold such items as handmade hats.[54] While most women still sold their wares within the country, both Ugandan women's organizations and international NGOs tried to develop outlets for their products in Europe and North America. Beauty and hairdressing salons multiplied, and a few Ugandan women found employment as models.[55] A handful of women trained as airplane pilots, and many did personnel work or public relations. A small number worked in factories, making such items as matches or textiles.[56] Others did unskilled work, sorting coffee beans or hand-winnowing rice or millet for agricultural firms. Girls and some adult women took positions as residential domestic workers, usually for a year or two before marriage but in some cases lasting for many years. Sex work was occasionally mentioned in the papers in 1995. They described round-ups of prostitutes at Gulu and teenage girls in Jinja who hung out at bars, picking up whites and Chinese workers.[57] Some enterprising women offered new services: one Kampala woman hired herself out to mourn loudly at burials but had some trouble keeping the supply of tears flowing; another offered herself as an 'auntie' to give young women the necessary traditional advice prior to marriage about how to please their husbands; and a third produced a powder that was said to correct male impotence.[58]

Women also entered types of work that had previously been reserved for men. They sold fuel at petrol stations, repaired car motors, painted houses, and made furniture.[59] They were involved in transport, such as working as a signals or telecommunications engineer for Uganda Railway or as a conductor on a taxi bus.[60] By 2000, a few women were starting to go into Information and Communication Technology fields or to make use of such technologies in other kinds of work.

An entrepreneurial approach

A vitally important feature of the NRM period was the increasing entrepreneurialism of some women active in the private sector, especially those who were educated, lived in towns, and had some access to capital.[61] Salaried women, including nurses and teachers, might employ their earnings to open a business. Women already involved in trade sometimes expanded into more lucrative activities or invested in property, using cash from their own savings, advanced by relatives, or obtained through a bank loan. Improved ownership rights over urban land made it possible for women to gain income from commercial or residential properties. Others introduced new products onto the market, taking advantage of services offered by the government or NGOs.[62]

The emergence of an entrepreneurially minded group of businesswomen able to compete at intermediate or upper levels holds great promise for women, the Ugandan economy, and the growth of a middle class. This is particularly true since Ugandan attitudes towards employment in the late twentieth century were not inherently conducive to either business or an entrepreneurial approach. Having a salaried job was generally thought to be better than running one's own business, and there was hesitation about taking economic risks. Women had previously been particularly cautious, since they were responsible for the daily provision of their families and commonly felt they could not afford to be caught without basic resources.

The women in our district sample provide many illustrations of a more venturesome attitude towards business. Nurses were setting up drug shops or going into private practice. A nurse in Arua who had gradually developed her professional qualifications and risen to being a senior nursing officer for the municipal council used her savings to open her own drug store next to the market and hoped to set up a private maternity home in the future.[63] A woman who had worked as a midwife at a hospital in Hoima for 16 years went into business as a private practitioner.

A movement into business was seen among other educated women as well. Grace Ssembatia (Profile 5.1), who had taught for some time at King's College, Budo, joined two other women in setting up her own private school in Kampala. They were able to finance the school thanks to commercial bank loans, which may have been granted more readily because they had their husbands' backing and were from well-known families. A doctor who had gone first to Kenya and then to London during the Amin/Obote II period returned to Kampala, where she and her husband invested heavily in real estate.[64] As well as residential properties, they obtained financing from Shelter Afrique in Nairobi to build a large office block in a prime location which in 2003 was rented to private firms and a government ministry. A teacher in Kampala who had studied accounting as part of her training course took a position as an accountant in a company dealing in motor cycles and then set up her own business.[65]

Women without professional skills were likewise thinking in entrepreneurial terms. Joyce Munduru (Profile 7.1) was planning to start providing food for schools and was building a house to rent out, though she continued to work as a driver. An account clerk with Masindi town council started a successful retail business in Hoima.[66] A Lira woman earned enough money from 13 years of traveling around to village markets by truck to buy produce which she then sold to army men that in 1996 she was able to build and start operating a small hotel.

Land too was being viewed in terms of its business potential. Fatuma Kasirye (Profile 2.2), who had been running a photography shop in Jinja with her husband, bought agricultural land and hired workers to grow food crops for sale. An article from 1989 described a visit by several government ministers to Jesa Mixed Farm, located about 30 miles from Kampala and owned by Mr and Mrs Mulwana.[67] Of the farm's 1.5 sq. miles, 400 acres had been developed and were used to run 160 Friesian milk cows. The farm was also growing bananas and maize, for sale and as supplementary feed for the cows. Because Mr Mulwana was managing director of a toothbrush factory in Kampala and chairman of the Uganda Manufacturers' Association, it was Sarah Mulwana who took charge of the farm. There she worked every day with her 75 employees, including a full-time veterinarian. By 2003, Jesa had expanded its range of products to include higher priced items desired by Kampala's middle-class residents, foreigners, and restaurants, including yogurt and ice cream.

The emerging women entrepreneurs attempted to strengthen their collective voice. In Kampala and to a lesser extent in other towns, entrepreneurs were obtaining personal support and training in practical skills from such organizations as Ugandan Women Entrepreneurs Association Ltd (UWEAL) and the Women Entrepreneurs Network of the UIA.[68] UWEAL was founded in 1987 for women with a registered business, but two years later it had only 35 members. It was headed in its earlier years by Theresa Mbire, who had moved from selling flowers on the street to running a bakery and tailoring establishment. Ida Wanendeya, who helped to found the UWFT, became its next director, and by 1998 it had several hundred members.[69] Sarah Kitakule, its head in 2002–3, was keenly aware of the importance of such factors as government economic policies, privatization, globalization, and access to information and foreign markets through computer-based technologies.

The Torchbearers thought that an important factor in women's increasing success in the economy during the NRM period was the government's support of women. Angela Nakafeero of CEEWA noted that women had been empowered by the government's affirmative action programs plus a generally favorable environment for women.[70] Not only were more women moving into the economy, some

---

Profile 9.1. A Rocky Road to Business Success: 'Margaret Birungi'

Margaret Birungi was a 37-year-old entrepreneur who was determined to move forward despite a series of setbacks in her business life.[71] A Catholic Munyoro, in 2003 she owned and operated a company that made fruit juices and baked goods, and she was busily diversifying her economic activities to provide long-term security. An articulate and self-assured person, she was interviewed at a multi-storey, custom-built structure on a hillside in a busy Kampala suburb. The ground floor and surrounding yards of Margaret's establishment served as the production site for her company, with offices upstairs; the top two floors contained comfortable living quarters for her family.

Margaret was born in 1965, in a village south of Hoima. Her father, a teacher, later founded his own school in Hoima, which had become the best one in the district by the time he retired 26 years later. Her mother made and sold a few small foodstuffs. Though they had many children and money was scarce, her parents gave Margaret a good education: she went all the way through primary and secondary school and passed her 'A-level' exams.

She had hoped to study further, but the war in the bush between the government and Museveni's forces was coming to a head in 1985, and her family's life was disrupted. She therefore moved to a trading center on the edge of Kampala to work for her brother, who had a small shop there. At first she was his assistant, but gradually she took charge of the business, buying produce from farmers and expanding the range of goods and services offered. Right from the beginning, she demonstrated the hard work, imagination, and entrepreneurial approach that were to characterize all her subsequent activities. 'Other women were in business at the time, but they were not very active the way I was. Me, I was determined. I used to wake up at 6 and I could close at midnight. As well as the long hours, I had a convincing tongue. Even though I was just a young girl, I could persuade people from the villages to buy and sell with me. We didn't have enough capital, but people learned that I was trustworthy in business, so they would bring me goods to sell and let me pay for them later.' Their shop was next to a stopping point for local and long-distance buses. 'I said, "Why can't I use that stop to get additional income for the shop?" So I would wait for the buses, go out to them with food, and sell. Some people coming from the villages, I would bring them into the shop, let them wash their hands and legs, give them breakfast. They used to be very happy.' After a year, her brother withdrew his money from the shop, whereupon she continued to run it on her own.

When she was 24, Margaret gave birth to a daughter by a man she decided not to marry. As a mother, 'I became serious about money'. Looking at the shop, she realized that, because it was so small, it would never produce a good income. She therefore began to explore other options. While the baby was young, she went back to her village near Hoima, working on the farm of another brother. He was raising tobacco, and she began to plant cassava as well, to increase their long-term income. But he did not like her approach and refused to pay her wages, so after some months they quarreled and she returned to Kampala.

Her next venture was 'a Busia business', trading across the border between Uganda and Kenya. Leaving the baby with a sister in Kampala, she moved to the eastern part of the country in 1990. Starting with the Ush 200,000 she had earned from her shop, she rose very early every morning and crossed over to

---

Malaba, located just on the far side of the border, while it was still dark. After buying wheat flour at a relatively low price there, she brought it back to Uganda and sold it for a profit. Because this was *magendo* (black market) trade, she had to avoid the border patrol, who would have demanded that she pay customs duties or a bribe. She made 6 trips per week, and within a few years she had Ush 3 million, despite the loss of much of her stock one night when a truck that was carrying her flour caught fire. At that point, tired of smuggling, she decided to move into legitimate trade.

Continuing to capitalize on differential prices for foodstuffs between Uganda and Kenya, Margaret began to deal in maize, this time going across the border in the opposite direction. In partnership with a man who had a truck, they went every day into villages deep in the countryside in the eastern region of Uganda, buying maize. They then drove to Malaba, where she still had contacts, to sell it. The vehicle was unreliable, and when it broke down, she and the driver carried the maize on their backs. Because there was high demand for maize in Kenya, they could afford to pay a little money at the border. Within three months she had increased her money to Ush 7 million. But she was exhausted, she had lost weight, and she was 'black like charcoal' because the only time she had time to bathe was if they stopped along the river at night. 'I said to myself, "I am not ready to die for money"' and she therefore changed her method of doing business.

Returning to Kampala to live, now aged 26, she hired someone to buy Ugandan maize and wheat flour and take it to a partner she had found in Kenya, who sold it. In three years her share in the business came to Ush20 million. She had meanwhile built a house on a plot of land given to her by her grandmother in a Kampala suburb. She has lived there ever since with her grandmother, and that is where her current building was later constructed. Her border trade collapsed in 1994 when her Kenyan partner backed out of their agreement and refused to deliver her share of the profits. 'Suddenly I was back to square one, without even a coin.' Determined to retrieve some of her money, Margaret went to Kenya and spent many days sitting at the man's house. 'Eventually his wife got tired of having me there and persuaded him to pay me 4 million out of what he owed.' Somewhat relieved, because now she could at least pay her debts, she set off for Kampala. On the way back, however, she was attacked at gunpoint by thieves, who took all her money. 'I cried a little but then began to think of how to start again.'

Because trade had proved so unreliable, Margaret decided in 1995, when she was 30, to start her own company, making and selling juice. 'People laughed at me, saying, "How can a woman start a company?" I said, "I WILL!"' Because she had no capital, she rented out rooms in the house she had built in Kampala, reserving just one for her grandmother and herself. She began by preparing juice the way she had learned at home, but it could only be kept for one week. So she went to government chemists to learn about preservatives. Every day she went on foot to a local market to buy fruit, carried it home in a wheelbarrow, boiled water, and made juice. She did her own advertising and distributing, going from shop to shop to tell people about her juices and encourage customers to try them and shopkeepers to sell them. 'God helped me, and slowly, slowly people started buying.' After six months she had accumulated enough money to be able to buy a whole bag of sugar at a time, and she hired a worker to help her. With characteristic foresight, she also registered the name of her company and its trademark.

The company henceforth prospered and grew. By 2003 Margaret employed 180 workers, who produced an array of juices and cakes and would soon start producing bread. It was her dream to make it one of the leading food manufacturing companies in the country, and she was proud that she had already won a National Enterprise Award. In 2002 a photograph of her talking with President Museveni at a trade fair appeared in a major national newspaper.[72]

In 1996, when she was 31, Margaret married a man of about her own age from eastern Uganda, his only wife. As of 2003 he had recently graduated from Makerere University and become a magistrate. They brought home Margaret's daughter, who had been living with an aunt, and then had two children of their own. At the time of the interview, their household also included Margaret's elderly grandmother, aged 102, her husband's younger sister, and two orphans (one of them the 5-year-old son of the first worker in her juice business, who had died from AIDS).

In recent years Margaret had been working to diversify her holdings. After her son was born, she went to her husband's area in Busoga and persuaded the clan elders to give them a tract of land, which was listed in the name of the baby boy. Her husband managed the farm, where they raised poultry, hiring 20 workers. 'I think of it as a demonstration farm to show people in that area what they could do.' In the future she wanted to expand the farm, supplying eggs and other poultry products to eastern and northern Uganda, Sudan, and Democratic Republic of. Congo, and starting a piggery. She had bought a piece of woodland, so she could avoid paying high prices for the fuel used to boil water for the juices. This supplemented her investment in expensive but high efficiency, environmentally friendly boiling vats. She had started building a hostel for students near the Makerere University campus. Though the structure would take three or four years to complete, it would eventually provide accommodation for nearly 100 rent-paying students. Margaret saw that as a way to ensure that she would be able to support her family as she got older.

Despite her business success, Margaret remained deeply embedded in her family. She helped her father set up a shop after he retired from teaching, and she educated all her younger brothers, one of whom was a veterinary doctor and another studying electrical engineering. Several brothers worked in her business, and she was paying for the education of the children of the brothers who were still in the village. She believed that many women who have succeeded economically 'have forgotten that you need to struggle for your family as well as for your business. We need to know our purpose, which is to benefit our families.' It was one of her greatest satisfactions that 'I have been able to uplift my people'.

were entering higher levels of business, such as owning and operating a bus company or constructing and renting out buildings in Kampala. Kitakule credited the NRM's policies for helping women to participate in trade and industry.[73] 'If the government had not said anything, had not done any affirmative action, had not said "Girls should go to school," the cycle [of female subordination] would have continued. Nobody would be talking about the importance of girls coming out and being economically empowered.' She pointed to the impact of these changes in the villages.

> The [local] councils and the women MPs, they have mobilized the women, they have made sure there are microfinance institutions within their constituency, they have sensitized them, so the women know that you can stand up and say whatever you want to say, which wasn't the case before. So it has given them some level of confidence, which is being built on. And there are now men who know that. 'Yes, I depend on my wife because she goes to that association and gets money, and we are able to educate our children.' So their respect for the wife goes up.

But Kitakule noted that the new climate had affected educated women like her as well. 'For me, if the empowerment thing hadn't come up, maybe I wouldn't be an activist in business and encouraging women. Probably I would still be in the Ministry of Trade, as a civil servant there, comfortably sitting at some desk and trying to see how can I manage and crying over little pay.'

The Torchbearers pointed to several additional factors that had helped women advance in the economy. Lydia Rugasira of UWFT noted that the growing availability of microfinance loans has enabled some women to come up with new ideas and start their own ventures.[74] One of the UWFT clients, a widow who initially worked as an unskilled laborer, now owned a stone quarry in Entebbe, where she supervised several male employees. Kitakule stressed that because many more women were getting educated, they wanted to earn their own living.[75] 'Once they are more exposed, they tend not to just sit at home and become housewives. They want to find a way of utilizing their education.' Another factor she identified was HIV/AIDS, which has 'forced women to go out and find a source of livelihood'. Retrenchment was important too. 'Government used to be the main employer, but now that has changed. People have to find alternatives, and they find them in the private sector.'

Women's ability to succeed outside the home was affected by their marital status. A number of the Torchbearers emphasized the involvement of single women, divorced or separated women, and widows, who were able to devote more of their time and energy to their businesses, thanks to their relative freedom from domestic responsibilities. Grace Mukasa of ACFODE said, 'I find that if a woman is not married, she is more open, takes more initiative, has more economic independence. This to me confirms that husbands actually put us out of competition.'[76] Nakafeero noted that many of the women succeeding at an intermediate level of business were not married. 'Because they have no one else to support them, they are forced into business full swing. They must make their own decisions, their own mistakes, and learn from them. So they become more independent, more confident.' Jackie Asiimwe of UWONET commented that marriage may hinder women's advancement in their business or profession 'because of the expectations. Your first responsibility must be to your family. But that is only for a woman, and not for a man. So while the man is out there doing what he has to do for his work, at whatever time it is, you still have to come home.'[77] Maggie Kigozi of the UIA, herself a widow, said she would have had difficulty in doing all the traveling required by her position if she were currently married or had young children at home.

Though marriage might be a handicap under some circumstances, it was a considerable asset for those few women who were successful at the top levels of the economy. Nakafeero pointed out that many of the leading women entrepreneurs were married to high-profile men (in government, the army, or large institutions) who provided capital and access to contacts and were willing to let them travel.[78] Olive Kigongo of the UNCCI said that partnership with her husband, a leading figure in the NRM, had been essential to her business success: 'I would never have been able to borrow the money from the World Bank for this big project [a complex of apartments and services] without his support.'

These entrepreneurial woman had succeeded without any economic assistance from the government. The NRM had done nothing to help women in economic terms comparable to its affirmative action policies in government or education. As a successful businesswoman in Kampala noted, 'It is very surprising that after the bush war there has been a lot of effort to get women into politics but very little effort to get women into business. Although the government has done a little to encourage women entrepreneurs, such as Maggie Kigozi leading the Uganda Investment Authority, really it's a half-hearted effort. Until women can access training, networking, and viable financing, it will be very difficult for them to succeed.'[79]

Portrayals of Women and their Issues

Public representations of women and their issues – like the political, educational, and economic opportunities open to them – were strongly influenced by the NRM's position. The government's advocacy of women's participation in the public domain, support that was forceful until the later 1990s, was an extension of the stance taken by the early Independence government during the 1960s. But now the range of occupations defined as acceptable for working women was widened even further. The NRM insisted that they be involved in politics at all levels, and it lessened the elitist assumptions that had been built into previous definitions. By around 2000, however, as we have seen, the government's support appeared to be weakening, and a backlash against affirmative action policies for women in government and education was visible. The media, even those with no connection to the NRM, reflected these changing attitudes. As was the case during the early Independence years, representations of women as full members of the nation were often far more positive than the views about women that many people still held in private. But public advocacy of women by the media – at least until the later 1990s – contributed to a climate conducive to their participation in the public domain.

The visibility of women was influenced also by an expansion of the press, radio, and television. While men had higher exposure to mass media than did women, by the turn of the century many women – especially in the towns – were in touch with wider events. In 2000–1, 44 percent of urban women read a newspaper at least once a week.[80] Local radio stations were abundant, and Ugandan television stations were active. Eighty-two percent of urban women and 47 percent of rural women listened to the radio at least once a week in 2000–1, while 37 percent of urban women and 4 percent of rural women watched TV on occasion.

The analysis below is based upon newspapers published in 1988–9, 1995, and 2002.[81] For the earlier years we looked only at English-language papers (three from 1988–9 and four from 1995). Because these papers deliberately covered all regions of the country and all of its ethnic groups, part of the NRM's efforts to reduce factionalism, local-language publications were of minor importance. *New Vision* was the government-affiliated paper, while by the mid-1990s the *Monitor* was presenting a more critical view. The government proclaimed freedom of the press, though it imposed some restrictions, such as reporting on the war in the north. For 2002, we looked at eight papers, five in English, three in local languages. The most widely read English ones were still *New Vision* and *Monitor*, both of which offered national coverage and aimed at a relatively educated and often urban readership that included both men and women. *East African* was a high-tone paper published in Nairobi, with articles of interest to the whole region, while *The Other Voice* presented reformist, sometimes radical positions. *Red Pepper* was a new and very popular mass circulation paper that contained lurid gossip about popular entertainers, important businesspeople, and politicians, plus explicitly sexual stories. The three local-language papers were *Bukedde* (in Luganda and featuring news from Buganda), *Orumuri* (in Runyankole, featuring news from the western region), and *Etop* (in Ateso, featuring news from Soroti). These papers were directed primarily at local readerships, though all were published by the same company that put out *New Vision*. Because of differential literacy levels and access to newspapers between men and women in smaller towns, their audience was more heavily male.

General representations of women and their issues

Throughout the NRM period all the papers gave extensive coverage to women's activities in the areas of government, education, health, organizations, and work. Articles about women make clear that nearly all kinds of activities were now acceptable, even sports formerly limited to men, like football, cricket, rugby, and boxing. Wealthier women were commended for their charitable work, and Ugandan women writers were getting published and gaining international recognition, thanks mainly to the organization called FEMRITE.

One sees, however, marked changes over time in how the papers represented women and their concerns. During the later 1980s and the first half of the 1990s, women were portrayed by the papers in a more positive manner than at any time in the past.[82] The press assumed that women were making valuable contributions outside the home, in many different spheres of life, and that the issues affecting women were important to the community as a whole. Newspapers made a conscious effort to correct stereotypes that obstructed women's advancement. An article about International Women's Day in 1989 refuted the claim that women are biologically and psychologically weaker than men and should therefore stay within the domestic context rather than going out to work.[83] If a newspaper slipped, presenting a negatively stereotypic picture of women, it was chastised. In 1989, Miria Matembe, then the women's representative for Mbarara in Parliament and newly elected chairperson of ACFODE, sent an angry letter to the *New Vision*, published under the title 'Women are not commodities'.[84] In it she complained about a recent *New Vision* article that had described 'the scary taxis, sweet tea and women of Western Uganda'. Matembe pointed out that the few women the author met in a pub were not representative of most western women, who were actively engaged in development projects. 'But that aside, what's wrong with a group of women sitting on stools in a pub. Why doesn't [the author] talk about all the men he boozed with in all the pubs he visited while in western Uganda. We the women of Uganda are not in any way amused at being made fun of and ridiculed in your paper. We are human beings in our own right, entitled to the dignity accorded to every citizen of this country. We need more of positive portrayal for the develop-ment of our country.'

The papers also provided serious discussion of issues important to women during the early NRM period. Late in 1988, ACFODE persuaded the *New Vision* to create a women's page, one that would address substantive matters, not just talking about cooking or fashion. ACFODE and other women's organizations supplied material, giving it a broad focus. On 17 April 1989, for example, the page included reports on the following topics: (i) An address given to women at an ACFODE retreat by a (male) lecturer at Makerere School of Law, who said that the benefits prescribed in the existing Ugandan constitution did not apply equally in practice to women and needed to be changed. Men needed to stop viewing women simply as child-bearers or sex symbols and acknowledge them as partners in development. (ii) A speech at that retreat by a (female) human rights com-missioner, stressing that women needed to be educated about their human rights and then be willing to stand up for them, including going to court. (iii) A speech by the director of women's affairs in the NRM secretariat, who encouraged women to get together to network and discuss serious issues. (iv) An announcement that the directorate of women's affairs was organizing an annual competition for women at the district, regional, and national levels. One of the themes was, 'Are men the only hindrance to women's development?,' while others addressed problems in the land law and women's inability to get credit from banks or financial institutions without title to property. (v) A speech by Loice Bwambale, a secondary school teacher who had been elected to represent Kasese women in Parliament (and was later to head the Uganda Women Parliamentarians Association), concerning the need for women's participation in tree planting and other activities to boost the national Environmental Protection Programme. A note in a box at the bottom of the page says: 'Ed: The Women's Vision page invites other women's organisations and RC secretaries for women to send their articles to Editor-in-chief, *The New Vision*.'

Up to around 1995, government and law were among the topics thought to be of interest to women. In an interview in 1989, Matembe said she wanted to see a forum developed in which all women could be educated 'about the unfair laws governing them so they can denounce them'.[85] In 1995, in addition to lengthy analysis of women's part in the constitution-building process, the papers explored whether the NRM and its women politicians were carrying out their designated roles.[86] Preparations for the Beijing Women's Conference of 1995 and the participa-tion of Ugandans in it received considerable attention.[87] After the meeting, however, there was little comment, apart from a rather perfunctory article saying Beijing had reaffirmed the rights of women.[88] Though the conference proved far less important for Ugandan women than its predecessor a decade before, it did encourage Uganda's Ministry of Gender to develop a National Gender Policy in 1997 and a National Action Plan on Women in 1999.[89]

By the end of the century, however, the papers had taken a step backwards. Women were portrayed in more conventional and often sexist terms, and discussion of the problems they faced had diminished. ACFODE's contributions to the *New Vision* had ended in 1993, when the page was replaced by a 'Women's Vision' pull-out, containing a more narrowly 'female' set of articles, focusing on appearance, shopping, and social relationships. Activists believed that this approach 'trivialized and marginalized women and women's issues and perpetuated their subordination'.[90]

In 2002, all the papers apart from *Etop* displayed a worrying tendency to portray women as sex objects. In some cases, this was fairly overt, even in the mainstream papers. The Miss Uganda and Miss Tourism competitions were reported in some detail, with illustrations; other opportunities for photographs of scantily clad young women were offered by a party celebrating the anniversary of a popular club and the launching of a new game by a casino that brought in models for the occasion.[91] Many editions of *Bukedde* included a suggestive photograph of a young woman together with her name, a brief account of her interests and activities, and where she worked.[92] *Red Pepper* included a section called 'Pepper Active: Girls You Must Meet Before You Die', showing sexually alluring photographs of girls, provided by themselves. The editor's note stated: 'If you are cute and would wish to have your best pictures to appear on this page, send them to us and we shall publish them'.[93] *Red Pepper* joined the mainstream papers in offering advertisements by people seeking relationships ('Connect to a love you need'). Some were young men, often secondary or university students who said that they were attractive but poor: they advertised for an older woman, sometimes explicitly calling her a 'sugar mummy', who would provide love and financial help. Like *Bukedde* and *Orumuri*, *Red Pepper* reported on marital infidelity by important women.

Red Pepper linked women, sex, and practices associated with witchcraft. One article described a woman living in the Mulago section of Kampala who was earning good money thanks to 'women and young girls who come to her house to seek blessings like how to get more sexual fluids, land rich men and prosper in their businesses'. Her rituals involved having the women undress (shown in the accompanying photograph) and then smoke special pipes prepared by the hostess, while mumbling their wishes in prayer.[94] Another article headed 'Juju men bed Coca Cola girls' discussed the recent introduction of a lie detector by the Century Bottling Company after the disappearance of a large amount of money from its factory. The 'witch doctors' of that area were said to have been making big money from employees who visited them 'to secure supernatural protection from the dreaded machine'. Most of the juju men insisted on taking female clients to bed before they would supply the magic.

The papers no longer provided thoughtful discussion of political and legal developments central to women's lives. In 2002, for example, the English-language papers gave spotty coverage to efforts to rectify women's inability to inherit and hold family land.[95] Only *The Other Voice* provided commentary on the situation, predicting that all such efforts would fail because 'Parliamentarians employ double standards over land for women'.[96] The local-language papers did not mention land rights at all, suggesting that publishers assumed that less educated men would not be interested.

Working women and their problems

Working women and the particular challenges they faced were likewise covered in differing ways over time and between the papers. During the first decade of the NRM period, women's economic contributions were valued highly. The papers stressed the importance for women of having an independent means of earning money, so as not to be totally dependent upon their husband, father, or brother. This point was emphasized in 1989 at a workshop on 'Women, Law and Development,' when the deputy prime minister said that women's liberation must take account of economic development.[97] Rural women were especially disadvantaged, despite the fact that they performed so much of the work. Emphasizing the importance of educating girls and attacking bridewealth, he said that married women should be able to enter into financial agreements on their own and that widows should have rights to land and moveable goods. An article published by the *Monitor* in 1995, entitled, 'The new reality men must face,' emphasized that women must have their own incomes, and pointed to the contributions of FIDA, the women lawyers' group, and UWFT and other MFIs in working toward that goal.[98]

For the first time, papers during the early NRM period addressed some of the special problems faced by working women. Among these was the difficulty of combining income-generating activities with family roles, including giving birth and caring for infants. A woman at Makerere University wrote to *New Vision* in 1989 calling for an extension of maternity leave from 45 days to 90 days.[99] Presenting cogent arguments in terms of the health of babies and the well-being of their mothers, she noted that the current situation placed such high demands upon working mothers that 'many women wonder whether it is not really a question of choice between having children and working'. She also pointed out that husbands or 'the whole clan' rarely understand how difficult limited maternity leave is for women. (This issue remained a problem throughout 2003, when the length of maternity leave and the amount of pay received by Ugandan women were very limited in comparison with other African countries.)[100]

Attention was drawn to the dissimilar conditions that women and men encountered on the job. An article in 1989 pointed out that the law governing employment in Uganda failed to provide for equal opportunities for women and did not outlaw sexual discrimination in recruitment and promotion.[101] Neither did it entitle women to equal pay with men for work of equal value. After describing women's exhaustion as the result of working 48 hours per week as employees plus doing all their household tasks, the female author argued that the concept of 'work/employment' must be redefined to include domestic chores so that the status of women could rise. So long as women who worked at home, especially rural women, continued to be exploited by their husbands and the government, not qualifying for a pension or social security, they would remain disadvantaged.

By 2002, in comparison, the newspapers expressed divergent and not always supportive views about working women. The local-language papers clearly had some reservations. *Bukedde* and *Orumuri* felt that women's primary attention should be focused on their homes and families, even if they had small income-generating activities or worked in respectable fields like teaching. They offered many articles for or about women engaged in small businesses, often linked to food, agriculture, or crafts, and they reported on women who had saved their money to buy a plot of land or build a house. If women were shown in atypical types of work, such as being a lorry driver or mechanic, the account suggested that they were rough and abnormal women. More important women, those who had succeeded in business or the government, were seldom mentioned. If women politicians appeared at all, they were usually shown addressing women's groups.

Etop had greater sympathy for working women but still assumed that most of them would be engaged in low-status work. Noting that women raised most of the food consumed by families or sent to market, it praised those who sold cooked food or local alcohol, some of whom it described as good businesswomen. An interview with a woman entrepreneur stressed that business is wrongly perceived as a man's field, and that even women who begin with little capital can gradually move ahead. Articles and letters pointed out that some women were forced to work because their husbands were no longer providing for the family, and that power relations within the household held back women's economic activities. In some families women did the work but did not receive any of the profits, while in others their work was actively opposed by their husbands: men did not want their wives to handle money, they took the women's earnings for their own activities, or they used violence against their wives.

In the mainstream English papers, women were often featured simply because they were successful. Articles might comment in a rather perfunctory manner on their qualifications, competence, or resilience, but the account generally focused on the women's physical attractiveness, fashionableness, or visible display of wealth. A new theme was the importance of the public image projected by a woman in business or a profession. One article, entitled, 'The psychology of sitting at the wheel,' showed a photograph of an attractive young woman over this caption: 'Sarah looks every inch the successful woman she is, down to the powerful cars she drives, like this Jeep Cherooke.'[102]

In 2002, the English papers offered a little discussion of the problems working women encountered. Shortly before International Women's Day, the Women's Vision section of *New Vision* mentioned the difficulties faced by businesswomen in accessing markets, due largely to lack of transport, and talked about opportunities for women in organic farming.[103] Other articles looked at women managers, asking whether they had a female style of handling people or must be 'macho', and giving tips for success.[104] The papers also drew attention to working women whom it presented as exploited or disadvantaged. While they praised the improved mobility for pedestrians that resulted from Kampala City Council's efforts to clear the sidewalks of vendors, they expressed sympathy for the women whose goods were confiscated.[105] Nurses were said to be overworked and underpaid; because they lacked adequate equipment and protective gear, such as gloves and rubber boots, thirteen nurses had died during a recent Ebola epidemic. The AGOA (African Growth and Opportunities Act) project, an American-based scheme which recruited girls from throughout the country to work in textile factories that produced clothing for export, was reported at first with some hope but later with growing skepticism; the girls were eventually described as little more than prisoners of their employers.[106] Other illustrated articles described the terrible working conditions and medical problems of the women and children who made salt at Lake Katwe.

For the first time, papers during the 1990s addressed the problems faced by housegirls. Concern with these young workers, often girls in their teens who had come from villages into the towns, reflected the diminished elitism of the NRM period. Though these live-in servants provided the domestic labor that allowed the wife or female head of the family to work away from home, they were open to sexual exploitation by men in the household as well as to economic exploitation by their employers. The many articles about housegirls in 1995 demonstrate their importance to the family economy but also show concern for the well-being of the servants. Husbands were reported for beating or raping housegirls, and a long article explored 'Why men sleep with their housegirls'.[107] The latter emphasized the harmful impact upon both the girls and marriages, forcing wives either to look the other way or to leave their husbands. A subsequent article pointed out that the difficulty of finding white-collar jobs was forcing even educated women to become housegirls.[108] A long article entitled 'Maids need day off' began: 'Power is about empowering others. In the bid to emancipate women an indispensable section of our community has been overlooked. *Women's Vision* carried out a random survey and this is what the house helpers say.' The women interviewed, ranging in age from 12 to middle age, described a variety of problems involving overwork, lack of respect and time off, and dependence upon the wishes or whims of their mistress and master. Contemporary fiction by Ugandan women likewise highlights the sexual attractiveness and/or vulnerability of housegirls.[109]

Discussion of prostitution provides an interesting reflection of changing attitudes towards women's work and sexuality. Although sex workers were some-times mentioned in the papers during the later 1980s and mid-1990s, their activity was not reported with the moral venom of the Amin period. A woman wrote to the *Monitor* in 1995 arguing that women had the right to sell sexual services for pay: 'My case for prostitution is that it helps the unemployed woman or one with less pay to earn a living wage. I don't see anything criminal with one offering what one has to earn a living! What is the difference between a sexual worker who offers her body to satisfy sexual desires of her customers, and a casual labourer who offers his (physical) labour for a few shillings?'[110] Attention was given also to the legal status of sex workers. Because prostitution was illegal, sex workers could be arbitrarily arrested and sentenced to time in jail for being 'idle and disorderly' or for 'loitering with immoral intentions'.[111] The Uganda Law Reform Commission urged the government to introduce laws to protect prostitutes from the police and their clients.

In 2002, a range of attitudes toward sex work was visible in the papers. The English-language papers generally approached prostitution indirectly. Prurient voyeurism is apparent in a series of illustrated articles in *New Vision* in which male and female reporters were sent out to investigate inexpensive places for sex in Kampala.[112] In a resurfacing of stereotypes from the Amin period, *New Vision* reported that Ugandan women were going to Dubai as sex workers, hoping to come home 'with suitcases full of clothes, CD changers and other items'. The article concluded, 'So, if your female relative tells you she flies between Entebbe and Dubai on business trips, you should watch out. She could be one of the girls clad in tight jeans with mosquito-thin waists now streaming to Dubai en-masse to hook a few dirhams from consumers of "women's flesh".'

As might be expected, *Red Pepper* capitalized on the sex trade. It claimed that it opposed the sale of sex but at the same time printed photographs of Kampala's 'Top 100 girls who sell the yo-yo'.[113] It decried the practice of sending photos of

Kampala sex workers to pimps in the Middle East and elsewhere, yet on the front page of one edition, under the heading 'Sex Rats Exposed', it printed photos of four such women, naked from the waist up. Other papers too used sex as a way of attracting readers. *Bukedde* published photographs of bare-breasted women in bars (and defended itself for doing so when some readers complained).[114] An illustrated article in *Orumuri* about a prostitute working in Mbarara and Kasese said that she had a good figure and her genitals were 'very wet and warm'.

Such representations were, however, joined in most of the papers by genuine concern about prostitution as a social problem. A particular worry was that girls – some as young as 10 years – were being pushed by poverty into sex work.[115] One report said that 97 percent of the street children in Kampala and Lira, amounting to 500 in total, were involved in the sex trade. Articles about the growing number of prostitutes in Masaka and Soroti were joined by a report that girls, some only 11 years old, were flooding into Busia and selling themselves to long-distance truck drivers.[116] The papers sometimes expressed sympathy for adult sex workers too. One article about 'Why daytime sex work is now a hit' noted that customers who came during the day were usually not drunk and therefore more gentle.[117]

Gender Tension

Although the papers normally did not discuss gender tension, other sources provide considerable evidence that increased female independence and the special advantages given to women through affirmative action were causing serious conflict between men and women, both outside the home and within the domestic context. The media's reluctance to explore the negative consequences of the tension between the new opportunities open to women in the public domain and the continuing force of Domestic Virtue thinking is an extension of the pattern we noted during the early years of Ugandan independence. When a government and the press are eager to present women as active contributors to the nation, they do not want to draw attention to the problems associated with those roles. Silence about gender tension was intensified by a strong sense in Uganda that marital conflicts and domestic violence were private matters that should not be discussed with anyone else. Nor did Christian and Muslim religious groups use their influence to promote open discussion of family relationships, though they did take a stand about poverty and some political issues.[118]

One does find in the papers some very general comments about uneven relations between men and women. In 1989 *New Vision* reported that the Minister for Women in Development had implored men to consider women as partners in development.[119] 'Women are major producers and processors but many men in our society never recognize the women's output.' The next day the lead editorial, entitled 'Let all men see the need for change', claimed that women's massive economic power in agricultural production 'should give them a special status where they are seen as equal partners in development. But on the contrary, they are regarded as beasts of burden.' It continued, 'Male chauvinism is the biggest factor giving rise to the exploitative tendency of regarding wives as mere sources of free labour. Ugandan women have failed to achieve equality and are being overtaken by women in other parts of the world who are advancing rapidly.' The

NRM was committed to improving their lot, and women must use that platform to liberate themselves. 'Men should not fear this. An active happy, prosperous, and well-educated woman will make a much better partner than an unhappy over-burdened illiterate woman. Both men and women should work hard to improve the lot of women in Uganda.'

When gender tension was mentioned at all in the papers during the later 1980s, it took the form of objections to women's movement into positions they had not formerly held. At the start of the NRM's rule the political authority of women was sometimes challenged. In Rakai District in 1988, for example, it was claimed that some government officials resented being led by a woman district administrator (DA) and refused to cooperate with her.[120] When asked about this problem, the DA herself curtly 'advised such people to seek employment elsewhere'. The following year, a letter to the paper from someone active in Rukungiri's district adminis-tration said that their female DA, who had only been in the district for a few months, was locally termed 'the untouchable'.[121] She was a despotic woman, who 'underlooks everybody in the district and has already conflicted with every head of department save the UCB boss'. A few weeks later, however, *New Vision* reported that women civil servants and the Rukungiri District Development Committee had condemned this letter, calling it malicious, unfounded, and character assassination; they pointed instead to the achievements of the DA in question.[122]

Some people feared that women politicians would forget their family roles. A Roman Catholic cardinal criticized the government in 1989 for appointing women to cabinet posts, claiming that when they held such positions, their children would be neglected and perhaps spend nights in discos and bars. In response, a woman wrote that most of the female ministers had high qualifications and long working experience.[123] 'They are mature and understanding ladies who can budget their time to suit their home needs. In fact most of them have grown-up children who need not be looked after like babies. It is not the sole responsibility of women to bring up children and look after homes. It should be shared like in most developed societies. We are now on the move. Women have a place in society. We are repre-sented at Cabinet level. We are developing but Cardinal wants to put us behind.'

After a conspicuous silence about gender tension during the mid-1990s, the newspapers included a few articles in 2002 that admitted that some working women faced troubled domestic relations. An article in the 'Lifestyle – Relation-ships' section of the *Sunday Monitor* discussed whether having a good job and being successful at work necessarily ruled out happiness at home for women.[124] Its answer to the question, 'Can marriage and a career be combined?,' was not encouraging. In its 'Women & Men' section a year later, the *Monitor* published a pair of responses, by a man and a woman, to the question, 'Has freedom provoked violence?' Whereas the man concluded that 'emancipation is breeding violence in our homes', the woman argued that women are better-off now because they can get an education and work. If they find themselves in abusive marriages, they can leave and look after their children on their own. She pointed out that men want to have it both ways: they seek educated women who can contribute to the economic well-being of the family, but at the same time they want their wives to be traditional at home. Marital problems turned up less directly too. Well into an article about education in Busia District, the *Monitor* noted that the district chairman had advised Functional Adult Literacy instructors to separate men from their wives during classes to avoid domestic violence in case the women proved to be brighter.[125] Parental violence against children was also thought to be a serious problem by social service workers, but was rarely mentioned by the press.

In contrast to the limited visibility of gender conflict in the papers, our interviews made clear that women's ability to generate their own income was a major source of tension with husbands and other relatives. This problem was highlighted by the Torchbearers, and a third of the women in our district sample reported serious conflict with their husbands concerning their work.[126] The percentage was highest among those who had been married but were now divorced or not living with their spouse, but more than a quarter of the currently married women also mentioned heated disputes with their husbands about their work.

Some men refused to allow their wives to continue working. They felt they should give their full attention and labor to the home, and they disliked the independence that having their own incomes gave them. They were especially likely to oppose activities that put the wife into contact with other men, took her away from home during the evenings, or involved traveling or going to meetings that meant being away overnight. Women who had enjoyed their jobs as teachers, nurses, or secretaries before marrying resented being told by their husbands that they must now stay at home.[127] In one poignant case, a woman who was interviewed in a setting in which her husband might have been listening said that she had stopped work so that she could look after her children better. But the next day she sought out the interviewer and slipped into her hand a written statement that explained that her husband had forced her to resign from her job: she objected to his demand, missed her work and the independence it had brought, and felt isolated at home. But if she had resisted, it would have broken up her family.

Other studies suggest that objection on the part of husbands to their wives' work may have been particularly strong in Muslim households.[128] One man refused to let his newly married wife continue her work as a medical doctor, despite the considerable resources that had been invested in her long training and the country's need for qualified female doctors. Faridah, a 28-year-old seller in Kampala's Bwaise market in 1998, said, 'My husband did not like the idea of my joining trade because I would be difficult to handle. He was also worried that other men would use me because I am still young.'[129] When she insisted upon working, in part because her husband was an alcoholic and she needed to take care of her six children, he withdrew all support for the household.

It was common for a husband to withhold money he had previously contributed to the household on the grounds that his wife now had her own income. A third of the women in our sample said that their husbands had decreased or ended their financial support of the family once the woman started earning money. The result was that the wife was working more hours – involved in both income generation and domestic responsibilities – but the net resources available to the household had increased little if at all. Equally troubling was what the men did with their extra money. A sixth of the women mentioned problems with their husbands' drinking, and the same proportion said that their husbands spent the money freed up by the income they produced on other women. A relevant factor here is the frequency of *de facto* polygamy in Uganda. Among the women in our sample, 31 percent said that their husband had other wives and families, a pattern that increased the chances that a husband who was unhappy about his wife's work

241

would shift his attention to another family or think about a second marriage. While in some cases the wife's work led to separation or divorce, the direction of causality often worked the other way: women who were no longer with their husbands for other reasons might then need to generate an income to support themselves and their children.[130]

Some of our interviews revealed more about these tensions. A nurse in Arua had married a much older man, a town official, when she was 22. She was his third recognized wife.[131] Together they had three children, who were aged 1-9 years at the time of the interview. At first her husband gave her at least Ush 30,000 (US$15) a week for housekeeping, but over time, as her work as a nurse and proprietress of a drug shop prospered, he gradually withdrew his support, apart from occasionally paying school fees for the children. He felt that since she was earning her own income, it was reasonable for him to spend his money on his other families. By 2003, her husband was living in Lira with his other wives and 'sends completely nothing for me and his children'. When Joyce Munduru (Profile 7.1) returned from exile, her husband became increasingly unhappy about her financial independence. He stood in the way of her business plans and cut back his support to the household, spending the money on drinking. Eventually she obtained a divorce.

Many women in our sample felt that their income promoted irresponsibility on the part of their husbands or partners. A woman living in a single room in Jinja with her two babies complained: 'When we were young, our fathers were responsible men. Now a woman has to look after herself and shoulder most of the problems. Take me, for instance. My children have fathers, but those men don't care, they have left all the responsibility to me. I am the one who is here, who is suffering with them. The men don't give any assistance even if they have money.'[132]

A primary school teacher in Jinja described the problem more fully.[133] Married to a man who was a builder, she had worked throughout their marriage, providing much of the income for their family (they had six children, aged 12–21 years at the time of the interview). She was also supporting the children of her late uncle. She believed that women were overworked because their husbands refused to fulfill their economic obligations to the family.

> Women used to depend on their husbands [for basic support]. If they wanted a little money, they could grow produce and use what they got from selling it. But today women are overworked: I want to tell you this! Before, men used to know that it was their responsibility to pay children's school fees, they used to take care of their responsibilities. But when we started coming up as women and trying to participate in making money, men have just sat. They are seated, they do not help. Like my husband, at times I get really annoyed and we quarrel. For him, he thinks his work is just to sit. He says, 'You are a teacher and at the end of the month you get a salary, but where do you expect me to get money?' Then I have to struggle and buy food, I have to struggle and pay school fees. I tell you, we are overworked. Men now sit aside and leave everything to women. Women are smart, we can now earn our own money, we can start projects, but there is always that extra weight added to us. Men need to be sensitized to do their part as men. When women live alone, they may struggle but they know they are independent. But when a woman is married and the man is not helping much, now that becomes a problem.

Female education as a protection against male unreliability was advocated by Merab Nambamu Kiremire in her novel *More Than a Woman?*[134] Based upon the belief that 'the Girl-child must start looking at herself in a more dynamic and positive manner, and place such a value to herself as will stand her in good stead should all else fail as she treads her life-span path,' the book tells the story of a woman whose prosperous husband gradually abandons her and their children in favor of other women. Eventually, drawing upon her earlier training in personnel management from a college of commerce and business studies, the mother sets off to create an independent life for herself and her children.

Male opposition to women's work could contribute to physical violence. Although domestic violence is difficult to measure in any society, indirect evidence suggests that it was rampant in Uganda at the turn of the century. Physical punishment of women by their husbands was accepted as legitimate by many women as well as by most men.[135] A government survey administered in 2000–1 asked women whether they agreed that a husband is justified in hitting or beating his wife for specific reasons.[136] Their responses were surprisingly tolerant of such treatment: 22 percent said he might do so if she burned the food, 24 percent if she refused sexual relations, 37 percent if she argued with him, 56 percent if she went out of the house or compound without telling him, and 67 percent if she neglected the children. Physical or psychological abuse is a common thread in the narratives in *Tears of Hope*, and a study of women who committed violent crimes showed that in many cases they were reacting to years of maltreatment by male relatives.[137]

Abused women faced strong social pressure to remain silent about their domestic situation even if they wielded considerable power in other aspects of their lives. In March, 2002, Dr Kazibwe, a surgeon who had been Vice President of Uganda since 1994, announced publicly that she had thrown her husband, an engineer, out of the home and was seeking a divorce because he beat her. (He replied that he had only slapped her a few times.) Her actions generated an over-whelmingly negative response among participants in radio talk shows and writers of letters to newspapers, on two main grounds: personal matters should be kept private within the home, not discussed openly; and women should remain in marriages for the sake of stability and their children, putting up with any mistreatment they might receive.[138]

Violence stemming from women's economic independence was mentioned by some of the women in our sample. It is significant that in each case the woman ultimately left her husband, a testimony to their refusal to accept physical punishment and to their ability to support themselves and their children. Women with abusive husbands or partners who did not have their own income would have been less able to walk out of the relationship (and probably less willing to talk about their problems to an unknown interviewer). A woman who traded and ran a small restaurant in Mpigi said, 'My husband [a businessman and farmer] was very bitter that I was working. He didn't want me to handle money, and he wanted more children. I already had seven and was tired. He was a very jealous man and used to beat me, so I had to leave.'[139] A dressmaker in Arua said, 'My husband and his relatives think I am a lazy women who can't stay home to do garden and house work. My husband used to beat me, telling me to go and do garden work. But instead I continued with my tailoring work and eventually he left me alone.' A teacher in Lira, whose husband was a teacher too, said 'We used to fight a lot. My husband denied me all kinds of business because he thought it would cause me to love other men. When I went to Masindi to upgrade as a teacher, my husband brought in other women to my house. I came back at the same grade he was, and the trouble became worse. He gave less money for the household and took to drinking, so I had to separate my income from his. When he burnt all my clothes, I took him to court for divorce.'¹⁴⁰ A woman who was an attendant in a bar in Arua said that her work had caused at least the threat of violence. 'My husband kept on telling me not to work, yet he was not contributing anything at all to the upkeep of the home so I had to get money. He was always drunk and coming to yell at me and threatened to beat me after people told him that I misbehaved at my work place. That was why we separated.'¹⁴¹ A nurse in Lira married to a businessman with several wives commented, 'My work caused conflict with my husband. He did not provide enough and expected me to pay. The rate of violence increased when I had to go for further studies. That led to our separation, which continues to date. Since then he has never contributed towards the children's upkeep.'

A woman doctor in Kampala suggested that domestic violence stemmed from the disparity between the changes in women's lives and the continuity of older attitudes among men. 'Women have been educated in Uganda, but the men have refused to move on. They want to behave like their own fathers behaved, like their own grandfathers behaved. That gap is a major issue, because a lot of educated women today refuse to live like their grandmothers did.'¹⁴² While she pointed out that cultural issues are very difficult to change, she emphasized the importance of working to increase male awareness of the issue. She cited her work with a crisis center for women and children who have experienced domestic violence, at which male counselors worked with abusive husbands and fathers ('Men ordinarily don't mind if a man tells them what to do, but they don't want women to be ordering them around'). When the counselors explained to men how their violence 'is affecting their families, what harm it is doing, and what other ways they could solve their problems, they often say, "We didn't know" or "We will make an effort to change." So I cannot condemn the men completely. With increased awareness, there is room for change.'

Domestic Virtue and Successful Entrepreneurs

During the NRM period, the Domestic Virtue model and its two variants retained their force for most Ugandan women.¹⁴³ Working and domestic patterns for rural women continued to be shaped by the assumptions of the original model, even if the women were providing labor for cash crops or bringing in a little income of their own through the sale of agricultural produce. The Service Career variation now extended to many women in professional or government positions, but it still required submissive behavior at home and often at work. The Petty Urban Trade version applied to the growing numbers of poor women engaged in subsistence-level businesses or providing unskilled or semi-skilled labor. The importance of this variation was intensified by the war in the north, which forced many women into towns and into any kind of work that allowed them to provide for their children.

Certain features of Domestic Virtue thinking were being enforced with particular vigor at the end of the twentieth century, part of the backlash against women's special privileges and enhanced opportunities outside the home. Because male identities had previously been defined as distinct from and often opposite to female roles, the ongoing expansion of women into male spheres constituted a severe threat to the gender security of many men. Women were now active in all areas of the economy, even those formerly reserved for men, and they were nominally equal – often favored – participants in education and government. In other areas too, they were de-mystifying male activities. In 1995, for example, Acholi women in Kitgum were learning male cultural dances so that ceremonies could be performed when the men were away, and a female football referee was recognized by the Ugandan football association.[144] In the face of these challenges to male identities, many men demanded that, when women were at home, they conform to the requirement for submissive behavior to their husbands, fathers, and other male relatives.[145] At work too, some women now experienced greater pressure to act in a 'womanly' fashion, refraining from direct challenges to male authority and remaining demure.

During the later 1990s, however, a new pattern of women's behavior was becoming visible. It was based upon the entrepreneurial working style and modified family relationships of a small group of confident and energetic women who were succeeding at the middle or upper levels of their chosen field. As we have seen, many of them were active in the private sector, but one finds similar patterns among some professional women, government officials, and politicians.[146] Although there had been occasional women in earlier generations who displayed some of the same features (for example, Mary Katushabe, Profile 2.4, and Grace Ssembatia, Profile 5.1), they were exceptions. By 2000, the attitudes and prominence of these women marked them out as a recognizable new breed, even though they were still limited in number.

Their entrepreneurial approach was quite different from that of their predecessors. These self-assured women were in charge of their own lives in the public domain, and they were ambitious, eager to expand the range and impact of their business or other activities. Taking advantage of the favorable climate for women created by the NRM, they competed with men for financial, professional, and political rewards. Thanks to their education (at least secondary schooling and in many cases well beyond), they had skills and knew how to obtain information. They were able to access capital: initially through their savings or the financial backing of husbands or other relatives, and later because their own personal credit was solid. Whereas earlier women working in service careers or in small-scale trade had not expected to get rich or famous, many of the new breed sought a high level of income and/or public recognition at the same time as they contributed to the economic, social, or political development of their community and country.

The domestic roles of these women also differed from previous generations. Within their extended families, they commonly played the role of a 'big man,' offering advice and economic support. They made effective use of the resources and personal connections offered by relatives. Married women were commonly joined in business by their husbands, or at least given financial backing by them, though the wife was in charge of the day-to-day operation of the venture. Unmarried women might gain support from fathers or brothers. Some of the most successful women in Uganda in 2003 were the wives, daughters, or sisters of powerful men in the government, business, or the professions. It is probably not coincidental that the first generation of teachers and nurses during the early colonial period likewise came from elite families. In both periods, the social respectability and economic security conferred by their family situation gave these pioneers the freedom to venture into new areas, while the connections provided by powerful relatives within a kin-based society contributed to their success.

The entrepreneurial group included women of all marital statuses. If a woman was married, she was usually either her husband's only wife or, in the case of a man with multiple wives, his 'official' or public wife. In most cases the relationship between wife and husband was more equal. Some couples shared a close emotional bond, which was frequently associated with the husband's involvement with their children and some degree of participation in household tasks like shopping. Even if the spouses did not have many interests in common, or if the husband had additional wives and families, the couple could still maintain an effective business relationship. Acknowledged or *de facto* polygamy might assist active participation in a competitive world: when the husband provided economic backing and contacts but spent only part of each week or month with that wife, she had more time and attention to devote to her business or career. In public contexts, however, these women were prepared to appear with their husbands and to act respectfully toward them and their relatives.

In the new approach, motherhood was not required for social acceptance, but neither were children a necessary obstacle to success. Although most of the women had children, they had generally either limited the size of their families or did not move into an energetic career mode until their children were older, having previously worked in a different occupation or taken a less aggressive approach to their work. Those who had only a few children might face some criticism, especially from rural relatives, but most of their peers recognized the wisdom of being able to provide well for a smaller family. (Their children commonly went to high-status boarding schools and to university.) Because the women were heavily involved in their business or other work, requiring long days and sometimes travel away from home, their ability to keep their households running depended on domestic help. For wealthier families, the staff might include a male driver to do errands and ferry the children to and from school as well as women to do the cooking, cleaning, and childcare.

The working lives and domestic relations of these entrepreneurial women offered an insuperable challenge to familiar gender roles as defined by Domestic Virtue thinking. Women had now assumed many of the functions formerly assigned to men, controlling resources and making their own economic decisions (though married women might consult with their husbands about major issues). Men, conversely, had lost most of the rights that had in the past been granted exclusively to them. While many of the husbands of the new style of women were secure enough in their own economic, social, and sometimes political roles that they could accept their wives' independent activities, the growing visibility of these women contributed to wider disquiet about the place of women and the future of marriage. The value of successful women's activities for Uganda's economic development was rarely admitted. Even those women who seemed most secure in their new roles might be knocked back by a sudden resurgence of older values, as seen in the furore evoked by Kazibwe's divorce announcement – despite the fact that she was a surgeon, a successful politician, and Vice President of the country. Conservatives viewed women who were successful in the private sector with particular disfavor. A woman engaged in a profession or the government was at least offering benefits to the community or nation, but a businesswoman was generating income that rightfully belonged to men.

Although the Domestic Virtue model had shown considerable adaptability in the past, it simply could not stretch far enough to accommodate the new entrepreneurial women. Most of them were solid members of their communities, some were married to (or widowed from) important men, and nearly all had children, so they could not be dismissed as bad women. Though they were educated and in some cases contributing through their professional or government careers, they were not content to work in the lower ranks of the service sector while maintaining a traditional posture at home, as the Service Career version required. Those who were in business operated at a level well above the subsistence pattern characteristic of the Petty Urban Trade variation.

A new set of gender expectations was therefore needed, one that allowed these high achieving, self-confident women to claim a positive identity. Demonstrating once again that ideological formulations could respond to practical changes, an alternative definition of roles was emerging by 2003. It said that successful female entrepreneurs could be regarded as good and proper women if they met expectations in only two domestically-focused areas:

• They must accept primary responsibility for the smooth operation of their households and, if they had children, for their care.
• If married, they must display appropriate respect for their husbands and their relatives in public settings.

Male roles were adjusted accordingly for their husbands, most of them educated men. They were now allowed to share an emotional partnership with their wives, spend time with their children, and help in the household without impairing their standing as males, so long as they had successful working lives of their own. We regard these attitudes as a promising example of how Ugandan women and women's roles can be defined in more constructive ways.

The NRM period thus brought considerable improvement to Uganda as a nation and to its women. By 2003 they participated far more fully in the country's government, educational system, and economy, though they continued to face significant challenges. Successful entrepreneurs offered hope that other women too would be able to rise within their chosen fields. The new gender formulation that supported their activity offered hope that attitudes would continue to evolve to match changing realities. In the final chapter we highlight the main features of women's situation in 2003 and present the recommendations that have emerged from this study.

Notes

1 UN, *WISTAT, 1999,* and UN, *The World's Women 2000,* p. 145. Among men, 17 percent were unpaid family workers, 62 percent were self-employed or employers, and 21 percent were waged.
2 *Monitor,* 23–5 August 1995.
3 Goldschmidt-Clermont, *Economic Evaluations,* Meagher, 'The Hidden Economy,' Bibangambah, 'Macro-Level Constraints,' Smith, 'Market Motives,' Byandaga, 'Under-

employment,' and UN Dept. of Economic and Social Information and Policy Analysis, *Methods of Measuring Women's Economic Activity.*

4   U. Bureau of Statistics, *Uganda Demographic and Health Survey 2000–2001*, p. 26. Among men, 63 percent were currently employed, 18 percent had been employed sometime during the year, and 19 percent were not employed at all. For below, see ibid., pp. 28–32.

5   U. Statistics Dept., *Uganda National Household Survey, 1995/96*, Vol. 2, *Summary Analytical Report*, Table 7.3.15, p. 66, as cited by Lucas, 'Locating Women,' p. 13.

6   Arua12. For below, see Kampala1.

7   Kampala3.

8   Lira16. For below, see Hoima20.

9   For the desire to build one's own house, found among very poor as well as more financially successful women, see, for example, Profiles 2.1, 2.4, 7.1, 7.2, and 9.1.

10 Kampala15. For below, see Jinja5.

11 Lira8. For below, see Arua5.

12 Bantebya, 'The Role of Women,' Snyder, *Women in African Economies*, chs. 2 and 4, Sorensen, 'Commercialization,' Tadria, 'Changing Economic and Gender Patterns,' Simwogerere, 'Cassava Processing,' and Nsubuga, 'Opportunities and Constraints.' For below, see Elson and Evers, 'Gender Aware Country Economic Reports.'

13 Maxwell, 'Urban Agriculture,' and Musiimenta, 'Urban Agriculture.'

14 *Monitor*, 26-29 May and 2-5 June 1995. For below, see *New Vision*, 17 January, 10 April, 20 February, and 14 August 1995.

15 Asowa-Okwe, 'Women Wage Workers,' Nyachwo, 'A Gender Analysis,' Basirika, *Gender Participation*, and Muzaki, 'Gender in the Rural Informal Labour Market'.

16 At Masese in 1992, for example, only one of 32 boat owners was female and none of 20 fishermen, but 18 of 26 processers and 18 of 38 traders were women (Mayende, 'Fish Production'). See also Mugisa, 'Exploration of Women Activities,' Olinga, *Gender Resource Allocation*, and Wekiya, 'Nkejje Fish.'

17 Elson and Evers, 'Gender Aware Country Economic Reports,' and Mwaka, 'Agricultural Production.' For below, see White et al., *Drawers of Water*, and World Bank, *Can Africa Claim the 21st Century?*, p. 140.

18 Batte, 'Constraints of Women's Involvement,' Lubega, 'Gender Division of Labour,' Kezaabu, 'Effects of Commercialisation,' Kapampara, 'Gender Differences,' and Nanteza, 'Gender Relations'. Men moved only 7 metric ton-kilometres.

19 CEEWA-U, 'The Relevance and Effectiveness of Agricultural Extension Services.'

20 See, more fully, Snyder, *Women in African Economies* and 'Women's Agency.' For women traders in Nairobi and Accra, see Robertson, 'Comparative Advantage.'

21 Micro-enterprises generally engage fewer than 5 people and are often related to self-employment and income generation; small enterprises, employing from 5 to either 19 or 49 people, are basically profit- and growth-oriented.

22 US Agency for International Development, *Micro- and Small-Scale Enterprises*, pp. 35 and 44. A lower proportion of women (38 percent) was found in a study of small-scale enterprises in Kampala done in 2002, presumably because it did not include micro-scale participants (Namayanja, 'The Impact of "Improve Your Business" Training Program'). Among male-owned businesses, 29 percent had under Ush 10,000 in current capital, and 38 percent had over Ush 200,000. For Nigerian women who traded while remaining secluded within their own homes, see VerEecke, 'Muslim Women Traders'.

23 Others include, for Uganda: Wanendeya, 'Women in Business,' Elson and Evers, 'Gender Aware Country Economic Reports,' and CEEWA-Uganda, 'Women and Trade'; more generally, International Labour Organization, *Employment Promotion of Women*, and Kevane, *Women and Development.*

24 Wandira-Kazibwe, 'Women in Business,' esp. pp. 73-4.

25 Snyder, *Women in African Economies*, for example, p. 38.

26 For example, Nantaba, 'A Study of the Self Employed Women's Aspirations.' But for a businesswoman keenly aware of the advantages of diversification, see Profile 9.1.

27 E.g. from 1995, *Sunday Vision*, 23 July and 29 December, *New Vision*, 11 July, 26 August, and 18 September; *New Vision*, 20 June and 21 July; see also Nalubwama, 'Cooked Food Vending.' For below, see *New Vision*, 17 November 1995, and *Monitor*, 25–28 August 1995. See also Bantebya Kyomuhendo, 'The Role of Women'.

28 Cf. Ojombo, 'The Implications of Informal Cross-border Trade.'

29 Nyakaana, 'Organisation and Regulation,' and Ahikire and Ampaire, *Vending in the City.*

30 Musisi, 'Baganda Women's Night Market Activities,' *New Vision,* 27 May and 18 July 1989, Willis, *Potent Brews,* Part Four, and Muzaki, 'Women Involvement.'

31 *East African,* 19–25 June 1995, and Kampala 17. For below, see Naluyiga, *Gender, Disability.*

32 *Monitor,* 14–16 June, and *New Vision,* 8 March and 5 April 1995. For below, see *Monitor,* 8–10 November, *New Vision,* 27 March and 29 July, and *Sunday Vision,* 3 December 1995, and *New Vision,* 31 May 1989.

33 E.g., Davis, 'Time Is Money?' For secondhand clothing in Zambia, see Hansen, *Salaula.*

34 *Sunday Vision,* 24 September, 9 July, 5 November, and 15 January, and *Monitor,* 15–17 November 1995.

35 *Commonwealth Businesswomen,* pp. 106–8 and 104–6.

36 For 1995, *New Vision,* 19 June and 5 October, *Monitor,* 12–14 July, and *New Vision,* 28 February. For below, see *New Vision,* 4 April, 19 January, and 17 August.

37 *New Vision,* 19 and 24 June, and *Monitor,* 6–9 February 1995.

38 *New Vision,* 13 February and 16 August 1995; TB4.

39 *New Vision,* 25 August, 21 January, and *Monitor,* 20–22 September.

40 For this and below, see U. Ministry of Education, 'Education Statistics Abstract, 1986' (typed figures kindly located and made available to Marjorie McIntosh by Mr Lule at the Ministry of Education), World Bank, *Africa DataBase, 2003,* UN, *WISTAT, 1999,* and U. Ministry of Gender and Community Development, *Women and Men in Uganda: 2000, Education.*

41 Ssekamwa, *History and Development of Education,* p. 210.

42 Mengo School of Nursing and Midwifery, *Register Book of Nurses,* Book A, and Mulago School of Nursing and Midwifery, *Register Book of Nurses and Midwives,* 1968–2002.

43 Five men out of a total of ten in 1996, and 22 men out of 36 total in the first four months of 2003 (UNMC, *Register of Enrolled Nurses,* Book III, *Register Book of Registered Nurses,* Book II, and *Register of Nurses with Comprehensive Qualifications*).

44 Bennett, *Ale, Beer, and Brewsters,* p. 10, quoting Joan Thirsk.

45 Namukasa, 'Mobility of Professionals,' and Kabale6.

46 *New Vision,* 25 April, 3 October, and 10 July 1995, *Sunday Vision,* 2 July, and *Monitor,* 23–25 August 1995; *New Vision,* 14 March, 23 February, 19 June, and 25 July 1995, and Kukunda, Kwarisiima, 'Breaking into the Male Domain.' As of 2001, only 10 percent of the police force and 18 percent of prison service employees were women (Asiimwe-Mwesige, 'Achievements and Challenges').

47 *New Vision,* 9 March 1988. Women were also active among groups that fought against the NRM government, including well-known leaders like Alice Lakwena and lesser-known people like the Muslim woman who was among the rebels captured near Hoima in 1995 (Behrend, *Alice Lakwena,* and *New Vision,* 3 March).

48 10 February 2002.

49 Arua13.

50 *New Vision,* 21 June 1995, and Kampala23.

51 Mukuma, 'Women Making a Difference,' and Ebila, 'Ugandan Women.' For below, see *New Vision,* 5 December 1989.

52 *Sunday Vision,* 25 June and 31 December, *New Vision,* 11 August, 7 January, and 13 January 1995.

53 *New Vision,* 2 May and 15 December 1995. For below, see *Monitor,* 20–22 September, and *New Vision,* 26 and 25 May 1995.

54 *New Vision,* 15 September, 3 May, and 18 October 1995. For below, see ibid., 29 and 15 June 1995 and 15 November 1989.

55 *New Vision,* 11 and 18 April and 2 May 1995, and *Monitor,* 4–6 September 1995. For below, see *Monitor,* 31 March–3 April 1995 and *New Vision,* 22 May and 15 November 1989, and *Monitor,* 17–20 November 1995.

56 *New Vision,* 28 February and 20 November 1989. For below, see ibid., 30 March, 22 August, and 17 November 1989.

57 *Monitor,* 9–11 January, *New Vision,* 14 March, and *Monitor,* 15–18 September. See also section B2 below.

58 *Bukedde,* 10 March, 9 April, and 24 September 2002.

59 *New Vision*, 31 January, 7 March, 25 April, and 30 June 1995 and 1 March 2002.
60 *New Vision*, 14 January 1995 and *Bukedde*, 31 March 2002. For below, see *Monitor*, 31 May 2002.
61 For further examples, see Snyder, *Women in African Economies*, esp. ch. 5.
62 See, for example, Profile 9.1.
63 Arua2. For below, see Hoima3.
64 Kampala17.
65 Kampala 21.
66 Hoima14. For below, see Lira4.
67 *New Vision*, 13 September 1989.
68 *Monitor*, 8 March and 30 September 2002. For below, see *New Vision*, 25 October 1989.
69 Snyder, *Women in African Economies*, pp. 215–17 and 28. For below, see TB7.
70 TB6.
71 Margaret was interviewed on 17 April 2003 by Marjorie McIntosh, in English (tape: Kampala15). The interviewer assessed her economic status as high.
72 *New Vision*, 18 September 2002.
73 TB7.
74 TB8.
75 TB7.
76 TB1. For below, see TB6.
77 TB3. For below, see TB5.
78 TB6. For below, see TB4.
79 Kampala17.
80 U. Bureau of Statistics, *Uganda Demographic and Health Survey, 2000–2001*, for this and below. For men, the figures were higher.
81 See Appendix A.
82 Tanzarn, 'Gender Portrayals in the Media' and her *Women and Men in the Media*, reporting research done in the early 1990s.
83 *New Vision*, 16 March 1989.
84 26 May.
85 *New Vision*, 31 May 1989.
86 31 January and 1 August 1995.
87 *New Vision*, 1 January, 28 February, 14 March, 28 July, 8, 22, and 28–9 August; and *Monitor*, 3–5, 10–12, 17–19, 21–24 July, 11–14 and 23–25 August 1995.
88 *New Vision*, 20 October. For other responses, see *New Vision*, 14 September, 10 and 31 October, *Sunday Vision*, 12 December, Kwesiga, 'The Meaning of Beijing,' and Snyder, 'What Did We Bring of Beijing.'
89 U. Ministry of Gender and Community Development, and U. Ministry of Gender, Labour and Social Development.
90 Mukama, 'Women Making a Difference,' p. 152.
91 *New Vision*, 22 May, *Monitor*, 20 April, and *Orumuri*, 2–8 December, *New Vision*, 2 July and 17 May.
92 E.g., 6, 11, 12, and 18 July 2002.
93 E.g., 8-14 Feb. For below, see, e.g., 4–10 January 2002.
94 11–17 January. For below, see 1–7 March 2002.
95 *Monitor*, 27 June and 23 July; *New Vision*, 13 May, 29 July, and 8 October; *Sunday Vision*, 2 June 2002.
96 16 June 2002.
97 *New Vision*, 8 November 1989.
98 13–15 September 1995.
99 28 February 1989.
100 In the late 1990s, the official length of maternity leave was 8 weeks (UN, *The World's Women 2000*, p. 141). The employer had to pay 100 percent of a woman's wages during the first month, but there was no obligation to pay anything during the second month. See Ampaire, 'Childcare Arrangements,' Bukirwa Sentamu, 'Challenges in Career Advancement,' and Namukasa, 'Mobility of Professionals'.
101 *New Vision*, 13 September 1989.
102 *Monitor*, 25 November 2002. See also *New Vision*, 1 and 22 November 2002.
103 5 March 2002.

104 E.g., *Monitor*, 4 April, *New Vision*, 7 May and 12 November 2002.
105 E.g., *Monitor*, 30 April, and *New Vision*, 2 May 2002. For below, see *Sunday Monitor*, 12 May (two articles)
106 E.g., *New Vision*, 3 and 7 May, 8 July, 27 September, and 8 October; *Monitor*, 22 May and 24 July; *Orumuri*, 20–26 May. For below, see *The Other Voice*, 16 June 2002, and *New Vision*, 23 July.
107 *Monitor*, 12–15 May, 8–10 March, and 12–14 June 1995.
108 *New Vision*, 19 September 1995. For below, see *ibid.*, 30 May.
109 E.g., Okurut, *The Official Wife*, and Barungi, 'The Last One to Know,' in Okurut and Barungi, *A Woman's Voice*, p. 54. Cf. Robertson, *Sharing the Same Bowl*, chs. 1 and 7. One woman in our sample had to quit her job as a housegirl when she refused to give in to the demands of her male employer (Hoima17).
110 20–22 September 1995.
111 *New Vision*, 8 January, and *Monitor*, 9 October 2002. For below, see *Monitor*, 10 April 2002
112 *Sunday Vision*, 17 February, and *Weekend Vision*, 15 March 2002. For below, see 7 March.
113 22–8 March. For below, see 15–21 March 2002.
114 1 March. For below, see 2–8 September.
115 *New Vision*, 14 September. For below, see *New Vision*, 22 October.
116 *New Vision*, 19 October, 18 August and 17 October.
117 *Monitor*, 17 March.
118 Tinkasiimire, 'Women's Contributions,' and Kassimir, 'Uganda: The Catholic Church'.
119 5 April 1989.
120 *Weekly Topic*, 21 September 1988.
121 *New Vision*, 14 April 1989.
122 Ibid., 4 May.
123 *New Vision*, 14 July 1989.
124 19 May 2002. For below, see 14 March 2003.
125 14 May 2002.
126 Similarly in Mozambique, 'The decades of emphasis on "revolutionary" ideals of womanhood have had little impact on the general public'. Many men still resisted having their wives work outside the home or their own fields; they were ashamed that they could not support their own families and mistrustful of women who traveled (Sheldon, *Pounders of Grain*, pp. 217–18 and 256).
127 E.g., Profile 8.1and Hoima4.
128 Nakamate, 'Challenges,' and Ssenyonjo, 'Factors Affecting the Performance.' For below, see TB3.
129 Kabundah, 'Problems of Women Market Traders,' p. 25.
130 Among women traders in Kampala's Bwaise market in 1998, for example, only 37 percent were currently married, with 44 percent separated/divorced and 19 percent widowed (Kabunduh, 'Problems of Women Market Traders'); among women brewing and selling alcohol in the Mulago slum area in 1997, 46 percent were married (Mukazi, 'Women Involvement'). See also Twongyeirwe, 'Where Do I Belong?,' in Wangusa and Barungi, *Tears of Hope*, pp. 1-24.
131 Arua7.
132 Jinja8.
133 Jinja10.
134 The author was raised in Uganda and trained as an administrative secretary by the East African Railways Corporation. She was living in Zambia at the time the book was published in 1992.
135 See Chapter 8.
136 U. Bureau of Statistics, *Demographic and Health Survey 2000–2001*, p. 37.
137 See, e.g., Ndagijimana, 'Frieda's World,' and Rwabukuku, 'Quest for Freedom,' in Wangusa and Barungi, *Tears of Hope*, pp. 25 and 93; Tibatemwa-Ekirikubinza, *Women's Violent Crime*.
138 Kwesiga, 'Leaders within Limits,' and, for example, *East African*, 25–31 March 2002, and *The Other Voice*, 31 March 2002.
139 Mpigi6. For below, see Arua11.
140 Lira11.

141 Arua13. For below, see Lira6.
142 Kampala17.
143 For the basic model, see Chapter 4; for its first two variations, see Chapters 4 and 7.
144 *New Vision*, 9 May and 7 March 1995.
145 Among the Iraqw of Tanzania in the 1990s, 'When women take up tasks which were formerly those of men, it does not mean that this shift allows them greater authority within the household' (Snyder, 'Gender Ideology,' in Moore et al., *Those Who Play with Fire*, pp. 225–53, esp. p. 235).
146 See first section of this chapter for entrepreneurial businesswomen.

Ten

Women & Work
in 2003
Assessment & Recommendations

This study has profound implications for contemporary public policy and development interventions. The summary and recommendations below offer a fresh approach to the question of how to facilitate African women's participation in the public domain. Rather than deriving from the assumptions of economists or political scientists, our suggestions are grounded in Ugandan women's experiences over the past century and their situation in 2003. Based upon the observations of the Torchbearers and women in our district sample as well as many other sources, they also reflect the combined perspective of a Ugandan anthropologist and a North American historian.

The primary recommendation to emerge from this study is that active intervention is needed to assist poor women to rise above subsistence level, to facilitate women's success at middle and higher levels, and to lessen destructive gender tension. If nothing is done, women will certainly continue to enter the cash-based economy, but most of them will stay at the bottom of the system. Their contributions to their families and the country's economic development will therefore be limited. If gendered expectations are not modified, women's productivity will be constrained and conflict between women and men will remain a serious problem.

Implementing our recommendations will require a joint effort among many groups. Although working women demonstrate great agency in their own lives, they cannot make the necessary changes on their own. Even educated and wealthy women and effective women's organizations lack the ability to reshape the powerful institutions, policies, structures, and attitudes that determine the context within which they operate. Programs designed to improve women's economic opportunities will require a coordinated campaign involving multiple organizations and individuals. The government will need to take the lead in creating a more conducive environment for women and rallying other groups and interests to join with it in promoting women's advancement. Other initiatives can be spearheaded by NGOs and CBOs, religious leaders and churches, and educators and schools. Some degree of financial support from international organizations will be necessary. Women must be centrally involved in the formulation and implementation of all aspects of this project.

The first section of this chapter addresses the seven material or practical factors influencing women's work that we have traced throughout the book, summarizing their role in 2003 and offering recommendations. The operation of these pressures is summarized visually in Figure 10.1. We turn then to the gender-based constraints that confront women at the workplace and at home. Most of these stem from that set of attitudes that we have labeled the Domestic Virtue model and its two variations: the Service Career and Petty Urban Trade versions.[1] A final section assesses the impact of Domestic Virtue thinking in 2003 and presents our recommendations for how to promote constructive change in gender definitions.

Material Factors

In this section, we highlight under each factor the main features in 2003, based upon the fuller discussions in Chapters 8 and 9. We then present recommendations for building upon strengths and tackling problems.

Women's education

Throughout the past century, women's education has been a major factor in pulling women into the market economy and enabling them to operate at a higher level within it. Professional women in particular were often eager to contribute to their communities and to gain the social rewards that accompanied their work. The NRM government's measures have greatly improved access to education for primary school girls and young women of university age. In 2003, however, studies were showing that girls attended school less regularly than boys and were more likely to drop out.

Recommendations
- The government should continue support for UPE, including enforcement of *attendance* (not just enrollment) by all children.
- Universities should continue to award extra points to female applicants so as to achieve and maintain more equal enrollment rates.
- If the country can afford it, presumably through the use of donor funding, expanded support for girls in secondary education would result in improved options for working women and a lowered birth rate.

Demographic and health factors

Geographic mobility for women and urbanization have promoted women's economic participation. The pressures that cause them remained strong in 2003 and need no reinforcement.

Women who head their own households, whether unmarried, separated/divorced, or widowed, are pushed strongly into the cash-based economy, if only to keep themselves and their children alive. Female-headed households were numerous in 2003, due in part to HIV/AIDS. However, such women often lack education and skills and hence have to enter the economy at the bottom level. Many of them remain stuck in subsistence-level petty trade for the rest of their lives.

Cultural expectations that women will have many children, when coupled with limited family planning facilities and poor reproductive health care, impede

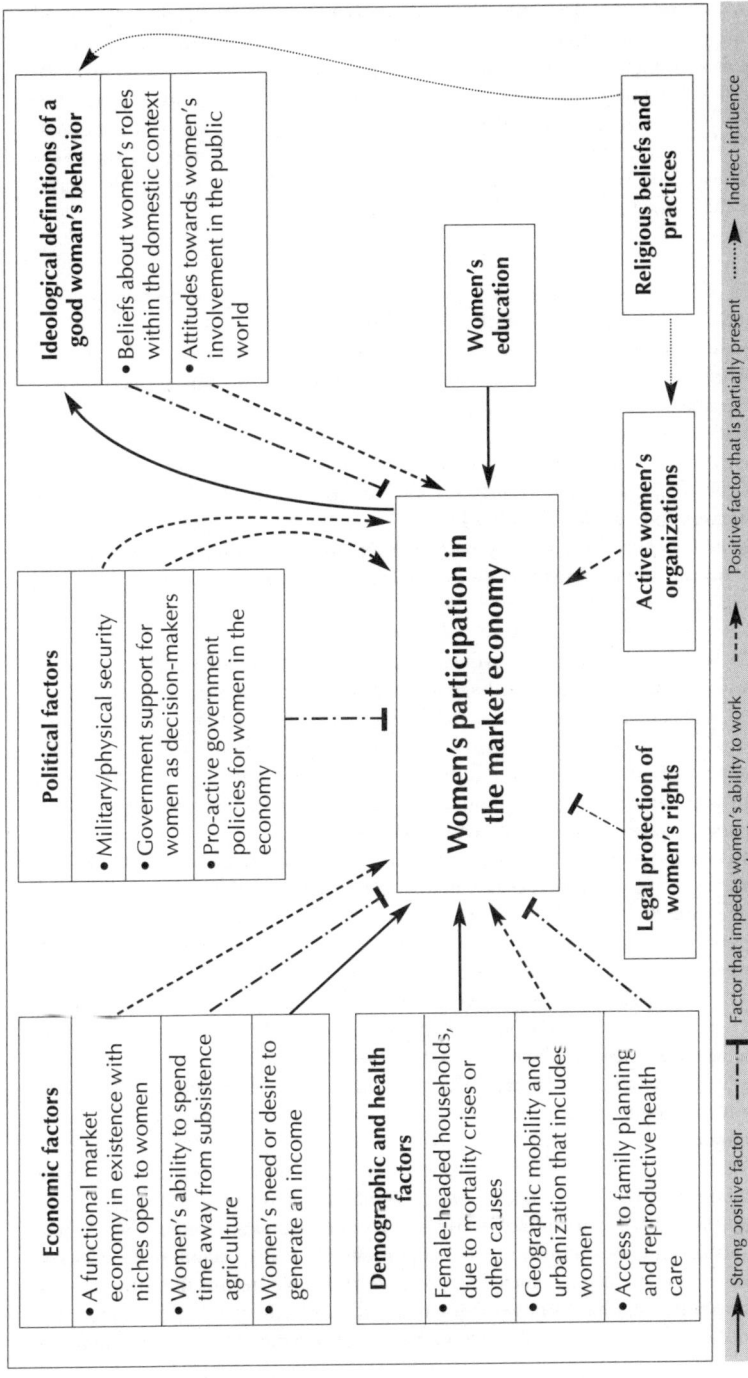

Figure 10.1 Ugandan women's participation in the market economy, 2003

women's ability to function effectively in the market economy. While motherhood is an important part of most Ugandan women's identity, large family sizes hamper their ability to provide well for their children.

HIV/AIDS takes a greater toll on women than men, due in part to their socially defined roles as carers. For working women, the illness and death of a male relative mean not only loss of his income but also an interruption of their own earning capacity. Women, especially those with cash resources, commonly assume responsibility for orphans.

Recommendations

- The government and women's groups should address the particular problems faced by female household heads, offering special training programs and increased access to credit. The minimum goal is to help these women provide better care for their children, including education, and acquire some degree of economic security.
- Family planning services and reproductive health care should be declared a priority by the government. This will assist all women but have a particularly beneficial impact upon women's contributions to the economy, and it will strengthen the quality of motherhood.
- HIV/AIDS programs should pay greater attention to women's roles as carers of sick people and orphans and provide more support for them.

Religion

In 2003, as in the past two generations, religion had little influence upon women's economic activities. Leaders of the mainstream churches spoke out boldly about poverty and certain political issues, and they made some effort to include more women within their own institutions. But none of the major faiths (Roman Catholic, Protestant, or 'born again' Christian denominations or Muslim communities) took a strong stand on women's issues. Although some religious women's groups were promoting income-generating activities, the churches did not use their official position to support women's work or to explain to their members why it benefits everyone in the family. Nor did they utilize their great potential influence to preach vigorously against domestic violence.

Recommendations

- The churches should advocate women's work as important to the well-being of the family and community, using the pulpit and other forms of communication.
- The churches should take a public stance that domestic violence is not consistent with Christian or Islamic definitions of a good marriage and employ all forms of persuasion at their disposal to reduce the problem among their own members.

Active women's organizations

In the later 1980s and early 1990s, women's organizations, including NGOs and CBOs, were numerous, vigorous, and cooperating fairly well together. They shared concerns in the areas of women's legal rights and poverty, including the goal of making credit available to poor women. Their own activities had an impact on women's lives and work, and they were able to put pressure on the government. By

2003, however, women's groups had lost their cohesiveness and sense of common purpose, their memberships were declining, and their external funding was insecure. The revival of party politics posed the threat that if leading women could not develop a shared agenda, one imposed upon all parties, women would be fragmented and hence marginalized.

Recommendations

- Women's organizations should continue to emphasize women's economic activities and find ways of addressing the needs of all groups: educated, urban women; poor women in towns; and village women.
- Women leaders should work together to develop a shared agenda of central issues that can be presented forcefully to the government and all political parties.
- Women's organizations must be able to function independently, without political interference.

Legal protection of women's rights

Despite the efforts of CBOs and NGOs, the legal situation of Uganda's women remained severely constrained. Educational activities on the part of such groups had resulted in improved knowledge on the part of women about the law and their status within it, but the laws themselves remained discriminatory. The two major areas of concern in 2003, as for much of the previous century, were women's inheritance and landholding rights, and marital and domestic relations. Unlike its earlier advocacy of women, the NRM government did not support revisions to the Land Act that would have given women a more secure claim to marital and family land or a proposed Domestic Relations Bill. Parliament had likewise turned down the former and never considered the latter.

Recommendations

- The government should take the lead in campaigning for revisions to the Land Act, helping to persuade men that the measure will have beneficial effects for their families.
- The government should back a Domestic Relations Bill that prohibits and imposes penalties for violence within the home, against both women and children.

Political factors

The NRM government has provided peace and physical security to much of the country, enabling women and men to live safely and engage comfortably in their economic activities. As of 2003, fighting in the north still continued after 17 years, and many questioned whether the government and military leaders were serious about trying to find a solution to the problem. In the disrupted areas, women faced tremendous challenges of all kinds, whether they remained at home, had fled to the towns, or were living in camps. Another kind of insecurity, one which damaged the market and those who participated in it, was corruption. This problem was increasing in 2003, at all levels of government.

The government provided outstanding support for women from its assumption of power in 1986 through to at least 1995. By naming women to important positions and introducing an affirmative action policy, the NRM created a climate in which women were accepted as decision-makers. It was rightly praised throughout the world for these measures. By 2003, however, government backing for women appeared to be weakening. Through its failure to support measures of key importance to them and its dismissal of some of the most visible women from office, the government contributed to the mounting backlash against women.

Recommendations
- The government should take urgent and effective action to bring the fighting in the north to an end.
- The government, assisted by Uganda's legal system and perhaps by outside organizations, should take effective steps to curb corruption.
- The government should resume its previous championship of women, demonstrating through the legislation it supports and the people it names to office that women share fully in all aspects of the nation's life.

Economic factors

The strongest single factor that has pushed women into the economy is the need or desire to generate income. Poor women needed money to keep themselves and often their families alive, but in general they had limited options about what kinds of work to pursue since they had few skills and little access to capital or credit. Despite the worthy goals of microfinance projects and their partial success in helping poor women to keep their families solvent, small loans for a few months have not succeeded in raising women out of poverty. Educated women commonly sought a higher standard of living for their households, including better schooling for their children, and/or a chance to serve the community. Women from important families had the added benefit of the credit and contacts that their position gave them, making it far easier for them to move into intermediate or upper positions in business, the professions, or government.

The majority of Ugandan women in 2003 continued to work in agriculture. In some cases they were paid for their labor, though more commonly it was done within the family. While some were able to raise extra produce for sale or pursue other small income-generating activities on the side, many devoted their full attention to raising food for their household. Due to the absence of draught animals in many parts of the country and of mechanized equipment on all but the largest commercial farms, human labor was essential to agriculture. Because men played only certain designated roles in the cultivation of crops in many of Uganda's cultures, women shouldered most of the burden. Even if a rural woman was eager to engage in the market economy, she might not have the time or energy to do so.

Women's ability to earn money was limited by certain features of Uganda's market economy that affected men as well. Structural problems included bad roads and inadequate transport within the country, weakly differentiated production and unspecialized markets, the inaccessibility of foreign consumers, unreliable or absent electricity and expensive petroleum fuels, and high rents, trading licenses, and taxes. Such difficulties made it almost impossible for women in many parts of the country to raise their production or marketing activities beyond a very modest level. Some of these problems were compounded by gender factors.

Improving the country's economy as a whole is an essential component of any attempt to improve the situation of working women. If the economic pie is not growing, women can only get a bigger piece at the expense of the share allocated to men, adding nothing to national development but contributing to gender hostility.

Because privatization and the pressures of a global economy have intensified the problems that businesswomen face in competing at middle and higher levels, affirmative action policies by the government are needed. Pro-active measures will hasten the ability of entrepreneurial women to succeed.

Recommendations

- Government agencies, NGOs, and commercial organizations should actively seek resources that will help to expand the scope and improve the efficiency of Uganda's market economy, benefiting both women and men.
- Agricultural experts should devote more attention to the use of animal power and labor-saving technologies that would free up rural women's time and encourage a more even division of labor between women and men.
- The government and NGOs should work together to increase the training available to poor women as a part of their poverty alleviation projects, enabling them to develop income-generating skills that will assist their entire household.
- The government should introduce economic affirmative action policies for women.
  These could include:
  - Extending incentives to women starting businesses similar to those given to foreign investors, such as tax breaks, guaranteed loans, and use of government facilities.
  - Giving some advantage to businesses owned and operated by women, similar to the extra points in university admissions, when awarding government tenders and purchasing contracts at all levels.
  - Insisting that businesses that accept contracts with the government have an affirmative action policy in their own hiring processes.

Gender-Based Constraints

In considering the gender-based problems faced by women who earned their own money, we look first at the handicaps they encountered at work and then at difficulties within the family context. In both areas, the values of the Domestic Virtue model are clearly visible. After assessing that model and its variations in 2003, we present recommendations for tackling the practical problems faced by women and for modifying gender expectations.

Within the workplace, an initial cluster of gender constraints stemmed from women's reproductive and nurturing roles, in biological and social terms. Although most Ugandan cultures encouraged women to downplay the impact of pregnancy and childbirth, biological factors commonly interrupted their ability to devote substantial and sustained attention to their income-generating activities. Because maternity leave was limited, and because few employers provided any kind of childcare facilities, motherhood constituted a practical and economic impediment to success at work. Breastfeeding meant either that the mother had to take the baby to work with her or have domestic help who would bring it to her workplace for feeding. In our district sample, women ranging from foodstuff vendors in urban markets to senior civil servants said they wished they had childcare facilities at their place of work. In the absence of household help, poor women were generally compelled to bring babies and young children with them to work.

Women with families invested less time in their work and faced interruptions that reduced their income and ability to succeed in careers. Professional women and civil servants commented that because they were unable to work flexible hours or take extra assignments due to their obligations at home, they did not advance.[2] Women operating small, informal enterprises in Lira town said that family responsibilities had harmed their businesses. Middle-level women managers said that the biggest problem they faced was conflict between their working and domestic roles.[3] They did not move forward on the job due to their family responsibilities, yet because they spent so much time at the work place, their families suffered.

Limited education and practical training, problems that affected men too but were magnified for women, stood in the way of women's success at work. Market traders and other poor women in business were held back by lack of basic skills like literacy and numeracy.[4] Women were less likely to receive the kinds of on-the-job training commonly provided to men: their employers felt that giving them specialized skills was not a good investment since they were unlikely to continue in their work and move up the ladder. Because so few businesswomen had been able to rise beyond a modest level, we give special recognition to Maggie Kigozi's energy in developing the capacity of women entrepreneurs through the UIA and to the training programs of organizations like UWEAL and CEEWA-Uganda.

Capital and credit were serious problems for many businesswomen. Insufficient credit was one of the causes of 'the missing middle class' among Ugandan women, keeping them from moving beyond subsistence activity.[5] People who started small-scale enterprises commonly derived their start-up capital from their personal savings, but women were less likely than men to have such resources.[6] Lenders were usually hesitant to grant credit to a married woman without knowing more about the financial situation of her husband and whether he was willing to back her project. Collateral in the form of land was a problem for women, due to legal restrictions on property ownership. But Islamic teachings prohibiting interest appear to have had little practical impact on Muslim businesswomen in terms of accessing credit.[7]

Women were subject to a variety of other practical problems. They had trouble lining up a reliable working partner or even finding someone to look after their business when they needed to be absent. They were more likely than men to be victims of petty theft, and when customers took items on credit but defaulted, they found it hard to force payment. Women who sold liquor or worked in bars complained of long working hours, lack of social respect because of the nature of their jobs, and sexual abuse from clients. Nurses were worried about the increased risk of contracting HIV/AIDS due to inadequate safety precautions in hospitals. Women engaged in unskilled labor or running small businesses mentioned unsanitary or dangerous working conditions, especially if they were producing food or drink with old or defective equipment.

Other types of handicaps stemmed from the ongoing impact of the attitudes promoted by the Domestic Virtue model, including its definition of appropriate roles for women and men. Gender stereotyping affected the kinds of work for which women were hired and the assignments they were given. Thus, police-women were typically sent to deal with women and children; female lawyers within a firm were handed cases dealing with gender, family, or HIV/AIDS; and journalists were directed to the women's page.[8] Because these were all low-prestige areas, not producing the kind of recognition and reward that many male assignments yielded, women's careers were held back. Even the army, which had previously boasted that it treated men and women equally, recalled 700 female soldiers from units scattered throughout the country in 2002 so that they could be reassigned to 'suitable jobs' at the main barracks in Bombo. These included duties in hospitals and offices.[9]

Women and men encountered divergent practices at work. Policewomen (but not policemen) had to get approval from the Inspector General before marrying.[10] Female candidates for political office had to campaign in ways different from men, and they were expected to behave differently once in office. Women who were successful in the professions, business, or politics were often regarded as excessively aggressive and unwomanly. Women were generally excluded from the informal drinking sessions or clubs where much discussion of job-related issues occurred and where information was shared.

Gaining respect from men could be a challenge. The women in our sample mentioned problems in hiring and supervising male employees, who refused to accept their authority. Some feared physical aggression. Women who operated small businesses might have trouble protecting themselves against harassment by local officials or the police.[11]

Sexual relations were a problematic area. Many women – even those in the police force – faced harassment at work, with employers often the major threat.[12] Women's participation in business or public life was still seen by many people as inseparable from promiscuity or infidelity, with a common suspicion that a woman who was succeeding in her work must have used her sexuality to move up.[13] Women who traveled on their own in connection with their work might be viewed as sexually available.

The way in which girls and young women were socialized, the education they received based upon Domestic Virtue assumptions, commonly impaired their ability to function effectively on the job. The message that girls and women should be submissive, docile, and non-aggressive was communicated within families, at school, and through the mass media.[14] Many working women were therefore constrained by lack of self-confidence and assertiveness.

Women's hesitation to join with others in business was a major detriment. Most women worked either on their own or with their husbands. Even successful women were often reluctant to join organizations like UWEAL or the Chamber of Commerce that gave businesspeople greater visibility and provided support for them. Some women did not want to spend the money or time associated with membership, while others feared their business would be swallowed up by the larger body. Unwillingness to work collectively has led women to miss out on opportunities that would have benefited their businesses, through informal networking and access to information, credit, and practical training.

Within the domestic context, the ways in which gender factors affected the lives of working women depended largely upon their marital situation. Married women might have greater economic security thanks to their husband's income and perhaps his financial assistance in their training or business, but they also faced strong pressure to conform to accepted roles within the family. Wives might also have to move to a new location or find another job if their husband's work changed.[15] Women who had not married or were separated, divorced, or widowed had greater freedom from restrictive gender expectations, but they were reliant upon their own earnings to maintain themselves and their families. Some successful businesswomen in Kampala in 2003 could focus upon their work because they were not currently married, but at the other end of the spectrum, many subsistence traders were also living without husbands. In all cases, working women were expected to be a major source of advice and practical assistance for their extended families. The time and money they could invest in their own economic activities were therefore curtailed.

A number of problems arose out of the ongoing expectation, central to Domestic Virtue thinking, that women were to assume full responsibility for caring for their household and children. Despite the huge increase in women's participation in the public domain across the twentieth century, a new pattern of domestic work shared between women and men had not emerged. Even women who were deeply engaged in business or the professions still had to shoulder the burden of running their households, on top of their income-generating activities.[16] Men were generally unwilling to assume what they saw as women's roles within the home, like cooking or washing dishes. Some men in towns, however, especially those who were educated, were beginning to spend more time with their children and helped with tasks like shopping.

Women described physical exhaustion and/or severe emotional pressure from trying to handle their domestic responsibilities while also working outside the home. Many were stretched thin, physically and emotionally, leading to health problems.[17] This complaint extended from poor women all the way to the country's female leaders, who pointed in 2003 to the impossibility of filling multiple roles adequately as one of the most severe problems confronting women.

Because many women did not have the time or energy to do all the household work themselves, they relied on domestic help. In the past poorer women commonly left an older daughter in charge of the house and family while they were away, but UPE now keeps many of these girls in school. This means that a growing proportion of working women must hire a domestic servant. Finding a reliable worker, often a village girl, and training and supervising her properly were major challenges.[18] Relatively little concern was expressed in the sources we used about the potential exploitation of housegirls, in economic, educational, and sexual terms.

Gender tension and sometimes domestic violence ensued when couples disagreed about the woman's work or how her income should be used. Even a highly educated woman holding an important job might have a husband who insisted that she be home to serve him his evening meal.[19] Men were often jealous when their wives spent time away from home in the presence of other men. Many husbands reduced their contribution to the family if their wife brought in an income of her own. Yet when women participated in the public arena, had their own incomes, and made important decisions at work, they were less willing to accept the authority of their husband when they came home. If domestic abuse occurred, they were in a better position to leave the relationship. Some people argued in 2003 that women's work was threatening the institution of marriage.

Recommendations

Our recommendations concerning gender-based constraints have two goals:
- to assist poor women to achieve basic economic security
- to help women compete successfully at higher levels in their careers or business.

The government, employers, and NGOs should work together in the following ways:
- Increase maternity leave from two to three months
- Provide daycare centers for women at work
- Offer increased training for women engaged in business and professional careers to help them compete with men
- With respect to credit:
  - Increase the size and length of microfinance loans
  - Advise women on how to utilize their loans
  - Develop mechanisms to enable women to access larger loans from commercial banks
- Define sexual harassment in the work place and create policies to reduce it
- Run short courses that train women to be more self-confident about their abilities and more assertive about their rights at work
- Encourage successful women to advise others in their type of work
- To lessen the class-based implications of the current reliance upon the cheap labor of housegirls:
  - Develop programs whereby adolescent girls and young women do part-time domestic work while continuing their own education or practical training
  - Develop appropriate technologies to lessen the domestic workload (e.g., better stoves and alternative fuels for cooking)

Domestic Virtue and the Future

The gendered expectations that most women faced at work and at home stemmed from the ongoing force of Domestic Virtue assumptions. Ugandan women were still defined primarily as wives and/or mothers, no matter how significant their participation in the public domain. This is illustrated by President Museveni's speech at the opening of the international women's congress held at Makerere University in July 2002. Although he was proud that women held important positions throughout Uganda's government (evoking sustained applause from the audience), he emphasized the importance of 'the African woman' to her family and referred to 'the Ugandan woman' as 'mother of the nation' (terms that offended some African and Western feminists).[20] Furthermore, he said that he had named Speciosa Kazibwe as Vice President as a symbol, without mentioning her own qualifications for the office.

In 2003, Domestic Virtue thinking continued to constrain the ability of many women to succeed in their income-generating activities, thereby reducing their contributions to their own households and to Uganda's economic development more generally. The weight of that model was felt especially strongly by rural women, who faced traditional expectations on the part of their male relatives and had fewer opportunities to enter the market economy. But many people in all settings still believed that women were solely responsible for the care of the household and children, that they should be submissive to their husbands and other men, and were not to make decisions within the family or control resources. Nor were they to compete with men in the public domain. Women's and men's roles were thus mutually exclusive. Women leaders concluded in 2003 that one of the most important problems faced by women was 'cultural beliefs about gendered rights and responsibilities that limit women's ability to take advantage of the new opportunities available to them'.[21] A contradiction between women's place in public settings and in the household has been described as characteristic of modern African states more generally.

The ideology of Domestic Virtue contributed also to gender tension and insecure male identities. Whereas women now enjoyed expanded opportunities, most men felt that they were progressively losing their accustomed roles and rights. Certain responsibilities previously assigned to men, such as hunting, fishing, and physical protection of their families, had diminished early in the twentieth century. Within the family, their place as household head and sole decision-maker was undercut by women's ability to generate their own income. Men's position as authority figures within the community was threatened by women's involvement in the public domain. Yet Domestic Virtue thinking prevented men from gaining new and more positive identity components in return. It is not surprising that many men resented women's growing power, in some cases expressing that resentment through verbal or physical abuse.

Because Domestic Virtue attitudes currently hamper women's effectiveness at work, promote gender conflict, and hamper the emergence of more positive identities for both women and men, new gender definitions are needed. To some extent, change will happen of its own accord, as women become better educated and more successful at work. Women who have been educated are likely to seek interesting jobs of their own and to want husbands who will accept their independence. Professional women and politicians will almost certainly become less willing to play second fiddle to men at work and may refuse to fill all the customary roles at home. As more women find lucrative forms of employment, their husbands may become persuaded that women's contributions to the family economy are worth the price of taking on some domestic duties themselves and accepting some loss of deference. The business page of *Sunday Vision* commented in 2002: 'Already there are women who earn more or the same amount of money as their husbands, and in the next decade, the number is expected to increase tremendously. It is anticipated that women will demand more, especially in the sharing of domestic chores, let alone parenting.'[22] But simply allowing matters to take their own course carries two risks: it may take several generations before women obtain a substantially higher level of equality at work and at home; and the gender tension that was limiting their productivity at work and breaking up marriages in 2003 is likely to remain high.

We believe that the development of more constructive gender definitions can be hastened by deliberate interventions. Deeply held beliefs about core issues like gender identities and domestic relations are, of course, hard to change. But this book has demonstrated that gender formulations are flexible, that they can and do respond to shifts in the material world around them. The arrows between the central box in Figure 10.1 and the upper right-hand box go in both directions. Even the powerful Domestic Virtue model was willing to make some compromises with the changing realities of women's lives, redefining several groups of female workers so that they could be regarded as good women though they did not conform to all features of the original model.

Efforts to improve the position of women in the early twenty-first century must include a campaign to promote more flexible definitions of women's and men's roles. One example of an alternative formulation arose in response to the practical success during the later 1990s of a small number of women active in the private sector and, to a lesser extent, in the professions, politics and government.[23] These women displayed an entrepreneurial approach at work, enlarging their activities and hoping to achieve a sizeable income and recognition even as they contributed to the broader community. They developed new relationships within the family, including with their husbands if they were married. Because such women could not be accommodated by any version of the Domestic Virtue model, a new set of definitions was beginning to emerge by 2003 that allowed women to compete vigorously in the public world so long as they accepted primary responsibility for their households and behaved respectfully to their husbands and other male relatives in public. Expectations for their husbands were likewise redefined: these men could interact more fully with their wives and children and help with some domestic activities while still being respected as males, provided they were successful in their own work. In this formulation, women's and men's roles were less rigidly defined; some overlap between them was accepted. Few Ugandan women will achieve the level of success of those entrepreneurs, but the revised gender definition that developed in response to their activity illustrates the kind of alternative norms that can replace the confining features of the Domestic Virtue approach.

Recommendations
Several goals should shape interventions designed to weaken the negative features of Domestic Virtue thinking and promote development of gender norms that provide greater flexibility in male and female roles.

• To open a public dialogue that persuades Ugandans that women's ability to generate their own income benefits everyone (their family, the community, and the nation), rather than forming a threat to the economic position, authority, and identities of men
• To demonstrate how Domestic Virtue expectations curtail women's productive capacity at work and in the home
• To highlight the adverse impact of Domestic Virtue thinking on the social interactions of women and men, and of parents and children, contributing to gender tension and domestic violence
• To promote the development of alternative gender definitions that will:
  ◦ improve women's ability to participate effectively in the economy while still being respected as good women
  ◦ help men gain a new and more positive identity

○ improve gender relations in all contexts and strengthen the institution of marriage

To achieve these goals, an educational campaign must be planned and implemented. It will require cooperation between many groups, who will need to agree to a long-term commitment, for the pace of change may well be slow. While women must be centrally involved in creating every component of the project, the audience must include men as well: as of 2003, women's thinking had in many cases changed more significantly than men's.

The campaign should be led by the government and introduced simultaneously by:

• the mass media, targeting a wide audience including young adults
• religious organizations, targeting people of all ages
• the Ministry of Education, local education officers, teacher training colleges, and schools, targeting children and teachers through revised curricula and textbooks
• NGOs and CBOs, targeting men and children as well as women

Such a program will require a substantial investment of time and money on the part of the multiple organizations involved. But if the will is there, this investment can be made. A good model is the successful educational initiative concerning HIV/AIDS during the 1990s, spearheaded by the government and joined by virtually every group in the country. As was the case with the HIV/AIDS initiative, Uganda will need financial and other types of support from international organizations for aspects of the project.

The benefits of this campaign far outweigh the costs. The gains are of two main types. If women's engagement in the market economy is facilitated, more women will have their own income (and in many cases a better income), increasing their economic and personal agency. Households and extended families will enjoy greater food security and a better standard of living, improved education and health care, and the ability to assist less fortunate relatives, including orphaned children. Economic growth and development for the country as a whole will be enhanced, especially if a higher proportion of working women are able to rise above a subsistence or unskilled level. In addition, if gender roles are modified so that men and women share responsibilities and rewards more evenly, they will be able to interact more productively at work, yielding clear economic benefits, and more harmoniously within the family setting, yielding clear social benefits.

Notes

1 See Chapters 4 and 7 above for the basic model and its variant forms.
2 Bukirwa, 'Challenges in Career Advancement,' Kukunda, 'Breaking into the Male Domain,' Namukasa, 'Mobility of Professionals,' Nantaba, 'A Study of the Self Employed Women's Aspirations,' and Musoke, 'Women in the Professions.' For below, see Onweng Angura, *Opportunities and Constraints*.
3 Musiimire, 'Inter-role Conflict'.

4   Nakamate, 'Challenges,' Bukirwa Sentamu, 'Challenges in Career Advancement,' and Namukasa, 'Mobility of Professionals'.

5   Snyder, *Women in African Economies*, ch. 5.

6   For this and below, see, e.g., Nakirunda, 'Factors Promoting Women-Operated Enterprises,' Ziwa, 'Peri-Urban Women's Home-Based Enterprises,' Onweng Angura, *Opportunities and Constraints*, and USAID, *Micro- and Small-Scale Enterprises in Uganda*, p. 72.

7   Kubiragume, 'Challenges and Prospects,' and Kabunduh, 'Problems of Women Market Traders'.

8   Kukunda, 'Breaking into the Male Domain,' *New Vision*, 11 June 2002, and TB3; Bukirwa Sentamu, 'Challenges in Career Advancement'.

9   *New Vision*, 9 January 2002.

10 *Bukedde*, 6 January 2002.

11 Nantaba, 'A Study of the Self Employed Women's Aspirations,' and cf. Okurut, 'The Tribe on Dewinton Road,' in her *Milking a Lioness*, p. 77.

12 *New Vision*, 31 December 2002, *Monitor*, 25 July 2002, Bukirwa, 'Challenges in Career Advancement,' and Kukunda, 'Breaking into the Male Domain'.

13 For 'bottom power' among elite Igbo women in Nigeria, see Okeke, 'Negotiating Social Independence'.

14 Tanzarn, 'Gender Portrayals in the Media in Uganda'.

15 Bukirwa Sentamu, 'Challenges in Career Advancement'.

16 Lubega, 'Gender Division of Labour'.

17 Bitunda, 'Problems and Prospects,' Nanteza, 'Gender Relations,' Bukirwa Sentamu, 'Challenges in Career Advancement,' and Basemera, 'Single Motherhood'. For below, see App. D.

18 Ampaire, 'Childcare Arrangements,' Basemera, 'Single Motherhood ,' Bitunda, 'Problems and Prospects,' Bukirwa Sentamu,' Challenges in Career Advancement,' and Namukasa, 'Mobility of Professionals'.

19 Okeke-Ihejirika likewise describes 'the patriarchal contract' that a successful Igbo career woman must accept in return for her participation in paid work, which includes preparing and serving certain foods to her husband in person (*Negotiating Power and Privilege*, p. 151).

20 Personal observation and Kwesiga, 'Leaders within Limits'.

21 See Appendix D. They cited men's insecurity and cultural factors that limit women's empowerment as significant underlying causes. For below, see Mikell, *African Feminism*, p. 333.

22 21 July 2002.

23 See Chapter 9.

Appendices

Appendix A. Newspapers Analyzed, by Year

Two graduate research assistants (Jean Kemitare and Deus Mukalazi) examined most of the papers listed below, for the full year unless otherwise noted. Moses Kadobera surveyed *Etop* for 2002. The papers are available in the Africana section of Makerere University Library. Our assistants looked for articles, photographs, cartoons, editorials, and letters to the editor concerning women's work and other activities, the factors that affected them, and attitudes towards women. All relevant material was photocopied; the copies are deposited in the library in the Dept. of Women and Gender Studies at Makerere University. The papers were published in Uganda and in English unless otherwise noted. Material from local-language papers was translated into English by our assistants or Grace Bantebya.

1915	*Uganda Herald*
1920	*Munno* (in Luganda)
1925	*Uganda Herald*
1930	*Munno* (in Luganda)
1935	*Uganda Herald*
1941	*Munno* (in Luganda)
1945	*Uganda Herald*
1950	*Munno* (in Luganda)
1955	*Uganda Argus*
	Uganda Herald
1960	*Ageteraine* (in Runyankore, published in Mbarara)
	Munno (in Luganda)
	Obugagga Bwa Uganda (in Luganda)
	Uganda Empya (in Luganda)
1965	*East African Standard* (published in Nairobi)
	Uganda Argus
1970	*Agerteraine* (in Runyankore, published in Mbarara)

	Munno (in Luganda)
	Taifa Empya (in Luganda)
	Taifa Uganda Empya (in Luganda)
1975	*Voice of Uganda*
1985	*The Star* (January-February)
	Weekly Topic (August)
1988	*Financial Times*
	New Vision
	Star
1989	*New Vision*
1995	*East African* (published in Nairobi)
	Monitor
	New Vision and *Sunday Vision*
	6th of February
2002	*Bukedde* (in Luganda)
	East African (published in Nairobi)
	Etop (in Ateso/Luo)
	Monitor
	New Vision and *Sunday Vision*
	Orimuri (in Runyankole)
	The Other Voice (March-June)
	Red Pepper

Appendix B. People Interviewed: Torchbearers, Cultural Historians, the District Sample, and Profiles

The tapes of all these interviews have been deposited in the library of the Department of Women and Gender Studies, Makerere University, Kampala.

1. Torchbearers

TB1. Grace Mukasa, executive director of Action for Development (ACFODE). Interviewed by Bantebya and McIntosh on 13 January 2003 in her office.

TB2. Peace Kyamureku, executive director of the National Association of Women's Organizations in Uganda (NAWOU). Interviewed by Bantebya and McIntosh on 14 January 2003 in Bantebya's office at Makerere University.

TB3. Jackie Asiimwe, executive director of UWONET, the Uganda Women's Organizations Network. Interviewed by McIntosh on 28 November 2002 in her office.

TB4. Olive Kigongo, director of the Uganda National Chamber of Commerce and Industry. Interviewed by Bantebya and McIntosh on 6 December 2002 in her business office at Mosa Court.

TB5. Dr Maggie Kigozi, executive director of the Uganda Investment Authority (UIA). Interviewed by McIntosh on 27 January 2003 in her office.

TB6.   Angela Nakafeero, executive director of the Uganda chapter of the Council for the Economic Empowerment of Women in Africa (CEEWA-U). Interviewed by Bantebya and McIntosh on 13 November 2002 in her office.

TB7.   Sarah Kitakule, director of the Uganda Women Entrepreneurs Association Ltd (UWEAL). Interviewed by Bantebya and McIntosh on 27 November 2002 in her office.

TB8.   Lydia Rugasira, Assistant General Manager of the Uganda Women's Finance Trust, Ltd (UWFT). Interviewed by Bantebya and McIntosh on 3 December 2002 in her office.

2. Cultural Historians

CultHist1. Festo Karwemera, a 78-year-old retired teacher and author of books about Bakiga culture and the Rukiga language, interviewed by McIntosh and Jean Kemitare at his home in Kabale, 4 February 2003.

CultHist2. Mustafa Mutyaba, Minister of Clan Homage and the Kabaka's Tours and author of books on Baganda history, interviewed by McIntosh in his office in Bulange, Mengo, 22 July 2003.

CultHist3. Philip Sseruwagi Namukadde, member of the Buganda Clan Tribunal, interviewed by McIntosh and Deus Mukalazi in his office in Bulange, Mengo, 9 July 2003.

CultHist4. Kabuuza Mukasa, Assistant Minister in Charge of Lukiiko and Cabinet Affairs, interviewed by McIntosh and Deus Mukalazi in his office in Bulange, Mengo, 27 June 2003.

3. The District Sample

The interviews are numbered within each place in the notes and on the tapes. The codebook identifying the women by name is on deposit at the library of the Department of Women and Gender Studies, Makerere University, should follow-up interviews ever be desired.

Arua: 15 women (and two men) interviewed by Judith Ruko, February–March 2003, in Lugbara and English

Hoima: 17 women (and three men) interviewed by Beatrice Tumushabe, March 2003, in Runyoro and English.

Jinja: 13 women (and three men) interviewed by Anita Mago-Sempa, February–March 2003, in Lusoga and Luganda.

Kabale: 16 women (and two men) interviewed by Jean Kemitare, February 2003, in Rukiga and English.

Kampala: 21 women (and two men) interviewed mainly by Jean Kemitare, January–May 2003, in Luganda and English; two interviews of women were done by Marjorie McIntosh, in English.

Lira: 17 women (and two men) interviewed by Sylvia Latigo-Olal, February–March 2003, in Luo and English.

Mpigi: 14 women (and five men) interviewed by Anita Mago-Sempa, March–April 2003, in Luganda.

4. Women in the District Sample Written Up as Profiles (all names are pseudonyms)

Profile 2.1   Angela Akello, a pioneer community development worker
Profile 2.2   Fatuma Kasirye, running a family shop
Profile 2.3   Fulgencia Apio, a life of limited opportunities
Profile 2.4   Mary Katushabe, a full and satisfying life
Profile 5.1   Grace Ssembatia, a member of the early educated elite
Profile 6.1   Eunice Kyamanya, a career in the media world
Profile 7.1   Joyce Munduru, working as a driver in the Amin/Obote II years
Profile 7.2   Jane Kamusiime, making ends meet by selling food and drink
Profile 8.1   Thereza Kamugasa, coping with HIV/AIDS
Profile 9.1   Margaret Birungi, a rocky road to business success

Appendix C. Quantitative Information about the District Sample

C1.   Ethnic Group and Religion by Place
C2.   Current Marital Status and Does Husband Have Multiple Families? by Religion
C3.   Current Age and Age at First Marriage
C4.   Number of Children and Number of Dependants
C5.   Educational Level of the Women and Highest Educational Level of Any of Their Children
C6.   Primary Type of Work Done Now by Type of Community
C7.   Self-Reported Earnings per Month vs. Interviewer's Assessment of Economic Level
C8.   Ethnic Group and Religion by Period in Which They Were Children
C9.   Primary Type of Work Done Now and Marital Status by Period in Which They Were Children

Appendix C1a   Ethnic group by place

	Arua	Hoima	Jinja	Kabale	Kampala	Lira	Mpigi	Total
Baganda	0	0	3	1	12	0	13	29
Banyoro	0	14	0	0	3	0	0	17
Bakiga	0	0	0	15	1	0	0	16
Ateso (Lango)	0	0	0	0	0	15	0	15
Lugbara	8	0	0	0	0	0	0	8
Basoga	0	0	6	0	0	0	0	6
Madi	3	0	1	0	0	0	0	4
Batoro	0	1	0	0	2	0	0	3
Other/mixed*	4	2	3	9	3	2	1	15
Total	15	17	13	16	21	17	14	113

* Other/mixed includes 2 Bakakwa, 2 Baringa, 2 Barwandese, 1 Basmia, 1 Bakumam, 1 Bajapadhola, 1 Banyankore, and 1 Bafumbira women, plus 3 of mixed ethnic parentage.

Appendix C1b Religion by place

	Arua	Hoima	Jinja	Kabale	Kampala	Lira	Mpigi	Total
Catholic	7	6	4	5	10	8	11	51
Protestant/ Anglican	6	8	7	9	6	8	1	45
Muslim	2	0	1	2	1	1	1	8
Pentecostal/ born again	0	3	1	0	4	0	1	9
Total	15	17	13	16	21	17	14	113

Appendix C2a Current marital status by religion

		Catholic	Protestant/ Anglican	Muslim	Pentecostal/ born again	Total
Single, probl. never married	Count	10	6	2	4	22
	% within religion	19.6	13.3	25.0	44.4	19.5
Married, living with spouse	Count	24	17	3	3	47
	% within religion	47.1	37.8	37.5	33.3	41.6
Separated/ divorced	Count	11	12	0	1	24
	% within religion	21.6	26.7	0	11.1	21.2
Widow	Count	6	10	3	1	20
	% within religion	11.8	22.2	37.5	11.1	17.7
Total	Count	51	45	8	9	113
	% within religion	100.0	100.0	100.0	100.0	100.0

Appendix C2b Does or did husband have multiple wives/families? by religion

		Catholic	Protestant/ Anglican	Muslim	Pentecostal/ born again	Total
No	Count	23	20	3	3	49
	% within religion	63.9	71.4	50.0	75.0	66.2
Yes with spouse	Count	11	8	3	1	23
	% within religion	30.6	28.6	50.0	25.0	31.1
No, but has relationships	Count	2	0	0	0	2
	% within religion	5.6	0	0	0	2.7
Total	Count	36	28	6	4	74
	% within religion	100.0	100.0	100.0	100.0	100.0

Appendix C3a Current age

	Frequency	%
20s	15	13.3
30s	26	23.0
40s	37	32.7
50s	21	18.6
60s	12	10.6
70s	1	0.9
90s	1	0.9
Total	113	100.0

Appendix C3b Age at first marriage

	Frequency	%
13–19 years	24	30.4
20–24 years	34	43.0
25–33 years	21	26.6
Total	79	100.0

Appendix C4a Number of children

	Frequency	%
0 children	13	11.5
1–2 children	26	23.0
3–5 children	34	30.1
6–10 children	35	31.0
Not asked	5	4.4
Total	113	100.0

Appendix C4b Number of dependants

	Frequency	%
0 dependants	12	10.6
1–4	46	40.7
5–9	33	29.2
10–18	14	12.4
many/unspecified	8	7.1
Total	113	100.0

Appendix C5a Educational level of the women

	Frequency	%
No formal education	4	3.5
Primary	27	23.9
Secondary	34	30.1
Sec. plus certif/diploma	35	31.0
BA/BS degree/post-graduate	13	11.5
Total	113	100.0

Appendix C5b Highest educational level of any of their children

	Frequency	%
Primary	6	9.8
Secondary	27	44.3
Sec. plus certif./diploma	4	6.6
BA/BS degree/postgraduate training	24	39.3
Total	61	100.0

Appendix C6 Primary type of work done now by type of community

	Type of community in which working				
	City (Kampala)	District headquarters	Peri-urban areas	Villages/very small towns	Total
Food/drink production or sale	2	5	4	7	18
Other types of production or sale	1	18	6	8	33
Teaching, nursing, secretarial work, or related business	0	15	12	3	30
Other professional, skilled or high status work	1	2	5	2	10
Unskilled or semi-skilled labor	0	10	5	4	19
Total	4	50	32	24	110

Appendix C7 Self-reported earnings/month vs. interviewer's assessment of economic level

	Interiewer's assessment of the woman's economic level, based on the standards of that community				
	very poor, living in hardship	poor but adequate	of middling level, living comfortably	Well off	Total
Under Ush 100,000	12	12	5*	2*	31
Ush 100,000–199,999	0	8	9	1	18
Ush 200,000–499,999	1	4	8	8	21
Ush 500,000–999,999	0	1	7	4	12
Ush 1,000,000 and over	0	0	0	5	5
Doesn't know/didn't answer	1	8	7	5	21
Total	14	33	36	25	108

* Most of the women in these two groups were retired, so their current earnings were low but they had other sources of income.

Appendix C8a Ethnic group by period in which they were children

	Period in which she was a child (aged 8 years or more)				
	Colonial period	Early independence	Amin/ Obote II	NRM	Total
Baganda	8	11	8	2	29
Banyoro	9	0	7	1	17
Bakiga	7	6	2	1	16
Ateso (Lango)	6	5	3	1	15
Lugbara	2	3	3	0	8
Basoga	1	3	2	0	6
Madi	1	1	2	0	4
Batoro	2	0	1	0	3
Other/mixed*	1	6	7	1	15
Total	37	35	35	6	113

* Other mixed includes 2 Bakakwa, 2 Baringa, 2 barwandese, 1 Basmia, 1 Bagisu, 1 Bakumam, 1 Bajapadhola, 1 Banyankore and 1 Bafumbira women, plus 3 of mixed ethnic parentage.

Appendix C8b Religion by period in which they were children

	Period in which she was a child (aged 8 years or more)				
	Colonial period	Early independence	Amin/ Obote II	NRM	Total
Catholic	16	16	16	3	51
Protestant/Anglican	19	11	14	1	45
Muslim	0	5	2	1	8
Pentecostal/born again	2	3	3	1	9
Total	37	35	35	6	113

Appendices

Appendix C9a Primary type of work done now by period in which they were children

| | Period in which she was a child (aged 8 years or more) | | | | |
	Colonial period	Early independence	Amin/ Obote II	NRM	Total
Food/drink production or sale	8	3	6	1	18
Other types of production or sale	8	13	12	1	34
Teaching, nursing, secretarial work, or related business	13	9	10	0	32
Other professional, skilled or high status work	5	2	3	0	10
Unskilled or semi-skilled labor	3	8	4	4	19
Total	37	35	35	6	113

Appendix C9b Current marital status by period in which they were children

| | Period in which she was a child (aged 8 years or more) | | | | |
	Colonial period	Early independence	Amin/ Obote II	NRM	Total
Single, probl. never married	2	6	9	5	22
Married, living with spouse	10	18	19	0	47
Separated/divorced	14	5	5	0	24
Widow	11	6	2	1	20
Total	37	35	35	6	113

Appendices

Appendix D. Report on Women Leaders' Meeting, 20 March 2003

At a meeting organized by the Department of Women and Gender Studies at Makerere University held at the Hotel Africana in Kampala, 20 Ugandan women leaders produced the following assessment.

A. What are the most important gains women have made since 1985?
1. Economic improvement
2. Improved visibility for women/gaining a voice
3. Political/legal gains
4. Education
5. Decision-making/leadership

B. What are the most important challenges or problems that women face today?
1. Problems in sustainability/lack of a shared vision/limited awareness and use of gender tools
2. Poverty/economic restraints
3. Cultural beliefs about gendered rights and responsibilities that limit women's ability to take advantage of the new opportunities available to them
4. The demands of multiple roles, at home and on the job
5. Limited education
6. Poor communication among women/lack of mutual support/isolation
7. Insufficient or ineffective government support for women's issues
8. Backlash against the gains made by women, on the part of men and some other women

C. What are the main underlying causes that contribute to those problems?
1. Men's insecurity
2. Cultural factors that limit women's empowerment
3. Inadequate laws on some matters of vital concern to women
4. Insufficient support for each other
5. Poor information flow among women, extending from the top all the way into the household and rural communities

D. Participants at the meeting
Joyce Mafabi Asenkenye, Uganda National Chamber of Commerce International, Katakwi District
Jackie Asiimwe, Uganda Women's Organisations Network (UWONET)
Dr Grace Bantebya Kyomuhendo, Dept. of Women and Gender Studies, Makerere University
Hon. Loice Bwambale, Uganda Women Parliamentarians Association
Hon. Rebecca Kadaga, Deputy Speaker, Parliament
Dr Sarah Kiguli, Association of Uganda Women Medical Doctors (AUWMD)
Mary Kusambiza, FIDA-Uganda (legal aid organisation for women)
Peace Kyamureku, National Association of Women's Organisations of Uganda (NAWOU)

Hon. Miria R. K. Matembe, Minister of Ethics & Integrity

Prof. Florence Mirembe, Dept. of Obst. & Gyn., Faculty of Medicine, Makerere University

Jane S. Mpagi, Ministry of Gender, Labour and Social Development

Maude Mugisha, East African Sub-Regional Support Initiative for the Advancement of Women (EASSI)

Irene Muloni, Uganda Electricity Distribution Company Ltd (UEDCL)

Hilda Musubira, Ministry of Public Service

Angela Nakafeero, Council for the Economic Empowerment of Women in Africa (CEEWA)

Christine Namatovu, Action for Development (ACFODE, representing Grace Mukasa)

Monica Azuba Ntege, Nile Hotel International Ltd (NHIL)

Julian A. Omalla, Uganda National Chamber of Commerce International

Rev. Canon Hellen Oneka, Provincial Mothers' Union, Church of Uganda, Namirembe

Margaret Sentamu, Uganda Media Women's Association (UMWA)

Facilitator: Violet Mugisa

Recorder: Marjorie McIntosh

Unable to attend that day but involved in subsequent meetings of the group:

Hon. Betty Akech, Minister of Higher Education

Hon. Namirembe Bitamazire, Minister of Primary Education

Hon. Zoe Bakoko Bakuru, Minister of Gender, Labour and Social Development

Dr Consolata Kabonesa, Dept. of WGS, Makerere University

Florence Kata, Uganda Export Promotion Board

Olive Kigongo, Uganda National Chamber of Commerce International

Dr Maggie Kigozi, Uganda Investment Authority

Sarah Kitakule, Uganda Women Entrepreneurs Association Ltd (UWEAL)

Florence Kuteesa, Budget Office, Ministry of Finance

Asst. Prof. Joy Kwesiga, Gender Mainstreaming, Makerere University

Ruth Ochieng, ISIS-WICCE

Margaret Ssekaja, Human Rights Commission

Bibliography

A. Manuscript Sources

Birmingham Univ. Library, UK. Church Missionary Society Archives, Uganda Missions, 1898-1934 (used via microfilm, Adam Matthew publishers).

Lukiiko Transcripts, 1895-1917, Kingdom of Buganda (on deposit in Africana section of Makerere Univ. Library). Produced for Dr. Lloyd Fallers in the 1950s; preserved by Dr. John Rowe; deposited by Prof. Holly Hanson in 2003.

Mengo School of Nursing and Midwivery, Kampala. *Register Books of Nurses and Midwives.*

Mulago School of Nursing and Midwifery, Kampala. *Register Books of Nurses and Midwives.*

Public Record Office (The National Archive), London (Kew), UK Colonial Office records, Uganda and East Africa.

Uganda Christian Univ., Bishop Tucker Campus, Mukono. Archives of the Church Missionary Society, Diocese and Province of Uganda, and Mothers' Union.

Uganda Nurses and Midwives Council, Min. of Health, Kampala. *Register Books of Nurses and Midwives.*

Uganda, Ministry of Education, 'Education Statistics Abstract, 1986' (handwritten).

B. Government Publications

1. Uganda Protectorate

UP, *Annual Medical and Sanitary Report for the Year 1912.* London: Waterlow & Sons., 1913.

UP, *Annual Medical and Sanitary Report for the Year ended 31st December, 1925.* Entebbe: Government Printer, 1926.

UP, *Annual Report of the Education Department for the Year ended 31st December, 1925.* Entebbe: Government Printer, 1926.

UP, *Annual Report of the Education Department for the Year ended 31st December, 1933.* Entebbe: Government Printer, 1934.

UP, *Blue Book for the Year ended December 31st, 1922.* Entebbe: Government Printer, n.d.

UP, *Blue Book for the Year ended December 31st, 1938.* Entebbe: Government Printer, 1939.

UP, *Census Returns, 1921.* Entebbe: Government Printer, 1921.

UP, *Development of African Teacher Training, Secondary Schools and the Education of Girls.* Entebbe: Government Printer, no date but 1954.

UP, *Education in Uganda* (Sessional Paper No. 2 of 1958/59). Entebbe: Government Printer, no date but 1959.

Bibliography

UP, *Official Bulletin*, Vol. 5, no. 9, Sept., 1954. Used at Uganda National Archives, Entebbe.

UP, *Report of the African Education Committee.* Entebbe: Government Printer, 1940.

UP, *Sessional Papers, 1932*, Agriculture (PRO CO 685/16).

UP, *Uganda Census, 1959: African Population*, Statistics Branch, Min. of Economic Affairs, Nairobi, 1961.

UP, *Uganda Census, 1959: Non-African Population*, East African Statistical Department, Nairobi/ Entebbe, 1960.

UP, *Uganda Government Gazette for 1905–6* (PRO CO 457/6).

UP, *Uganda Official Gazette, 1908* (PRO CO 612/1).

UP, *Uganda Official Gazette, 1920* (PRO CO 612/8).

UP, *Uganda Official Gazette, 1933* (PRO CO 612/15).

2. Uganda, Republic of

The Local Governments Act, 1997. No place or date of publication shown, but after 27 July 2001.

U. Bureau of Statistics. *2002 Statistical Abstract.* Entebbe, November, 2002.

U. Bureau of Statistics. *Uganda Demographic and Health Survey, 2000–2001.* Entebbe, Dec., 2001.

U. Bureau of Statistics. *Uganda DHS EdData Survey, 2001: Education Data for Decision-Making.* Entebbe, Feb., 2002

U. Ministry of Education. 'Education Statistics Abstract, 1978.' Compiled by the Educational Planning and Statistics Unit, typescript.

U. Ministry of Education and Sports. *Education Statistical Abstract, 2001.* Kampala, 2001.

U. Ministry of Finance, Planning and Economic Development. *Challenges and Prospects for Poverty Reduction in Northern Uganda.* Discussion Paper 5. Kampala, March 2002.

U. Ministry of Finance, Planning and Economic Development. *Draft Policy Paper on Micro and Small Enterprise Development.* Kampala, January 1999.

U. Ministry of Finance, Planning and Economic Development. *National Program for Good Governance in the Context of PEAP.* Kampala, 2001.

U. Ministry of Finance, Planning and Economic Development. *An Overview of the National Economy.* Discussion Paper 7, Kampala, 2004.

U. Ministry of Finance, Planning and Economic Development. 'Strategic Plan for Expanding the Outreach and Capacity of Sustainable Microfinance in Uganda,' Microfinance Forum, APEX Subcomittee on Rural Finance, Kampala, 27 June 2002.

U. Ministry of Finance, Planning and Economic Development. *Uganda Participatory Poverty Assessment Process: Kalangala District Report*, Kampala, January 2000.

U. Ministry of Finance, Planning and Economic Development. *Uganda Participatory Poverty Assessment Process: Kampala District Report*, Kampala, January 2000.

U. Ministry of Gender and Community Development and Min. of Planning and Economic Development. *The National Gender Policy.* Kampala, 1997.

U. Ministry of Gender, Labour and Social Development. *The National Action Plan on Women: Follow up to the Fourth World Conference on Women, Beijing, 1995.* Kampala, May 1999.

U. Ministry of Gender, Labour and Social Development, Ministry of Finance, Planning and Economic Development, and UK Department for International Development (DFID). 'Engendering Uganda's Poverty Eradication Initiatives: A Desk Review on Gender and Poverty,' prepared by Bonnie Keller, March 2002.

U. Ministry of Gender and Community Development. *Women and Men in Uganda. Facts and Figures, 2000. Sectoral Series: Education.* Kampala, November 2000.

U. Ministry of Information and Broadcasting. *Uganda's Economic War.* Kampala, January 1975.

U. Ministry of Planning and Economic Development. *High Level Manpower Survey, 1967, and Analyses of Requirements, 1967–1981.* Entebbe, Govt. Printer, 1968.

U. Ministry of Planning and Economic Development. *National Manpower Survey, Census of Civil Servants.* Kampala: February 1988.

U. Ministry of Women in Development, Culture, and Youth. 'Women's Informal Credit Groups: An Exploratory Study of Some Experiences in Kampala.' September 1994 (Typescript).

U. Ministry of Works, Housing and Communications, The President's Office, National Council for Science and Technology. 'National Information and Communication

Bibliography

Technology Policy' [draft], May, 2002.

U. President's Office, Statistics Division. *Report on the 1969 Population Census: Vol. IV, The Analytical Report.* Entebbe: January 1976.

U. Statistics Dept. *Uganda National Household Survey, 1995/96.* Vol. 2, *Summary Analytical Report.* Entebbe, 1996.

3. Other bodies and Ugandan parastals

East African Governments. *Report of the Working Party on Higher Education in East Africa, July-August, 1958.* Nairobi: Government Printer, 1959.

East African Royal Commission. *Report, 1953-55.* London: HMSO, 1955.

International Labour Organization, *Employment Promotion of Women in Uganda: From Disabling to Enabling Environment.* Report on ILO/UNDP TSS1 Mission on Women's Employment Promotion to Uganda. No date for the report, but after October/November 1994.

IMF (International Monetary Fund). *Uganda: Adjustment with Growth, 1987–94,* by Robert L. Sharer, H. R. deZoysa, and C. A. McDonald. Occas. Paper 121. Washington, DC: IMF, March, 1995.

Uganda National Agricultural Research Organization. 'Outreach and Partnership Initiative: A Strategy for Decentralisation and Mutual Institutional Learning,' Working Paper No. 1, October, 2001.

Uganda National Council for Children. *Equity and Vulnerability: A Situation Analysis of Women, Adolescents and Children in Uganda, 1994.* Written by Tom Barton and Gimono Wamai of the Child Health and Development Centre. Kampala: UNCC, 1994.

UN (United Nations). *The World's Women 2000: Trends and Statistics.* Social Statistics and Indicators, Series K, no. 16. New York: United Nations, 2000.

UNDP (United Nations Development Program), *Uganda Human Development Report, 2002.* Kampala: UNDP, 2002.

UNICEF (United Nations Children's Fund). *Children and Women in Uganda: A Situation Analysis.* Kampala: UNICEF, 1989.

United Nations Dept of Economic and Social Information and Policy Analysis, Statistical Division. *Methods of Measuring Women's Economic Activity: Technical Report,* Studies in Methods, Series F, No. 59. New York: United Nations, 1993.

United Nations, Dept. of Public Information, Division for Economic and Social Information. *Convention on the Elimination of All Forms of Discrimination against Women,* April, 1984.

United Nations. *WISTAT, 1999 (Women's Indicators and Statistics Database,* Version 4, 1999). CD.

United States Agency for International Development. *Micro- and Small-Scale Enterprises in Uganda. A Report of the National Baseline Survey, 1995.* Kampala, July, 1995.

World Bank. *Africa DataBase, 2003.* CD.

World Bank. *African Development Indicators, 2000.* Washington, DC: World Bank, 2000.

World Bank. *Can Africa Claim the 21st Century?* Washington, DC: World Bank, 2000.

World Bank. *Gender, Growth, and Poverty Reduction (Special Program of Assistance for Africa, 1998 Status Report on Poverty in Sub-Saharan Africa).* Washington, DC: World Bank, 1999.

World Bank. Human Development Network, Education Notes, April 2002: www1.worldbank.org/education/pdf/EduNotesUganda.pdf, accessed 15 January 2004.

World Bank. *Uganda: The Challenge of Growth and Poverty Reduction.* Washington, DC: World Bank, 1996.

World Bank. *Uganda: Growing Out of Poverty (A Country Study).* Washington, DC: World Bank, 1993.

World Bank. *Uganda: Social Sectors.* Washington, DC: World Bank, 1993.

World Bank. *Uganda's Recovery: The Role of Farms, Firms, and Government* (ed. R. Reinikka and P. Collier). Washington, DC: World Bank, 2001.

World Bank and Uganda Ministry of Gender and Community Development. 'Report of Study on Legal Constraints to the Economic Empowerment of Ugandan Women.' Prepared by Jennifer Okumu Wengi and Elizabeth Kyasimire. Kampala, October 1995.

C. Other Printed Works and Dissertations

ActionAid Uganda. *Footprints in Social Transformation: Efforts of Civil Society Organizations to Promote Gender Equality and Women's Empowerment in Uganda.* Kampala: ActionAid 2002.

ActionAid Uganda. *Sisterhood?: Policy Advocacy by Gender-Focused NGOs and the Reality for Women at the Grassroots of Uganda.* Kampala: ActionAid 2002.

Afonja, Simi. 'Changing Modes of Production and the Sexual Division of Labor among the Yoruba.' *Signs* 7 (1981):299–313.

Ahikire, Josephine. *Gender, Political Space and Electoral Processes: An Overview of the 1996 Presidential and Parliamentary Elections in Uganda*, Research Paper No. 1, Dept. of Women and Gender Studies, Makerere Univ., July 2001.

Ahikire, Josephine. 'Of Local Democracy and Grassroots Tyranny: Gender and Local Council Elections in Uganda.' Unpubl. paper delivered at Dept. of Women and Gender Studies, Makerere Univ., 3 December 2002.

Ahikire, Josephine. 'Worker Struggles, the Labor Process and the Question of Control: The Case of the United Garments Industry Ltd,' in *Uganda: Studies in Living Conditions, Popular Movements and Constitutionalism* (ed. M. Mamdani and J. Oloka-Onyango), Vienna: Centre for Basic Research, 1994:183–226.

Ahikire, Josephine, and Christine Ampaire, *Vending in the City: A Gendered Perspective of Policy, Conditions, and Organizational Capacity of Vendors in Kampala, Uganda.* Final Draft Report prepared under the WIEGO (Women in Informal Employment, Globalising and Organising) Project on Street Vendors. Kampala: Centre for Basic Research, March 2003.

Ahluwalia, D. P. S. *Plantations and the Politics of Sugar in Uganda.* Kampala: Fountain, 1995.

Allen, M. B. E. 'The Women and Girls of Uganda,' *Uganda Church Review* 20 (1930):115–17.

Allman, Jean. 'Rounding Up Spinsters: Gender Chaos and Unmarried Women in Colonial Asante,' in *"Wicked" Women and the Reconfiguration of Gender in Africa* (ed. D. L. Hodgson and S. A. McCurdy), Portsmouth, NH: Heinemann, 2001: 130–48.

Allman, Jean, and Victoria Tashjian. *"I Will Not Eat Stone": A Women's History of Colonial Asante.* Portsmouth, NH: Heinemann, 2000.

Allman, Jean, Susan Geiger, and Nakanyike Musisi, eds. *Women in African Colonial Histories.* Bloomington, IN: Indiana Univ. Press, 2002.

Ampaire, Christine. 'Childcare Arrangements and Implications for Working Mothers in Uganda.' M.A. Diss.,Women and Gender Studies, Makerere Univ., 1997.

Andama-Harmsworth, Josephine W. 'The Economic Status of Rural Women in Uganda.' Research Report, c. 1986.

Apter, Andrew. 'Atinga Revised: Yoruba Witchcraft and the Cocoa Economy, 1950–1951,' in *Modernity and Its Discontents: Ritual and Power in Postcolonial Africa* (ed. J. Comaroff and J. Comaroff), Chicago: Univ. of Chicago Press, 1993: 111–28.

Apter, David E. *The Political Kingdom in Uganda.* Princeton, NJ: Princeton Univ. Press, 1961.

Asiimwe, Jacqueline. 'Making Women's Land Rights a Reality in Uganda: Advocacy for Co-Ownership by Spouses,' *Yale Human Rights and Development Law Journal* 4 (2001):1–17.

Asiimwe, Jacqueline. 'Women and the Struggle for Land in Uganda,' in *The Women's Movement in Uganda: History, Challenges, and Prospects* (ed. A. M. Tripp and J. C. Kwesiga) Kampala: Fountain, 2002: 119–45.

Asiimwe-Mwesige, Jacqueline. 'The Achievements and Challenges Facing the Women's Movement in Uganda Since 1995.' Unpubl. report, 2004.

Asowa-Okwe, C. *The Dynamics of Women's Participation in Workers' Struggles in Uganda: A Case Study of the National Union of Clerical, Commercial, Professional and Technical Employees (NUCCPTE).* Centre for Basic Research Working Paper No. 40. Kampala: CBR, 1991.

Asowa-Okwe, C. *Women Wage Workers in Plantation Estates in Uganda.* Final report for OSSREA Project on Gender, 1990/91. Presented also at workshop on 'Women and Work: Historical Trends,' Centre for Basic Research, Kampala, 1992.

Ayuru, Rose N. 'Sensitised Women as a Development Strategy: The Uganda Case.' Unpubl.

Bibliography

paper given at the OSSREA 1983 Congress on Alternative Development Strategies for Eastern Africa held at Addis Ababa, Ethiopia, June 1983.

Bagaya, Elizabeth. *Elizabeth of Toro: The Odyssey of an African Princess: An Autobiography*. New York: Simon & Schuster, 1989.

Bakwesegha, Christopher J. *Profiles of Urban Prostitution: A Case Study from Uganda*. Nairobi: Kenya Literature Bureau, 1982.

Bantebya Kyomuhendo, Grace. 'Decision-Making in Poor Households: the Case of Kampala, Uganda,' in *Urban Poverty in Africa* (ed. S. Jones and N. Nelson), London: Intermediate Technology Publs., 1999:113–25.

Bantebya Kyomuhendo, Grace. 'Low Use of Rural Maternity Services in Uganda: Impact of Women's Status, Traditional Beliefs and Limited Resources,' *Reproductive Health Matters* 11, 21 (2003):16-26.

Bantebya Kyomuhendo, Grace. 'The Role of Women in Petty Commodity Production and Commerce: A Case Study of Rural Peasant Women in Uganda,' *Eastern Africa Social Science Research Review* 8 (1992):1-19.

Bantebya Kyomuhendo, Grace. 'Treatment Seeking Behaviour among Poor Urban Women in Kampala, Uganda.' Ph.D. thesis, Univ. of Hull, 1997.

Bantebya Kyomuhendo, Grace, and Jessica Ogden. 'Six Women: Individual Women's Accounts of Treatment Seeking,' in *Kampala Women Getting By: Wellbeing in the Time of AIDS* (ed. S. Wallman), London: James Currey, 1996:189–205.

Banugire, Firimooni. 'Towards an Appropriate Policy Framework for a Magendo Economy,' *Eastern Africa Social Science Research Review* 2 (1986):77–107.

Barnes, Teresa, 'Virgin Territory? Travel and Migration by African Women in Twentieth-Century South Africa,' in *Women in African Colonial Histories* (ed. J. Allman, S. Geiger, and N. Musisi), Bloomington, IN: Indiana Univ. Press, 2002: 164–90.

Barrett-Gaines, Kathryn. 'Katwe Salt in the African Great Lakes Regional Economy, 1750–1950s,' Ph.D. thesis, Stanford University, 2001.

Barton, Tom, and Gimono Wamai. *Equity and Vulnerability: A Situation Analysis*. See under Govt. Publications, 3, Uganda National Council of Children.

Barungi, Violet, ed. *Words from A Granary: An Anthology of Short Stories by Ugandan Women Writers*. Kampala: FEMRITE Publs., 2001.

Baryaruha, A. *Factors Affecting Industrial Employment: A Study of Uganda Experience, 1954–1964*. Nairobi: Oxford Univ. Press, no date. (East African Inst. of Social Research Occas. Paper No. 1.)

Basemera, Laetitia. 'Single Motherhood in Urban Uganda: A Case Study of Fort Portal Municipality.' M.A. Diss., Women and Gender Studies, Makerere Univ., 1995.

Basirika, Edith. *Gender Participation in the Rural Labor Market: The Case for Kabarole District, Uganda*. Addis Ababa: OSSREA (Organisation for Social Research in Eastern and Southern Africa), 1995.

Basirika, Edith. 'Structural Adjustment, the Informal Sector and Market Women,' in *Empowerment, Poverty, and Structural Adjustment in Uganda* (ed. J. C. Munene), Kampala: Friedrich Ebert Foundation, no date: 85–113.

Bastian, Misty L. '"Vultures of the Marketplace": Southeastern Nigerian Women and Discourses of the *Ogu Umunwaanyi* (Women's War) of 1929,' in *Women in African Colonial Histories* (ed. J. Allman, S. Geiger, and N. Musisi) Bloomington, IN: Indiana Univ. Press, 2002: 260–81.

Batte, Patrick Ssozi. 'Constraints of Women's Involvement in Agricultural Income Generating Activities in Mpigi District.' B.A. Diss., Dept. of Social Work and Social Admin., Makerere Univ., 1993.

Behrend, Heike. *Alice Lakwena and the Holy Spirit: War in Northern Uganda, 1987–97*. Oxford: James Currey, 1999.

Belshaw, Deryke. 'Agriculture-Led Recovery in Post-Amin Uganda,' in *Uganda Now: Between Decay and Development* (ed. H. B. Hansen and M. Twaddle) London: James Currey, 1988: 111–25.

Bennett, F. J. A. 'A Muganda Housewife's Day and Its Health Implications,' *Makerere Journal* 9 (1964): 63–70

Bennett, Judith M. *Ale, Beer, and Brewsters in England*. New York: Oxford Univ. Press, 1996.

Bibliography

Berger, Iris. 'Women in East and Southern Africa,' in *Women in Sub-Saharan Africa: Restoring Women to History* (ed. I. Berger and E. F. White), Bloomington, IN: Indiana Univ. Press, 1999), 5–62.

Bibangambah, J. R. 'Macro-Level Constraints and the Growth of the Informal Sector in Uganda,' in *The Rural-Urban Interface in Africa: Expansion and Adaptation* (ed. J. Baker and P. O. Pedersen), Uppsala: Scandinavian Inst. for African Studies, 1992: 303–13.

Bigsten, Arne, and Steve Kayizzi-Mugerwa. *Crisis, Adjustment and Growth in Uganda: A Study of Adaptation in an African Economy.* Basingstoke: Macmillan, 1999.

Birungi, Harriet. 'Perspectives for the Evolvement of Kinship Credit Systems: A Study of Two Communities in Busoga,' in *Constraints to and Scope for Rural Development in Uganda* (ed. E. Nabuguzi), Kampala: Makerere Inst. of Social Research, 1991.

Bitamazire, Geraldine. 'The NGO Perspective at the 4th World Conference on Women,' *Uganda Journal* 44 (1997):131-2.

Bitunda, Anne J. 'Problems and Prospects of Self Employed Women in Masaka Municipal Council,' B.A. Diss., Social Work and Social Admin., Makerere Univ., 1996.

Boyd, R. E. 'Empowerment of Women in Contemporary Uganda: Real or Symbolic?,' *Labour, Capital and Society* 22 (1989):19-40.

Brandt, Hartmut. 'The Organization of Peasant Farms under the Influence of Industrial Towns: The Case of Jinja/Uganda,' in *The Industrial Town as Factor of Economic and Social Development: The Example of Jinja* (ed. H. Brandt, B. Schubert, and E. Gerken), Afrika-Studien, no. 77. Munich: Weltforum Verlag, 1972: 25–137.

Brown, Winifred. *Marriage, Divorce and Inheritance: The Uganda Council of Women's Movement for Legislative Reform.* Cambridge African Monographs No. 10. Cambridge: African Studies Centre, 1988.

Bukirwa Sentamu, Margaret N. 'Challenges in Career Advancement in Uganda: A Study of Journalists with Emphasis on Women in New Vision and Monitor Newspapers.' M.A. Diss., Women and Gender Studies, Makerere Univ., 1997.

Bunker, Stephen G. *Peasants against the State: The Politics of Market Control in Bugisu, Uganda, 1900-1983.* Chicago: Univ. of Chicago Press, 1991 (orig. publ. 1987).

Burke, Timothy. '"Fork Up and Smile": Marketing, Colonial Knowledge and the Female Subject in Zimbabwe,' in *Gendered Colonialisms in African History* (ed. N. R. Hunt, T. P. Liu, and J. Quataert), Oxford: Blackwell, 1997:118–34.

Burke, Timothy. *Lifebuoy Men, Lux Women: Commodification, Consumption, and Cleanliness in Modern Zimbabwe.* Durham, NC: Duke Univ. Press, 1996.

Busingye, Winnie. *The Impact of Structural Adjustment Programs on Women and Gender Relations in the Household: The Case of Kabale District.* Network of Uganda Researchers and Research Users, Working Paper No. 11, Kampala: NURRU, 2002.

Butegwa, Florence, Taaka Awori, and Stella Mukasa. 'Private Sector Development in Uganda: Making Room for Gender on the Economic Reform Agenda,' in *Demanding Dignity: Women Confronting Economic Reforms in Africa* (ed. D.Tsikata and J. Kerr), Ottawa: The North-South Inst., 2000: 201–20.

Byandaga, Livingstone. 'Underemployment in the Informal Sector of Kampala District.' M.A. Diss., Economic Policy and Planning, Makerere Univ., 1996.

Byanyima, W. Karagwa, 'Women in Political Struggle in Uganda,' in *Women Transforming Politics: Worldwide Strategies for Empowerment* (ed. J. M. Bystydzienski), Bloomington, IN: Indiana Univ. Press, 1992: 129–42.

Byanyima, Winnie, and Richard Mugisha, eds. *The Rising Tide: Ugandan Women's Struggle for a Public Voice, 1940–2002.* Kampala: Forum for Women in Democracy, 2003.

Chanock, Martin. *Law, Custom and Social Order: The Colonial Experience in Malawi and Zambia.* Cambridge: Cambridge Univ. Press, 1985

CMS (Church Missionary Society). *Extracts from the Annual Letters of the Missionaries for the Year 1903.* London: CMS, 1904.

CMS. *Extracts from the Annual Letters of the Missionaries for the Year 1904.* London: CMS, 1905.

CMS. *Letters from the Front, Being a Selection from the Annual Letters from the Missions, 1911, I: Africa.* London: CMS, 1912.

CMS. *Letters from the Front, 1912.* London: CMS, 1913.

Clark, Gracia. 'Gender and Profiteering: Ghana's Market Women as Devoted Mothers and

Bibliography

"Human Vampire Bats",' in *"Wicked" Women and the Reconfiguration of Gender in Africa* (ed. D. L. Hodgson and S. A. McCurdy), Portsmouth, NH: Heinemann, 2001: 293–312.

Clark, Gracia. *Onions Are My Husband: Survival and Accumulation by West African Market Women.* Chicago: Univ. of Chicago Press, 1994.

Clark, Gracia, and Takyiwaa Manuh. 'Women Traders in Ghana and the Structural Adjustment Program,' in *Structural Adjustment and African Women Farmers* (ed. C. H. Gladwin), Gainesville, FL: Univ. of Florida Press, 1991: 217–34.

Cock, Jacklyn. 'Domestic Service and Education for Domesticity: The Incorporation of Xhosa Women into Colonial Society,' in *Women and Gender in Southern Africa to 1945* (ed. C. Walker), Cape Town: David Philip, 1990: 76–96.

Commonwealth Businesswomen: Trade Matters, Best Practices & Success Stories (ed. T. Johnson and J. Bartlett). London: Commonwealth Secretariat, 2002.

Coquery-Vidrovitch, Catherine. *African Women: A Modern History* (trans. B. G. Raps). Boulder, CO: Westview, 1997.

CEEWA–U (Council for Economic Empowerment for Women of Africa–Uganda Chapter). *A Baseline Study on Economic Empowerment of Women through the Use of ICTs in Uganda.* Final report, Oct. 2000.

CEEWA-U. *Gender Analysis for Economic Decision-Making in Selected Government Departments.* Final report of the Needs Assessment, February 1999.

CEEWA-U. 'Information Communication Technology Project, Evaluation Report.' Final draft., June 2002.

CEEWA-U. *The Relevance and Effectiveness of Agricultural Extension Services to the Gender Differentiated Activities and Needs of Small-Holders in Uganda.* Final report, November 1999.

CEEWA-U. 'Women and Trade in Uganda.' Paper presented at a seminar on 'Women and Trade in SADC: Women in the Global Market-Trade in the African Women's Eyes', June–July, 1998.

Cox, Jeffrey. *Imperial Fault Lines: Christianity and Colonial Power in India, 1818–1940.* Stanford, CA: Stanford Univ. Press, 2002.

Davis, Paula Jean.'Time Is Money? Women's Time Allocation to Market Trading and to Infant Feeding in Kampala, Uganda.' Ph.D. thesis, Johns Hopkins Univ., 1997.

Davison, Jean. *Gender, Lineage, and Ethnicity in Southern Africa.* Boulder, CO: Westview, 1997.

Decalo, Samuel. 'Military Coups and Military Régimes in Africa,' *Journal of Modern African Studies* 11 (1973):105–27.

Denzer, LaRay. 'Domestic Science Training in Colonial Yorubaland, Nigeria,' in *African Encounters with Domesticity* (ed. K. T. Hansen), New Brunswick, NJ: Rutgers Univ. Press, 1992: 116–39.

Dicklich, Susan. 'Indigenous NGOs and Political Participation,' in *Developing Uganda* (ed. H. B. Hansen and M. Twaddle), Oxford: James Currey, 1998: 145–58.

Dimock, Elizabeth. 'The Silence of African Women? A 1931 Protest of Christian Women in Uganda,' in *The Post-Colonial Condition: Contemporary Politics in Africa* (ed. D. P. S. Alhuwalia and P. F. Nursey-Bray), Connack, NY: Nova Science Publishers 1997: 55–66.

Dimock, Liz. 'Women's Leadership Roles in the Early Protestant Church in Uganda: Continuity with the Old Order,' *Australasian Review of African Studies*, 25 (2003):8-22.

Duara, Prasenjit, ed. *Decolonization: Perspectives from Now and Then.* London: Routledge, 2004.

Ebila, Florence. 'The Portrayal of Gender Relations in Lango Oral Poetry and Its Part in the Socialization Process.' M.A. Diss., Women and Gender Studies, Makerere Univ., 1997.

Ebila, Florence. 'Ugandan Women Watering the Literary Desert,' in *The Women's Movement in Uganda: History, Challenges, and Prospects* (ed. A. M. Tripp and J. C. Kwesiga), Kampala: Fountain, 2002: 162–73.

Edel, May Mandelbaum. *The Chiga of Western Uganda.* 2nd edn, New Brunswick, NJ: Transaction, 1996 (orig. publ. 1957).

Edmonds, Keith. 'Crisis Management: The Lessons for Africa from Obote's Second Term,' in *Uganda Now: Between Decay and Development* (ed. H. B. Hansen and M. Twaddle), London: James Currey, 1988: 95–110.

Ehrlich, Cyril. 'Cotton and the Uganda Economy, 1903–1909,' *Uganda Journal* 21 (1957): 162–75.

Ehrlich, Cyril. 'The Marketing of Cotton in Uganda, 1900–1950: A Case Study of Colonial

Bibliography

Government Economic Policy.' Ph.D. thesis, Univ. of London, 1958.

Ekechi, Felix K. 'Gender and Economic Power: The Case of Igbo Market Women of Eastern Nigeria,' in *African Market Women and Economic Power* (ed. B. House-Midamba and F. K. Ekechi), Westport, CT: Greenwood Press, 1995: 41–58.

Elkan, Walter. *An African Labour Force.* East African Inst. of Social Research/East African Studies Series No. 7, 1956; summarized in *Developing the Underdeveloped Countries* (ed. A. B. Mountjoy), London: Macmillan, 1971: 240–46.

Elkan, Walter. 'The Employment of Women in Uganda.' Typescript, 1956; also publ. in *Bulletin de l'Institut Inter Africain du Travail* [Brazzaville] 4 (1957):8–23.

Elkan, Walter. *Migrants and Proletarians: Urban Labour in the Economic Development of Uganda.* London: Oxford Univ. Press, 1960.

Elkan, Walter. 'Review of East Africa Royal Commission, 1953–1955 Report,' *Uganda Journal* 20 (1956):100–1.

Elkan, Walter. 'Trade in Ankole.' Typescript, undated, but probably c. 1958.

Ellyne, Mark J. 'The Economic History of Uganda and Progress under Its Structural Adjustment Programme,' *Uganda Journal* 42 (1995):16–31.

Elson, Diane, and Barbara Evers. 'Gender Aware Country Economic Reports: Working Paper Number 2, Uganda.' Revised version, Univ. of Manchester, Graduate School of Social Sciences, July, 1997.

Encyclopedia of World Cultures: Supplement (ed. M. Ember et al.). New York: Gale Group, 2002.

Evans, David R. 'Image and Reality: Career Goals of Educated Ugandan Women,' *Canadian Journal of African Studies* 6 (1972):213–32.

'Extracts from 'Mengo Notes' – VIII.' *Uganda Journal* 13 (1949):211–29.

'Extracts from Lt.-Col. C. Delmé-Radcliffe's Diary.' *Uganda Journal* 11 (1947):9–29.

Falola, Toyin. 'Gender, Business, and Space Control: Yoruba Market Women and Power,' in *African Market Women and Economic Power* (ed. B. House-Midamba and F. K. Ekechi), Westport, CT: Greenwood, 1995: 41–58.

Few, H. S. S. 'On Avoiding Detection,' *Uganda Journal* 23 (1959):85–7.

FIDA Uganda. *Annual Report, 1998.* Kampala: FIDA, 1998.

Fisher, A. B. *Twilight Tales of the Black Baganda.* London: Marshall Brothers, n.d. but prob. 1911.

FOWODE (Forum for Women in Democracy). 'Ugandan Women in Public Life, 1940–2002' (collection of photographs). Kampala: FOWODE, n.d. but 2003–4.

FOWODE . 'What a Pity This Child Was Born a Girl!' [collection of cartoons]. Kampala: FOWODE, n.d. but 2003–4.

Geiger, Susan. *TANU Women: Gender and Culture in the Making of Tanganyikan Nationalism, 1955–1965.* Portsmouth, NH: Heinemann, 1997.

Gerken, Egbert. 'Social Structure and the Industrial Town: The Case of Social Change in Jinja and Busoga/Uganda,' in *The Industrial Town as Factor of Economic and Social Development: The Example of Jinja* (ed. H. Brandt, B. Schubert, and E. Gerken), Afrika-Studien, no. 77. Munich: Weltforum Verlag, 1972: 291–433.

Gladwin, Christina H., ed. *Structural Adjustment and African Women Farmers.* Gainesville, FL: University of Florida Press, 1991.

Glazer, Ilsa M. 'Alcohol and Politics in Urban Zambia: The Intersection of Gender and Class,' in *African Feminism: The Politics of Survival in Sub-Saharan Africa* (ed. G. Mikell), Philadelphia: Univ. of Pennsylvania Press, 1997: 142–58.

Goldschmidt-Clermont, Luisella. *Economic Evaluations of Unpaid Household Work: Africa, Asia, Latin America and Oceania.* Women, Work and Development, Vol. 14. Geneva: International Labour Office, 1987.

Good, Charles. M. *Rural Markets and Trade in East Africa.* Dept. of Geogr., Univ. of Chicago, Research Paper no. 128. Chicago: Univ. of Chicago Press, 1970.

Gordon, April A. *Transforming Capitalism and Patriarchy: Gender and Development in Africa.* Boulder, CO: Lynne Rienner, 1996.

Gutkind, P. C. W. 'Notes on the Kibuga of Buganda,' *Uganda Journal* 24 (1960): 29–43.

Gutkind, P. C. W. 'Town Life in Buganda,' *Uganda Journal* 20 (1956): 37–46.

Guyer, Jane I. 'Food, Cocoa, and the Division of Labour by Sex in Two West African Societies,' *Comparative Studies in Society and History* 22 (1980): 355-73.

Bibliography

Hale, Angela. 'What Does Trade Liberalisation Mean for Women's Work?,' in *Trade Myths and Gender Reality: Trade Liberalisation and Women's Lives* (ed. A. Hale), Uppsala: Global Publs. Foundation, 1998: 18–26.

Hale, Angela. 'Women Workers and the Social Clause Debate,' in *Trade Myths and Gender Reality: Trade Liberalisation and Women's Lives* (ed. A. Hale), Uppsala: Global Publs. Foundation, 1998: 27–33.

Hale, Sandra. 'Feminist Method, Process, and Self-Criticism: Interviewing Sudanese Women,' in *Women's Words: The Feminist Practice of Oral History* (ed. S. B. Gluck and D. Patai), New York: Routledge, 1991: 121-36.

Hansen, Holger Bernt. *Mission, Church and State in a Colonial Setting: Uganda, 1890–1925*. London: Heinemann & New York: St. Martin's, 1984.

Hansen, Holger Bernt, and Michael Twaddle. 'Introduction' in *Changing Uganda: The Dilemmas of Structural Adjustment and Revolutionary Change* (ed. H. B. Hansen and M. Twaddle), London: James Currey, 1991: 1–19.

Hansen, Holger Bernt, and Michael Twaddle, eds. *Changing Uganda: The Dilemmas of Structural Adjustment and Revolutionary Change*. London: James Currey, 1991.

Hansen, Karen Tranberg. 'The Black Market and Women Traders in Lusaka, Zambia,' in *Women and the State in Africa* (ed. J. L. Parpart and K. A. Staudt), Boulder, CO: Lynne Rienner, 1989: 143–60.

Hansen, Karen T. *Salaula: The World of Secondhand Clothing and Zambia*. Chicago: Univ. of Chicago Press, 2000.

Hansen, Karen T., ed. *African Encounters with Domesticity*. New Brunswick, NJ: Rutgers Univ. Press, 1992.

Hanson, Holly E. *Landed Obligation: The Practice of Power in Buganda*. Portsmouth, NH: Heinemann, 2003.

Hanson, Holly. 'Queen Mothers and Good Government in Buganda: The Loss of Women's Political Power in Nineteenth-Century East Africa,' in *Women in African Colonial Histories* (ed. J. Allman, S. Geiger, and N. Musisi), Bloomington, IN: Indiana Univ. Press, 2002: 219– 36.

Hanson, Holly. 'Sleeping Sickness Deaths and Women's Access to Land in Early Colonial Buganda.' Unpubl. paper given at the African Studies Association, Washington, DC, Dec., 2002.

Harmsworth, Josephine W. 'The Ugandan Family in Transition,' in *Beyond Crisis: Development Issues in Uganda* (ed. P. D. Wiebe and C. P. Dodge), Kampala: Makerere Inst. of Social Research, 1987: 91–100.

Hawkins, Sean. *Writing and Colonialism in Northern Ghana*. Toronto: Univ. of Toronto Press, 2002.

Hawkins, Sean. ''The Woman in Question': Marriage and Identity in the Colonial Courts of Northern Ghana, 1907–1954,' in *Women in African Colonial Histories* (ed.. J. Allman, S. Geiger, and N. Musisi), Bloomington, IN: Indiana Univ. Press, 2002: 116–43.

Holden, Pat. 'Colonial Sisters: Nurses in Uganda,' in *Anthropology and Nursing* (ed. P. Holden and J. Littlewood), London: Routledge, 1991: 67–83.

Hoover, Sandra. 'Aspects of Village Structure and Mobility in Toro.' Typescript headed 'Sociology Working Paper No. 130, 16 November 1972'.

Hughes, Heather. '"A Lighthouse for African Womanhood": Inanda Seminary, 1869–1945,' in *Women and Gender in Southern Africa* (ed. C. Walker), Cape Town: David Philip, 1990: 197–220.

Hutton, Caroline. 'Unemployment in Kampala and Jinja, Uganda,' *Canadian Journal of African Studies* 3 (1969): 431–40.

Isegawa, Moses. *Abyssinian Chronicles: A Novel*. New York: Knopf, 2000.

IWGGT. 'Gender and Trade: Some Conceptual and Policy Links, an IWGGT Statement,' in *Trade Myths and Gender Reality: Trade Liberalisation and Women's Lives* (ed. A. Hale), Uppsala: Global Publs. Foundation, 1998: 8–17.

Jackson, R. T., ed. *Essays on Rural Marketing in West Nile*. Dept. of Geography, Occas. Paper no. 47, Kampala: Makerere Univ., 1972.

Jamal, Vali. 'The Agrarian Context of the Uganda Crisis,' in *Changing Uganda: The Dilemmas of Structural Adjustment and Revolutionary Change* (ed. H. B. Hansen and M. Twaddle), London:

Bibliography

James Currey, 1991: 78–97.

Jamal, Vali. 'Changes in Poverty Patterns in Uganda,' in *Developing Uganda* (ed. H. B. Hansen and M. Twaddle), Oxford: James Currey, 1998: 73–97.

Jamal, Vali. 'Taxation and Inequality in Uganda, 1900–1964,' *Journal of Economic History* 38 (1978):418–38.

Jamal, Vali. 'Ugandan Economic Crisis: Dimensions and Cure,' in *Beyond Crisis: Development Issues in Uganda* (ed. P. D. Wiebe and C. P. Dodge), Kampala: Makerere Inst. of Social Research, 1987: 121–36.

Jeater, Diana. 'The British Empire and African Women in the Twentieth Century,' in *Black Experience and the Empire* (ed. Philip D. Morgan and Sean Hawkins), Oxford: Oxford Univ. Press, 2004: 228–57.

Jeater, Diana. *Marriage, Perversion, and Power: The Construction of Moral Discourse in Southern Rhodesia, 1894–1930*. Oxford: Clarendon, 1993.

Jørgensen, Jan Jelmert. *Uganda: A Modern History*. New York: St Martin's, 1981.

Kabundah, Annet. 'Problems of Women Market Traders in Kawempe Division: A Case Study of Bwaise Market.' B.A. Diss., Sociology, Makerere Univ., 1998.

Kaggwa, Apolo. *The Kings of Buganda*. Trans. of his *Basekabaka be Buganda* (ed. M. S. M. Kiwanuka), Nairobi: East African Publishing House, 1971.

Kandiyoti, Deniz. 'Identity and Its Discontents: Women and the Nation,' in *Colonial Discourse and Post-Colonial Theory* (ed. P. Williams and L. Chrisman), New York: Columbia Univ. Press, 1994: 376–91.

Kapampara, Esther. 'Gender Differences that Affect Women's Participation in the Marketing of Maize and Beans: The Case of Kabarole District.' M.A. Diss., Women and Gender Studies, Makerere Univ., 1996.

Karugire, S. R. *A Political History of Uganda*. Nairobi: Heinemann, 1980.

Kasisira, Grace Lubulwa. 'Credit to Ugandan Women: The Experience of the Uganda Women's Finance and Credit Trust Ltd.' M.A. Diss., Economic Policy and Planning, Makerere Univ., 1992.

Kassimir, Ronald. 'Uganda: The Catholic Church and State Reconstruction,' in *The African State at a Critical Juncture* (ed. L. A. Villalón and P. A. Huxtable), Boulder, CO: Lynne Rienner, 1998: 233–53.

Kateregga, Elizabeth G. 'Women's Experience with Credit: A Case Study of Credit Institutions and Women Borrowers in Masaka District (Uganda).' M.A. Diss., Women and Gender Studies, Makerere Univ., 1997.

Kateregga, Rosette Mulinde. 'A Gender Assessment of the Housing Situation in Urban Areas: A Case Study of Kamwokya II, in Kampala.' M.A. Diss., Women and Gender Studies, Makerere Univ., 1996.

Kevane, Michael. *Women and Development in Africa: How Gender Works*. Boulder, CO: Lynne Rienner, 2004.

Kezaabu, Rosemary Kakwanzi. 'Effects of Commercialisation of Milk Production on Gender Relations at the Household Level: A Case of Kashari County, Mbarara District.' M.A. Diss., Women and Gender Studies, Makerere Univ., 1997. Publ. as *Commercialisation of Milk Production in Households: A Gender Perspective*. Occas. Paper No. 12., Dept. of Women and Gender Studies, Makerere Univ., 2001.

Kharono, Elizabeth. 'Imperatives for International Donor Action,' *Uganda Journal* 44 (1997):138–40.

Kiggundu, Rose. 'Women and Trade: The Case of Uganda,' in *Trade Myths and Gender Reality: Trade Liberalisation and Women's Lives* (ed. A. Hale), Uppsala: Global Publs. Foundation, 1998: 53–63.

Kiguli, Susan N., and Juliet Kiguli. 'Representations of Women Leaders in the Uganda Press,' in *Africa in World Affairs: Challenges to Humanities* (ed. E. Wamala et al.), Kampala: Faculty of Arts, Makerere Univ., 2004:146–53.

Kiiza, Enid, Winifred Kwe-Beyanga, and Agnes Kamya. 'Accounting for Gender: Improving Ugandan Credit Policies, Processes, and Programs,' in *Demanding Dignity: Women Confronting Economic Reforms in Africa* (ed. D. Tsikata and J. Kerr), Ottawa: The North-South Inst., 2000: 48–56.

Kikampikaho, Margaret, and Joy C. Kwesiga. 'Contributions of Women's Organisations to

Bibliography

Girls' Education in Uganda,' in *The Women's Movement in Uganda: History, Challenges, and Prospects* (ed. A. M. Tripp and J. C. Kwesiga), Kampala: Fountain, 2002: 40–57.

Kiremire, Merab Nambamu. *More Than A Woman?* Lusaka: UNZA, 1992.

Kirunda, M. F. 'Women's Education in Buddo and its Social Consequences.' M.Ed. Diss., Makerere Univ., 1976.

Kisaka, John Frederick. 'The Uganda Teachers Association and the Teachers of Uganda,' in *Labour Problems in Uganda*. Kampala: Uganda Press Trust, for the Milton Obote Foundation, 1966: 73–81.

Kisekka, Mere. 'El Papel de la Mujer en el Desarrollo Socioeconómico: El Caso de Nigeria y de Uganda,' *Estudios de Asia y Africa* 21 (1986): 413–41.

Kisubika, Ruth. 'Contributions of Pre-independence Women's Organizations to the Empowerment of Women in Uganda.' M.A. Diss., Women and Gender Studies, Makerere Univ., 1993.

Kiteme, Kamuti. 'The Socioeconomic Impact of the African Market Women Trade in Rural Kenya.' *Journal of Black Studies* 23 (1992): 135–51.

Knight, J. B. 'The Determination of Wages and Salaries in Uganda,' *Bulletin of the Oxford Univ. Inst. of Economics & Statistics* 29 (1967): 234–64.

Kubiragume, Amelia A. 'Challenges and Prospects of Women Traders in Peri-Urban Kampala: A Case Study of Horticulture Traders in Nakawa Division.' B.A. Diss., Sociology, Makerere Univ., 1998.

Kukunda Kwarisiima, Jennifer. 'Breaking into the Male Domain: A Case of Police Women in Kampala.' M.A. Diss., Women and Gender Studies, Makerere Univ., 1998. Publ. under same title as Occas. Paper No. 15, Women and Gender Studies, Makerere Univ., 2001.

Kwagala, Betty, Hope Kabuchu, Lydia Kapiriri, and Rebecca Wasswa. 'Health and the Economic Empowerment of Women: Life in a Kampala Unplanned Settlement,' in *Demanding Dignity: Women Confronting Economic Reforms in Africa* (ed. D. Tsikata and J. Kerr), Ottawa: The North-South Inst., 2000: 166–80.

Kwesiga, Joy. 'Leaders within Limits: Gender Ideologies and Identities in Uganda Today.' Unpubl. report, 2004, part of study of 'Public Policy, Changing Gender Relations, Ideologies and Identities in Uganda' carried out at Makerere Univ.

Kwesiga, Joy. 'The Meaning of Beijing for Higher Education in Uganda,' *Uganda Journal* 44 (1997):133–7.

Kwesiga, Joy C. *Women's Access to Higher Education in Africa: Uganda's Experience*. Kampala: Fountain, 2002.

Kwesiga, Joy. 'The Women's Movement in Uganda: An Analysis of Present and Future Prospects,' *Uganda Journal* 42 (1995):54–74.

Kwesiga, Joy. 'The Women's Movement in Uganda Revisited: Will the Twenty-First Century Create a Different Strand?,' *Uganda Journal* 50 (2003): 20–40.

Kyasimire, Elizabeth. 'The Role of Women in Economic Development,' in *Ugandan Women in Development* (ed. A. A. H. Abidi), African Development Series No. 1, Kampala: Foundation for African Development, 1990: 69–71.

Lateef, K. Sarwar. 'Structural Adjustment in Uganda: The Initial Experience,' in *Changing Uganda: The Dilemmas of Structural Adjustment and Revolutionary Change* (ed. H. B. Hansen and M. Twaddle), London: James Currey, 1991: 20–42.

Lawrance, J. C. K. 'A History of Teso to 1937,' *Uganda Journal* 19 (1955):7–40.

Lindsay, Lisa A. *Working with Gender: Wage Labor and Social Change in Southwestern Nigeria*. Portsmouth, NH: Heinemann, 2003.

Lovett, Margot. 'Gender Relations, Class Formation, and the Colonial State in Africa,' in *Women and the State in Africa* (ed. J. L. Parpart and K. A. Staudt), Boulder, CO: Lynne Rienner, 1990: 23–46.

Lovett, Margot. '"She Thinks She's Like a Man": Marriage and (De)constructing Gender Identity in Colonial Buha, Western Tanzania, 1943–1960,' in *"Wicked" Women and the Reconfiguration of Gender in Africa* (ed. D. L. Hodgson and S. A. McCurdy), Portsmouth, NH: Heinemann, 2001: 47–66.

Lubega, Monnie. 'Gender Division of Labour and Differences in Income Generating Activities of Rural People in Kalungu County in Masaka District.' M.A. Diss., Women and Gender Studies, Makerere Univ., 1993.

Lucas, Linda. 'Locating Women: Structure and Work in the Uganda Macroeconomy.' Unpubl. paper presented at Women's Worlds 2002.

Lusembo, Mathias. *The Transformation of the Status and Role of the Ganda Married Woman since 1877.* Rome: Pontifica Universitas Gregoriana, 1990.

Mafatle, Hazel Tebello Refiloe. 'Determinants of Women Enrolment at University Level in Uganda.' M.A. Diss., Economic Policy Management, Makerere Univ., 2000.

Magyezi, Raphael Tibaingana, 'The Role of Informal Credit Schemes in Poverty Alleviation in Uganda: A Case Study of Savings and Credit Associations in Mukono District.' M.A. Diss., Economic Policy and Planning, Makerere Univ., 1997.

Mair, Lucy P. *An African People in the Twentieth Century.* London: George Routledge and Sons, 1934.

Makerere University. *Installation and Graduation Ceremony, 9 October 1971; Graduation Ceremony, 7 October 1978; Graduation, 17ᵗʰ January 2003.*

Makerere University College, University of East Africa. *Report for the Year 1969-70.*

Mama, Amina. 'Sheroes and Villains: Conceptualizing Colonial and Contemporary Violence against Women in Africa,' in *Feminist Genealogies, Colonial Legacies, Democratic Futures* (ed. M. J. Alexander and C. T. Mohanty), New York: Routledge, 1997: 46–62.

Mamdani, Mahmood. *Citizen and Subject: Contemporary Africa and the Legacy of Late Colonialism.* Princeton, NJ: Princeton Univ. Press and Oxford: James Currey, 1996.

Mamdani, Mahmood. *Politics and Class Formation in Uganda.* New York: Monthly Review, 1976.

Mandeville, Elizabeth. 'Poverty, Work and the Financing of Single Women in Kampala,' *Africa* [UK] 49 (1979): 42–52.

Mann, Kristin. 'The Dangers of Dependence: Christian Marriage among Elite Women in Lagos Colony, 1880–1915,' *Journal of African History* 24 (1983): 37–56.

Mann, Kristin. *Marrying Well: Marriage, Status, and Social Change among the Educated Elite in Colonial Lagos.* Cambridge: Cambridge Univ. Press, 1985.

Mann, Kristin. 'Women, Landed Property, and the Accumulation of Wealth in Early Colonial Lagos.' *Signs* 16 (1991): 682–706.

Manyire, Henry. *Gender and Housing Development in the Low Income Suburbs of Jinja Municipality, Uganda.* Organization for Social Science Research in Eastern and Southern Africa, Gender Issues Research Report Series, no. 17, Addis Ababa, 2002.

Martin, Doris M., and Fatuma Omar Hashi. *Law as an Institutional Barrier to the Economic Empowerment of Women.* Working Paper No. 2, Poverty and Social Policy Division, Technical Department, Africa Region. Washington, DC: World Bank: June 1992.

Martin, Susan M. *Palm Oil and Protest: An Economic History of the Ngwa Region, South-Eastern Nigeria, 1800–1980.* Cambridge: Cambridge Univ. Press, 1988.

Matembe, Miria. *Gender, Politics, and Constitution Making in Uganda.* Kampala: Fountain, 2002.

Maxwell, Daniel G. 'Urban Agriculture: Unplanned Responses to the Economic Crisis,' in *Developing Uganda* (ed. H. B. Hansen and M. Twaddle), Oxford: James Currey, 1998: 98–108.

Mayende, Stephen Nabangi. 'Fish Production, Processing and Marketing at Masese and the Impact of Integrated Fisheries Development Project.' M.A. Diss., Economic Policy and Planning, Makerere Univ., 1992.

Mbilinyi, Marjorie. 'This Is an Unforgettable Business: Colonial State Intervention in Urban Tanzania,' in *Women and the State in Africa* (ed. J. L. Parpart and K. A. Staudt), Boulder, CO: Lynne Rienner, 1989: 111–29.

McCurdy, Sheryl A. 'Urban Threats: Manyema Women, Low Fertility, and Venereal Diseases in Tanganyika, 1926–1936,' in *"Wicked" Women and the Reconfiguration of Gender in Africa* (ed. D. L. Hodgson and S. A. McCurdy), Portsmouth, NH: Heinemann, 2001: 212–33.

Meagher, Kate. 'The Hidden Economy. Informal and Parallel Trade in Northwestern Uganda,' *Review of African Political Economy* 47 (1990): 64–83.

Mengo Hospital Centenary Magazine, 1897–1997: A Century of Christian Medical Witness. Kampala, 1997.

Mianda, Gertrude. 'Colonialism, Education, and Gender Relations in the Belgian Congo:

Bibliography

The *Évolué* Case,' in *Women in African Colonial Histories* (ed. J. Allman, S. Geiger, and N. Musisi), Bloomington, IN: Indiana Univ. Press, 2002: 144–63.

Middleton, John. *The Lugbara.* 2nd edit., Fort Worth, TX: Harcourt Brace Jovanovich, 1992; orig. publ. 1965.

Middleton, John. 'Trade and Markets among the Lugbara,' in *Markets in Africa* (ed. P. Bohanen and G. Dalton), Evanston, IL: Northwestern Univ. Press, 1962: 560–79.

Mikell, Gwendolyn, ed. *African Feminism: The Politics of Survival in Sub-Saharan Africa.* Philadelphia: Univ. of Pennsylvania Press, 1997.

Mkandawire, Thandika, and Charles C. Soludo. *Our Continent, Our Future: African Perspectives on Structural Adjustment.* Dakar: Council for the Development of Social Science Research in Africa, 1999.

Moore, Henrietta L., Todd Sanders, and Bwire Kaare, eds. *Those Who Play with Fire: Gender, Fertility and Transformation in East and Southern Africa.* London: Athlone, 1999.

Mugisa, Simoli Margaret. 'Exploration of Women Activities in the Fishing Community and the Availability of Food in the Household: A Study of Kasenyi Landing Site, Mpigi District.' B.A. Diss., Social Sciences, Makerere Univ., 1998.

Mugyenyi, Joshua B. 'IMF Conditionality and Structural Adjustment under the National Resistance Movement,' in *Changing Uganda: The Dilemmas of Structural Adjustment and Revolutionary Change* (ed. H. B. Hansen and M. Twaddle), London: James Currey, 1991: 61-77.

Mugyenyi, Mary R. 'The Impact of Structural Adjustment Programmes on Ugandan Rural Women in the 1980s: Prospects for Empowerment in the New Decade.' Unpubl. report, 1992.

Mugyenyi, Mary R. 'Towards the Empowerment of Women: A Critique of NRM Policies and Programmes,' in *Developing Uganda* (ed. H. B. Hansen and M. Twaddle), Oxford: James Currey, 1998), 133–44.

Muhumuza, John, Maria Musoke, and Patrick Bazalaki. *Uganda Cooperative Alliance: Three Research Reports.* Kampala, 1992.

Mukama, J. B. 'An Old Busoga Market,' *Makerere College Magazine* 2 (1938):158–9.

Mukama, Ruth. 'Women Making a Difference in the Media,' in *The Women's Movement in Uganda: History, Challenges, and Prospects* (ed. A. M. Tripp and J. C. Kwesiga), Kampala: Fountain, 2002: 146–61.

Mukasa, Stella, and Nite B. Tanzarn, eds. *Celebrating 10 Years of Existence: Department of Women and Gender Studies, Makerere University.* Kampala: Women and Gender Studies, n.d. but 2002.

Mukazi, Odeta Mutanguha. 'Women Involvement in the Brewing and Selling of Local Alcohol in Mulago Slum Area: Constraints and Prospects,' B.A. Diss., Social Work and Social Admin., Makerere Univ., 1997.

Mukwaya, A. F. 'Katwe Markets.' Typescript dated 29 September 1955.

Mukwaya, A. F., 'The Marketing of Staple Foods in Kampala, Uganda,' in *Markets in Africa* (ed. P. Bohannan and G. Dalton), Evanston,IL: Northwestern Univ. Press, 1962: 643–66.

Mupawaenda, Anna. 'Problems Faced with Women Co-operatives in Uganda and Some Remedial Measures for Improvement,' in *Counting the Cost: Women, Politics and Production in Africa* (ed. T. Berhane-Selassie), London: Institute for African Alternatives, 1987: 1–14.

Mupedziswa, Rodreck, and Perpetua Gumbo. *Women Informal Traders in Harare and the Struggle for Survival in an Environment of Economic Reforms.* Research Report No. 117. Uppsala: Nordiska Afrikainstitutet, 2001.

Museveni, Yoweri Kaguta. *Sowing the Mustard Seed: The Struggle for Freedom and Democracy in Uganda.* Basingstoke: Macmillan, 1997.

Musiimenta, Peace. 'Urban Agriculture and Women's Socio-Economic Empowerment: A Case Study of Kiswa and Luwafu Areas in Kampala City.' M.A. Diss., Women and Gender Studies, Makerere Univ., 1997.

Musiimire, Charity. 'Inter-role Conflict: A Study of Middle Level Women Managers in the Uganda Civil Service.' M.A. Diss., Women and Gender Studies, Makerere Univ., 1995.

Musisi, Nakanyike B. 'Baganda Women's Night Market Activities,' in *African Market Women and Economic Power* (ed. B. House-Midamba and F. K. Ekechi), Westport, CT: Greenwood, 1995: 121–39.

Bibliography

Musisi, Nakanyike B. 'Colonial and Missionary Education: Women and Domesticity in Uganda, 1900–1945,' in *African Encounters with Domesticity* (ed. K. T. Hansen), New Brunswick, NJ: Rutgers Univ. Press, 1992: 172–94.

Musisi, Nakanyike B. 'Gender and the Cultural Construction of "Bad Women",' in *'Wicked' Women and the Reconfiguration of Gender in Africa* (ed. D. L. Hodgson and S. A. McCurdy), Portsmouth, NH: Heinemann, 2001: 171–87.

Musisi, Nakanyike B. 'A Personal Journey into Custom, Identity, Power, and Politics: Researching and Writing the Life and Times of Buganda's Queen Mother Irene Drusilla Namaganda (1896–1957),' *History in Africa* 23 (1996):369-85.

Musisi, Nakanyike B. 'The Politics of Perception or Perception and Politics? Colonial and Missionary Representations of Baganda Women, 1900–1945,' in *Women in African Colonial Histories* (ed. J. Allman, S. Geiger, and N. Musisi), Bloomington, IN: Indiana Univ. Press, 2002: 95–115.

Musisi, Nakanyike B. 'Transformations of Baganda Women: From the Earliest Times to the Demise of the Kingdom in 1966.' Ph.D. thesis, Univ. of Toronto, 1991.

Musisi, Nakanyike B. 'Women, "Elite Polygyny", and Buganda State Formation,' *Signs* 16 (1991): 757–86.

Musoke, Maria G. N. *Research on Women in Uganda: An Annotated Bibliography*. Dept. of Women Studies, Makerere Univ., March 1993.

Musoke, Maria G. N. 'Women in the Professions: Challenges and Prospects of Careerism in Uganda since Independence.' Unpubl. report, 1990.

Musoke, Maria G. N., and Mary Amajo. 'Women's Participation in Existing Credit Schemes in Uganda.' Unpubl. report, 1989.

Mutyaba, Mustafa, and S. Namukade. *Chwa II ne Muteesa II*. Kampala: Crane, 2001.

Muwanika, Harriet Kiwemba. 'Empowerment of Women through Credit Facilities: A Case Study of FINCA in Jinja District.' M.A. Diss., Women and Gender Studies, Makerere Univ., 1998.

Muzaale, Patrick J. 'A Study of Women Involvement/Participation in the Co-operative Movement in Uganda.' Unpubl. report sponsored by the Uganda Co-operative Alliance Ltd, December 1989.

Muzaki, Sarah. 'Gender in the Rural Informal Labour Market: The Case of Budadiri County, Mbale District.' M.A. Diss., Women and Gender Studies, Makerere Univ., 1998.

Mwaka, Victoria M. 'Agricultural Production and Women's Time Budgets in Uganda,' in *Different Places, Different Voices. Gender and Development in Africa, Asia and Latin America* (ed. Janet H. Momsen and Vivian Kinnaird), London: Routledge, 1993: 46–51.

Nabunya, A. N. 'A Survey into the Socio-Economic Conditions of Working Mothers.' B.A. Diss., Social Work and Social Admin., Makerere Univ., 1979.

Nakamate, Zaamu. 'Challenges Facing Muslim Women Entrepreneurs: The Case of Micro and Small Scale Enterprises in Kampala District.' M.A. Diss., Women and Gender Studies, Makerere Univ., 2002.

Nakirunda, Maureen. 'Factors Promoting Women-Operated Home-Based Enterprises (HBEs) in Kampala City.' M.A. Diss., Women and Gender Studies, Makerere Univ., 1996.

Nalubwama, Esther. 'Cooked Food Vending in Kampala City: An Exploration Study.' B.A. Diss., Social Work and Social Admin., Makerere Univ., 1997.

Naluyiga, Hasifa. *Gender, Disability and Work in the Urban Informal Sector in Kampala City*. Occas. Paper No. 11, Dept. of Women and Gender Studies, Makerere Univ., 2001.

Nalwanga-Sebina, Abby. 'Report on a Five-Day Survey on the Needs of Widows and Other Disadvantaged Groups in Selected Counties in Luweero District.' Typed report for USAID, Kampala. N.d. but probably late 1980s.

Nalwanga-Sebina, Abby J. 'Women and AIDS in Uganda.' Unpubl. report prepared for UNICEF Situation Analysis for 1995–2000, 1992.

Nalwanga-Sebina, Abby J., and Edith R. Natukunda. 'Uganda Women's Needs Assessment Survey, 1988.' Unpubl. report.

Namayanja, Jane. 'The Impact of "Improve Your Business" Training Program on Small-Scale Enterprises in Kampala District.' M.A. Diss., Economic Policy Management,

Bibliography

Makerere Univ., 2002.

Namukasa, Suzette K. 'Mobility of Professionals: A Gendered Study of Agricultural Officers in Kampala and Mpigi Districts.' M.A. Diss., Women and Gender Studies, Makerere Univ., 1997.

Nankunda, Hilda. *Civil Service Reforms and the Living Standards of Retrenched Civil Servants: A Case Study of Kampala District.* Working Paper No. 18, Kampala: NURRU, 2002.

Nantaba, Barbara. 'A Study of the Self Employed Women's Aspirations, Perceptions and Problems in the Central Division of Kampala District.' B.A. Diss., Social Work and Social Admin., Makerere Univ., 1997.

Nanteza, Diana. 'Gender Relations and the Effectiveness of the Heifer Project for Women Farmers in Mpigi District, Uganda.' M.A. Diss., Women and Gender Studies, Makerere Univ., 1995.

Natukunda, Edith, and Harriet Birungi. 'Women at War: A Study of Women's Involvement in War and Its Implications.' Unpubl. paper, Department of Languages, Makerere Univ., Kampala, 1990.

Neema, Stella. 'Women's Organisations: A Gateway to Women's Health in Uganda,' in *The Women's Movement in Uganda: History, Challenges, and Prospects* (ed. A. M. Tripp and J. C. Kwesiga), Kampala: Fountain, 2002: 58–71.

Newman, Constance, and Sudharshan Canagarajah. *Gender, Poverty, and Nonfarm Employment in Ghana and Uganda.* World Bank Working Papers, Labor & Employment, No. 2367. Washington, DC: World Bank, 2002.

Newspapers: see Appendix A (available in Africana section of Makerere Univ. Library).

Norris, Pippa. *Digital Divide: Civic Engagement, Information Poverty, and the Internet Worldwide.* Cambridge: Cambridge Univ. Press, 2001.

Nsimbi, M. B. 'Village Life and Customs in Buganda,' *Uganda Journal* 20 (1956): 27–36.

Nsubuga Lubyayi, Geraldine. 'Opportunities and Constraints for Women's Participation in Bee Keeping: Case Study of Katikamu Sub-County, Luwero District in Uganda.' M.A. Diss., Women and Gender Studies, Makerere Univ., 2000.

Ntege, H. 'Women and Urban Housing Crisis: Impact of Public Policies and Practices in Uganda,' *Economic and Political Weekly*, 28/44 (30 October 1993): WS 46–62.

Nyachwo, Frances. 'A Gender Analysis of the Effects of Adopting Clonal Coffee Production on Household Workload: A Case Study of Ntenjeru Sub-County, Mukono District.' M.A. Diss., Women and Gender Studies, Makerere Univ., 2000.

Nyakaana, J. B. 'Organisation and Regulation in the Informal Sector: The Street Traders of Kampala City, Uganda,' *Eastern and Southern African Geographical Journal* 4 (1993): 17–22.

Obbo, Christine. *African Women: Their Struggle for Economic Independence.* Johannesburg: Ravan, 1981.

Obbo, Christine. 'East African Women, Work and the Articulation of Dominance', in *Persistent Inequalities: Women and World Development* (ed. Irene Tinker), New York: Oxford Univ. Press, 1990: 210–22.

Obbo, Christine. 'Gender and Urban Poverty in the Days of AIDS in Uganda,' in *Urban Poverty in Africa* (ed. S. Jones and N. Nelson), London: Intermediate Technology Publs, 1999: 149–59.

Obbo, Christine. 'Sexuality and Economic Domination in Uganda,' in *Woman-Nation-State* (ed. N. Yuval-Davis and F. Anthias), London: Macmillan, 1989: 79–91.

Obbo, Christine, 'Stratification and the Lives of Women in Uganda,' in *Women and Class in Africa* (ed. Claire Robertson and Iris Berger), New York: Africana Publishing, 1986: 178–94.

Obbo, Christine. 'What Women Can Do: AIDS Crisis Management in Uganda,' in *Women Wielding the Hoe: Lessons from Rural Africa for Feminist Theory and Development Practice* (ed. D. F. Bryceson), Oxford: Berg, 1995: 165–78.

Obbo, Christine. 'Who Cares for the Carers? AIDS and Women in Uganda,' in *Developing Uganda* (ed. H. B. Hansen and M. Twaddle), Oxford: James Currey, 1998: 207–14.

Ochieng, E. O. 'Economic Adjustment Programmes in Uganda, 1985–8,' in *Changing Uganda: The Dilemmas of Structural Adjustment and Revolutionary Change* (ed. H. B. Hansen and M. Twaddle), London: James Currey, 1991: 43–60.

O'Connor, Anthony. 'Uganda: The Spatial Dimension,' in *Uganda Now: Between Decay and*

Bibliography

Development (ed. H. B. Hansen and M. Twaddle), London: James Currey, 1988: 83–94.

Ojo, Olatunji. 'Writing Yoruba Female Farmers into History: A Study of the Food Production Sector,' in *Africanizing Knowledge* (ed. T. Falola and C. Jennings), New Brunswick, NJ: Transaction Publishers, 2002: 387–404.

Ojombo, Stephen. 'The Implications of Informal Cross-border Trade on Household Welfare in Busia District.' M.A. Diss., Women and Gender Studies, Makerere Univ., 1997.

Okeke, Philomena E. 'Negotiating Social Independence: The Challenges of Career Pursuits for Igbo Women in Postcolonial Nigeria,' in *"Wicked" Women and the Reconfiguration of Gender in Africa* (ed. D. L. Hodgson and S. A. McCurdy), Portsmouth, NH: Heinemann, 2001: 234–51.

Okeke-Ihejirika, Philomena E. *Negotiating Power and Privilege: Igbo Career Women in Contemporary Nigeria*. Athens, OH: Ohio University Press, 2004.

Okereke, Okoro. 'The Role of the Co-operative Movement in the Economic Development of Uganda.' MA thesis, Univ. of East Africa, 1968.

Okurut, Mary Karooro. *The Invisible Weevil*. Kampala: FEMRITE, 1998.

Okurut, Mary Karooro. *Milking a Lioness and Other Stories*. Kampala: Monitor, 1999.

Okurut, Mary Karooro. *The Official Wife*. Kampala: Fountain, 2003.

Okurut, Mary Karooro, and Violet Barungi, eds. *A Woman's Voice: An Anthology of Short Stories by Ugandan Women*. Kampala: FEMRITE, 1998.

Olinga, Forough Ehsani. *Gender Resource Allocation and Fisheries Development: The Case of Buvu and Lulamba Islands, Lake Victoria*. Occas. Paper No. 8, Dept. of Women and Gender Studies, Makerere Univ., 2000.

Oliver, Roland. *The Missionary Factor in East Africa*. 2nd edn, London: Longman, 1965.

Oloya, J. J., and T. T. Poleman. *The Food Supply of Kampala: A Study in the Marketing of Basic Food-Stuffs in an African Metropolitan Area*. Kampala: Makerere Inst. of Social Research, 1972.

Omitta, Sulaiman. 'Challenges of Empowering Women Economically by NGOs in Uganda: A Study of FINCA in Kakira Subcounty.' MA Diss., Sociology, Makerere Univ., 1999.

Onweng Angura, Tobias. *Opportunities and Constraints to Informal Sector Activities in Northern Uganda: A Comparative Study of Women and Men in Informal Enterprises in Lira Town*. Report submitted to OSSREA, Makerere Inst. of Social Research, 1993.

Opolot, Jethro A. 'Occupational Aspirations of Primary School Leavers in Uganda,' *Uganda Journal* 41 (1984):1-7.

Parkin, David. *Neighbours and Nationals in an African City Ward*. Berkeley, CA: Univ. of California Press, 1969.

Parpart, Jane L. '"Wicked Women" and "Respectable Ladies": Reconfiguring Gender on the Zambian Copperbelt, 1936–1964,' in *"Wicked" Women and the Reconfiguration of Gender in Africa* (ed. D. L. Hodgson and S. A. McCurdy), Portsmouth, NH: Heinemann, 2001: 274–92.

Patai, Daphne. 'U.S. Academics and Third World Women: Is Ethical Research Possible?' in *Women's Words: The Feminist Practice of Oral History* (ed. S. B. Gluck and D. Patai), New York: Routledge, 1991: 137–53.

Peel, John D. Y. *Religious Encounter and the Making of the Yoruba*. Bloomington, IN: Indiana Univ. Press, 2000.

Perlman, Melvin L. 'The Changing Status and Role of Women in Toro (W. Uganda),' *Cahiers d'Etudes Africaines*. 6 (1966): 564–91.

Perlman, M. L. 'Some Aspects of Marriage Stability in Toro.' Unpubl. paper read at conf. of the East African Inst. of Social Research, Makerere Univ. College, held in Kimuru, Kenya, 1962.

Pickering, Helen, Ellen Kajura, George Katongole, and James Whitworth. 'Women's Groups and Individual Entrepreneurs: A Ugandan Case Study,' *Gender and Development* 4 (1996): 54–60.

Porter, Marilyn, and Ellen Judd, eds. *Feminists Doing Development: A Practical Critique*. London: Zed Books, 1999.

Presley, Cora Ann. *Kikuyu Women, the Mau Mau Rebellion, and Social Change in Kenya*. Boulder, CO: Westview, 1992.

Prunier, G. 'La 'Magendo' en Uganda (1972–1989),' in *Histoire Sociale de l'Afrique de L'Est*

Bibliography

(XIXe–XXe Siècle), Paris: Karthala, 1991: 319–34.

Purseglove, J. W. *Tobacco in Uganda*. Entebbe: Government Printer, 1951.

Rathgeber, Eva M. and Edith Ofwona Adera, eds. *Gender and the Information Revolution in Africa*. Ottawa: Internatl. Devel. Research Centre, 2000.

Redding, Sean. 'South African Women and Migration in Umtata, Transkei, 1880-1935,' in *Courtyards, Markets, City Streets* (ed. K. Sheldon), Boulder, CO: Westview, 1996: 31–46.

Reid, Richard J. *Political Power in Pre-Colonial Buganda*. Oxford: James Currey, 2002.

Reinikka, Ritva, and Paul Collier, eds. *Uganda's Recovery: The Role of Farms, Firms, and Government*. See under Government Publications, 3, World Bank.

Robertson, Claire. 'Comparative Advantage: Women in Trade in Accra, Ghana, and Nairobi, Kenya,' in *African Market Women and Economic Power* (ed. B. House-Midamba and F. K. Ekechi), Westport, CT: Greenwood, 1995: 99–120.

Robertson, Claire. 'The Death of Makola and Other Tragedies.' *Canadian Journal of African Studies* 17 (1983): 469–95.

Robertson, Claire. *Sharing the Same Bowl: A Socio-Economic History of Women and Class in Accra, Ghana*. Bloomington, IN: Univ. of Indiana Press, 1984.

Robertson, Claire. 'Traders and Urban Struggle: Ideology and the Creation of a Militant Female Underclass in Nairobi, 1960–1990,' *Journal of Women's History* 4 (1993): 9–42.

Robertson, Claire C. 'Transitions in Kenyan Patriarchy: Attempts to Control Nairobi Area Traders, 1920–1963,' in *Courtyards, Markets, City Streets: Urban Women in Africa* (ed. K. Sheldon), Boulder, CO: Westview Press, 1996, 47–71.

Robertson, Claire. *Trouble Showed the Way: Women, Men, and Trade in the Nairobi Area, 1890–1990*. Indianapolis, IN: Indiana Univ. Press, 1997.

Robertson, Claire C. and M. A. Klein, eds. *Women and Slavery in Africa*. Madison, WI: Univ. of Wisconsin Press, 1983.

Roscoe, John. *The Baganda: An Account of their Native Customs and Beliefs*. 2nd edn, New York: Barnes and Noble, 1966 (orig. publ. 1911).

Schiller, Laurence D. 'The Royal Women of Buganda,' *International Journal of African Historical Studies* 23 (1990): 455–73.

Schmidt, Elizabeth. '"Emancipate Your Husbands!" Women and Nationalism in Guinea, 1953–1958,' in *Women in African Colonial Histories* (ed. J. Allman, S. Geiger, and N. Musisi), Bloomington, IN: Indiana Univ. Press, 2002: 282–304.

Schmidt, Elizabeth. *Peasants, Traders, and Wives: Shona Women in the History of Zimbabwe, 1870-1939*. Portsmouth, NH: Heinemann, 1992.

Sebina-Zziwa, Abby J. *Gender Perspectives on Land Ownership and Inheritance in Uganda*. Research Paper 16, Makerere Inst. of Social Research and the Land Tenure Center, 1995.

Sebina-Zziwa, Abby J. Nalwanga. 'The Paradox of Tradition: Gender, Land and Inheritance Rights among the Baganda.' Ph.D. Diss., Univ. of Copenhagen, 1998.

Sekabanja, Florence. 'Situational Gender Analysis of Financial Sector Policy and the Plan for Expansion of Outreach of Micro Finance in Uganda.' Unpubl. report commissioned by ACFODE, 2003.

Sen, Gita, and Caren Grown. *Development, Crises, and Alternative Visions: Third World Women's Perspectives*. New York: Monthly Review, 1987.

Senyondo, Vincent. 'Female Absenteeism in Industry: An Exploratory Study of Causes.' B.A. Diss., Social Work and Social Administration, Makerere Univ., 1982.

Sharer, Robert L. et al. *Uganda: Adjustment with Growth, 1987–94*. See under Government Publications, 3, IMF.

Sheldon, Kathleen E. *Pounders of Grain: A History of Women, Work, and Politics in Mozambique*. Portsmouth, NH: Heinemann, 2002.

Sheldon, Kathleen. 'Urban African Women: Courtyards, Markets, City Streets,' in *Courtyards, Markets, City Streets* (ed. K. Sheldon), Boulder, CO: Westview, 1996: 3–27.

Shields, Francine. 'Palm Oil and Power: Women in an Era of Economic and Social Transition in 19th Century Yorubaland (South-Western Nigeria).' Ph.D. thesis, Univ. of Stirling, 1997.

Shiroya, Okete. 'Northwestern Uganda in the Nineteenth Century.' Research Paper, Dept. of History, Makerere Univ., 1971. Discussed extensively by Jackson, *Essays in Rural Marketing*, but no copy could be found at Makerere Libraries in April 2003.

Bibliography

Simwogerere, Erioth. 'Cassava Processing in Uganda,' in *Do It Herself: Women and Technical Innovation* (ed. H. Appleton), London: Intermediate Technology Publs., 1995: 181–4.

Smith, James D. 'Market Motives in the Informal Economy,' in *The Economics of the Shadow Economy* (ed. W. Gaertner and A. Wenig), Berlin: Springer Verlag, 1985, 161–77.

Snyder, Katherine A. 'Gender Ideology, and the Domestic and Public Domains among the Iraqw,' in *Those Who Play with Fire* (ed. H. L. Moore et al.), London: Atholone, 1999: 225–54.

Snyder, Margaret. 'What Did We Bring of Beijing to Uganda: A Conversation on the United Nations Fourth World Conference on Women, Beijing, 1995,' *Uganda Journal* 44 (1997):128–30.

Snyder, Margaret. *Women in African Economies: From Burning Sun to Boardroom.* Kampala: Fountain, 2000.

Snyder, Margaret. 'Women's Agency in the Economy: Business and Investment Patterns,' in *The Women's Movement in Uganda: History, Challenges, and Prospects* (ed. A. M. Tripp and J. C. Kwesiga), Kampala: Fountain, 2002: 76–89.

Sofer, Cyril, and Rhona Sofer. *Jinja Transformed: A Social Survey of a Multi-Racial Township.* Kampala: East African Inst. of Social Research, 1955.

Sofer, Cyril, and Rhona Sofer. 'Recent Population Growth in Jinja,' *Uganda Journal* 17 (1953): 38–50.

Sorensen, Pernille. 'Commercialization of Food Crops in Busoga, Uganda, and the Renegotiation of Gender,' *Gender and Society* 10 (1996): 608–23.

Southall, A. W. 'Alur Migrants,' in *Economic Development and Tribal Change* (ed. A. I. Richards), Cambridge: W. Heffer, 1954: 141–60.

Southall, A. W. 'Kinship, Friendship, and the Network of Relations in Kisenyi, Kampala,' in *Social Change in Modern Africa* (ed. A. Southall), London: Oxford Univ. Press for the International African Inst., 1961: 217–29.

Southall, A. W., and P. C. W. Gutkind. *Townsmen in the Making: Kampala and its Suburbs.* Kampala: East African Inst. for Social Research, 1957.

Ssekamwa, J. C., *History and Development of Education in Uganda.* Kampala: Fountain, 1997.

Ssemogerere, Germina. 'Mobilisation of Domestic Financial Resources in Uganda: Commercial Banks versus the Uganda Cooperative Savings and Credit Union,' in *Saving for Economic Recovery in Africa* (ed. J. H. Frimpong-Ansah and B. Ingham), London: James Currey, 1992: 93–118.

Ssenyonjo, Jamil. 'Factors Affecting the Performance of Muslim Women in Trade.' B.A. Diss., Social Work and Social Admin., Makerere Univ., 1993.

Stacey, Judith. 'Can There Be a Feminist Ethnography?,' in *Women's Words: The Feminist Practice of Oral History* (ed. S. B. Gluck and D. Patai), New York: Routledge, 1991:111–20.

Staudt, Kathleen. 'The Impact of Development Policies on Women,' in *African Women South of the Sahara* (ed. M. J. Hay and S. Stichter), 2nd edn, Harlow: Longmans, 1995: 225–38.

Steiger-Hayley, T. T. 'Wage Labour and the Desire for Wives among the Lango,' *Uganda Journal* 8 (1940): 15–18.

Sudarkasa, Niara. *Where Women Work: A Study of Yoruba Women in the Marketplace and in the Home.* Ann Arbor, MI: Univ. of Michigan, Museum of Anthropology, 1973.

Summers, Carol. 'Intimate Colonialism: The Imperial Production of Reproduction in Uganda, 1907–1925,' *Signs* 16 (1991): 787–807.

Syahuka-Muhindo, Arthur. *Understanding Women's Participation in Artisanal Salt Production at Lake Katwe in Western Uganda, 1970–1990.* Addis Ababa: OSSREA, 1996.

Tadria, Hilda M. K. 'Changes and Continuities in the Position of Women in Uganda,' in *Beyond Crisis: Development Issues in Uganda* (ed. P. D. Wiebe and C. P. Dodge), Kampala: Makerere Inst. of Social Research, 1987, 79–90.

Tadria, Hilda M. K. 'Changing Economic and Gender Patterns among the Peasants of Ndejje and Sseguku in Uganda.' Ph.D. Diss., Univ. of Minnesota, 1985.

Tamale, Sylvia. *When Hens Begin to Crow: Gender and Parliamentary Politics in Uganda.* Boulder, CO: Westview, 1999.

Tanzarn, Nite Baza. 'Gender Portrayals in the Media in Uganda: A Study of Female-Male Images in Newspapers in English.' M.A. Diss., Women and Gender Studies, Makerere Univ., 1995. Publ. as *Women and Men in the Media: Analysis of Gender Portrayal in Selected*

Bibliography

Newspapers in Uganda, Occas. Paper No. 18, Dept. of Women and Gender Studies, Makerere Univ., 2002.

Tanzarn, Nite. 'The Link between the Domestic Relations Bill (DRB) and the Poverty Eradication Action Plan (PEAP),' Unpubl. report for Uganda Women's Network, 2004.

Taylor, Brian K. *Tropical Toro: A Ugandan Society*. Brighton: Pennington Beech, 1998.

Temple, P. H. 'Nakasero Market, Kampala,' *Uganda Journal* 28 (1964): 165–78.

Temple, Paul H. 'The Urban Markets of Greater Kampala,' *Tijdschrift voor Economische en Sociale Geografie* 60 (1969): 346–59.

Thomas, Lynn F. *Politics of the Womb: Women, Reproduction, and the State in Kenya*. Berkeley, CA: Univ. of California Press, 2003.

Thompson, Gardiner. *Governing Uganda: British Colonial Rule and Its Legacy*. Kampala: Fountain, 2003.

Tibatemwa-Ekirikubinza, Lillian. *Women's Violent Crime in Uganda: More Sinned Against Than Sinning*. Kampala: Fountain, 1999.

Tinkasiimire, Therese. 'Women's Contributions to Religious Institutions in Uganda (1962–2001),' in *The Women's Movement in Uganda: History, Challenges, and Prospects* (ed. A. M. Tripp and J. C. Kwesiga), Kampala: Fountain, 2002: 138–45.

Tourigny, Yves. *So Abundant A Harvest: The Catholic Church in Uganda, 1879–1979*. London: Darton, Longman & Todd, 1979.

Tripp, Aili Mari. 'Gender, Political Participation and the Transformation of Associational Life in Uganda and Tanzania,' *African Studies Review* 37 (1994): 107–31.

Tripp, Aili Mari. 'Local Women's Associations and Politics in Contemporary Uganda,' in *Developing Uganda* (ed. H. B. Hansen and M. Twaddle), Oxford: James Currey, 1998, 120–32.

Tripp, Aili Mari. *Women and Politics in Uganda*. Oxford: James Currey, 2000.

Tripp, Aili Mari, and Joy C. Kwesiga, eds. *The Women's Movement in Uganda: History, Challenges, and Prospects*. Kampala: Fountain, 2002.

Tripp, Aili Mari, with Sarah Ntiro. 'Women's Activism in Colonial Uganda,' in *The Women's Movement in Uganda* (ed. A. M. Tripp and J. C. Kwesiga), Kampala: Fountain, 2002: 23–39.

Tukahebwa, Geoffrey B. 'Privatization as a Development Policy,' in *Developing Uganda* (ed. H. B. Hansen and M. Twaddle), Oxford: James Currey, 1998: 59–72.

Tumusiime, James, ed. *Uganda 30 Years, 1962–1992*. Kampala: Fountain, 1992.

Turrittin, Jane. 'Colonial Midwives and Modernizing Childbirth in French West Africa,' in *Women in African Colonial Histories* (ed. J. Allman, S. Geiger, and N. Musisi), Bloomington, IN: Indiana Univ. Press, 2002: 71–91.

Uganda Council of Women. *Laws about Marriage in Uganda*. No date, but reviewed in *Uganda Journal* 26 (1962): 220–21.

Uganda Education Association. *Bulletin*, Vol. I (1940).

Uganda Teachers' Journal, Vols. II (1940) and III (1941).

Unterhalter, Elaine. 'Constructing Race, Class, Gender and Ethnicity: State and Opposition Strategies in South Africa,' in *Unsettling Settler Societies* (ed. D. Stasiulis and N. Yubal-Davis), London: Sage, 1995: 207–40.

Urdang, Stephanie. 'Women in National Liberation Movements,' in *African Women South of the Sahara* (ed. M. J. Hay and S. Stichter), Harlow: Longman, 1995: 213–24.

Uzoigwe, G. N., 'Precolonial Markets in Bunyoro-Kitara,' *Comparative Studies in Society and History* 14 (1972): 422–55.

Van Allen, Judith. '"Aba Riots" or Igbo "Women's War"? Ideology, Stratification, and the Invisibility of Women,' in *Women in Africa: Studies in Social and Economic Change* (ed. N. Hafkin and E. Bay), Stanford, CA: Stanford Univ. Press, 1976: 59–86.

Van Allen, Judith. '"Sitting on a Man": Colonialism and the Lost Political Institutions of Igbo Women,' *Canadian Journal of African Studies* 6 (1972): 165–81.

VerEecke, Catherine. 'Muslim Women Traders of Northern Nigeria: Perspectives from the City of Yola,' in *African Market Women and Economic Power* (ed. B. House-Midamba and F. K. Ekechi), Westport, CT: Greenwood, 1995: 59–80.

Wakoko, Florence, and Linda Lobao. 'Reconceptualizing Gender and Reconstructing Social Life: Ugandan Women and the Path to National Development,' *Africa Today* 43 (1996): 307–22.

Bibliography

Walker, Cherryl. 'Gender and the Development of the Migrant Labour System, c. 1850–1930: An Overview,' in *Women and Gender in Southern Africa to 1945* (ed. C. Walker), Cape Town: David Philip, 1990: 168–96.

Wallace, Christine C. and Sheldon G. Weeks. *Success or Failure in Rural Uganda: A Study of Young People.* Kampala: Makerere Inst. of Social Research, 1974.

Wallman, Sandra, ed. *Kampala Women Getting By: Wellbeing in the Time of AIDS.* London: James Currey, 1996.

Wandira-Kazibwe, S. 'Women in Business and Industry,' in *Ugandan Women in Development* (ed. Ayed A. H. Abidi). African Development Series No. 1. Kampala: Foundation for African Development, 1990: 73–4.

Wanendeya, Ida M. 'Women in Business: Problems and Prospects, Uganda Country Paper.' Prepared for Roundtable for Women in Business in the PTA Subregion, Lusaka, Zambia, 1992.

Wangusa, Ayeta Anne and Violet Barungi, eds. *Tears of Hope: A Collection of Short Stories by Ugandan Rural Women.* Kampala: FEMRITE, 2003.

Wanyoto, Lydia. 'Retrenchment in Uganda's Civil Service: A Gender Focused Study of the Experiences of the Retrenched Employees in Kampala and Mbale Districts.' M.A. Diss., Women and Gender Studies, Makerere Univ., 1998.

Watson, Catharine. 'Uganda's Women: A Ray of Hope,' *Africa Report* 33 (1988): 29–32.

Wavamuno, Clare. 'Women Credit Situation in the Development Finance Department of the Bank of Uganda.' Research report, 1991.

Wekiya, Irene Florence. 'Nkejje Fish in Lake Victoria,' in *Do It Herself: Women and Technical Innovation* (ed. H. Appleton), London: Intermediate Technology Publs., 1995: 185–7.

White, Gilbert F., David J. Bradley, and Anne U. White. *Drawers of Water: Domestic Water Use in East Africa.* Chicago: Univ. of Chicago Press, 1972.

White, Luise. *The Comforts of Home: Prostitution in Colonial Nairobi.* Chicago: Univ. of Chicago Press, 1990.

White, Luise. '"They Could Make Their Victims Dull": Genders and Genres, Fantasies and Cures in Colonial Southern Uganda,' *American Historical Review* 100 (1995): 1379–1402.

Whitehead, Ann. 'Rural Women and Food Production in Sub-Saharan Africa,' in *The Political Economy of Hunger,* Vol. I (ed. J. Drèze and A. Sen), Oxford: Clarendon, 1990: 425–73.

Willis, Justin. 'The Only Money A Woman Can Claim: A History of Distilling in Bunyoro,' *Uganda Journal* 46 (2000): 1–16.

Willis, Justin. *Potent Brews: A Social History of Alcohol in East Africa, 1850–1999.* London: British Inst. in East Africa, 2002.

Wright, Graham A. N., Deborah Kasente, Germina Ssemogerere, and Leonard Mutesasira. 'Vulnerability, Risks, Assets and Empowerment – The Impact of Microfinance on Poverty Alleviation,' in *World Development Report,* New York: World Bank, 2001.

Ziwa, Magdalene. 'Peri-Urban Women's Home Based Enterprises: An Exploratory Study.' B.A. Diss., Social Work and Social Admin., Makerere Univ., 1993.

Index

abduction 149
abortion 70, 163
accounting 227
ACFODE x, 24, 169, 191, 194, 203, 204,
  205, 233, 234
Action for Development *see* ACFODE
advertising, Western standards/domesticity
  in 137
affirmative action 9, 111; backlash against
  199-200; economic 259; gender tension
  caused by 239; in education 193, 255;
  NRM government 3, 16, 17, 184, 190,
  227, 231, 258
African Growth and Opportunities Act 237
Ageteraine (Ankole) 108, 110, 111, 135, 136
agriculture 20-21; subsistence 46, 117; (as
  women's work) 13, 51, 55, 80, 87, 98,
  99, 104, 106, 123, 152, 153, 169-70,
  175, 211, 221, 258, 259; (undervaluation
  of) 16, 49, 116, 133, 170, 239; *see also*
  cash crops
'Akello, Angela' 33-5, 128, 186, 204, 208,
  220
alcohol, disapproval of women producing
  and selling 57, 77, 90, 125, 132; linked
  to sex work 107, 135-6; production and
  sale of 38, 77, 89, 99, 100-1, 104, 107,
  108, 125, 132, 170, 171, 223, 260
Amin, Idi x, 9, 156, coup of 117, 146,
  'Economic War' of 17, 36, 51, 153-4;
  policies on female appearance and
  behavior 163, 164; and IWY 166, 175
Ankole 14, 16; progressive beliefs regarding
  women's issues 105, 108
'Apio, Fulgencia' 38, 125, 155, 176
arts 131, 225
Arua, district of 23

Asiimwe, Jackie 25, 120, 128, 231
ayah x *see also* housegirls

Ba x
Baganda *see* 'Kasirye, Fatuma'; 'Ssembatia,
  Grace'
Bagaya, Elizabeth (formerly princess of
  Toro) 127-8, 164-5
Bagenda, Rose Mary 128
Bahima 55
Bakakole (born-again Christian) 123
Bakiga *see* 'Mary Katushabe'; 'Kamusiime,
  Jane'
banking 224
Banyoro *see* 'Kamugasa, Thereza';
  'Birungi, Margeret'
Batoro, *see* 'Kyamanya, Eunice'
beauty/hairdressing 125, 175, 225
beer *see* alcohol
Beijing Women's Conference 218, 234
birthrates 10, 18, 206, 254; declining 77-8
'Birungi, Margaret' 160, 211, 223, 228-30
bishops (Church of Uganda), role in shifting
  gender expectations 15, 80; *see also*
  Stuart, Bishop; Tucker, Bishop; Willis,
  Bishop
Bitamazire, G. N. 192
black market *see magendo*
bridewealth, x, 67, 68, 70, 78, 106, 135,
  136, 157, 201; challenges to 108, 110,
  121, 135, 136, 236
Bu x
Buganda 13-14, 92; Agreement of 1900 48,
  66, 67, 73; gender expectations of
  15,16, 80, 81, 117; evidence available
  for 66; *see also Kabaka, Lukiiko*
Bukedde (Luganda) 225, 233, 235, 236, 239

300

Index

'Munduru, Joyce' 158-9, 211, 225, 227, 242

Munno 71, 73, 105, 107, 110, 135

munno mukabi 203-4

Muolwana, Sarah 227

Museveni, Yoweri Kaguta xi, 3, 13, 147, 148, 160, 184, 185-6, 189, 225, 228, 230, 263 pro-women stance of 190-1, 206, talk of term limiting of 198, and HIV/AIDS 208

Musisi, Nakanyike 7, 54, 68-9, 97, 103, 134

mwenge 100

Nakacwa, Theresa 131

Nakafeero, Angela 26, 227, 231, 232

Namaganda, Irene 109-10

Namagembe, Sarah 131

Namale, Hadijah 131

Namasole (Queen Mother) affair 109

namasole xi

Namugenyi, Hawa 123

National Action Plan on Women 234

National Association of Women's Organizations in Uganda *see* NAWOU

National Gender Policy 234

National Resistance Army *see* NRA

National Resistance Movement *see* NRM

nationalism 92

NAWOU xi, 24, 34, 225

NCW establishment of 165

New Vision 199-200, 225, 233, 236, 237, 238, 239, 240

newspapers *see Ageterain, Bukedde, The East African, East African Standard, Ebifa, The [London] Times, Monitor, Munno, New Vision, The Other Voice, Red Pepper, Sunday Vision, Tafia Empya, Uganda Herald, Uganda Argus, Uganda Empya, Voice of Uganda,*

NGOs xi, 10, 17, 187, 192-3, 200, 201, 204, 203, 205, 208, 210, 211, 226, 256, 257, 259, 266, 263, employment of women by 225

Nkokonjeru College, teacher training at 60

non-governmental organization *see* NGO

NRA xi, xii, 160; methods of 185; the 'bush war' 147; women's participation in 151, 191, 225

NRM xi, 147, 178; positive international attention to 21; pro-women policies of, 151, 190-5, 218, 232, 240, 257-8; disillusionment with 195-9; backlash against 196, 199-200, 244, economic impact of 227, 231; stability provided by 257; support for education 10, 254,

women's perceptions of 35, 37, 38, 40-1, 159, 171, 194-5

Nsambya Hospital (Kampala) 104

Nsambya Materinity Training School 61

Nsambya School of Nursing 174

Nsereko, Margaret N. 127

Nsibirwa, Prime Minister of Buganda, assassination of 91

Ntiro, Sarah Nyedwoha 97, 106-7, 120, 157

NUCCPTE 175

nuns 107

nursing 58, 61-2, 82, 83, 101-2, 104, 108, 126, 128, 139, 174, 237, 242; perceptions of 58, 132, 160-1; and business 226; and HIV/AIDS 211-12, 260; and Service Career variation 15, 82, 83, 107-8; enrollment in nursing schools 174, 224

Obbo, Christine 7, 133, 147, 170, 173

Obote II xi

Obote, Apolo Milton xi, 9, 116, 117-18, 146-7; economic policies of 152, 156-7; on women's issues 122-3, 169

Obote, Miria 122

Okello, Tito 146, 147, 150, 166

organization, labor 124, 125, 127, 128, 175, 202, cooperatives 202

organizations, of women 96-8, 111, 121-122, 130, 168, 200-6; (Christianity) 121, 122, (craftwork) 126, (practical education) 121, 194, 202, (benefits) 10, (entrepreneurial) 227, (suspicion of) 135, 136, (political) 98, (problems ailing) 204-6, 261, (recommendations) 256-7; (repression of) 146, 165

orphans 9; of HIV/AIDS 21, 28, 208, 256

Orumuri (Runyankole) 233, 235, 236

Owen Falls Dam 24, 88, 90

Pandya, Ansuya 137

parastatals xii

Parliament 235, 257; suspension of under Amin 164; women in 17, 122, 164, 191, 233, 234

patriarchy, 14; as a bulwark to colonial economy 80

peanuts *see* groundnuts

periods, early Independence (1962-1971) 16, 116-39; NRM (1986-2003) 17-18, 184-212, entrepreneurial activity of women in 226-32; Amin/Obote II (1971-86) 16-17, 34, 38, 39, 146-79; early colonial (1900-39) 13-15, 44-62, 65-83; late colonial (1940-62) 15-16, 87-112